Cut Flowers
of the World

Cut Flowers
of the World

Johannes Maree

Ben-Erik van Wyk

TIMBER PRESS
Portland • London

Published in 2010 by
Timber Press, Inc.

The Haseltine Building
133 S.W. Second Avenue, Suite 450
Portland, Oregon 97204-3527
www.timberpress.com

2 The Quadrant
135 Salusbury Road
London NW6 6RJ
www.timberpress.co.uk

First edition, first impression, 2010

ISBN: 978-1-60469-194-8

Project manager: Reneé Ferreira
Design and layout: Melinda Stark, Lebone Publishing
   Services, Cape Town
Reproduction: Resolution Colour, Cape Town
Printed and bound by Tien Wah Press (Pte.) Ltd,
   Singapore

CONTENTS

PREFACE

This is the fourth title in a series on useful plants of the world. It follows on *Medicinal Plants of the World* (2004), *Food Plants of the World* (2005) and *Mind-altering and Poisonous Plants of the World* (2009), all written and presented in the same style and layout. These books now cover all the basic human interactions with plants – medicine, food and decoration. It is intended to give a bird's eye view of the diversity of cut flowers, foliage greens and potted flowers that are sold in florist shops all over the world. It is also intended to be a source of accurate basic information on the plant species that are used, including aspects of their origin, history, cultivation, properties, quality criteria, main uses, care and handling.

Part of the beauty of florist flowers lie in their extreme diversity – an aspect that is exploited by breeders in their efforts to create an ever-increasing number of colourful and often bizarre new forms. This is at the same time a frustrating aspect of florist flowers, as it is practically impossible to account for the full diversity in a single book! There are many thousands of cultivars for roses alone! The best we could do within the limitation of 400 pages (and this was our intention) was to provide an overview at the species level. Some exceptions were made in cases where there are very distinct cultivar groups that most people would recognise as separate entities. For many of the 330 entries, the original parentage of the commercially used flower has been obscured by a long period of hybridisation and back-crossing, often involving several species. In such cases we have simply listed them under the relevant genus.

A second feature that makes a comprehensive treatment quite difficult is the dynamic nature of the flower business. Flowers are truly on the move, with new species and new cultivars coming and going at an ever-increasing pace. The extreme biodiversity of many countries (such as Australia and South Africa) is not only historically the source of many everyday florist flowers, but provides an almost unlimited source of novel shapes and colours. The element of fashion certainly plays an important role – shapes and colours also come and go. As a result, important species may have been overlooked here simply because they are very new. We would therefore appreciate any suggestions for improvement and additional species to keep in mind for possible future editions. Offers of high-quality photographs would also be greatly appreciated.

In the treatment of species we have followed the internationally accepted binomial Latin names given to plants. For all the species, the best-known common name or names are also provided. Some florist flowers simply do not have a common name and are "commonly" known by their botanical name. Furthermore, the authors realise that common names for the same flower may differ from country to country. Adding to this is the fact that completely different plants can have the same common name, which usually causes some confusion. For example, *Rudbeckia*, *Echinacea* and *Ratibida* are all commonly known as "coneflower". Since common names are open to criticism and correction, we would appreciate any comments, additions or suggestions for improvements.

People all over the world are becoming more sophisticated and demanding about what they buy and use. This is particularly true in the florist industry, where high quality and novelty are increasingly important elements. By giving critical information in a user-friendly way, we hope that this book will not only inform but also add to the joy and pleasure of giving and receiving flowers.

Johannes Maree and Ben-Erik van Wyk
January 2010

INTRODUCTION

To be healthy and to stay healthy, humans need food and medicine. But there is more to life than simply surviving. We also need to enrich our lives with objects of beauty, such as works of art or the masterpieces of creation, namely colourful flowers. Since time immemorial, flowers have served to decorate and inspire.

This is the fourth volume in a series on the useful plants of the world, following on *Medicinal Plants of the World* (first published in 2004), *Food Plants of the World* (first published in 2005) and *Mind-altering and Poisonous Plants of the World* (2009). These books summarise the three basic human needs related to plants: medicine to treat disease, food to stay healthy and now flowers, to admire and enjoy. The book is intended to be a user-friendly but scientifically accurate, quick reference guide to all the most important commercial cut flowers, foliage greens and potted flowers that are sold in florist shops all over the world. It can be viewed as a compact, full-colour encyclopaedia that summarises the main important points about cut flowers – their history, cultivation, properties, uses, care and handling.

General aspects such as the history of cut flowers, the so-called "language of flowers" and the regions of origin of cut flowers are briefly introduced in the first pages. This is followed by short reviews of the modern cut flower industry, followed by a short introduction to the main production areas. The process and movement of a cut flower from the breeder (where it was created through modern breeding techniques) all the way to the home of the end consumer are highlighted. This logical flow of activities is then further elaborated, including such topics as cultivars and breeding, the cultivation process, harvesting and post-harvest treatments and the marketing of cut flowers. Basic concepts about the properties of cut flowers are introduced, followed by practical hints on how to recognise good quality and how to go about selecting superior flowers. An important part of the introductory pages, useful to both the professional florist and the lay person, is the section on the care and handling of fresh cut flowers, dried flowers, cut greens and foliage, and also potted flowers.

Since all flowers and foliages are arranged alphabetically in the book by their botanical (scientific) names, some readers may find it difficult to locate a particular species of interest. For this reason, additional indices to common names (vernacular names) are provided as a quick reference. The most common and well-known cut flowers, foliages and potted flowers are each listed in a separate common name index that gives the scientific name. The reader is advised, however, to also use the comprehensive index in the back of the book to locate a species. The main part of the book comprises short treatments of 330 of the most commonly used and best-known florist flowers (and their close relatives). Photographs are included to show the flower or foliage as an aid to identification. Unfortunately, space does not allow us to display the fantastic diversity of shape and colour that is found in most florist flowers. The best we could do is to show a typical example (or a few examples). There are many specialist books on roses, tulips, chrysanthemums and other main categories of flowers where readers can find more information (and photographs) of the cultivars and cultivar groups. A treatment at this level would have required a very thick book for roses alone!

Also included are a short glossary of terms and a list of references for further reading.

It is hoped that this book will fulfil its proposed function as an "illustrated encyclopaedia" and provide easy access to useful, practical and scientifically accurate information (and photographs) on all or most of the commercially relevant florist flowers of the world.

HISTORY OF FLOWERS

The early history of cut flowers is not documented and there is no definite starting point, but we see their outline on ancient pottery, rock art, Egyptian tomb walls, Inca and Aztec temples, Greek pillars and Roman frescoes. There is no doubt that the beauty of flowers has fascinated people throughout the ages. This is highlighted in stories such as the one about Queen Anne's lace (named after the wife of King James I of England). The queen's friends challenged her to try to create lace as beautiful and delicate as the flower itself. To give a glimpse of the fascinating history of flowers, some of the most famous examples are briefly discussed here.

TULIPS AND OTHER BULB FLOWERS. Many ancient civilisations, such as the Egyptians, grew and used bulbs for medicinal purposes. However, already by the 3rd century BC, the Greeks were cultivating hyacinths, narcissi and ranunculi for their beauty alone, as well as decorating their vases and other goods with floral designs. After the fall of the Roman Empire, bulbs lost their popularity and were mainly found growing in monasteries. There is a historical record of Sultan Selim II issuing an order in 1574 for the purchase of 50 000 tulip bulbs to be planted in the royal gardens. By the early 1700s there were already more than 1 300 documented tulip cultivars in the courts of the sultans. Many flower bulbs (including tulips and hyacinths) were first introduced into Western Europe by Carolus Clusius, a pharmacist in charge of the Imperial Medicinal Gardens of Emperor Maximilian II in Vienna. He had obtained a number of bulbs from a friend who was a consul at the court of the sultan. In 1573, when Maximilian II died, Carolus was dismissed and moved to Holland, taking along many of his bulbs.

In the 17th century, "tulip mania" gripped Holland and trading in bulbs literally became frenzied, with rare varieties being sold over and over again, before they had even flowered. In 1637 it all ended, in what could well have been the first recorded stock market crash. A similar thing happened with hyacinths a century later, even though the bulbs were introduced into Europe at around the same time as tulips, both from the region of Turkey. Throughout the 18th century, the hyacinth reigned supreme amongst bulbs and at the court of Louis XVI of France, hundreds of flowers were ordered on a daily basis from florists to decorate and fill the palaces with beautiful flowers and perfume. By the 1720s, around 2 000 cultivars were being traded, with novelties fetching ridiculous prices. This was all before specialists had discovered how to propagate bulbs on large scale and in a short time as is done today.

Pictures of lilies were discovered in a villa in Crete and date back to around 1580 BC. The flowers are mentioned in the Old and New Testaments of the Bible and they symbolise chastity and virtue. In Greek marriage ceremonies the bride would wear a crown of lilies and wheat, symbolising purity and abundance and these beautiful flowers were at one time routinely placed on the graves of children.

ROSES. No florist flower is as well known as the rose, or has been cultivated, manipulated and traded as extensively. From as far back as 1600 BC it can found in all forms of art and literature. This and the natural ability of roses to interbreed, has made it very difficult to accurately trace the lineage of many species. Original rose species had five petals, except *Rosa sericea*, which had four. Roses occur naturally only in the northern hemisphere and in four regions, namely Europe, North America, Asia and the Middle East. The Chinese were probably the first to cultivate and interbreed them in the early 6th century BC. In the West, roses were grown more for making rose water and perfumes, in an age where lack of bathing was common.

Some sources claim that the first cultivated roses appeared in Asian gardens more than 5 000 years ago. Be that as it may, in ancient Mesopotamia, Sargon I, King of the Akkadians (2684–2630 BC) brought back "vines, figs and rose trees" from a military expedition beyond the River Tigris. Confucius wrote that during his life (551–479 BC), the Emperor of China owned over 600 books relating to roses and their cultivation. The Chinese extracted oil from roses grown in the Emperor's garden for use by nobles and dignitaries of the court. If a commoner were found in possession of even the smallest amount, he was condemned to death.

Roses were first introduced to Rome by the Greeks. Roses collected in the wild and from Turkish gardens first started to arrive in Europe through Vienna around 1600. The yellow rose, *Rosa foetida*, was one of the first. It was not until the mid-1700s that Chinese garden roses ("tea

"Flowers in a vase" by Jan Brueghel (ca. 1607)

"Flowers in a wooden vessel" by Jan Brueghel (ca. 1606/07)

roses") and new species from North America began to arrive in Europe. The hybrids between these eastern diploid "tea" roses and the western tetraploid "cabbage" roses resulted in plants that were able to flower more than once during a season. Later a French breeder, Guillot, developed the first recognised hybrid tea and polyantha roses. Hybrid teas, although generally considered to be modern roses, were first developed in the 1860s. Some breeders use 1920 as the cut-off point between old and new roses. Besides being grown as a horticultural crop, roses were used medicinally to make soothing eyewashes and headache remedies, not forgetting rose petal oil used in the perfume industry.

CARNATIONS. Originating from the Near East, it appears that carnations have been cultivated for at least 2 000 years. The name originally applied only to *Dianthus caryophyllus* but nowadays is more loosely used as a common name for the various hybrids and cultivars, especially those between *D. caryophyllus* and other species. It is commonly believed that the name comes from the word "coronation" and was used as one of the flowers in ancient Greek ritual crowns. An alternative view is that the name comes from the word *carnis*, which means flesh, and reflects the flesh-toned colour of the original *D. caryophyllus* species.

CHRYSANTHEMUMS. The Chinese considered chrysanthemums the highest of all flowers and named their royal throne after them. Originating from China, it is also the national flower of Japan. The name comes from the Greek *krus anthemon*, meaning "gold flower". The original, small yellow or gold flower has been known since 5000 BC. The ancient Chinese named the chrysanthemum ("chu hua") as their official "Flower for October", and it was also the official badge of the Chinese army. Ordinary Chinese people were not permitted to grow them in their gardens. Around AD 400 the chrysanthemum was brought to Japan by visiting Buddhist monks. Japanese emperors so loved this flower that it became a symbol of the country and was featured on the Imperial Crest of Japan. In Italy, however, chrysanthemums are associated with death. Chrysanthemums have become a very popular florist flower because they have many desired characteristics. Growers like them because they grow well and their flowering time can be manipulated to the day. Florists and the general public like them because they are available in so many shapes and colours and have a very good vase life.

THE LANGUAGE OF FLOWERS

Flowers are strongly associated with sentiments or virtues – often of love, romance, appreciation and friendship. The art of sending messages through flowers is said to have originated from the Turkish or Persian "language of flowers and objects", known as *selam*. To some extent, all cultures of the world, including the Chinese, Japanese, Middle Eastern, Greek and Roman cultures, have some form of symbolism associated with flowers, at least as part of the literary tradition. The so-called language of flowers was introduced into England by Lady Mary Wortley Montagu, after a visit to the Turkish Court in 1716 to 1718. The idea also became popular in France – more so after the publication in 1819 of Madame Charlotte de Latour's book on the subject, entitled *Le Langage des Fleurs*. During the 19th century (especially during Victorian times) publishers in many countries produced hundreds of editions of "language of flowers" books. A famous example is the 1884 Routledge edition of *The Language of Flowers*, illustrated by Kate Greenaway. The idea has appeal even today, as is evident from the large number of websites devoted to the subject.

Plants and flowers are deeply engrained in everyday life and even in the language we speak. We talk about Nobel *laureates* and Bacca*laureus* degrees without even thinking of the connection with plants – the bay leaf or laurel (*Laurus nobilis*) has always been associated with the reward of merit. In Greek times, winners of contests (e.g. the marathon) were rewarded with a wreath of laurel. This practice was revived in the Athens Olympics in 2004 (but it seemed that there was a problem with the supply of laurel leaves, so that the wreaths were actually made from olive branches – therefore signifying peace, not merit). Different flowers and flower colours are also linked to months of the year in various cultures. Traditionally, the symbol for the fourth wedding anniversary is flowers. An iris still suggests that a message is being sent, as Iris was the messenger of the gods in Greek mythology. Myrtle is a symbol of marital love. Princess Diana followed a royal tradition started by Queen Victoria and included myrtle in her bridal bouquet.

Flowers are used as national symbols, such as the Australian golden wattle, Canadian maple leaf, Chinese narcissus, Egyptian and Indian lotus, English and Persian rose, French fleur-de-lis (iris), German cornflower, Greek violet, Dutch and Turkish tulip, Irish shamrock, Italian poppy or white lily, Jamaican and Malaysian hibiscus, Japanese chrysanthemum, Scottish thistle, Singapore orchid, South African protea, Spanish pomegranate, Swiss edelweiss, the American rose, Welsh leek and daffodil and the Zimbabwean flame lily.

In the United States, each state has a designated floral emblem. Flowers were chosen because they are typical of that state or because they played a role in the history of the state. These are Alabama – Camilla (*Camellia*), Montana – bitterroot (*Lewisia rediviva*), Alaska – forget-me-not (*Myosotis alpestris*), Nebraska – goldenrod (*Solidago gigantea*), Arizona – Saguaro cactus (*Carnegiea gigantea*), Nevada – sagebrush (*Artemisia tridentata*), Arkansas – apple blossom (*Malus coronaria*), New Hampshire – purple lilac (*Syringa vulgaris*), California – golden poppy (*Eschscholzia californica*), New Jersey – purple violet (*Viola sororia*), Colorado – columbine (*Aquilegia caerulea*), New Mexico – yucca (*Yucca glauca*), Connecticut – mountain laurel (*Kalmia latifolia*), New York – rose (genus *Rosa*), Delaware – peach blossom (*Prunus persica*), North Carolina – dogwood (*Cornus florida*), Florida – orange blossom (*Citrus sinensis*), North Dakota – wild prairie rose (*Rosa arkansana* or *Rosa blanda*), Georgia – Cherokee rose (*Rosa laevigata*), Ohio – scarlet carnation (*Dianthus caryophyllus*), Hawaii – yellow hibiscus (*Hibiscus brackenridgei*), Oklahoma – mistletoe (*Phoradendron serotinum*), Idaho – syringa (*Philadelphus lewisii*), Oregon – Oregon grape (*Mahonia aquifolium*), Illinois – native violet (*Viola sororia*), Pennsylvania – mountain laurel (*Kalmia latifolia*), Indiana – peony (genus *Paeonia*), Rhode Island – violet (*Viola sororia*), Iowa – wild rose (*Rosa arkansana, Rosa blanda* and *Rosa carolina*), South Carolina – yellow jessamine (*Gelsemium sempervirens*), Kansas – sunflower (genus *Helianthus*), South Dakota – pasque flower (*Pulsatilla hirsutissima*), Kentucky – goldenrod (genus *Solidago*), Tennessee – iris (genus *Iris*), Louisiana – magnolia (*Magnolia grandiflora*), Texas – blue bonnet (*Lupinus texensis*), Maine – white pine cone (*Pinus strobus*), Utah – Sego lily (*Calochortus nuttallii*), Maryland – black-eyed Susan (*Rudbeckia hirta*), Vermont – red clover (*Trifolium pratense*), Massachusetts – may flower (*Epigaea repens*), Virginia – dogwood (*Cornus florida*), Michigan – apple blossom (*Malus coronaria*), Washington – rhododendron (*Rhododendron macrophyllum*), Minnesota – lady slipper (*Cypripedium reginae*), West Virginia – big rhododendron (*Rhododendron maximum*), Mississippi – magnolia (*Magnolia*

"Flora" by Guiseppe Archimboldo (1591)

grandiflora), Wisconsin – wood violet (*Viola papilionacea*), Missouri – hawthorn (genus *Crataegus*) and Wyoming – Indian paintbrush (*Castilleja linariaefolia*).

"Say it with flowers." The language of flowers, also called floriography, is said to be a means of communication in which not only single flowers conveyed messages, but entire floral arrangements, which could be interpreted as sentences. Red and white roses together, for example, signify unity. The tendrils of climbing plants such as Virginian creeper, when added to a garland, suggest family ties or marital ties. The hand – left or right – that offers (or receives) the flowers is supposed to give additional meaning: an affirmative by the right, a negative by the left. The more subtle nuances of this "language" are now long forgotten, but most people still have a vague idea about the symbolism of certain flowers or flower colours. Red roses mean romantic love, while white roses symbolise chastity, purity and innocence. To some, yellow roses signify platonic love, infidelity or jealousy, while others regard it as a message of friendship and devotion. Giving a red tulip is a clear declaration of love, while a red rosebud means "you are young and beautiful". In the same way, marigolds signify grief, nasturtiums patriotism, hibiscus delicate beauty, wheat prosperity, fennel (or cedar) strength, yew sadness, white lily modesty and purity, ivy marital faithfulness and zinnia thoughts of absent friends.

"How the universal heart of man blesses flowers! They are wreathed round the cradle, the marriage-altar, and the tomb… Flowers should deck the brow of the youthful bride, for they are in themselves a lovely type of marriage. They should twine round the tomb, for their perpetually renewed beauty is a symbol of the resurrection. They should festoon the altar, for their fragrance and their beauty ascend in perpetual worship before the Most High." (P.F. Collier, 1882)

REGIONS OF ORIGIN

Famous cut flowers of the world originated from all regions of the globe. During the age of discovery, people were fascinated by exotic and colourful flowers from all corners of the earth. It is reasonable to assume that the "hotspots" of biological diversity in the world also contributed the largest number of species used as commercial cut flowers today. Due to many centuries of breeding, cultivation and trading it is not always possible to pinpoint exactly where a specific cut flower originated from, but only the general region. The main geographical sources of cut flowers are briefly discussed here.

China and Japan

China and Japan are not just regions where some famous cut flowers originally grew in the wild, but are well known for having cultivated and grown flowers for many centuries. Flowers were grown specifically for their beauty and pleasure and not simply for their medicinal or food value. Examples include many orchids, roses and chrysanthemums. Chrysanthemums were cultivated in Chinese gardens for more than 2 000 years before they were first exhibited in England in 1795. Buddhist monks introduced chrysanthemums into Japan around AD 400. The tropical regions of China and Asia still hold a vast wealth of stunning plants that will one day in the future adorn florist shops and dining-room tables.

Near East

Many of the most popular florist flowers available today either originated from the Fertile Crescent, or were first cultivated as cut flowers in that region. These include the rose, the tulip, carnation and hyacinth. More than a thousand years ago, tulips grew wild in Persia. The great Mogul Baber recorded 33 different species near Kabul. The tulip was so often represented and mentioned in Persian poetry, songs and art that Europe considered it to be the symbol of the Ottoman-Persian Empire.

Mediterranean region

Many perennials used in the florist and garden industries today either originated from the Mediterranean region, or have parentage from the region. These include famous flowers such as delphiniums, ranunculi, roses and veronicas. Although the origin of snapdragons is not conclusive, many botanists believe that they came from Italy and Spain, and were already common in the earliest of European gardens. Other well-known and beautiful cut flowers that have their origins in Europe include anemones, cyclamens, muscari, daffodils, bellflower (*Campanula* species) and sea holly (*Eryngium maritimum*).

South Africa

The Fynbos or Cape flora is famous all over the world for the extreme species diversity, and many well-known cut flowers and potted flowers originated here. When explorers and collectors came to southern Africa in the 1700s and 1800s, they were overwhelmed by the wealth of bulbs and other flora they found. Many of these were exported back to the Netherlands and are still favourites amongst florists today, such as calla lilies, *Gladiolus*, *Freesia*, *Sparaxis*, *Gerbera* and *Ornithogalum*. Another important Cape plant is *Pelargonium* (so-called geranium). As bedding and pot plants, more than 35 million pelargoniums of about 250 cultivars are now sold every year in the United States alone.

North America

Many important and well-loved florist flowers have their roots in North America. The number of different geographical and climatic regions allow for a vast spectrum of very different species to thrive there. Over the years many of these beautiful wild species have been identified, bred and cultivated as cut flowers that can be found in florist shops in any part of the world. Some of these

Chrysanthemum   Tulip   Daffodil   Gerbera

Lisianthus   Poinsettia   Alstroemeria   Geraldton waxflower

well-known and economically important flowers include lisianthus, Michaelmas daisy, dahlias, delphiniums, goldenrod, liatris, sunflower and phlox.

Central America

The sunflower, which comes from Central and North America, is relatively new as florist flower on the international market. Yet, centuries ago the Aztecs already appreciated its beauty and adorned their temples, clothes and household goods with it. Many potential cut flowers from Central America were first brought to Europe, where they were bred, cultivated and introduced into the world as florist flowers. Nearly all cacti (many of which are found in florists, nurseries and wholesalers) are restricted to the Americas. Other popular cut flowers and potted flowers native to this region are amaryllis, bouvardia, tuberose, poinsettia, gloxinia, flossflower, flamingo flower and zinnia.

South America

The tropical forests of South America are arguably the richest regions on earth when it comes to biodiversity of fauna and flora. There are not many places in the world that can boast the number of plant species per area than that of the Amazon jungle. Some of these regions are not only the origin of well-known and established florist flowers in the world today, but potentially are rich sources of many future florist flowers. Some of the well-known and internationally used flowers that have originated from South America include alstroemeria, bougainvillea, saffron spike, various bromeliads (e.g. guzmania) and amaryllis.

Australia and New Zealand

There is a wealth of potential cut flowers in Australia and New Zealand. It is, however, only in the last few decades that many of the native flowers of these regions have started to be cultivated for the international florist industry. Well-known examples of flowers from these regions include banksias, waxflowers, drumsticks, waratahs and kangaroo paws. Many of these potential and existing commercial plants tend to be seen more as fillers and cut foliage than true cut flowers.

THE MODERN CUT FLOWER INDUSTRY

In the 1960s most demand for cut flowers was satisfied by local production. In Europe and Japan, the per capita consumption was significant, and the consumer culture demanded a large and ever increasing supply of cut flowers for gifts, occasions, and everyday use. As transportation systems developed throughout Europe, it became possible to distribute cut flowers grown in southern areas of Europe to northern areas. Consequently, the European flower industry began to extend its boundaries and along with this expansion grew the influence of the European flower industry. This could probably be considered the beginning of the international commercial flower trade as we know it today.

With the world energy crisis in 1973, distributing cut flowers grown in different European countries to the Netherlands for sale through the Dutch flower auctions (and back to markets throughout Europe) became a significant production opportunity for southern European growers. Increasingly larger quantities of cut flowers were grown in southern Europe to meet the demand for cut flower sales through the Netherlands. Growers in the southern regions had a price advantage over growers located in northern regions because cut flower production was more expensive there because of higher energy costs to obtain quality flowers in controlled temperature greenhouses.

Competition intensified when Israeli growers entered the market through the Dutch flower auctions. Israeli growers had a climatic advantage for most of the year over many European growers, allowing them to produce cut flowers in open fields or plastic tunnels year round, eliminating many overhead expenses for greenhouses and heating systems. Transportation costs (which offset growers' cost advantages in terms of energy compared to growers in southern Europe) were government subsidised. The reduced shipping costs helped to maintain a competitive cost advantage over European growers.

During the 1970s, the activities of the European flower industry had begun to influence cut flower production and sales beyond the borders of Europe. Cut flower sales through the Dutch flower auctions had gained a market share in the United States, with most flowers airfreighted to and through New York. At the same time, Miami was becoming a key import distribution base for cut flowers being grown in Colombia. This caused considerable competition for local cut flower growers in the United States.

In the 1980s, the European flower industry began expanding into Asia – at first into Japanese markets and later into Korea, Taiwan and Hong Kong. Since the early 1990s, the European flower industry, as a worldwide leader in commercial floriculture, has been impacting the rest of Asia with cut flower imports from the Netherlands. This includes sales of new flower cultivars, production equipment and the necessary specialised technology for new production operations in Asia. Israeli cut flower producers, manufacturers, and suppliers have followed, but one step behind.

Interestingly enough, only about 20 florist flowers account for more than 90% of the total world market value. However, within each of these flower types there are many types and cultivars, and each year new ones are released.

Worldwide trade in floriculture products was estimated at over US$14 billion in 2008, with cut flowers accounting for 50% and cut foliage for 10% of sales. Seven countries exported 70% of the value of the world's floriculture crops: The Netherlands, Colombia, Italy, Belgium, Denmark, the United States and Ecuador. It was estimated that in the year 2008, almost 50% of exported floriculture products came from the Netherlands. This figure includes crops that are grown domestically and crops that are imported, brokered, and then resold. Colombia was the second largest exporter at approximately 7%. Italy, Belgium, Denmark, the United States, Ecuador and Germany followed, with each accounting for approximately 3% of the total exported products. Kenya, Costa Rica, Israel and Spain produced about 2% each. Major markets are Germany, the United States, Britain, France and the Netherlands. These five countries account for almost 70% of all imports of floriculture products.

The top 20 commercial cut flowers of the world

Rose	Chrysanthemum	Carnation	Oriental lily
Gerbera	Tulip	Asiatic lily	Freesia
Alstroemeria	Hypericum	Iris	Asiflora (L/A) lily
Gypsophila	Daffodil	Longiflorum lily	Michaelmas daisy
Lisianthus	Statice	Gladiolus	Solidago

MAIN PRODUCTION AREAS
OF CUT FLOWERS

Most countries of the world produce floral products of some sort for domestic consumption. Approximately 80 countries are involved in the international trade of florist flowers, but only about 30 play a significant role. The Netherlands, Colombia, Italy, Kenya and Israel account for the bulk of global exports, with approximately 16 other countries accounting for the remaining few percentage points. Cut flowers are an internationally traded, high value commodity. Worldwide, retail trade is worth over US$40 billion per annum, and growing. Presently, the largest markets are China, the United Kingdom, Germany, Japan, the United States and the Netherlands. Other important markets are the individual countries of Western Europe, which have the highest per capita consumption of cut flowers in the world. According to the statistics available from the Flower Council of the Netherlands, Switzerland, Norway, Austria and Germany are the countries with highest per capita consumption of floriculture products. Traditionally the Japanese market, although very large, was supplied by a large number of very small local growers. In contrast, production in Colombia, Ecuador, Zimbabwe and Kenya is on a few very large farms. The United States is a large consumer market, and imports over half of its total floricultural products consumed. The European Union consumes over 50% of the world's flowers and includes many countries with a relatively high per capita consumption of cut flowers. There is strong demand in Germany, the Netherlands, the United Kingdom, Switzerland, Italy and France. Germany and the United Kingdom are the two largest importers of floral products, with up to half of the United Kingdom's sales taking place through supermarkets and chain stores.

PRODUCTION IN THE NORTHERN HEMISPHERE. The leading production countries in floriculture are China, Japan, the Netherlands and the United States. With rapid development in recent years, China has become the largest flower producer in terms of production area and yield, but presently only a very small percentage of this large production is exported. Japan's production area is nearly three times that of the Netherlands. However, productivity, quality and yields on Dutch farms are very high. Most Dutch flowers come from the Westland. This region is often called the "the garden of Europe" or "the city of glass" because the landscape is covered with glasshouses.

PRODUCTION IN THE SOUTHERN HEMISPHERE. Cut flower production in Israel, Colombia, Kenya and other South American or African countries (with the exception of South Africa) is virtually entirely for export. Most of these countries have an ideal growing climate or low labour costs, which outweigh many of the disadvantages of airfreight. The general movement of export flowers is from developing countries to the richer markets of North America and Western Europe. The Dutch flower industry still plays a central role in global trade and controls about 55–65% of the international wholesale trade.

PRODUCTION VS EXPORT AND IMPORT. Production and export volumes do not necessarily coincide. For example, nearly all of production in Kenya and Colombia is for export, while nearly all of production in Australia, China, Japan and the United States is for local consumption. The Netherlands is the world's largest exporter of floral crops, while the United States ranks near the bottom of the top ten. Yet, the United States is the world's largest producer of floral crops, with the Netherlands second. The Netherlands has a surplus from both domestic production and imports, which it exports worldwide. The top five floral producers (including cut flowers, foliages and pot plants) are the United States, the Netherlands, Germany, France and Italy. With the exception of Germany, these top producers are also in the top ten exporters. The countries that import the greatest number of floral products are Germany, the United States, France, Switzerland, the Netherlands, the United Kingdom, Austria, Belgium / Luxembourg and Sweden. The United States gets most of its imports from Colombia and Ecuador, while the Netherlands gets most of its imports from Israel and Kenya. Otherwise, the Netherlands is the major supplying country to the remaining importing countries.

Field of tulips   Greenhouse production of chrysanthemums

AUSTRALIA. Australia produces mainly traditional florist flowers but there is an upsurge in the cultivation and trade of indigenous flowers and foliages. Around 90% of flowers produced are for domestic consumption. In terms of Australian exports, over 50% of exported flowers are destined for markets in Japan, with 30% to the United States, 11% to the Netherlands and 3% to Germany.

AFRICA. Kenya is currently the fourth largest exporter of cut flowers in the world and accounts for around a quarter of all exports into Europe. In 2003, Zimbabwe was the eighth largest exporter of cut flowers (10th in 2004). South Africa is in 21st place; other exporting countries are Zambia (23rd), Tanzania (29th) and Mauritius (38th). South Africa ranks 15th largest in world terms, and is the only significant exporter of foliage within southern Africa. South Africa has a relatively large local market, which consumes approximately 50% of local production. The main export destination is the Dutch auctions; with Germany and the United Kingdom being important export destinations as well. Some 80% of South African exports go to Western Europe, 12% to the United States and 8% to Japan, with exports to Dubai growing steadily.

REGIONAL TRADE. International trade is predominantly along regional lines. Asia-Pacific countries are the main suppliers to Japan and Hong Kong. New Zealand sells 70–80% of its exports to Japan; Taiwan more than 90% and Australia 50%. Hong Kong's principal suppliers are China, Taiwan, Malaysia, Singapore and New Zealand. African and other European countries are the principal suppliers to Europe's main markets. Kenya sends over 60% to the Dutch auctions; Zimbabwe 80%, Zambia over 90% and South Africa 90% to EU markets. The United States is supplied mainly by Colombia, Ecuador and Mexico.

FROM BREEDER TO CONSUMER

Cut flower production is a specialist, capital-intensive industry that is often high-tech. It is probably the most intensive and high yielding of all the agricultural disciplines. There are several different industries within the production chain, with possible overlap between some of them.

Breeders ➤ Propagators ➤ Growers ➤ Distributors ➤ Wholesalers ➤ Retailers ➤ Consumers

BREEDERS. Companies that develop and breed new hybrids and cultivars. It often takes many years of cross-pollination and back-crossing, followed by selection and evaluation, to develop a new cultivar that is significantly better than those already on the market. New cultivars are then registered and the breeders (who are usually the owners of the breeder's rights) make licensing agreements with propagators and growers, who propagate and multiply the plants. The breeders receive a royalty on each plant grown or flower sold.

PROPAGATORS. Propagating companies that multiply stock purchased from breeders and sell plant material to growers. Depending on the species and local conditions, the plant material may be in the form of rooted cuttings or seedlings (often in plugs). Tissue culture has also become popular as a means of mass production of single, desirable clones (but is relatively expensive). Sometimes the breeder is also the propagator. There is a large demand for quality plants each year. For example, approximately one billion carnation plants are used each year.

GROWERS. Individuals or companies supplying local and/or export markets. Production set-up, methods and size vary considerably, especially from country to country and are also very much related to the type of cut flowers that are being grown. Flowers and other products may be wild-harvested to some extent, but the overwhelming majority is mass cultivated. Production methods range from open fields (the cheapest), to shade cloth houses to highly sophisticated and often automated greenhouses, which are also the most expensive.

DISTRIBUTORS. Individuals or companies transporting flowers by road, rail, sea or air, depending on location and destination. For local markets and distribution within Europe and the United States, road transport is used. The cut flower industries in countries such as Israel, Colombia and Kenya are established primarily for export and in these cases transport is via air. There are two important issues in the transport and distribution of cut flowers from the source to their final destination – doing it in the shortest time possible and keeping the flowers cool along the entire journey. By using cool-rooms and refrigerated containers, the cold chain is maintained.

WHOLESALERS. Flowers are sold through wholesalers or at wholesale markets or auctions, which provide retailers with a large range and volume of flowers. Wholesalers are mostly based at many of the world's large auctions. The Dutch clock system of auctioning is mostly used, during which all transactions are electronically recorded by registered buyers. The "clock" is set at a high price and slowly moves to a lower and lower price. Individual bidders (retailers and florists) can stop the clock electronically at the price point of their choice (for that particular batch of flowers) and the bid is automatically registered against their name or number. If you stop the clock too quickly, you may pay too much, but if you wait too long, the opportunity may be lost and others will buy the flowers.

RETAILERS. In all developed markets, florists are still the main retail outlet for flowers to the consumer. The advantage is that individual care and attention can be given to the proper treatment and storage of the flowers to ensure that they reach the consumer in the best possible state of freshness. However, there is an international trend towards supermarket or chain store outlets.

CONSUMERS. Finally, it is the consumer (whether it is the home owner or the organiser of a large wedding or conference) that drives the flower industry. Giving and receiving flowers have become part of everyday life. Like most industries, it is very much about supply and demand. Fashion and colour play a very important role in the demand for certain cut flowers.

Cuttings of cone bush (*Leucadendron*)

Production area

Refrigerated truck

The clock system of auctioning

Flowers on the floor

Flowers for sale

CULTIVARS AND BREEDING

A comparison of cultivated flowers with their original (wild) counterparts shows the remarkable effects of human selection and breeding on the size, shape and colour of flowers. More subtle differences include a longer vase life, improved resistance against diseases, transportability, uniformity of growth and higher productivity (more stems with more buds per unit area of greenhouse). There is a natural tendency to select unusual colour forms ("pigment mutants"). In earlier years breeders would pamper new potential selections but nowadays they select the ones that show maximum vigour and resistance to stresses such as diseases and temperature fluctuations. A new cultivar has to stay true to type once propagated and cultivated. This is especially of concern in flowers that are propagated from seed.

BREEDING OF NEW CULTIVARS. Breeding is a specialised activity that calls for patience, dedication and hard work over many years. Commercial flower growers often have a small greenhouse on the side where they experiment with new hybrids and selections. Hybrid breeding is the most common and obvious way to create new forms. Hybrid seed is produced on the so-called "pod parent" after cross-pollination with pollen from the "pollen parent". A common strategy in breeding is to create two distinct lineages of heavily inbred plants – the plants are repeatedly hybridised with themselves until they are genetically (and morphologically) absolutely uniform. When two such inbred lines are finally crossed, exceptionally vigorous hybrids are often produced (a phenomenon known as "hybrid vigour"). The more deeply inbred the two parental lines, the more likely and more pronounced the hybrid vigour effect. The resultant plants are called F_1 hybrids. The seeds of F_1 hybrids are not useful because the offspring usually lack uniformity and show a random combination of the traits present in the two parental lineages. This means that you have to buy F_1 seed from the breeder.

New cultivars can also be developed by subjecting seeds or cuttings to non-lethal levels of radiation. This causes a higher rate of mutation than would normally occur in nature. The vast majority of such random mutants have to be discarded, but a few of them typically show interesting new traits that can be used in further breeding work. These changes are totally unpredictable and may include new colour patterns in flowers and foliage, increased stem length, larger flowers or taller plants. Nowadays it is also possible to create new cultivars by genetic engineering, where the desired traits are introduced by way of gene transfer. This process occurs totally random when we hybridise plants but can be highly predictable when specific target genes (for flower colour, for example) are transferred. There is some resistance to genetically modified organisms (so-called GMOs) but most people have no objections when the new organism is not used as food but only for decoration.

BOTANICAL NAMES AND CULTIVAR NAMES. It may be useful to consider here the correct terminology and the correct way of writing plant and cultivar names. In botanical nomenclature, the correct scientific name for a plant species is a combination of the genus name (e.g. *Rosa*) and a descriptive term known as the specific epithet (e.g. *chinensis*). *Rosa chinensis* is therefore the Latin botanical name that translates to "the Chinese rose". Sometimes a species is subdivided into naturally occurring varieties (e.g. *Rosa chinensis* var. *alba* – "the white form / variety of the Chinese rose"). The abbreviation "var." means a botanical variety but this term is often also used for artificial or cultivated varieties. We recommend that the term "cultivar" (derived from the words cultivated and variety) be used for all forms of a species that does not occur in nature but which resulted from selection and breeding.

The correct way to write a cultivar name is to combine the botanical name with the "fancy" (non-botanical) name of the cultivar, such as *Rosa chinensis* 'Emperor's Gold'. In the case of hybrids, many different species may be involved and then we simply write the genus name (e.g. *Rosa* 'Peace'). Hybrids are sometimes described as new botanical genera or species. The hybrid origin is indicated by a multiplication sign (×) placed before the genus name (in the case of intergeneric hybrids) or before the specific epithet in the case of interspecies hybrids. For example, the name ×*Cattleytonia* is used for the new genus created by crossing a *Cattleya* orchid with a *Broughtonia* orchid. The name *Lilium* ×*testaceum* is used for the nankeen lily (a hybrid between *Lilium candidum* and *L. chalcedonicum*).

Gerbera (wild form)   Gerbera cultivar

Gerbera cultivars: 'Frenzy pink', 'Ruby red', 'Serena', 'Dana Allen' and 'Showgirl'

REGISTRATION OF CULTIVARS. Breeders often register their cultivars in order to be granted "plant breeder's rights" (also called "plant variety rights" in some countries). This is a form of intellectual property rights that are closely related to patent law (but it is not possible to patent a living organism such as a plant). The International Union for the Protection of New Varieties of Plants (UPOV) is responsible for an international convention on plant breeder's rights. Most countries of the world are signatories to the convention and have national laws aimed at protecting breeders' rights.

PLANT BREEDER'S RIGHTS. Plant breeder's rights are typically granted for a period of 20 years (or 25 years for woody vines and trees). In order to register a new cultivar, the breeder has to prove that it is (1) new and distinct (different from all forms found in nature and different from all other cultivars); (2) uniform (that all individuals are the same – often a problem with seedlings) and (3) stable (that it retains the unique traits through several generations). After a lengthy process of evaluation (by a special Registrar, usually residing in the National Department of Agriculture) the new cultivar may then be listed and registered. The process usually takes one to three years. National or international plant breeder's rights are then granted to the breeder (or to someone assigned by the breeder in the form of a deed of assignment) and a registration certificate is issued. There is an annual fee to keep the plant breeder's right in force. The holder of the rights is obliged to issue licences to all producers who wish to use the cultivar and is entitled to collect a royalty payment (per plant or stem sold) to recover the costs of research and development.

CULTIVATION OF CUT FLOWERS

CULTIVATION FACILITIES. Cut flowers are cultivated under a number of conditions and in a variety of facilities. These include greenhouses, shade structures, tunnels and open fields. The advantage of greenhouses is that the growing environment (temperature, humidity, light) can be controlled, which is not possible in open field production. The harvesting of flowers in the wild is also very much a part of the flower industry, but it represents only a small part of the total production.

PLANT MATERIAL. It is impossible to produce top quality flowers if the grower is starting with poor quality plant material. Plant material includes seed, seedlings, cuttings and young established plants. The starting point for many of the main flower lines tends to move away from seeds or seedlings and more towards cuttings and established plants in plugs or containers, to ensure that plants remain true to the original cultivar. Seed is often used for many of the less important speciality or summer flower crops that are grown in open fields. Greenhouse space is expensive, so growers prefer larger plantlets in order to minimise the time to harvest.

SOIL. Proper and thorough preparation of the soil prior to planting is critical to final flower quality. The roots of a plant need oxygen to be healthy and grow well. If the soil is poorly prepared then often the drainage is not good and soils can become waterlogged. Soils may also become too compact and then the roots do not get sufficient oxygen for premium growth. Soil preparation also includes the introduction of compost or other organic fertilisers, the introduction of soil microbes needed for healthy plant growth, the adjusting of the acidity of the soil and the shaping and making of beds. Many modern cut flower facilities no longer use soil; they have changed to artificial growth mediums in which to grow their flowers.

IRRIGATION. How much water to give and when to give it are carefully controlled in cut flower cultivation. Various types of irrigation systems are used, often depending on the type of flower being grown. The main difference is that some systems give water from the top (overhead watering) and some give from the bottom (e.g. drip lines). The quantity and quality of the irrigation water have a direct effect on the final quality of the harvested flowers. Too much water is just as problematic as too little water. Water quality is reduced as a result of a too high salt content or if it is too alkaline. In many areas of the world, river water is used for irrigation and often this water carries pollutants and diseases which affect flower quality. Growers need to regularly test the quality of their irrigation water.

FERTILISATION. Plants differ with regard to their feeding (nutritional) needs. For example, some flower types are heavy nitrogen feeders while others are not. All plants need nitrogen (N), phosphorus (P) and potassium (K), but they often require them in different ratios and concentrations at different growth stages. These nutrients are not only worked into the soil prior to planting, but are continually fed to the plants through the irrigation system. The term fertigation is used when irrigation and fertilisation is combined into a single system. Some growers use hydroponic systems in which fertigation is done without the use of soil.

LIGHT AND DAY LENGTH. All plants need light to grow and produce flowers. Growers often speak of light quality, which relates to how much actual energy the plants are getting from the available light. Flowering is induced in many plants by the number of daylight hours (day length). For example, under long day conditions (summer) chrysanthemums grow tall but do not flower, but once the daylight hours shorten (winter) flowers start to form. Growers can force flowers that are sensitive to day length to flower by artificially creating long or short days. This process is achieved by switching on lights to illuminate and so break the dark cycle, or by drawing screens to darken and increase the dark cycle.

TEMPERATURE. Plants are affected by temperature in a number of ways. All plants have an ideal temperature range at which optimal growth and flower quality is achieved. Certain plant types, such as bulbous plants (e.g. lilies and alstroemerias), only flower once a certain sequence of warm

Pest control

and cold temperatures has taken place. Some plants require a winter chilling period, while others (often tropical plants) prefer high temperatures without fluctuations.

FLOWER FORCING. Through the years much research has been done to determine exactly which factors are directly involved in the flowering process of many different flower types (e.g. light, temperature, hormones). Then, by artificially manipulating these factors, growers literally force plants to flower outside of their natural cycle and can then meet consumer demand by producing flowers all year round or at peak seasons such as Christmas or Valentine's Day.

PESTS AND DISEASES. As in food plants, pests (insects, mites) and diseases (mould, mildew, virus infections) have to be carefully controlled. A proper spray programme needs to be in place, and maintained, if top flower quality is to be realised. A preventative programme is recommended. In other words, it is easier to prevent a plant from getting a fungal or insect infection, than to have to deal with the problem later. Usually when there is an outbreak of a disease or infection, the chemicals needed to solve the problem are quite aggressive and also very expensive. There is then the risk of causing physical damage through burning when using these stronger chemicals. *Prevention is the best cure.* Also try to limit the use of chemicals because they may have a negative effect on plant growth and quality. To really maintain healthy, pest and disease-free plants on an ongoing basis, one needs to use a spay programme specifically designed for the flowers you are growing. It does not always pay to continually use a generalised, all-purpose programme.

HYGIENE. Hygiene is another important part of cut flower cultivation, especially with regard to keeping plants healthy and producing top quality flowers. Hygiene includes maintaining weed-free production areas; removing or quarantining sick or diseased plants; controlling pests that cause damage and disease; and cleaning and sterilising greenhouses / tunnels, pack-houses, cool-rooms, implements, tools, buckets and clothing on a regular basis.

HARVESTING OF CUT FLOWERS

The harvesting of cut flowers is in most cases labour intensive. All of this handling often results in physical damage to the flowers. To minimise damage, growers are continually trying to reduce the number of times a flower is physically touched by a person. Cut flowers are not only harvested on cut flower farms, but also from the wild. In many countries, cut flowers and to even greater extent foliage, is harvested from their natural habitat. If not properly controlled this sort of cut flower industry can cause damage to the environment and will not be sustainable. In countries such as Australia and South Africa, where wild-harvesting is regularly practised because of the incredibly rich floral diversity, regulations are in place to ensure that biodiversity is not lost and that sustainability is maintained. Wild-harvested flowers often have problems such as pests and diseases, as well as lack of desired characteristics found in cultivated flowers, such as crooked stems, limited colours and shorter vase life. Therefore research is continually being done on naturalising, breeding and cultivating potential species harvested from the wild.

STAGE OF HARVEST. The opening stage at which flowers are harvested has an influence on their vase life and how well the flowers will continue to open. If the flowers are harvested too early, the carbohydrate (starch and sugar) reserves are too low. These carbohydrates are a source of energy or food needed by the flower to live and to continue to open. Furthermore, carbohydrates help to maintain turgidity, thus preventing the flower from drooping or wilting too quickly.

If flowers are harvested too late, they would have passed their prime and also have a shorter vase life at the consumer. It is not always easy to determine the exact stage at which a flower must be harvested. Besides the carbohydrate factor, there is also the market demand factor. Different markets or customers want their flowers at different opening stages. Flowers harvested for local consumption are often harvested more open than those harvested for export.

TIME OF HARVEST. Flowers should be harvested in the cool of the day. This is usually early morning or late afternoon. Early in the morning flowers are still fully turgid. That is they are full of water and firm. During the heat of the day, cut flowers lose a lot of water through transpiration. Often more water is lost than can be taken up and thus temporary wilting takes place. Even if these flowers are picked and immediately placed in water, the results are not as good and quality is lost. The flowers might stand up again, especially when placed in a cool-room, but a lot of unseen damage may already have been done and flowers picked in the heat of the day will never last as long as flowers harvested in the early, cool morning or late afternoon. Many researchers recommend that the best time to harvest flowers is late in the day when the carbohydrate reserves are at their highest, but this may not be practical. However, water reserves are usually best in the early morning. Both times are fine for harvesting. The timing and frequency of harvesting per day also depends on the type of flower grown and the size of the operation.

TEMPERATURE. Heat kills flowers. At high temperatures flowers respire much faster than at lower temperatures. Respiration and transpiration lead to a significant loss of water. This excessive water loss causes severe damage to cell walls, leading to permanent wilting. Temperature is a critical factor in the whole quality chain. For every 10-degree temperature decrease, the speed of the physiological processes in plants is on average reduced by two to three times. Field heat needs to be removed from flowers as soon as possible after harvesting and a cold chain maintained. Each flower type has a minimum temperature at which it can be stored and anything below this could result in cold damage.

A primary factor determining the consumer quality of cut flowers is temperature management during handling and transportation. It is therefore of utmost importance to try to maintain the cold chain as efficiently and as long as possible. Transporting cut flowers in water does not replace the need to transport the flowers at low temperatures. The main emphasis in maintaining the cold chain is to ensure flower quality, freshness and vase life.

Most flowers are best stored at 4–6°C (39–43°F) and at 90% relative humidity. This does not mean that they can be stored indefinitely at those temperatures. They still need to be sold as

Harvesting of cut flowers

soon as possible. Preferably, flowers should not be held for longer than 3–4 days in a cool-room. After that many flower types start to lose quality rapidly.

For florists who work with a variety of cut flowers but have only one cool-room, it is best to set the temperature at 4–6°C (39–43°F) and the relative humidity at 90%. However, tropical flowers still need to be stored at a higher temperature of 13–15°C (55–59°F) and a relative humidity of 90%.

AIR HUMIDITY. Even in storage, transpiration continues and this can lead to unacceptable moisture loss that cannot be effectively replaced, leading to premature wilting and death of the flower. The main cause of transpiration is the vapour pressure deficit (VPD), which is the combined effect of temperature and relative humidity. When the VPD is high, the transpiration rate of flowers is also high. A low transpiration rate, which is ideal, can be obtained by a combination of low temperature and high humidity. Therefore, there should be some mechanism for controlling humidity in flower cool-rooms. If the humidity is set too high (over 95%) other problems arise such as condensation on the cool-room ceilings and walls. This causes a lot of damage to flowers as the condensation drips onto the flowers, and also creates an ideal environment for the outbreak of diseases such as botrytis.

SANITATION AND HYGIENE. Flower quality and vase life are dramatically affected by the level of sanitation and hygiene. The main areas to focus on are working surfaces, tables, cool-rooms, equipment and tools, and vehicles. All of these need to be cleaned daily and regularly sterilised. Washing with soap and water means it may be clean, but it is not disinfected. To achieve full hygiene, a disinfectant needs to be used as well.

GRADING. The proper grading according to market standards and demands is vital. Grading affects the overall quality of flowers. Flowers in a bunch should be uniform in all aspects. That is in their opening stage, length, colour and grade. Few things irritate a buyer or end-consumer more than a poorly graded bunch of flowers. They often regard this as poor quality or dishonesty on the part of the supplier. Presentation forms a vital part of perceived and real quality of cut flowers.

POST-HARVEST TREATMENTS
OF CUT FLOWERS

All cut flowers, foliages and cut greens should be treated at grower and retail level. This treatment usually involves placing an additive (commonly known as a cut flower preservative) in the water in which the flowers are kept. Florists should also urge their clients to use cut flower preservatives so that maximum enjoyment can be obtained from their purchase. Keep in mind that post-harvest treatments do not improve but simply help to maintain quality. These treatments also help flowers cope with the stresses of handling and transportation.

Good quality water is needed for cut flower preservatives to be effective. Water is of a suitable quality for cut flowers when it has very little dissolved salts in it, including fluoride. Hard water, which is often water with a high concentration of calcium carbonates in it, will also render cut flower preservatives less effective.

There are a number of different types of floral treatments, the use of which depend on the type of flower as well as where in the marketing chain the flower is.

PULSING MEDIUMS. These are typically used by growers after harvest to hydrate and condition flowers to help them cope with the stresses of handling and transportation. These mediums usually break down water tension to facilitate water uptake by the flowers and also contain a sugar to supply energy. If the flowers are sensitive to ethylene, then growers will also treat them with an anti-ethylene agent, which either prevents the production of ethylene by the flower itself or helps the flower to withstand damage from external ethylene sources. Pulsing mediums are usually highly concentrated and flowers will typically only stand in them for a few minutes or a few hours.

HYDRATING SOLUTIONS. They assist and improve water uptake by the flowers. Hydrating solutions drastically lower the pH of the water and make it very acidic (pH 3–3.5). These solutions work best if there are no sugar additives in the solution. They are used by growers, wholesalers and florists.

HOLDING PRODUCTS. These usually contain a bactericide to keep the water clean and a sugar (sucrose or fructose) in low concentrations to assist in maintaining the source of food (energy) for the flowers. If the sugar concentration is too high, it can cause buds to open too quickly, thus shortening vase life.

CUT FLOWER PRESERVATIVES. Many cut flower preservatives have been specially formulated for specific flowers or groups of flowers. This is aimed at directly combating particular problems these flowers may have, such as ethylene sensitivity or yellowing of leaves.

All of the above products or mediums contain anti-bacterial components to suppress growth of micro-organisms in the water as well as in the stems of the flowers themselves. Microbes that grow and multiply in the water also infect and block the vessels inside the flower stems, thereby preventing the necessary uptake of water.

Flowers that respond well to commercial slow-release chlorine solutions and aluminium sulphate-based hydration solutions include ageratum, allium, calendula, echinops, eremurus, eryngium, eupatorium, frittelaria, gerbera, helipterum, hydrangea, hypericum, lavender, liatris, lobelia, lupine, lysimachia, pelargonium, molucella, monarda, nandina, nicotiana, nigella, oregano, papaver (poppy), penstemon, phlox, photinia, ranunculus, salvia, saponaria, tagetes (marigold), tanacetum (matricaria), trachelium, verbascum, xeranthemum and zinnia.

Flowers that respond best to a quaternary ammonium-based hydration solution include aster, bupleurum, dahlia, gentian, helianthus (sunflower), limonium and all daisy-type flowers (Asteraceae).

Flowers that require a low sugar pre-treatment include calla lilies, lisianthus, lilac, mimosa, stock, sunflower and viburnum.

Flowers that require a high sugar pre-treatment include proteas, leucadendrons, leucospermums and tuberoses.

A modern cool-room

COLD TREATMENT. The "cold chain" refers to keeping the flowers cold at all times as they move from the field to the flower market and then to the wholesaler, retailer and finally the vase in the flower-lover's home.

Recommended storage temperatures for cut flowers depend on the particular species and cultivar, but generally vary between 0–4°C (32–39°F) for traditional flowers and 12–15°C (54–59°F) for tropical flowers. Cut stems could either be stored wet in water and preservative solutions or dry in a polyethylene plastic or wax-lined box. It is recommended that wholesalers and florists store most flowers wet, which results in less damage if not done 100% correctly. However, many cut greens inherently have a long vase life and can be stored dry without major loss of quality as long as a high humidity is maintained (e.g. kept in plastic bags or water-retentive boxes).

There are essentially two types of coolers used by florists: storage coolers for holding or storing flowers and display coolers for displaying flowers and bouquets. Standard beverage coolers and the like are not suitable for flowers, as they do not have humidifiers. Cold air will dehydrate flowers and flower coolers need to have humidifiers so that not only temperature, but also humidity can be controlled. The low temperature slows down respiration and bud opening, and the high air humidity slows down transpiration (water loss and resultant wilting). Relative humidity is just as important in a cooler as temperature. Avoid or reduce botrytis and other infections by keeping the cool-room temperatures from going above 6°C (43°F). Do not place wet flowers in the cooler, but first allow them to dry at room temperature. Do not overcrowd buckets or cool-rooms but allow for ventilation. Remove damaged, diseased and decaying plant material, as it is most vulnerable to infection and promotes the spread of disease. Keep buckets, work surfaces, tools, cool-room floors and walls clean and sterilise them regularly.

Some flowers and florist greens are tropical in origin and are very sensitive to chill injury if held or transported at low temperatures. These tropical and other chill-sensitive flowers and florist greens include anthurium, bird-of-paradise, camellia, cattleya orchid, chamaedora, cordyline (ti), dieffenbachia, eucharis, euphorbia, ginger, godetia, heliconia, palm, poinsettia, protea, staghorn fern and vanda orchid.

MARKETING OF CUT FLOWERS

Marketing forms an integral part of any business, including florists and flower retailers. Florists spend much time face to face with their customers in the shop and this creates important marketing opportunities. Some basic tips for florists are: Clearly display signs and prices. Maintain a good volume and colour mix of flowers. Sell only top quality flowers and greens. Keep display areas and buckets clean, tidy and hygienic (as well as the shop in general). Continually remove old or dying flowers from potted plants. Give customers advice on how to handle and care for the flowers they purchase.

LIGHTING. Lighting in shops is important not simply because plants and flowers require it but also because the proper lighting can go a long way to bring out the best colour in the flowers. Lighting should be as close to natural daylight as possible. Fluorescent lights are usually the best for this purpose. Fluorescent lights also give off very little heat, which is important. Incandescent light bulbs often produce a yellowish, unnatural light, as well as give off a lot of heat that can damage and dry out flowers and plants. It is also important for cool-rooms to have proper lighting. Roses should be conditioned in a dark cooler. All other flowers should be conditioned for 1–2 hours in light outside the cooler.

MARKETING BASICS. The basics of marketing for florists should revolve around quality, consistency and communication. High-quality flowers are important, but such quality needs to be constant to keep customers coming back for more. You, as the florist or retailer, need to be able to trace each and every flower sold to your customers back to your source. Should there be any complaints from your customers, the flowers can be traced back to a specific supplier. Do not oversupply or present customers with too many choices. Novelty is also an important factor in the successful marketing of new cultivars, as the cut flower industry is very much driven by fashion. In the past, trends in flowers, such as colour, did not originate in the cut flower industry itself, but have been set by other industries such as fashion, interior design, magazines and television.

SPECIAL OCCASIONS. Festive occasions play an important role in the cut flower industry. On most of these special occasions, cut flower sales increase dramatically. Florists need to have an understanding of the reasons for the celebration and the colour, or colours, associated with it. Prices for certain colours reach a peak during festive and ceremonial occasions. In many countries, the three peak flower delivery periods for florists are Mother's Day (2nd Sunday of May), Saint Valentine's Day (14 February; 12 June in Brazil) and Christmas Day (25 December). Mother's Day was recognised as a public holiday in the United States in 1914 after a campaign by Anna Jarvis of West Virginia. Mother's Day is associated with carnations, symbolic of love and gratitude (pink) or admiration (red). Saint Valentine's Day (or simply Valentine's Day) is a day on which lovers express their love for each other by presenting flowers and other gifts. The red rose is symbolic of romantic love. Christmas Day is also a very important day on the florist's calendar in many countries. The poinsettia has become a preferred Christmas flower. Flower symbols associated with Thanksgiving Day, a harvest festival in the United States (4th Thursday in November) and Canada (2nd Monday in October), include autumn foliage, decorative pumpkins or gourds and bunches of wheat.

TOP-SELLING FLOWERS. It is impossible to be completely accurate about the best-selling flowers. These are constantly changing because production can be affected by adverse or favourable weather conditions in many parts of the world, and because market forces control which products are imported from where and in what quantities. As a rough guide, the following are often amongst the bestsellers in most countries: roses (60% of all flowers!), chrysanthemums (15%?), carnations (10%), lilies (5%), tulips (4%), and then followed by alstroemeria, gerbera, freesia, gladiolus, snapdragons, daffodils, delphinium, tuberose, Michaelmas daisy and statice. Among the top-selling potted flowers are kalanchoe, African violets, begonias, rhododendrons, chrysanthemums, roses, orchids and pelargoniums. The most popular foliages and fillers include leatherleaf, aspidistra, asparagus ferns, butcher's broom, twisted willow, florist gum, gypsophila, golden rod, pittosporum and hypericum.

Typical outdoor display

Diversity of products

PROPERTIES OF CUT FLOWERS

Market research has shown on numerous occasions and in many countries that the most popular flower colour is blue and that the most popular cut flower is the rose. Interestingly enough, when people are asked to quickly think of a flower and its colour, they generally come up with a red rose. Perhaps this is why the red rose is the most famous of all florist flowers and why there is a strong desire for breeding a blue rose!

GENERAL APPEARANCE. Flowers are often bought on impulse. Even those of us who intentionally go into a florist shop to buy flowers, often buy a certain flower, bunch or bouquet on impulse. Therefore, the overall appearance (aesthetic value) of a flower or mix of flowers is important. This includes the length of the stems, the colour and shape of the leaves and even the packaging and presentation of the flowers.

COLOUR. One of the most important properties of a cut flower is its colour. This is also why certain flowers are in demand for certain festive occasions, such as red roses for Valentine's Day, white lilies for weddings or blue flowers as a novelty. Colour is due to various pigments in the petals, of which anthocyanins, flavonoids and betacyanins are the main groups. There is always a demand for new, novel colours, as well as a continuous search for rare or as yet unknown flower colours such as a genuine black tulip or a really blue rose.

STEM LENGTH. Stem length is usually seen as an important indicator of quality. Certain flowers such as daffodils (*Narcissus*) and hyacinths (*Hyacinthus*) are naturally short-stemmed, but the market knows and accepts this. However, even these still need to meet the minimum stem length requirements for those species to be viewed as good quality.

VASE LIFE. The length of time a flower lives after it has been harvested and put in plain water is the primary determining factor of quality used in the industry. There are numerous factors that influence the vase life of a flower. The real vase life of a flower should be seen as the number of days the flower remains in an acceptable state at the end consumer. If a flower lasts one week at the end consumer, this is viewed as acceptable and is seen as an average vase life. There are, however, some exceptions of flowers that the market accepts as having a shorter vase life.

ETHYLENE SENSITIVITY. Ethylene is a natural occurring colourless and odourless gas that has an adverse affect on the life of cut flowers. The atmospheric concentrations of ethylene are highest during autumn and winter. Ethylene in the atmosphere results from natural sources (production by plants, micro-organisms and volcanoes), as well as from industrial activity and internal combustion engines (smoke, cigarettes, general pollution). Ethylene is also a plant growth regulator (hormone) that is directly associated with ripening, maturation and aging of flowers, fruits, leaves, etc. In flowers, a sharp increase in ethylene production is observed just prior to wilting and aging. Different flowers and even different cultivars of the same flower, exhibit varying degrees of sensitivity to ethylene, but all flowers become more sensitive as they age. Symptoms and rate of onset also vary and include, but are not necessarily restricted to leaf drop, flower and/or bud drop (abscission, bud abortion), rapid or premature flower ageing, epinasty (sleepiness) or shrinkage of flowers, and reduced vase life. Flowers absorb external ethylene, which then speeds up the ageing process. Concentrations as low as 0.1 parts per million (ppm) can have a negative effect on ethylene-sensitive flowers. Ethylene generally causes less damage to potted plants. However, there are also possible negative effects on potted flowers, resulting in many of the same symptoms as with cut flowers. Ethylene induced injury to potted flowers is more serious during high temperatures, low light intensities and after excessive over-watering or drying.

FRAGRANCE. The effect of flowers on the senses and emotions of humans is undoubtedly also related to their fragrance. Besides the visual aspects of bright colours, varying forms and textures that place many flowers in demand, the sweet scent of some flowers is also an important selling

White lilies are popular for weddings

point. Sweet peas, tuberoses, bouvardias, spring blossoms, lilies and cattleya orchids are examples of flowers that are sometimes bought as much for their fragrance as for their colour or shape. A strong fragrance is often found in flowers that open in the evening and that are adapted to pollination by moths. Unfortunately, many modern cultivars have lost their fragrance during commercial breeding. Old English roses, for example, are commonly grown in home gardens for their exquisite fragrance, while many of the modern rose cultivars are almost totally devoid of fragrance. Some flowers, although beautiful, can have unpleasant or irritating aromas. Examples are alliums (they have an onion or garlic smell due to the presence of sulphur compounds) and some statice cultivars. Carrion flowers (e.g. *Stapelia gigantea*) are commonly cultivated despite their unbelievably foul smell that serves to attract flies and blowflies as pollinating agents.

STAGE OF HARVEST. It is difficult to routinely harvest flowers at exactly the right stage of maturity. Not only do different flowers have different optimum harvesting stages, but the stages also vary among cultivars of the same flower type. Furthermore, cutting stages usually differ during winter and summer. The main aim is trying to ensure that the flowers arrive at the customer at just the right opening stage as demanded by them.

As a rule of thumb, the best stage to harvest any flower is "as closed as possible to open". In other words, picking the flower as closed as possible to limit handling damage and maximise vase life, but at the same time at a sufficiently advanced stage of development so that a grower knows the flower will still open to its full potential. This of course is the case not only for single-stemmed flowers but sprays, spikes and inflorescences as well, where most, if not all of the flowers on the stem should open fully. This said, different countries or consumers often want their flowers at different opening stages. For example, the United States typically requires export flowers to be in partial bloom, while they need to be tightly closed buds for the Japanese market and wide open for the Russian market.

QUALITY CRITERIA – HOW TO SELECT A SUPERIOR FLOWER

Quality and cut flowers are synonymous, but it is very difficult to comprehensively define cut flower quality in a single sentence or by a single factor. The industry (and consumers) tend to measure the quality of cut flowers primarily by how long they will last once harvested and sold (or bought and arranged), namely vase life. Different types of flowers last different lengths of time. For example, under similar conditions, chrysanthemums last, on average, much longer than roses or tulips. Over a period of time, the average vase life for each cut flower type and cultivar is established in the market place. The market then expects and demands that a top quality flower, which receives a premium price, should, on average and under normal circumstances, last a minimum of so many days.

Besides vase life, other factors that are also indicators of quality are the following:

BUD / FLOWER SIZE AND COUNT. Generally speaking the bigger the buds the better the quality of the flowering stem. Bud count is also important, but obviously not with standards (single stem and flower), such as is often found in roses, chrysanthemums and carnations. Bud size and count are crucial in flowers such as lilies and orchids, but much less so in many of the filler flowers.

SHADE, INTENSITY AND SHARPNESS OF FLOWER COLOUR. One of the most important characteristics of a florist flower is its colour. For this reason, uniformity, intensity and sharpness of the colour of the flower/s are seen as a measure of quality. Flower colour is often adversely affected by poor cultivation conditions such as excessive heat, and florists, retailers and consumers are also aware of this. Sometimes a cultivar might be healthy and of top quality but still have a naturally poor, or washed out colour. Typically such cultivars do not fare well in the industry and are not popular amongst flower buyers so that they are soon discarded.

LEAF COLOUR AND SIZE. The results of poor cultivation practices and disease are quick to show in the leaves of a plant. Lack of certain nutrients quickly shows as yellowing along leaf veins, tips or edges. Excessive heat results in burnt tips, while pests and disease can cause leaves to curl, discolour or die. Healthy plants tend to have larger leaves and a more vibrant and uniform colour. It is therefore important to always look at the leaves when buying flowers, even if you intend to strip them all off. The quality of the leaves will suffer first at the expense of the actual flower.

STEM THICKNESS, STRAIGHTNESS AND LENGTH. The stem of a flower must be able to support the flower head. Healthy plants will produce thicker stems. Proper cultivation practices (regular irrigation, proper fertilisation, adequate light and pest management) will ensure that stems are strong, straight and of good length.

WEIGHT OF CUT FLOWER. A healthy cut stem typically weighs more than a poor quality one. This is simply because the healthy stem will be thicker and have larger flowers, more buds and more leaves. Many cut flowers (e.g. chrysanthemums) are often graded according to weight.

ABSENCE OF SPRAY RESIDUE, PESTS AND HANDLING DAMAGE. A top quality cut stem is one that has no signs of pests and diseases, handling damage or spray residue on the leaves, stem or flowers. This is simply a sign that the utmost care has been taken in the cultivation, management, processing and transporting of the cut flower, foliage or filler.

GENETIC MAKEUP. There are internal and external factors that influence the vase life of cut flowers. External factors include temperature, irrigation, light, treatment, handling, etc. Internal factors include the genetic makeup of the plant or flower. For this reason different flowers, even when grown under optimal conditions, will have different vase lives (e.g. irises compared to chrysanthemums). However, just because a plant inherently has a short vase life does not necessarily mean that it is of poor quality. The industry has set a standard for various flower types and consumers soon learn that a quality flower of a certain type must have a vase life of so many days, or else it was a poor quality flower. Because of the short vase life of certain florist flowers they cannot be transported over long distances. These flowers are very seldom exported and are typically produced for local markets only.

The various factors discussed here once again highlight the fact that the quality of a florist flower or florist green is not determined by a single factor, but by a combination of many factors.

Common defects in roses (from left to right): high quality; crooked stem; flower too open and botrytis damage; bent neck; bud too closed and damaged foliage

CARE AND HANDLING OF FRESH CUT FLOWERS

There is no post-harvest procedure that can improve the quality of cut flowers or potted flowers. After production, quality may, at best, be maintained as the flowers move through the marketing chain to the flower vase. The quicker the flowers are sold and leave the florist shop the better. Their vase life is limited and the more time they spend in the home, the better. Each flower has a normal, genetically determined maximum vase life. However, there are many factors (over which we have control) that reduce vase life. These include food depletion, attack by fungal and bacterial diseases (especially botrytis, see later), fluctuations in temperature, mechanical damage (e.g. bruising due to careless handling), poor water quality, wilting and general water stress and the accumulation of ethylene (see later). Some important considerations for maintaining or improving vase life are given here.

MAINTAIN THE COLD CHAIN. Keep flowers cool. Vase life drastically decreases as flower temperatures increase. Flowers should be transported and stored within recommended temperature ranges. Do not purchase flowers from growers that you know do not transport flowers in cooled trucks. Lowering the temperature of the flower slows down metabolism, thereby maintaining stored energy levels (carbohydrates). Most flowers are best stored at 1–2°C (34–36°F), except tropical flowers such as anthurium, ginger, proteas, orchids and strelitzia, which should be stored at 10–13°C (50–55°F).

PAY ATTENTION TO HYGIENE. Keep tools, equipment, cool-rooms and work surfaces clean and sterilised. Use alcohol, bleach or other disinfectants. Micro-organisms, such as botrytis, thrive in damp, dirty conditions and easily spread from dirty containers to flowers or from flower to flower. They spoil the appearance of the petals or, when present in the cut ends, prevent uptake of water. Botrytis is a fungus, commonly known as grey mould, which causes a lot of damage in florist flowers. Common symptoms are grey or brown spots on the petals or leaves that typically start off as small circular blemishes and then enlarge. Only purchase quality flowers and greens and inspect them for signs of disease and infection. After flowers have been unpacked, they should be prepared for conditioning in a preservative solution. As a first step, any damaged foliage or flowers should be removed because this will begin to decay and emit higher levels of ethylene than fresh foliage or flowers.

RECUT STEMS. Removing the bottom 20–50 mm (1–2") of the stem improves water uptake in three different ways: (1) It removes the natural seal that has formed over the cut (wound); (2) It removes possible bacterial infections that may block the stem ends; (3) It removes air embolisms or air bubbles that may have formed in the stem ends. Make sure that the cut is clean – use sharp secateurs or a knife – ordinary scissors will bruise or crush the stems. It is not necessary to cut stems under water, as this does not improve vase life, especially if cut flower foods and preservatives are used. If you insist on doing so make sure the cutting tank is regularly sterilised and the water replaced to prevent re-infection from the water.

Crushing stems with a hammer has been used in the past with chrysanthemums and other flowers to "open up" the stems for easier water uptake. However, nowadays this practice is generally considered inappropriate for any flower because it damages the water-carrying vessels in the stem. Before cutting the fleshy, hollow stems of tulips, daffodils, irises and calla lilies, it is best to wrap the individual stem bases with string. These stems will soften and split when placed in water, and the string (placed just above the point where the stem will be cut) will prevent this damage.

Some flower stems, for example euphorbia and poinsettia, contain a milky sap (latex) that will continue to flow from the cut stem. This will lead to wilting of the flower, fouling of the storage water, and interference with water absorption by other flowers in the container. The sap flow may be stopped by sealing the stem end-cut (congealing the latex) by either searing the latex droplet with a flame, dipping the stem into boiling water for less than a minute, or soaking the stem end in ice water for several minutes. Normal water uptake will take place through the stem end after the latex has been sealed.

Re-cut stems

Botrytis damage

How much of the stem to cut off will vary from flower to flower, and also depend on how much stem is available or needed. It may be as little as 5 mm (¼") for anthurium or up to 100–150 mm (4–6") for gladiolus, but the usual cut length will be about 25–50 mm (1–2"). In all cases the cut should be made diagonally across the stem rather than straight across. An angled cut does not increase the amount of water a stem is able to take up, but it does prevent stems from resting flat against the bottom of the container and possibly blocking water uptake.

Water in the flower stem vessels is under natural tension; this is how the water is moved through the stem. As the flower and stem dehydrate, the remaining water is under even greater tension. When the stem is cut, that tension will pull the water back away from the new cut end and draw in air. This creates an air "bubble" or embolism that must be absorbed or broken up before water can flow into and up the stem. Thus, it is generally recommended that flower stems should be recut underwater so that water, rather than air, will be drawn in at the new stem end. When the stems are removed from the container where they were recut, enough water will cling to the stem end to block the entry of air as the stems are moved quickly to the container of preservative solution. Underwater recutting of stems is not a universal practice. It is an awkward and messy task that has not been proven as significantly adding to the floral vase life. Roses, with their high value and shorter than desirable vase life, are particularly advocated for underwater stem cutting, and the practice does appear to provide some benefits. It is particularly inefficient during the design process when using a knife, and the practice appears to be less beneficial when the stems are fully hydrated. Recutting stems underwater in the case of dehydrated, "dry pack" flowers, even if the benefit is only limited, should be considered an inexpensive bonus to the customer when it can be reasonably done. There are commercially available underwater flower cutters that consist of a large knife attached to the inside of a tank filled with water. These make it possible to very efficiently cut a large number of flowers.

REMOVE FOLIAGE BELOW THE WATER LINE. Remove any foliage that will be below the water line when the stems are placed in the preservative solution. The leaves release phenoles into the water which block the vessels, hinder the development of the buds and accelerate the withering of the flower. They also pollute the water and encourage growth of micro-organisms. Foliage left below the water line will begin to rot and encourage bacterial growth in the water and affect flower vase life by promoting stem blockage. Lower foliage should be gently stripped off to avoid bruising or cutting the stem. In the case of roses, preferably do not remove the thorns with a mechanical stripper as these cause open wounds that can infect easily.

PAY ATTENTION TO WATER QUALITY AND TEMPERATURE. Hard, alkaline water shortens the vase life. If you live in an area with hard water, you can use a deioniser or add some citric acid to the water. Too much sodium in the water is poisonous to carnations and roses while too much fluoride will damage gerbera, gladioli and freesia. Lukewarm water is recommended for just a few flower types, such as heliconia. It can be very damaging for some other kinds of flowers. Never use hot water – this will damage any type of flower. In most cases simply use tap water at the temperature at which it comes out of the tap. Never mix old water with new, clean water. Never place fresh flowers in old water or dirty buckets and vases.

REHYDRATE FLOWERS. Flowers can easily lose 5–10% of their water during transportation and storage. Do not place the flowers in a draught and keep the wrapping around the bouquet as long as possible. Dehydration can lead to the formation of air-bubbles in the water vessels, which will hinder the flow of fluids even after the flowers are put into water again. The quicker they are hydrated the less water stress they will suffer and the better the vase life will be. This can be done by using hydrating solutions, lowering water pH with acids such as citric acid, or simply recutting and placing in a preservative for one to two hours at room temperature.

Generally, when flowers are placed in a preservative solution they should be left to stand at room temperature for an hour or two before moving them to the cool-room. They should be in a draught-free location, away from radiators or other sources of heat or cold, out of direct sunlight, and away from any fruit or evergreens, as these emit high levels of ethylene. This conditioning period allows the flowers to take up the "warm" preservative food and water quickly, whereas placing them directly in the cool-room can slow down the process. "Warm" flowers take up water faster than "cool" flowers, and the aim is to get as much water as possible into the flowers as quickly as possible. After standing at room temperature for an hour or more, the containers of flowers should be moved into a cool-room or floral cooler. Roses are a notable exception to this and should be placed directly into the cool-room. When properly prepared, they will hydrate fast enough in the cool-room while avoiding further water loss and bud opening that would occur at room temperature.

During the processing and conditioning of flowers, any damaged flower heads or wilted petals should be removed. However, if flowers are to be stored in a cool-room rather than on display, these petals may be better left on to protect the flower head until it is moved to a display cooler or is to be used in an arrangement.

AVOID ETHYLENE. Ethylene prematurely ages, damages and shortens the vase life of many, but not all flowers. Typically, ethylene exposure increases with increased temperatures. Sources of ethylene in the home are micro-organisms (bacteria and fungi), ripening fruit, exhaust fumes, cigarette smoke and the flowers themselves. Handle flowers with care – injury produces more ethylene – and provide good ventilation. It is very important to avoid contact with sources of ethylene. The use of cut flower preservatives containing anti-ethylene agents is recommended. During shipment in boxes and other packaging, or storage in confined environments, ethylene is trapped and concentrations increase. Small packets of ethylene-absorbing granules can be placed in the boxes to reduce ethylene concentrations and ventilation can be improved. Fruits and vegetables produce high amounts of ethylene as they mature, and flowers should not be transported or stored with them.

USE CUT FLOWER PRESERVATIVES AND FOODS. Nearly all florist flowers benefit from the use of preservatives and foods (sugars) in the water. Preservatives typically have an anti-bacterial effect (to keep the water fresh) and they usually have a surfactant to break any air bubbles that may form (which may prevent water uptake). Another benefit is that they typically contain an energy source (mainly sugar such as sucrose or fructose) that provides the flower with additional energy, which it no longer gets from the parent plant. Furthermore, they often contain anti-ethylene agents that prevent ethylene damage. These include salts of silver (STS – silver thiosulphate or silver

Keep buckets clean

Avoid sources of ethylene

Floral preservatives

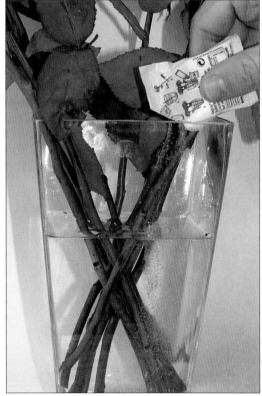

Use of preservatives

nitrate) or hormones such as cytokinins. Using preservatives goes a long way to maintaining vase life and helping flowers cope with the general stress of lack of water, handling, ethylene, etc. Just keep in mind that preservatives are not "miracle" products and can only do so much. Using them does not mean the other general rules and practices of care and handling should be neglected.

CONSIDER TEMPERATURE. Avoid temperature fluctuations – gradually introduce flowers from a cold room (or cold vehicle) to a warm room. During winter, it is advisable to allow flowers to adjust in a place not heated directly, at about 15°C (59°F), before placing them in a heated room. Never leave flowers in a closed car or in any other place that is too hot. Avoid freezing temperatures. Some types of flowers will die within seconds at such temperatures. Also avoid displaying flowers in direct sunlight.

ENSURE SUFFICIENT AIR CIRCULATION. A certain amount of air circulation is necessary to avoid the build-up of high concentrations of ethylene produced by the flowers. Cigarette smoke, exhaust gases or ripe fruit, especially strawberries and tomatoes, in the vicinity can also release large quantities of ethylene. Good ventilation is necessary, but avoid a direct draught on the flowers, which will dehydrate them.

PROVIDE NATURAL LIGHT. Lighting should be as close to natural daylight as possible. Not only does it display the flowers to the best advantage, it also provides the natural stimulus to keep flowers alive and to maintain pigment levels. However, some flowers, such as roses, should be conditioned and stored in a dark cooler and then moved to the illuminated display cooler as needed. Fluorescent lights are preferred for floral coolers as they produce very little heat, which helps to maintain the proper temperatures without lowering the efficiency of the cooler operation. Incandescent light bulbs produce a great deal of heat and can be harmful to the flowers if they are too close to them.

USE ONLY TOP QUALITY FLOWERS. Some cultivars do not last as long as others. Find out which cultivars are more long lasting and attempt to purchase these whenever possible. Get to know which growers, wholesalers or florists supply quality flowers.

Tips on working with floral foams

First and foremost, be aware of the importance of properly conditioning the flowers before placing them in an arrangement. This involves giving the flowers a fresh cut at the stem, removing the foliage that would fall below the water line, and placing the flowers in a clean bucket filled with water and a floral food or hydration solution. In a commercial retail florist shop, the flowers are then "hardened" by placing them in a cooler at the proper temperature. Home-based designers should simply allow their flowers to drink water for several hours before styling begins.

Floral foams saturate best when allowed to float freely in a tub of water in a flat position. There should be enough water to fill the brick and also allow it to float freely when fully saturated. While all foams soak in a few minutes, the lighter foams soak more quickly than the heavier foams. Do not force bricks under the water in an attempt to get them saturated quickly, as this has the opposite effect of trapping air and reducing water uptake and saturation. Floral foods or preservatives should be used in preparing the soaking solution. The first 24 hours is the critical period in the use of floral preservatives. The use of preservatives gives the designer the added assurance of more brilliant colours and larger, longer lasting blooms.

Floral foam is not a substitute for water! The water lost by evaporation or consumed by the flowers must be replaced. When the design does not call for a container, the brick should be wrapped in foil or other nonporous material in order to minimise water loss. To make sure that the flowers always have an adequate water supply, choose containers that provide a reservoir for water. If it is difficult to add water to the arrangement, it is certain the flowers will become thirsty and will not survive for long.

Allow the floral foam to aid the design. Many florists cut floral foam level with the top of the container. Instead, cut the foam so that it extends above the rim of the container. This will allow you to place the flower stems horizontally over the edge of the container and thus permitting much greater design flexibility. Foam has a wicking or capillary action, which will draw water into the flower cell as long as there is a readily available supply of water.

Float foam bricks (do not submerge)

Use of floral foams

Saturate foam before use

Floral foam

CARE AND HANDLING
OF DRIED FLOWERS

Dried flowers are very much part of the florist's flower trade. It is therefore important to highlight some care and handling aspects of this discipline.

GENERAL CONSIDERATIONS. Use high quality flowers. Do not try to "salvage" poor quality flowers by drying them. Flowers to be dried must not be moist or wet. Young, but mature flowers work best. When flowers are too old they tend to lose their colour when dried. A large percentage of the volume of a flower is water. So when they are dried they shrink and become smaller in size. Flowers with a high water content such as lilies or peonies do not dry as well as those with a moderate to low water content. Tropical flowers do not air-dry well. Flowers that do not air-dry well are usually also difficult to preserve properly by means of glycerine treatments. Sunlight causes colours to fade when drying. Dry in the dark to retain colour. Faded dry flowers are, however, advantageous when they are to be coloured. The exceptions are eucalyptus and gypsophila, which give the best results when dried in the light. A dried flower should feel stiff and dry and not soft or moist. Examples of flowers that preserve well by air-drying are gypsophila, cattail, limonium, celosia, dock, solidago, heather and pussy willow. Flowers dried in this manner are extremely stiff once dried. Blue and yellow flowers retain their colours when air-dried, but pink flowers tend to fade. Roses and peonies shrink somewhat when air-dried. Dried flowers should have a "vase life" of at least one year. Routine dusting can be accomplished using a real feather duster or hairdryer on the lowest setting. To store dried flowers, wrap them in newspaper and place in a cardboard box. Do not store the box in unusually damp (some basements) or dry (some attics) areas. Temperature is not that important. Depending on the storage area, take care to protect the flowers from rodents and insects.

There are many methods to dry fresh flowers. Some of the most popular ones with regard to florists are air-drying, pressing, silica gel or other brand name desiccants, silica sand, borax and maize meal or something similar, glycerine solution and microwave treatment.

AIR-DRYING. Prepare proper facilities for the air-drying of flowers. Avoid direct sun, wind, water and dust. Dust particles can attach permanently to flowers that have been treated with sealants or flame-retardants. Good air-movement accelerates drying time and removes the build-up of moisture that can lead to flowers becoming mouldy. The rate of drying increases with an increase in temperature but decreases with humidity. Many, but not all, florist flowers are suitable for drying.

The simplest way to air-dry flowers is to tie them into small, loose bunches and to hang them upside down in a well-ventilated, dark area. Cut stems to a uniform length. Make small, loose bunches to avoid crushing or deforming and to improve air circulation around the individual flowers. Tie together with twine or rubber bands that will hold but not crush the stems. Lack of ventilation or high humidity (more than 65%) could result in flowers becoming mouldy. Sunlight usually causes flower colours to fade.

Most flowers take one to three weeks to dry properly, depending on moisture content and the procedure that is followed. Some flowers continue to open while drying and these should be obtained for drying at the bud stage or partially open stage. Growers that produce flowers for drying usually pick most flowers once fully open. Failure to dry flowers adequately can lead to mould problems when packed or stored.

Flowers ideal for air-drying include gypsophila, celosia (crested and plume types), globe amaranth, solidago, solidaster, hydrangea, salvia, limonium, xeranthemum, proteas, astilbe, everlastings, false indigo, okra, bee balm, gaillardia, allium, ornamental grasses, poppies, calendula, Queen Anne's lace, larkspur, lavender, verbena, marigolds, meadow-rue and yarrow.

PRESSING. Flowers can also be preserved by the classical method of simply pressing them between sheets of drying paper. However, this method is seldom used by florists because the three-dimensional form of the flower is lost. Unglazed paper should be used, such as newsprint paper.

Glycerine-dried roses   Dried flowers can be colourful

Alternating layers of flowers and paper are placed between two boards. A heavy object is then placed on the top board. Special plant presses are also available – the ones botanists use when they collect plant specimens. Drying papers must be regularly replaced with new (dry) ones to avoid mould – at first on a daily basis and later, when the moisture content is lower, every three days. The process should be complete within two to four weeks and varies with flower type and the water content of the tissue.

Flowers ideal for pressing include aster, bleeding heart, buttercup, chrysanthemum, columbine, cosmos, dahlia, English daisy (*Bellis perennis*), geranium, lily-of-the-valley, marigold, pansy, poppy, rose, sweet pea, violet and zinnia.

GLYCERINE-DRYING. Another approach to preserve flowers is to use glycerine, but this is trickier than other methods. The procedure is as follows: use fresh, fully hydrated (unwilted) flowers. Use a glycerine solution of about 1:3 (one part glycerine to three parts hot water) plus a surfactant to help with the uptake of the solution. Stand flowers in approximately 80–100 mm (3–4") of solution for 3–7 days, in a well-ventilated area, using shallow buckets to help with air movement around the leaves. Water-soluble dyes could be added during this process if desired. Remove flowers, cut off the part of the stem that was in the solution and hang to dry using normal air-drying procedures. Duration is approximately 1–2 weeks. If the drying flowers are not soft enough after 4–5 days, then the leaves can be given a light misting with glycerine. Some flowers do not absorb glycerine very well and will need to be immersed in the solution for 1–2 days (if unheated) or 6–12 hours (if heated – to approximately 82°C / 180°F). Afterwards, remove and rinse the flowers and hang to dry.

SILICA GEL OR OTHER DESICCANTS. Silica gel is an excellent drying agent for florist flowers. It rapidly absorbs moisture and preserves colour well. Sand or borax can be used in the same way but is less effective. The procedure is as follows: Place flowers in a sealed container otherwise moisture from the air will be absorbed. Flowers dried using silica gel will sometimes reabsorb moisture and wilt. Flowers dried in this manner should therefore be stored and displayed in a closed container to keep out moisture.

Flowers ideal for silica-drying include aster, carnation, chrysanthemum, dahlia, delphinium, geranium, larkspur, marigold, rose and zinnia. Flowers that dry well in sand or borax include aster, balloon-flower, balsam, candytuft, Canterbury bell, carnation, chrysanthemum, columbine, coneflower, coreopsis, cornflower, cosmos, daffodil, dahlia, delphinium, geranium, gladiolus, iris, liatris, lilac, loosestrife, lupine, pansy, peony, rose, shasta daisy, snapdragon, stock, tulip and zinnia.

CARE AND HANDLING OF CUT GREENS AND FOLIAGE

Cut greens and cut foliage are not nearly as important to the cut flower industry in terms of volumes traded and monetary value, as are cut flowers. However, they are still important and form an integral part of a florist or flower trader's business.

CUT GREENS AND FOLIAGE. These are very loose terms that relate to a large number of plant species. Cut greens or foliage are basically plant leaves which are predominantly green and are used by florists in the making up and presentation of bouquets or mixed bunches. Good examples of true cut greens are leather leaf fern, aspidistra, ruscus and anthurium leaves. As the industry developed, many more exciting leaf forms and colours have become available. Although still generally referred to as cut greens, foliage or florist greens, not all of these leaves are green. Examples of variegated forms are croton leaves, ti leaves, hosta leaves, variegated pittosporum and variegated ivy leaves.

FILLERS. "Fillers" is another loosely used term that can literally refer to any part of a plant that is used to "fill" out an arrangement or bouquet. Typically, florists would use a few specific cut flower stems (e.g. roses, lilies and/or chrysanthemums) and then add a variety of fillers to increase the volume of the bouquet and add visual interest. Some of these fillers are just leaves, while others may be leafy sprays with small flowers (e.g. heather, baby's breath, goldenrod and Michaelmas daisies). The concept of "filler" even includes unusual elements such as dry willow twigs (*Salix*) or maize cobs. The distinction between cut flower and filler is sometimes not very clear. Asters, for example, are sometimes viewed as cut flowers, while at other times they are used to fill out bouquets and are then regarded as fillers.

Cut greens and fillers are often less expensive and usually have a longer vase life than many of the traditional cut flowers. In most cases it is a mistake to handle or treat them any different to standard cut flowers. It is best to put them through the same basic procedures of unpacking, cutting, hydrating and storing at the right temperatures, as is done with cut flowers. Specifics on the care and handling of important florist greens and fillers are discussed under the appropriate plant species in the book.

UNPACK. On arrival immediately open the boxes and packaging and inspect the general condition for quality, damage and disease. Verify that the correct products and volumes have been received. Contact suppliers immediately should there be any discrepancies.

PROCESS AND HYDRATE. A number of cut greens such as leather leaf, aspidistra and holly can be kept in their shipping boxes or bags (to maintain high humidity) in the cooler. Other cut greens (especially those with sufficiently long stems or stalks such as ruscus, papyrus, florist gum or strelitzia leaves) can be recut and placed in water, with a bactericide or floral preservative, in the cooler at a high relative humidity (90–95%). Remove foliage below the water line. Check individual species for specific requirements.

Many cut greens are long lasting (e.g. ruscus, ivy, New Zealand flax, pittosporum and aspidistra), but many of the cut foliages, especially those with fine leaves and small flowers are not and need to be properly hydrated on arrival before they are stored or used. These should be placed in a floral preservative, bactericide or hydrating solution, in clean, sterilised buckets and allowed to hydrate for 2–4 hours at room temperature prior to use or cold storage. Check individual species for requirements.

STORING. Some foliage types will store as well or better with their stems out of water as long as they are kept cold and at high humidity in the shipping box or plastic bag. If unsure, it is best to handle and care for cut greens and foliage in the same way as quality cut flowers. That is, unpack, hydrate and store in a floral preservative at low temperatures (2–4°C / 36–39°F) and high relative humidity (90–95%). The exception is to store fillers such as grasses, dry twigs and dry branches (e.g. bamboo, twisted willow, papyrus and pampas grass) dry and at a low relative humidity. As

Cut foliage (from left to right): parlour palm, leather leaf fern, butcher's broom and broom fern

with cut flowers, good ventilation is necessary to avoid the build-up of ethylene or fungal spores. Also ensure that no condensation falls from the ceiling of the cooler onto the cut greens and foliage, as this will quickly cause deterioration.

DAILY MAINTENANCE. Inspect all foliage and cut greens on a daily basis. Remove any damaged or dying leaves and stems to prevent ethylene build-up and damage to other products. Damaged or decaying plant material also creates a potential source of disease. Check that there is enough water in the buckets and that it is still clean (clear and not cloudy). Remove any debris in the water. Replace water and buckets every few days.

HOW TO SELECT A SUPERIOR CUT GREEN. As with cut flowers, the quality of cut greens is important. Do not settle for poor or mediocre quality with the idea that they are insignificant or usually longer lasting than cut flowers. Make sure leaves such as ruscus, aspidistra, anthurium, hosta and the like are fully mature, but do not show any signs of ageing. Leaves that are still too young when harvested tend to be soft and will often lack good vase life and wilt easily. With variegated forms, such as dieffenbachia, calathea, fragrant dracaena and ti leaves, make sure that the colours are clean, sharp and well-defined, as this is the real attraction of such foliage. Small-flowered, leafy or branching fillers, such as heathers, tea bushes and wax flowers, need to be inspected carefully for blemishes, ageing and disease. Flowers typically need to be one-third to fully open, but once again not showing any signs of ageing. Woody fillers should be well branched with the main stems not too thick or too woody, as this will often have a negative effect on water-uptake and vase life. Species of shrub from which foliage is wild-harvested can vary significantly in vase life and care must be taken to obtain high quality material, which should be properly hydrated and treated on arrival and prior to use. As with cut flowers, cut greens benefit from being stored at reduced temperatures and high humidity.

All selected cut greens should be mature, well formed and well coloured. Where relevant, foliage and blooms must be evenly dispersed and all products should be at the correct stage of development when purchased. As with cut flowers, process all cut greens as quickly as possible and handle with care.

CARE AND HANDLING
OF POTTED FLOWERS

A potted flower is simply a flowering plant, usually small and compact, that is grown in a pot. Potted flowers are often discarded by the buyer after they have finished flowering. Popular examples include chrysanthemums, cyclamen, lisianthus, curcuma and daffodils. However, some potted flowers such as orchids and bromeliads are usually kept as permanent indoor plants and allowed to reflower. Not all plants grown and sold in pots have flowers, or are small enough to be placed on a desk or kitchen table. These are usually described as pot plants, indoor plants or container plants (e.g. draceana, ficus and many of the ferns).

The handling and care of potted flowers is slightly different to cut flowers or greens. The following hints serve as a general guide.

DEVELOPMENT STAGE. The stage of growth (development) at which potted flowers are packaged and sold by growers has a direct impact on the lasting quality of the plant and flowers. If sold too soon (e.g. when the buds are small and not showing any colour) then often buds fail to open properly, or drop off or the colour of the flowers that do open is faded (especially true of dark flowers). If sold too late then the plant, or flowers, may have passed its prime or simply does not last as long as customers would expect. Growers try to dispatch plants with enough colour and maturity to catch the customer's attention, but early enough to ensure maximum shelf life and enjoyment by the end-user. Different potted flowers are sold at different stages of development. Flowers can generally be traded at a less developed stage as potted flowers than as cut flowers. Market demands also influence the stage of development at which potted flowers are sold. For example, American markets generally want plants showing more colour, while European markets will accept plants showing less colour. Kalanchoes, for example, last longer when shipped with only a few flowers open, but American markets prefer them more colourful, with 50% of flowers open.

PACKAGING. The primary purpose of packaging is to protect the potted flower during shipping and handling. Ironically, this packaging often has a negative effect on longevity and quality. This occurs when plants are kept too long in closed boxes, or when humidity builds up in plastic sleeves.

TRANSPORTING OR SHIPPING. The transporting of potted flowers from the grower to the market or florist is inevitable. The three main factors that have an influence on quality and longevity during shipping are temperature, duration of shipping and exposure to ethylene due to a closed environment (trucks and boxes).

QUALITY CRITERIA. The more that is known about the potted flowers purchased the better. Preferably keep records for future reference. Select potted flowers that have the following characteristics:
1   The cultivar is known to be less sensitive to ethylene.
2   The grower treated the plants against ethylene.
3   The pots were transported at reduced temperatures (2–4°C / 36–39°F for most plants, but 13–15°C / 55–59°F for tropical plants such as orchids and including calla lilies, begonias, bougainvillea, poinsettias, clerodendrum, schlumbergera, African violets and gloxinias).
4   Plants have not been in transit and/or boxed for more than six days.
5   The plant is at the proper stage of development at the time of purchase.
6   The plant is well formed, compact, full of buds and free from any diseases or blemishes.
7   There is no moisture on the sleeving.
8   The potting medium or soil is slightly dry to dry, and not very wet.

ETHYLENE. Quality and longevity of many potted flowers (not only cut flowers) is negatively affected by ethylene exposure. The effect varies from buds, leaves and/or flowers dropping off the plant, to leaves curling or yellowing, to buds failing to open. Fully opened flowers are more sensitive to ethylene than closed buds.

Potted flowers: begonia, poinsettia, kalanchoe and guzmania

ON ARRIVAL. Unpack plants immediately. Preferably remove all packaging, including sleeving. However, understandably many florists and retailers would want to retain sleeves to protect plants during transport by clients. It is, however, important to realise that sleeves do not improve shelf life – in fact they usually reduce it, except when it comes to protection from physical damage during handling and shipping. Carefully inspect the plants for poor quality, damage, disease and correct development stage. Remove broken or diseased leaves and flowers. Remove plants that are diseased. Give feedback to the supplier or florist and report on the quality of the shipment. Keep records.

INITIAL WATERING. Incorrect watering shortens the life of the plant and negatively affects flowering. Check the moisture level of the potting mix. Only water those plants where the medium is dry to the touch. Do not water plants that are already too wet. Water well and allow water to drain out of the bottom of the pot.

DISPLAY AND STORAGE. Display plants in the correct environment, be it high light or low humidity. Most potted flowers do not like to stand in a direct draught, but need good ventilation. Obtain specifics from suppliers and inform clients as well. Do not display plants near ethylene-forming agents such as fruit. In most cases potted flowers should not be stored in the dark or in the cooler at low temperatures such as 1–2°C (34–36°F). Preferably display them at an optimum temperature of 18–21°C (64–70°F), or at room temperature. Bulb plants should be kept and displayed at low temperatures (4°C / 39°F), to maintain shelf life and to prevent flowers from opening too quickly.

DAILY MAINTENANCE. Inspect the soil or growing medium in the pot to a depth of about 20 mm (1"). If the soil still feels damp, then do not water; if it feels dry then water thoroughly. In most cases it is best to avoid wetting the foliage when watering. Keep in mind that water requirements vary from species to species and sometimes even from cultivar to cultivar. There is no need to fertilise potted flowers in the florist shop. Low light, low temperature and high humidity all result in lower water needs by the potted flower. Inspect daily for problems and remove any dead, dying or diseased leaves and flowers.

COMMON NAME INDEXES

Cut flowers

African corn lily (*Ixia* cultivars)
African lily (*Agapanthus* species)
African marigold (*Tagetes erecta*)
amaryllis (*Hippeastrum* cultivars)
Amazon lily (*Eucharis grandiflora*)
American marigold (*Tagetes erecta*)
anise hyssop (*Agastache foeniculum*)
anthurium (*Anthurium* species)
artichoke (wild) (*Cynara cardunculus*)
arum lily (*Zantedeschia aethiopica*)
Asiatic lily (*Lilium* cultivars)
aster (*Aster* species)
Australian sword lily (*Anigozanthus flavidus*)

beaked heliconia (*Heliconia rostrata*)
baby's breath (*Gypsophila paniculata*)
balisier (*Heliconia bihai*)
balloon flower (*Platycodon grandiflorus*)
banksia (*Banksia* species)
Barberton daisy (*Gerbera jamesonii*)
bachelor's button (*Gomphrena globosa*)
bachelor's buttons (see drumsticks)
beard tongue (*Penstemon hartwegii*)
bearded protea (*Protea neriifolia*)
bee balm (*Monarda didyma*)
beehive ginger (*Zingiber spectabile*)
belladonna lily (*Amaryllis belladonna*)
bellflower (*Campanula persicifolia*)
bellflower (Chinese) (*Platycodon grandiflorus*)
bells-of-Ireland (*Moluccella laevis*)
bergamot (*Monarda didyma*)
billy buttons (see drumsticks)
bird-of-paradise (*Strelitzia reginae*)
black-eyed Susan (*Rudbeckia hirta*)
blanket flower (*Gaillardia grandiflora*)
blazing star (*Liatris spicata*)
blue beard (*Caryopteris* species)
blue false indigo (*Baptisia australis*)
blue lace flower (*Trachymene coerulea*)
blue lily (*Agapanthus* species)
blue spiraea (*Caryopteris* species)
blue throatwort (*Trachelium caeruleum*)
blushing bride (*Serruria florida*)
bottlebrush (*Callistemon speciosus*)
bougainvillea (*Bougainvillea buttiana*)
bouvardia (*Bouvardia longiflora*)

brodiaea (*Triteleia laxa*)
bugle lily (*Watsonia* cultivars)
buttercups (*Ranunculus asiaticus*)
butterfly bush (*Buddleja davidii*)
butterfly weed (*Asclepias tuberosa*)

calla lily (*Zantedeschia* species)
cambria orchid (*Vuylstekeara* cultivars)
camellia (*Camellia japonica*)
candytuft (*Iberis umbellata*)
Cape jasmine (*Gardenia augusta*)
cardinal flower (*Lobelia cardinalis*)
cardoon (*Cynara cardunculus*)
carnation (*Dianthus caryophyllus*)
cat's tail (*Amaranthus caudatus*)
cat's tail (*Bulbinella* species)
cattleya orchid (*Cattleya* cultivars)
China aster (*Callistephus chinensis*)
chincherinchee (*Ornithogalum thyrsoides*)
Chinese bellflower (*Platycodon grandiflorus*)
Chinese hibiscus (*Hibiscus rosa-sinensis*)
Chinese jasmine (*Jasminum polyanthemum*)
Chinese lantern lily (*Sandersonia aurantiaca*)
Christmas bells (*Sandersonia aurantiaca*)
chrysanthemum (*Chrysanthemum morifolium*)
cluster rose (*Rosa* cultivars)
cockscomb (*Celosia argentea*)
columbine (*Aquilegia* cultivars)
common lilac (*Syringa vulgaris*)
coneflower (purple) (*Echinacea purpurea*)
coneflower (yellow) (*Rudbeckia hirta*)
coral bells (*Heuchera sanguinea*)
coral flower (*Hesperis matronalis*)
corn cockle (*Agrostemma githago*)
cornflower (*Centaurea cyanus*)
cosmea (*Cosmos bipinnatus*)
cosmos (*Cosmos bipinnatus*)
crane flower (*Strelitzia reginae*)
crinum (*Crinum japonicum*)
crown imperial (*Fritillaria imperialis*)
Cuban lily (*Scilla peruviana*)
culver's root (*Veronicastrum virginicum*)
cymbidium orchid (*Cymbidium* cultivars)

daffodil (*Narcissus* cultivars)
dahlia (*Dahlia hortensis*)
damask flower (*Hesperis matronalis*)

dancing doll orchid (*Oncidium flexuosum*)
delphinium (*Delphinium elatum*)
dendranthema (*Chrysanthemum morifolium*)
dendrobium orchid (*Dendrobium bigibbum*)
desert candle (*Eremurus stenophyllus*)
didiscus (*Trachymene coerulea*)
dogwood (*Cornus alba*)
dove orchid (*Phalaenopsis* cultivars)
drumsticks (*Craspedia globosa*)
Dutch iris (*Iris hollandica*)
dyer's chamomile (*Anthemis tinctoria*)

Easter lily (*Lilium longiflorum*)
echinacea (*Echinacea purpurea*)
Eucharist lily (*Eucharis grandiflora*)
European globe flower (*Trollius europaeus*)
everlasting (*Helichrysum bracteatum*)
everlasting (winged) (*Ammodium alatum*)

falling stars (see montbretia)
false bishop's weed (*Ammi majus*)
false blue indigo (*Baptisia australis*)
false goat's beard (*Astilbe arendsii*)
false Queen Anne's lace (*Ammi majus*)
feverfew (*Chrysanthemum parthenium*)
firebird (*Heliconia bihai*)
flame lily (*Gloriosa superba*)
flame of the woods (*Ixora coccinea*)
flaming freesia (*Tritonia crocata*)
flamingo flower (*Anthurium andraeanum*)
flannel flower (*Actinotus helianthi*)
florist allium (*Allium giganteum*)
florist chrysanthemum (*Chrysanthemum
    morifolium*)
florist's genista (*Genista canariensis*)
flossflower (*Ageratum houstonianum*)
forget-me-not (*Myosotis dissitiflora*)
foxglove (*Digitalis purpurea*)
foxtail lily (*Eremurus stenophyllus*)
freesia (*Freesia hybrida*)

garden montbretia (*Tritonia crocata*)
garden ranunculus (*Ranunculus asiaticus*)
gardenia (*Gardenia augusta*)
gayfeather (*Liatris spicata*)
gerbera (*Gerbera jamesonii*)
giant hyssop (*Agastache foeniculum*)
giant onion (*Allium giganteum*)
giant protea (*Protea cynaroides*)
giant thistle (*Onopordum acanthium*)
ginger (beehive) (*Zingiber spectabile*)

ginger lily (*Alpinia purpurata*)
ginger lily (white) (*Hedychium coronarium*)
gingerwort (nodding) (*Zingiber spectabile*)
gladiolus (*Gladiolus* cultivars)
globe amaranth (*Gomphrena globosa*)
globe flower (*Trollius europaeus*)
globe thistle (*Echinops bannaticus*)
glory lily (*Gloriosa superba*)
godetia (*Clarkia amoena*)
golden aster (*Solidaster luteus*)
goldenrod (*Solidago canadensis*)
gooseneck loosestrife (*Lysimachia clethroides*)
grassnut (*Triteleia laxa*)
gravel root (*Eupatorium purpureum*)
Guernsey lily (*Nerine bowdenii*)
gypsophila (*Gypsophila paniculata*)

hanging lobster claws (*Heliconia rostrata*)
harlequin flower (*Sparaxis tricolor*)
heliopsis (*Heliopsis helianthoides*)
helmet flower (*Aconitum* species)
hibiscus (*Hibiscus rosa-sinensis*)
hollyhock (*Alcea rosea*)
honesty (*Lunaria annua*)
hortensia (*Hydrangea macrophylla*)
hyacinth (*Hyacinthus orientalis*)
hybrid tea rose (*Rosa* cultivars)

ice plant (*Sedum spectabile*)
Iceland poppy (*Papaver nudicaule*)
immortelle (common) (*Xeranthemum annuum*)
Inca lily (*Alstroemeria* cultivars)
iris (*Iris hollandica*)

Jacob's ladder (*Convallaria majalis*)
Japanese crinum (*Crinum japonicum*)
Japanese toad lily (*Tricyrtis hirta*)
Japanese thistle (*Cirsium japonicum*)
japonica (*Camellia japonica*)
jasmine (*Jasminum polyanthemum*)
Jersey lily (*Amaryllis belladonna*)
Joe Pye weed (*Eupatorium purpureum*)
jungle flame (*Ixora coccinea*)

kangaroo paw (*Anigozanthos flavidus*)
king protea (*Protea cynaroides*)

lace flower (*Ammi majus*)
lace orchid (*Odontoglossum crispum*)
lady's mantle (*Alchemilla mollis*)
larkspur (*Consolida ajacis*)

lenten rose (*Helleborus orientalis*)
lilac (*Syringa vulgaris*)
lily-of-the-valley (*Convallaria majalis*)
lion's ear (*Leonotis leonurus*)
lisianthus (*Eustoma grandiflorum*)
lobster claws (*Heliconia bihai*)
lobster claws (hanging) (*Heliconia rostrata*)
loosestrife (*Lysimachia clethroides*)
lotus (*Nelumbo nucifera*)
love-in-a-mist (*Nigella damascena*)
love-lies-bleeding (*Amaranthus caudatus*)
lupin (lupine) (*Lupinus hartwegii*)
lychnis (*Silene chalcedonica*)

macaw flower (*Heliconia bihai*)
magnolia (*Magnolia grandiflora*)
mallow (*Lavatera trimestris*)
Maltese cross (*Silene chalcedonica*)
marguerite (*Argyranthemum frutescens*)
marigold (*Calendula officinalis*)
masterwort (*Astrantia major*)
Mexican hyssop (*Agastache foeniculum*)
Mexican bush sage (*Salvia leucantha*)
Michaelmas daisy (*Aster ericoides*)
milkweed (*Asclepias tuberosa*)
money plant (*Lunaria annua*)
monkshood (*Aconitum* species)
montbretia (*Crocosmia crocosmiiflora*)
moth orchid (*Phalaenopsis* cultivars)
mullein (nettle-leaved) (*Verbascum chaixii*)

New England aster (*Aster novae-angliae*)
New York aster (*Aster novi-belgii*)

obedient plant (*Physostegia virginiana*)
oleander leaf protea (*Protea neriifolia*)
onion (ornamental) (*Allium giganteum*)
oriental lily (*Lilium* cultivars)
ornamental onion (*Allium giganteum*)
Oswego tea (*Monarda didyma*)
ox-eye (*Heliopsis helianthoides*)

pagoda flower (*Mimetes hirtus*)
painted tongue (*Anthurium* species)
paper daisy (*Rhodanthe manglesii*)
parakeet flower (*Heliconia psittacorum*)
parrot's flower (*Heliconia psittacorum*)
peace lily (*Spathiphyllum wallisii*)
penny flower (*Lunaria annua*)
penstemon (*Penstemon hartwegii*)
peony (*Paeonia* species)

Peruvian lily (*Alstroemeria* cultivars)
Peruvian scilla (*Scilla peruviana*)
Philippine ground orchid (*Spathoglottis plicata*)
phlox (*Phlox paniculata*)
pincushion (*Leucospermum cordifolium*)
pincushion flower (*Scabiosa caucasica*)
pineapple lily (*Eucomis comosa*)
pink everlasting (*Rhodanthe roseum*)
pinks (*Dianthus barbatus*)
poppy anemone (*Anemone coronaria*)
pot marigold (*Calendula officinalis*)
prairie gentian (*Eustoma grandiflorum*)

queen lily (*Curcuma petiolata*)

ranunculus (*Ranunculus asiaticus*)
red ginger (*Alpinia purpurata*)
red hot poker (*Kniphofia* species)
red ixora (*Ixora coccinea*)
rocket larkspur (*Consolida ajacis*)
rose (*Rosa* cultivars)
rose mallow (*Lavatera trimestris*)

sacred lotus (*Nelumbo nucifera*)
safflower (*Carthamus tinctorius*)
sage (*Salvia leucantha*)
satin flower (*Clarkia amoena*)
scarlet lobelia (*Lobelia cardinalis*)
scarlet plume (*Euphorbia fulgens*)
sea holly (*Eryngium planum*)
sea lavender (*Limonium perezii*)
shasta daisy (*Leucanthemum superbum*)
silver thistle (*Onopordum acanthium*)
snapdragon (*Antirrhinum majus*)
sneezeweed (-wort) (*Helenium autumnale*)
snowdrop (*Galanthus nivalis*)
spathoglottis (*Spathoglottis plicata*)
speedwell (garden) (*Veronica longifolia*)
spirea (*Astilbe arendsii*)
spray rose (*Rosa* cultivars)
St Joseph's lily (*Lilium longiflorum*)
star-of-Bethlehem (*Ornithogalum thyrsoides*)
statice (*Limonium sinuatum*)
stock(s) (*Matthiola incana*)
strawflower (*Helichrysum bracteatum*)
sugarbush (*Protea repens*)
summer aster (*Callistephus chinensis*)
summer lilac (*Buddleja davidii*)
summer orchid (*Angelonia angustifolia*)
summer snapdragon (*Angelonia angustifolia*)

sun spurge (*Euphorbia fulgens*)
sundrops (*Oenothera fruticosa*)
sunflower (*Helianthus annuus*)
Swan River everlasting (*Rhodanthe manglesii*)
sweet pea (*Lathyrus odoratus*)
sweet rocket (*Hesperis matronalis*)
sweet scabious (*Scabiosa caucasica*)
sweet william (*Dianthus barbatus*)
Swiss mountain thistle (*Onopordum acanthium*)
sword lily (*Gladiolus* cultivars)

tanacetum (see *Chrysanthemum parthenium*)
tassle flower (*Amaranthus caudatus*)
Texas bluebell (*Eustoma grandiflorum*)
thistle (*Cirsium japonicum*)
thoroughwax (*Bupleurum rotundifolium*)
throatwort (*Trachelium caeruleum*)
tickseed (*Coreopsis grandiflora*)
toad lily (*Tricyrtis* species)
torch ginger (*Alpinia purpurata*)
torch ginger (red) (*Etlingera elatior*)
torch lily (*Kniphofia* species)
triplet lily (*Triteleia laxa*)
tritonia (*Tritonia crocata*)
tuberose (*Polianthes tuberosa*)
tulip (*Tulipa* cultivars)
tweedia (*Tweedia caerulea*)

vanda orchid (*Vanda coerulea*)
velvet flower (*Amaranthus caudatus*)
vuylstekeara orchid (*Vuylstekeara* cultivars)

wallflower (*Centranthus ruber*)
wand flower (*Ixia* cultivars)
waratah (*Telopea speciosissima*)
water lily (*Nymphaea* cultivars)
watsonia (*Watsonia* cultivars)
waxflower (*Chamelaucium uncinatum*)
white ginger lily (*Hedychium coronarium*)
windflower (*Anemone coronaria*)
winged everlasting (*Ammodium alatum*)
wild garlic (*Tulbaghia violacea*)

yarrow (*Achillea* species)
yellow chamomile (*Anthemis tinctoria*)
youth-and-old-age (*Zinnia elegans*)

zinnia (*Zinnia elegans*)

Cut greens, foliage and fillers

anthurium (*Anthurium* species)
artichoke (wild) (*Cynara cardunculus*)
asparagus fern (*Asparagus* species)
aspidistra (*Aspidistra elatior*)
Australian bracken (*Pteris tremula*)

Baker fern (*Dryopteris erythrosora*)
balisier (*Heliconia bihai*)
balsam fir (*Abies balsamea*)
bamboo (*Bambusa vulgaris*)
banksia (*Banksia* species)
bar room plant (*Aspidistra elatior*)
bachelor's buttons (see drumsticks)
bear grass (*Xerophyllum tenax*)
beard tongue (*Penstemon hartwegii*)
beautyberry (*Callicarpa* species)
beehive ginger (*Zingiber spectabile*)
beetle weed (*Galax urseolata*)
bell reed (*Cannomois virgata*)
bella palm (*Chamaedorea elegans*)
bells-of-Ireland (*Moluccella laevis*)
berzelia (*Berzelia lanuginosa*)
billy buttons (see drumsticks)
bird-of-paradise (*Strelitzia reginae*)
bird's nest fern (*Asplenium nidis*)
blanket flower (*Gaillardia grandiflora*)
blue lace flower (*Trachymene coerulea*)
blue wattle (*Acacia dealbata*)
Boston fern (*Nephrolepis exaltata*)
bottlebrush (*Callistemon speciosus*)
bougainvillea (*Bougainvillea buttiana*)
bowstring hemp (*Sansevieria* species)
box (boxwood) (*Buxus sempervirens*)
broom (*Cytisus scoparius*)
bulrush (lesser) (*Typha angustifolia*)
bupleurum (*Bupleurum* species)
burrawang (*Macrozamia communis*)
butcher's broom (*Ruscus* species)
bush cherry (Chinese) (*Prunus glandulosa*)
butterfly bush (*Buddleja davidii*)

cabbage (ornamental) (*Brassica oleracea*)
calathea (*Calathea lancifolia*)
camellia (*Camellia japonica*)
Californian huckleberry (*Vaccinium ovatum*)
Cape heather (*Erica coriifolia*)
Cape myrtle (*Phylica ericoides*)
cardinal flower (*Lobelia cardinalis*)
cardoon (*Cynara cardunculus*)

carrot (wild) (*Daucus carota*)
cast iron plant (*Aspidistra elatior*)
cattail (narrow leaf) (*Typha angustifolia*)
cedar (*Cedrus deodara*)
ceriman (*Monstera deliciosa*)
Chinese bush cherry (*Prunus glandulosa*)
Chinese fountain grass (*Pennisetum alopecuroides*)
Chinese hibiscus (*Hibiscus rosa-sinensis*)
Chinese lantern (*Physalis alkekengi*)
Chinese wormwood (*Artemisia annua*)
club moss (*Lycopodium* species)
cluster rose (*Rosa* cultivars)
coconut palm (*Cocos nucifera*)
columbine meadow-rue (*Thalictrum aquilegiifolium*)
common ivy (*Hedera helix*)
common lilac (*Syringa vulgaris*)
conebush (*Leucadendron salignum*)
coneflower (purple) (*Echinacea purpurea*)
coral bells (*Heuchera sanguinea*)
coral flower (*Hesperis matronalis*)
corkscrew hazel (*Corylus avellana*)
corn (*Zea mays*)
corn cockle (*Agrostemma githago*)
crampbark (*Viburnum opulus*)
crane flower (*Strelitzia reginae*)
croton (*Codiaeum variegatum*)
cycas (*Cycas revoluta*)

dagger plant (*Yucca aloifolia*)
damask flower (*Hesperis matronalis*)
deodar (*Cedrus deodara*)
didiscus (*Trachymene coerulea*)
dill (*Anethum graveolens*)
dogwood (*Cornus alba*)
dracaena (fragrant) (*Dracaena fragrans*)
drumsticks (*Craspedia globosa*)
dumb cane (*Dieffenbachia maculata*)

echinacea (*Echinacea purpurea*)
elk grass (*Xerophyllum tenax*)
English ivy (*Hedera helix*)
everlasting (winged) (*Ammobium alatum*)

feather-head (*Phylica plumosa*)
fennel (*Foeniculum vulgare*)
fern leaf yarrow (*Achillea* species)
fir (*Abies* species)
firebird (*Heliconia bihai*)
famingo flower (*Anthurium* species)

flame of the woods (*Ixora coccinea*)
flaming freesia (*Tritonia crocata*)
flannel flower (*Actinotus helianthi*)
flax (see New Zealand flax)
florist gum (*Eucalyptus cinerea*)
flowering maple (*Abutilon hybridum*)
forget-me-not (*Myosotis dissitiflora*)
fragrant dracaena (*Dracaena fragrans*)
furze (*Ulex europaeus*)

garden montbretia (*Tritonia crocata*)
garden orache (*Atriplex hortensis*)
Geraldton waxflower (*Chamelaucium uncinatum*)
German statice (*Goniolimon tataricum*)
ginger (beehive) (*Zingiber spectabile*)
ginger lily (*Alpinia purpurata*)
gingerwort (nodding) (*Zingiber spectabile*)
golden bell (*Forsythia intermedia*)
gorse (*Ulex europaeus*)
gourd (ornamental) (*Cucurbita pepo*)
grass tree (*Xanthorrhoea australis*)
gravel root (*Eupatorium purpureum*)
greenbrier (*Asparagus asparagoides*)
Guelder rose (*Viburnum opulus*)

hare's ear (*Bupleurum rotundifolium*)
hazel (*Corylus avellana*)
heather (*Calluna vulgaris*)
heather (Cape) (*Erica coriifolia*)
heliopsis (*Heliopsis helianthoides*)
hibiscus (*Hibiscus rosa-sinensis*)
holly (*Ilex aquifolium*)
honesty (*Lunaria annua*)
honeycomb (*Grevillea whiteana*)
honeywort (*Cerinthe major*)
horsetail (*Equisetum* species)
huckleberry (*Vaccinium ovatum*)
hypericum (*Hypericum androsaemum*)

immortelle (common) (*Xeranthemum annuum*)
Indian basket grass (*Xerophyllum tenax*)
iron plant (*Aspidistra elatior*)
ivy (*Hedera helix*)

Japanese mock orange (*Pittosporum tobira*)
Japanese pittosporum (*Pittosporum tobira*)
Japanese shield fern (*Dryopteris erythrosora*)
Japanese toad lily (*Tricyrtis hirta*)
japonica (*Camellia japonica*)

jasmine (*Gardenia augusta*)
Joe Pye weed (*Eupatorium purpureum*)
jungle flame (*Ixora coccinea*)
juniper (*Juniperus communis*)

kale (ornamental) (*Brassica oleracea*)
kusamaki (*Podocarpus macrophyllus*)

lace fern (*Asparagus setaceus*)
lady's mantle (*Alchemilla mollis*)
lanuginosa (*Berzelia lanuginosa*)
lavender (*Lavandula angustifolia*)
leather leaf fern (*Rumohra adiantiformis*)
lemon leaf (*Gaultheria shallon*)
lilac (*Syringa vulgaris*)
lobster claws (*Heliconia bihai*)
love-in-a-mist (*Nigella damascena*)
lychnis (*Silene chalcedonica*)
lycopodium (*Lycopodium* species)

macaw flower (*Heliconia bihai*)
magnolia (*Magnolia grandiflora*)
maize (*Zea mays*)
Maltese cross (*Silene chalcedonica*)
manuka (*Leptospermum scoparium*)
meadow-rue (*Thalictrum aquilegiifolium*)
Meyer's fern (*Asparagus densiflorus*)
mimosa (*Acacia dealbata*)
miniature date palm (*Phoenix roebelinii*)
Ming fern (*Asparagus densiflorus*)
money plant (*Lunaria annua*)
mother-in-law's tongue (*Sansevieria trifasciata*)
mountain spinach (*Atriplex hortensis*)
mullein (nettle-leaved) (*Verbascum chaixii*)
myrtle (*Myrtus communis*)

New Zealand flax (*Phormium tenax*)
noble fir (*Abies procera*)

orache (*Atriplex hortensis*)
oregano (*Origanum vulgare*)
ox-eye (*Heliopsis helianthoides*)

palmetto palm (*Sabal palmetto*)
pampas grass (*Cortaderia selloana*)
papyrus (*Cyperus papyrus*)
parakeet flower (*Heliconia psittacorum*)
parlour palm (*Chamaedorea elegans*)
parrot's flower (*Heliconia psittacorum*)
penny flower (*Lunaria annua*)

penny gum (*Eucalyptus cinerea*)
penstemon (*Penstemon hartwegii*)
pepper (ornamental) (*Capsicum annuum*)
philodendron (*Philodendron pinnatifidum*)
pincushion tree (*Hakea victoria*)
pineapple (*Ananas comosus*)
pittosporum (Japanese) (*Pittosporum tobira*)
plantain lily (*Hosta sieboldiana*)
plumosa (*Asparagus setaceus*)
purple top (*Verbena bonariensis*)
pussy willow (*Salix discolor*)
pygmy date palm (*Phoenix roebelinii*)

Queen Anne's lace (*Daucus carota*)

rattlesnake plant (*Calathea lancifolia*)
red ginger (*Alpinia purpurata*)
red ixora (*Ixora coccinea*)
red valerian (*Centranthus ruber*)
reed mace (narrow-leaved) (*Typha angustifolia*)
rekoala (*Cannomois virgata*)
rice flower (*Ozothamnus diosmifolius*)

salal (lemon leaf) (*Gaultheria shallon*)
scarlet lobelia (*Lobelia cardinalis*)
Scotch broom (*Cytisus scoparius*)
sea holly (*Eryngium planum*)
shaking brake (*Pteris tremula*)
shallon (*Gaultheria shallon*)
shellflower (*Moluccella laevis*)
shot huckleberry (*Vaccinium ovatum*)
silver wattle (*Acacia dealbata*)
smilax (*Asparagus asparagoides*)
smoke tree (*Cotinus coggygria*)
sneezeweed (-wort) (*Helenium autumnale*)
snowball (*Viburnum opulus*)
snowberry (*Symphoricarpos albus*)
snow-on-the-mountain (*Euphorbia marginata*)
Spanish bayonet (*Yucca aloifolia*)
spelt (spelt wheat) (*Triticum spelta*)
spider flower (*Grevillea whiteana*)
spineless butcher's broom (*Ruscus hypoglossum*)
split-leaf philodendron (*Philodendron pinnatifidum*)
spray rose (*Rosa* cultivars)
sprenger fern (*Asparagus densiflorus*)
statice (see tartarian statice)
statice (*Limonium* species)

steel grass (*Xanthorrhoea australis*)
stoebe (*Stoebe plumosa*)
string smilax (*Asparagus asparagoides*)
sun spurge (*Euphorbia fulgens*)
sundrops (*Oenothera fruticosa*)
swamp foxtail grass (*Pennisetum alopecuroides*)
sweet Annie (*Artemisia annua*)
sweet rocket (*Hesperis matronalis*)
sweet wormwood (*Artemisia annua*)
Swiss-cheese plant (*Monstera deliciosa*)
sword fern (*Nephrolepis exaltata*)

tartarian statice (*Goniolimon tataricum*)
tea bush (*Leptospermum scoparium*)
thoroughwax (*Bupleurum rotundifolium*)
ti leaves (*Cordyline terminalis*)
tickseed (*Coreopsis grandiflora*)
toad lily (*Tricyrtis hirta*)
tobira (*Pittosporum tobira*)
torch ginger (*Alpinia purpurata*)
trembling brake (*Pteris tremula*)
tritonia (*Tritonia crocata*)
tutsan (*Hypericum androsaemum*)
tweedia (*Tweedia caerulea*)

Venetian sumach (*Cotinus coggygria*)
verbena (tall) (*Verbena* species)

wand plant (*Galax urseolata*)
wattle (*Acacia* species)
whin (*Ulex europaeus*)
white phylica (*Phylica ericoides*)
white pine (*Pinus strobus*)
wild carrot (*Daucus carota*)
wild garlic (*Tulbaghia violacea*)
wild marjoram (*Origanum vulgare*)
willow (*Salix* species)
windowleaf (*Monstera deliciosa*)
winged everlasting (*Ammodium alatum*)

yarrow (*Achillea* species)
yew pine (*Podocarpus macrophyllus*)

Potted flowers

abutilon (*Abutilon hybridum*)
African marigold (*Tagetes erecta*)
African voilet (*Saintpaulia ionantha*)
amaryllis (*Hippeastrum* cultivars)
Amazon lily (*Eucharis grandiflora*)
American marigold (*Tagetes erecta*)

anthurium (*Anthurium* species)
arum lily (*Zantedeschia aethiopica*)
asiatic lily (*Lilium* cultivars)
aster (*Aster* species)
Australian sword lily (*Anigozanthus flavidus*)
azalea (*Rhododendron simsii*)
baby's breath (*Gypsophila paniculata*)

balloon flower (*Platycodon grandiflorus*)
Barberton daisy (*Gerbera jamesonii*)
bead plant (*Nertera granadensis*)
begonia (*Begonia hiemalis*)
bellflower (*Campanula persicifolia*)
bellflower (Chinese) (*Platycodon grandiflorus*)
black-eyed Susan (*Rudbeckia hirta*)
blanket flower (*Gaillardia grandiflora*)
blazing star (*Liatris spicata*)
blue throatwort (*Trachelium caeruleum*)
blushing bride (*Serruria florida*)
bougainvillea (*Bougainvillea buttiana*)
bouvardia (*Bouvardia longiflora*)
bromeliad (*Guzmania lingulata*)
broom (*Cytisus scoparius*)
browallia (*Browallia speciosa*)
brunia (spray) (*Brunia nodiflora*)
bush lily (*Clivia miniata*)
bush violet (*Browallia speciosa*)
busy lizzie (*Impatiens hawkeri*)
buttercups (*Ranunculus asiaticus*)

cabbage (ornamental) (*Brassica oleracea*)
calandiva (*Kalanchoe blossfeldiana*)
calla lily (*Zantedeschia* species)
cambria orchid (*Vuylstekeara* cultivars)
candytuft (*Iberis umbellata*)
Cape cowslip (*Lachenalia aloides*)
Cape heather (*Erica coriifolia*)
Cape jasmine (*Gardenia augusta*)
Cape primrose (*Streptocarpus hybridus*)
cardinal flower (*Lobelia cardinalis*)
carnation (*Dianthus caryophyllus*)
cattleya orchid (*Cattleya* cultivars)
Chinese bellflower (*Platycodon grandiflorus*)
Chinese hibiscus (*Hibiscus rosa-sinensis*)
Chinese jasmine (*Jasminum polyanthemum*)
Chinese lantern (*Abutilon hybridum*)
Christmas cactus (*Schlumbergera buckleyi*)
Christmas rose (*Euphorbia pulcherrima*)
chrysanthemum (*Chrysanthemum morifolium*)
cineraria (*Pericallis hybrida*)

clivia (*Clivia miniata*)
cockscomb (*Celosia argentea*)
columbine (*Aquilegia vulgaris*)
conebush (*Leucadendron salignum*)
coneflower (*Rudbeckia hirta*)
coral moss (*Nertera granadensis*)
crocus (*Crocus vernus*)
crown imperial (*Fritillaria imperialis*)
culver's root (*Veronicastrum virginicum*)
curcuma (see queen lily)
cyclamen (*Cyclamen persicum*)
cymbidium orchid (*Cymbidium* cultivars)

daffodil (*Narcissus* cultivars)
dahlia (*Dahlia hortensis*)
damask violet (*Hesperis matronalis*)
dancing doll orchid (*Oncidium flexuosum*)
dendranthema (*Chrysanthemum morifolium*)
dendrobium orchid (*Dendrobium bigibbum*)
dove orchid (*Phalaenopsis* cultivars)
Dutch iris (*Iris hollandica*)
dyer's chamomile (*Anthemis tinctoria*)

Easter lily (*Lilium longiflorum*)
English babytears (*Nertera granadensis*)
erica (see Cape heather)
Eucharist lily (*Eucharis grandiflora*)

false goat's beard (*Astilbe arendsii*)
feverfew (*Chrysanthemum parthenium*)
flaming Katy (*Kalanchoe blossfeldiana*)
flaming sword (*Vriesia splendens*)
flamingo flower (*Anthurium* species)
floradora (*Marsdenia floribunda*)
florist cineraria (*Pericallis hybrida*)
florist gloxinia (*Sinningia speciosa*)
florist streptocarpus (*Streptocarpus hybridus*)
florist verbena (*Verbena hybrida*)
florist violet (*Viola odorata*)
flowering maple (*Abutilon hybridum*)
forget-me-not (*Myosotis dissitiflora*)
freesia (*Freesia hybrida*)
French marigold (*Tagetes patula*)
fuchsia (*Fuchsia* cultivars)

garden nasturtium (*Tropaeolum majus*)
garden ranunculus (*Ranunculus asiaticus*)
gardenia (*Gardenia augusta*)
gayfeather (*Liatris spicata*)
Geraldton waxflower (*Chamelaucium uncinatum*)

geranium (ivy-leaved) (*Pelargonium peltatum*)
geranium (regal) (*Pelargonium domesticum*)
geranium (zonal) (*Pelargonium zonale*)
gerbera (*Gerbera jamesonii*)
ginger lily (*Alpinia purpurata*)
gloxinia (*Sinningia speciosa*)
godetia (*Clarkia amoena*)
gooseneck loosestrife (*Lysimachia clethroides*)
grape hyacinth (*Muscari* species)
gypsophila (*Gypsophila paniculata*)

harlequin flower (*Sparaxis tricolor*)
heather (*Calluna vulgaris*)
heather (Cape) (*Erica coriifolia*)
hibiscus (*Hibiscus rosa-sinensis*)
hyacinth (*Hyacinthus orientalis*)
honeywort (*Cerinthe major*)
hortensia (*Hydrangea macrophylla*)
hypericum (*Hypericum androsaemum*)

ice plant (*Sedum spectabile*)
Iceland poppy (*Papaver nudicaule*)
impatiens (*Impatiens hawkeri*)
Inca lily (*Alstroemeria* cultivars)
Indian azalea (*Rhododendron simsii*)
Indian cress (*Tropaeolum majus*)
iris (*Iris hollandica*)
ivy-leaved geranium (*Pelargonium peltatum*)

Jacob's ladder (*Convallaria majalis*)
jasmine (*Jasminum polyanthemum*)
Jerusalem cherry (*Solanum pseudocapsicum*)
Johnny jump-up (*Viola wittrockiana*)

kale (ornamental) (*Brassica oleracea*)
kangaroo paw (*Anigozanthus flavidus*)

lace orchid (*Odontoglossum crispum*)
lachenalia (*Lachenalia aloides*)
lady's mantle (*Alchemilla mollis*)
lavender (*Lavandula angustifolia*)
lenten rose (*Helleborus orientalis*)
lily-of-the-valley (*Convallaria majalis*)
lisianthus (*Eustoma grandiflorum*)
loosestrife (*Lysimachia clethroides*)

Madagascar jasmine (*Marsdenia floribunda*)
Madeira winter cherry (*Solanum pseudocapsicum*)
marguerite (*Argyranthemum frutescens*)
marigold (*Calendula officinalis*)

marigold (*Tagetes* species)
Mexican bush sage (*Salvia leucantha*)
Michaelmas daisy (*Aster ericoides*)
mini rose (*Rosa* cultivars)
moss rose (*Portulaca grandiflora*)
moth orchid (*Phalaenopsis* cultivars)
muscari (*Muscari* species)

nasturtium (garden) (*Tropaeolum majus*)
New Guinea impatiens (*Impatiens hawkeri*)

oriental lily (*Lilium* cultivars)

pansy (*Viola wittrockiana*)
paper daisy (*Rhodanthe manglesii*)
peace lily (*Spathiphyllum wallisii*)
peony (*Paeonia* species)
pepper (ornamental) (*Capsicum annuum*)
Persian violet (*Cyclamen persicum*)
Peruvian lily (*Alstroemeria* cultivars)
Philippine ground orchid (*Spathoglottis plicata*)
phlox (*Phlox paniculata*)
pincushion (*Leucospermum cordifolium*)
pincushion flower (*Scabiosa caucasica*)
pink quill (*Tillandsia cyanea*)
pinks (*Dianthus barbatus*)
pitcher plant (*Nepenthes* cultivars)
pitcher plant (yellow) (*Sarracenia flava*)
pocketbook plant (*Calceolaria* species)
poinsettia (*Euphorbia pulcherrima*)
polyanthus (*Primula vulgaris*)
portulaca (*Portulaca grandiflora*)
pot marigold (*Calendula officinalis*)
pot rose (*Rosa* cultivars)
prairie gentian (*Eustoma grandiflorum*)
primrose (*Primula vulgaris*)

queen lily (*Curcuma petiolata*)

ranunculus (*Ranunculus asiaticus*)
red ginger (*Alpinia purpurata*)
regal geranium (*Pelargonium domesticum*)

saffron spike (*Aphelandra squarrosa*)
sage (*Salvia leucantha*)
sapphire flower (*Browallia speciosa*)
satin flower (*Clarkia amoena*)

scarlet lobelia (*Lobelia cardinalis*)
scarlet star (*Guzmania lingulata*)
Scotch broom (*Cytisus scoparius*)
sea lavender (*Limonium sinuatum*)
slipper flower (*Calceolaria* species)
slipper orchid (*Paphiopedilum* cultivars)
sneezeweed (-wort) (*Helenium autumnale*)
snowdrop (*Galanthus nivalis*)
spathoglottis (*Spathoglottis plicata*)
speedwell (garden) (*Veronica longifolia*)
spirea (*Astilbe arendsii*)
spray brunia (*Brunia nodiflora*)
St Joseph's lily (*Lilium longiflorum*)
statice (*Limonium sinuatum*)
stephanotis (*Marsdenia floribunda*)
streptocarpus (*Streptocarpus hybridus*)
summer azalea (*Godetia amoena*)
summer orchid (*Angelonia angustifolia*)
summer snapdragon (*Angelonia angustifolia*)
sunflower (*Helianthus annuus*)
Swan River everlasting (*Rhodanthe manglesii*)
sweet rocket (*Hesperis matronalis*)
sweet scabious (*Scabiosa caucasica*)
sweet violet (*Viola odorata*)
sweet william (*Dianthus barbatus*)

Texas bluebell (*Eustoma grandiflorum*)
tillandsia (*Tillandsia cyanea*)
tom thumb (*Kalanchoe blossfeldiana*)
torch ginger (*Alpinia purpurata*)
tulip (*Tulipa* cultivars)
tutsan (*Hypericum androsaemum*)

vanda orchid (*Vanda coerulea*)
Venus's slipper (*Paphiopedilum* cultivars)
verbena (common) (*Verbena hybrida*)
violet (sweet) (*Viola odorata*)
vuylstekeara orchid (*Vuylstekeara* cultivars)

winter cherry (*Solanum pseudocapsicum*)

yellow chamomile (*Anthemis tinctoria*)
yellow pitcher plant (*Sarracenia flava*)
yellow trumpet (*Sarracenia flava*)

zebra plant (*Aphelandra squarrosa*)
zonal geranium (*Pelargonium zonale*)

CUT FLOWERS
IN ALPHABETICAL ORDER

Abies procera
noble fir

Abies procera foliage and cone

Abies procera leaves

DESCRIPTION Noble fir is a large tree of up to 70 m (more than 200′). The needle-like leaves are about 35 mm (1½″) long and are arranged along the sides and top of the branches. The leaves are generally a glossy blue-green colour and have silvery grey stomatal bands below. The attractive cones are cylindrical and more than 200 mm (8″) long. *Abies balsamea* (balsam fir), also often known as "Christmas greens" can be used and treated in the same way as noble fir. There are numerous cultivars that differ in the shape and colour of the foliage. These include 'Aurea' and 'Sherwoodii' (both with bright golden yellow leaves) and 'Glauca' (with silvery blue leaves). Particular emphasis in cultivar selection is on creating dwarf cultivars for use in gardens.

ORIGIN & HISTORY North-western parts of the United States. The trees have become popular as Christmas trees and foliage plants.

PARTS USED The fresh leafy branches are used as foliage (these are generally known as "Christmas greens").

CULTIVATION Propagation is from seeds or cuttings. Trees are easy to grow in almost any soil but require cold winters and moderate summer temperatures. Plants are cultivated for use as Christmas trees but foliage is often wild-harvested.

PROPERTIES Vase life is very good (21–28 days). This type of greens is sensitive to ethylene, so try to avoid poor ventilation and contact with sources of ethylene such as ripening fruits and ageing flowers.

QUALITY CRITERIA Select stems with leaves in full colour. Dropping of needles (leaves) is an indication of dry stems or incorrect care and handling. Younger, well-branched stems are of much better quality than older or sparser ones.

CARE & HANDLING Store separately from cut flowers to avoid ethylene damage. Keep cool for immediate use. If material has to be kept for later use, recut and place in water with a bactericide.

Abies procera Rehd. (=*A. nobilis*)   family: Pinaceae
coniferen (Dutch); *sapin* (French); *Edle Tanne* (German)

Abutilon hybridum

flowering maple • Chinese lantern • abutilon

Abutilon 'Bella'

Abutilon 'Bella' mixed colours

DESCRIPTION A shrub of up to 5 m (about 16') but dwarf forms have become popular as pot plants. The light green, multi-lobed leaves resemble those of a maple tree. The solitary bell-shaped or lantern-shaped flowers face outwards. The venation of the petals is often very distinct and adds to the attraction of the flowers. Not many cultivars are available, but those that are have a wide range of colours and generally produce compact, well-branched plants that work very well as a potted flower. Cultivars are basically bred and sold as F_1 seed hybrids.

ORIGIN & HISTORY Tropical regions of the Old World. The plant originated as a garden hybrid.

PARTS USED Whole plants are used as potted flowers.

CULTIVATION Most cultivars are grown from seed, except variegated abutilon, which is usually propagated vegetatively. Many potted flowers have their central growing points pinched out during production to create full, well-branched plants. This is generally not necessary in the case of flowering maple, where the best branching is achieved by proper spacing between the pots. *Abutilon* prefers cool production temperatures (15–21°C; 59–70°F), which results in more intense colours of the flowers. Excessively high temperatures (>30°C; >85°F) can result in abortion of flower buds.

PROPERTIES Plants usually flower continually for weeks on end. They are ethylene sensitive.

QUALITY CRITERIA Pots or baskets are sold with about 1–6 plants each, depending on the size of the container. Carefully check and select plants with 3–4 uniform branches each. Make sure leaves do not have any brown spots or the flowers any marks, as these are often signs of botrytis infection.

CARE & HANDLING Regularly remove dead flowers and leaves to promote continued flowering. Display pots in a cool, low-light area and definitely not in direct sunlight. Avoid draughts. Keep potting medium moist.

Abutilon ×hybridum Hort.   family: Malvaceae

abutilon, lanterne chinoise (French); *Samtpappel* (German); *abutilo* (Italian)

Acacia dealbata

silver wattle • mimosa • wattle • blue wattle

Acacia dealbata leaves and flowers

DESCRIPTION The silver wattle is a tall, evergreen tree of up to 30 m (more than 100') high. The leaves are twice compound and have a feathery appearance. Minute flowers are borne in small, rounded heads. They are pale yellow and highly fragrant. No cultivars are known except 'Pendula', a form with weeping branches. Several other species are also used as fillers, including *A. mearnsii* (blackwattle).

ORIGIN & HISTORY Tasmania and Australia. The tree has become an aggressive invader in southern Africa. Several species are used.

PARTS USED Stems with leaves and flowers are used as florist foliage.

CULTIVATION Acacias are often viewed as easy to grow. However, to obtain good quality foliage, a sandy, well-drained soil is required. Plants prefer full sun and have low water requirements. Young plants are very sensitive to frost damage. Material is predominantly wild-harvested.

PROPERTIES Vase life is rather poor (3–5 days). Flowers dry out fairly quickly and lose their fluffy appearance. They have a subtle, pleasant fragrance. Flowers (or the pollen) may cause allergies in some people.

QUALITY CRITERIA Select stems with flowers in full bloom. Make sure the blossoms are free of brown spots or have not dried and shrivelled up. Look for well-shaped branches that are not too woody. Check that stems are free of pests and diseases.

CARE & HANDLING Unpack, recut stems and hydrate immediately. Hydrate foliage for at least 2 hours (or until flowers and leaves are turgid) in warm water (38–40°C/100–105°F) that has been acidified to pH 3.5. Remove any foliage that will be under water. After hydrating, place foliage in a preservative and preferably hold at 2–4°C (36–39°F) and 90% relative humidity until used, or else display in a cool place out of any draughts. Avoid unnecessary changes in temperature. Do not store the stems but use them quickly. Flowering stems can be air-dried. However, actual flowers tend to lose their fluffy appearance when dried.

Acacia dealbata Link.   family: Fabaceae

mimosa (Dutch); *acacia, mimosa* (French); *Silberakazie* (German); *mimosa* (Italian)

58

Achillea filipendulina
yarrow • fern leaf yarrow

Achillea filipendulina

Achillea millefolium 'Cassis'

Achillea millefolium mixed colours

DESCRIPTION Fern leaf yarrow is a perennial herb with flowering stems of up to 1 m (40") tall. The compound leaves are feathery and loosely hairy. Tiny florets are borne in minute flower heads, which in turn are arranged in many-headed, flat-topped clusters. Several cultivars are available, with names mostly reflecting the typical golden yellow colour of the flower heads (such as 'Cloth of Gold', 'Altgold', 'Gold Plate'). Hybrids with A. ptarmica have become popular and include cultivars such as 'Schwefelblüte' ("flowers of sulphur"). A. millefolium is also an important commercial species that is nowadays available in a wide range of flower colours. Numerous cultivars have been derived from hybrids between A. millefolium and a cultivar known as A. 'Taygetea'.
ORIGIN & HISTORY Central Europe (Caucasia), West Asia (Iran to Afghanistan) and Central Asia. Yarrows are old favourite ornamental plants.
PARTS USED The fresh or dried flower heads.
CULTIVATION Mostly in open fields or under shade cloth (greenhouse cultivation is normally not viable). Plants prefer well-drained, low salt-content soils. A cold period (vernalisation) of below 4°C (39°F) is beneficial in increasing plant vigour and uniformity of flowering. Light intensity, planting density and age of the plant affect stem length. Growers normally lift, separate and replant plants after the second year of production.
PROPERTIES Vase life is poor to good (5–10 days), depending on the species and cultivar. Grey-green foliage is fragrant, but not necessarily pleasing.
QUALITY CRITERIA Select stems that are long, straight and sturdy, with well-formed flower heads that are in full colour. Look for florets that are fully open, with pollen visible. When harvested too soon, the vase life is reduced – flower heads can drop or stems tend to wilt in the vase.
CARE & HANDLING Recut stems and place in water with an all-purpose preservative. Remove foliage below the water line. Loosen tight bunches to improve air-circulation. The flower heads are excellent for drying.

Achillea filipendulina Lam.   family: Asteraceae

duizendblad (Dutch); *millefeuille* (French); *Schafgarbe* (German); *millefoglie* (Italian); *milenrama* (Spanish)

Aconitum napellus

monkshood • helmet flower

Aconitum dark blue

Aconitum tricoloured

Aconitum pale blue

DESCRIPTION A biennial or perennial herb with flowering stems of 1 m (40") high. The leaves are up to 100 mm (4") wide, with 5–7 lobes, each with three smaller lobes which may be deeply divided or lacerated. Flowers are borne in branched clusters. They are about 40 mm (just over 1½") long and usually white, but sometimes red, blue, purple, bicoloured or variegated, depending on the species and cultivar. Examples are 'Bicolor' (white and blue), 'Caeruleum' (deep blue), 'Doppelgänger' (dark blue), 'Grandiflorum Album' (white) and 'Nachthimmel' (dark violet).

ORIGIN & HISTORY Europe. The main commercial species are *A. napellus* (common monkshood) and a hybrid with *A. variegatum* (eastern monkshood) which has become known as garden monkshood (*A. ×cammarum*). *A. napellus* also has numerous other common names, including friar's-cap, soldier's-cap, turk's-cap and bear's-foot.

PARTS USED The fresh flowers are used as cut flowers.

CULTIVATION The size of the flowering stem depends on tuber size and weight. Plants are productive for at least 5 years, but are usually lifted, separated and replanted after 3 years. Tubers planted in greenhouses need vernalisation (period of cold) to induce proper flowering. Growers try to harvest flowers as high as possible because leaf mass affects tuber formation.

PROPERTIES Warning: All parts of the plant are extremely poisonous. Vase life is poor to average (5–7 days). Flowers are sensitive to ethylene.

QUALITY CRITERIA Quality is measured by stem length, raceme length, flowers per stem and stem thickness. Make sure actual flowers are undamaged. Select stems with flowers open to within 30–50 mm (1–2") of the tip. If cut too early (with no flowers open), then most of the buds will fail to open properly.

CARE & HANDLING Use a preservative with an anti-ethylene agent. Flowers can be stored for 2–3 days at 2–4°C (36–39°F), but do not store above 21°C (70°F). Wash hands thoroughly after working with flowers and warn customers or other people that the flowers are poisonous. The flowers can be dried, but strip off leaves prior to drying.

Aconitum napellus L.   family: Ranunculaceae

monnikskap (Dutch); *aconit* (French); *Eisenhut* (German); *aconito* (Italian); *acónito* (Spanish)

Actinotus helianthi
flannel flower

Actinotus helianthi flower heads

DESCRIPTION A woolly perennial herb of up to 0.6 m (2') high bearing bi- or tripinnately compound leaves with narrow ultimate segments. The white flower clusters (dense umbels) are borne on short stems. These flower heads are surrounded by about 15 to 18 large, white, leaf-like and attractive woolly bracts, so that the whole inflorescence resembles a single flower. Each of the petal-like bracts is about 50 mm (2") long, with a long drawn out tip. The flowers themselves are small and rather inconspicuous. There are as yet no named or well-known cultivars. The most immediate problem is finding cultivars that are resistant to *Fusarium* pathogens.

ORIGIN & HISTORY The species originated in Australia and has been used extensively as cut flowers since the 1800s when stems were harvested from natural stands along the New South Wales coast. The commercial cultivation of this species began in the 1990s and *Actinotus* is still in its infancy as a florist flower but has become popular in recent years.

Actinotus helianthi Labill.

actinotus (Dutch, French, Italian, Spanish); *Actinotus* (German)

PARTS USED Flowering stems are used as florist flowers or fillers.

CULTIVATION Plants can be cultivated in a range of soils, as long as they are very well drained and acidic (pH 4.5–4.8). Plants do well in hot weather but are susceptible to fungal attack if overhead watering is used. Most flowers are wild-harvested.

PROPERTIES Vase life is very good (14–21 days). Handling of flowers can cause skin irritations due to fine hairs on the stem. Plants and flowers are susceptible to botrytis infection.

QUALITY CRITERIA Flowers are graded and sold on stem length. Select straight, sturdy stems. Make sure flower heads are free of disease and general damage. Select stems with 15–30 of the florets in the centre of the main disc of the flowering head open.

CARE & HANDLING Recut stems and place in water with a bactericide and a low sugar concentration. Flower heads can be stored in water for 7 days at 4°C (39°F) and a relative humidity of 90%.

family: Apiaceae (Umbelliferae)

Agapanthus africanus

African lily • blue lily

Agapanthus africanus blue

Agapanthus africanus white

DESCRIPTION *Agapanthus* species are robust perennial herbs with thick, fleshy rhizomes and strap-shaped leaves. The trumpet-shaped flowers occur in umbels (all flower stalks are of equal length and they arise at the same point). Umbels are borne on long slender stalks of up to 0.6 m (2") long (in the case of *A. africanus*) or up to 1 m (40") long in *A. praecox* and numerous hybrids and cultivars. Although known as blue lilies, some flowers are white. Various shades of blue are encountered. Cultivars derived from *A. africanus* include 'Albus' (white flowers), 'Albus Nanus' (dwarf plant, white flowers) and 'Sapphire' (dark blue flowers). *Agapanthus praecox* cultivars include 'Variegatus' (leaves striped with silver) and 'Plenus' (with double flowers). Cultivars of unknown or hybrid origin include 'Maximus Albus' (white) and 'Blue Giant' (blue).

ORIGIN & HISTORY South Africa. They are popular garden plants in many parts of the world.

PARTS USED Fresh flowers are used as cut flowers.

CULTIVATION Deciduous types are divided and transplanted in early spring (evergreen types just after flowering in late summer). They grow well in most soils but prefer light loam that contains plenty of humus. Plants prefer full sun or light shade, but not full shade.

PROPERTIES Vase life is average (5–8 days), with florets continually opening over a 3–4 day period. There is no noticeable fragrance.

QUALITY CRITERIA Purchase stems with a tight cluster of mainly closed flowers, but showing colour. Select strong straight stems with no lesions or soft spots where stems may buckle.

CARE & HANDLING Recut the stems and place them in water as soon as possible. Use an all-purpose preservative, which will also assist in flower opening. *Agapanthus* flowers respond very well to anti-ethylene treatment. A storage temperature below the optimum of about 4–5°C (39–41°F) can result in reddish-tinted florets.

Agapanthus africanus (L.) Hoffm.   family: Agapanthaceae (or Amaryllidaceae)

Afrikaanse lelie (Dutch); *Afrikanische Lilie* (German); *agapanto* (Italian); *agapanto* (Spanish)

Agastache foeniculum
anise hyssop • giant hyssop • Mexican hyssop

Agastache foeniculum 'Liquorice Blue'

Agastache foeniculum 'Liquorice White'

DESCRIPTION Anise hyssop is an uncommon perennial herb of nearly 1 m (40") high. It has slender flowering spikes borne above mint-like leaves. The flowers are usually violet-blue but sometimes white or red in modern cultivars. They are borne in regular clusters along the spikes. A number of hybrids and cultivars are available. Even though some of them are excellent as florist flowers it must still be kept in mind that *Agastache* cultivars are mainly bred and cultivated for the garden industry. Cultivar names include 'Firebird' (0.6 m or 2' high, coppery red flowers), 'Alabaster' and 'Alba' (both with white flowers) and the multi-coloured and sweet-smelling 'Fragrant Delight'.

ORIGIN & HISTORY North America. The plant has become a popular border perennial and is also cultivated as a cut flower.

PARTS USED The fresh flower spikes are used as cut flowers.

CULTIVATION Anise hyssop is easy to grow from seed sown in spring. For good production and quality flowers, well-drained soils and a high light intensity are essential. *Agastache* is usually grown outdoors during the summer months when the days are longer. Even so, ideal production temperatures are in the range of 15–21°C (59–70°F). The crop is seldom grown in greenhouses for cut flowers as it has a relatively low value.

PROPERTIES Vase life is slightly poor to above average (6–10 days). Foliage is scented. The leaves of *A. foeniculum* have a liquorice scent.

QUALITY CRITERIA Select inflorescences with 50–75% of flowers open. Look for sturdy stems with long, well-developed flower spikes. Make sure that the leaves have good colour and are free from damage or disease.

CARE & HANDLING Recut and place in water with a general all-purpose preservative. Make sure all the leaves below the water line are removed. Flowers can be stored for 2–3 days at 5–6°C (41–43°F).

Agastache foeniculum (Pursh) Kuntze

family: Lamiaceae

hysope anisée (French); *Anis-Ysop, Duftnessel* (German)

Ageratum houstonianum

flossflower • floss flower

Ageratum 'Red Sea'

Ageratum 'High Tide Blue'

Ageratum 'High Tide White'

DESCRIPTION An annual of about 0.7 m (28") high with broad, heart-shaped leaves. The flower heads are grouped into loose, round-topped clusters with a tassle-like appearance. The original flower colour was mostly lavender, but nowadays a range of colours are available, including white, lilac, blue, pink and violet. A number of seed strains, cultivars and hybrids are available. Taller cultivars with blue flowers include 'Blue Horizon' and 'Blue Banquet'. Cultivar selection focuses on stem length and yields per plant, which is more of interest to the grower than the florist.

ORIGIN & HISTORY Mexico. The Greek "a" meaning *not* and "geras" meaning *old age* could refer to the flowers persisting and retaining their colour for a long time while on the plant. Flossflower is well known in the bedding plant trade. It is only more recently that cultivars have been bred for the florist industry.

PARTS USED Stems with leaves and flowering heads are used as cut flowers. Dwarf cultivars have been used as potted flowers.

CULTIVATION Flowering is most proficient within a temperature range of 15–21°C (59–70°F), while temperatures consistently below 10°C (50°F) or above 32°C (90°F) inhibits flowering. Plants are grown in open fields and planting starts after the danger of frost has passed. Flowers are normally supported with netting because they collapse easily during and after rainy weather. Some growers pinch young plants to produce extra shoots.

PROPERTIES Vase life is slightly poor to average (5–7 days). There is very little or no ethylene sensitivity.

QUALITY CRITERIA Flowers do not store or last all that well. Therefore, it is best to purchase locally grown flowers. Select flower heads with the central floret open and the other florets showing colour but still closed. Check leaves and flowers for disease and general damage.

CARE & HANDLING Recut stems immediately and place in a preservative. Flower heads can be air-dried, but the colour often fades.

Ageratum houstonianum Mill.

family: Asteraceae

agérate (French); *Leberbalsam* (German); *agerato* (Spanish)

Agrostemma githago
corn cockle

Agrostemma githago wild form

Agrostemma atrosanguinea

DESCRIPTION An erect, weedy annual of about 1 m (40") high with narrow opposite leaves and attractive flowers. The wild form has pink flowers, but breeding and selection have resulted in a few cultivars with pink, lilac, purple-rose and white flowers. *Agrostemma atrosanguinea* is also used as a cut flower.

ORIGIN & HISTORY Corn cockle occurs naturally in Western Europe, where it is considered little more than a weed and not necessarily thought of as a florist flower. It is naturalised in the United States and has been introduced into cereal growing regions of the world along with poorly cleaned seed.

PARTS USED Flowering stems are used as foliage and filler.

CULTIVATION The best flower quality and yields are achieved under cool growing conditions, long days, high light intensity, regular watering and well-drained soils. Flowers are usually grown in open fields, as market prices are too low for greenhouse cultivation. Due to its poor vase life, flowers need to be harvested only when it is cool and immediately placed into a preservative. Most growers harvest by pulling out the whole plant, stripping off the leaves and bunching the stems, as it is usually not viable to harvest stems individually over a period of time.

PROPERTIES Vase life is poor to average (5–7 days). Stems do not transport particularly well over long distances. Seeds are poisonous if eaten.

QUALITY CRITERIA Single stems should be harvested when only 1–2 flowers are open. However, because most stems are harvested simultaneously, growers wait for more flowers to first be open. Therefore, select bunches with preferably 30% of flowers open. Make sure flowers and leaves (if present) are healthy with a uniform colour.

CARE & HANDLING Recut stems and immediately place in a preservative. Remove any leaves that might be below the water line. Storage is not recommended, but if necessary store for 2–4 days at 4°C (39°F) in a preservative.

Agrostemma githago L.   family: Caryophyllaceae

bolderik (Dutch); *nielle de champs, gerzeau* (French); *Kornrade* (German); *gittaione, mazzetone* (Italian)

Alcea rosea

hollyhock

Alcea rosea pink

Alcea rosea 'Happy Lights'

DESCRIPTION A short-lived biennial or perennial with broad, hairy leaves and erect (usually single) flowering stems of up to 3 m (10′) high. The flowers are large (80–120 mm or 3–5″ in diameter) and may be single or double. Flower colour varies from white to pink, purple, red or pale yellow. Several cultivars and seed races have been developed, including Chater's Double Hybrids (with peony-like, double flowers in a range of colours) and 'Indian Spring' (single flowers in white, yellow or pink). Majorette Mixed and Pinafore Mixed are semi-double, lace forms. Of particular interest is 'Nigra', a cultivar with dark maroon flowers, used as a source of natural colour for herbal teas.

ORIGIN & HISTORY The western parts of Asia (possibly Turkey). Hollyhock has been cultivated in gardens in Europe for a long time.

PARTS USED The fresh flowers are used as cut flowers.

CULTIVATION Hollyhock grows best when cultivated in full sun or partial shade and in a deep, rich soil with good drainage. Flowering stems become extremely tall and 2–3 layers of support are usually required.

PROPERTIES Flower stems and leaves are hairy and may cause some skin irritation. There is no noticeable fragrance.

QUALITY CRITERIA Look for straight, sturdy stems containing a good volume of evenly spaced flowers. Preferably choose stems that are not too thick or too large. Make sure the flowers and leaves are free of disease and general damage. Check that leaves and stems have a good green colouration and are not pale or blotchy.

CARE & HANDLING Immediately recut stems and place in a hydrating solution for 1–2 hours at room temperature. Stems can be recut by at least 50–100 mm (2–4″). Afterwards place in a preservative with a bactericide and sugar. Stems pollute water easily so do not keep in the same water as pollutant-sensitive flowers. Storage is not recommended.

Alcea rosea L.   family: Malvaceae

stokrose (Dutch); *rose trémière* (French); *Gewöhnliche Stockrose* (German); *malva rósea* (Spanish)

Alchemilla mollis

lady's mantle

Alchemilla mollis 'Robusta'

Alchemilla mollis leaves and flowers

DESCRIPTION A robust perennial herb with large leaves and flowering stems of up to 0.8 m (32") high. The leaves are typically circular, with about 10 rounded lobes, each of which has 7–9 unequal teeth. The spreading hairs on the leaves are characteristic. Small greenish yellow flowers are borne in large showy clusters. There are hardly any cultivars except 'Variegata', a form of which the leaves are variously marked with yellow. The cultivar 'Robusta' is said to be indistinguishable from the wild form.

ORIGIN & HISTORY Eastern Europe (Caucasia and the eastern Carpathians). It has become a popular garden subject and is often used as a border plant in Europe. The plant was reputed to have healing powers and was popular amongst alchemists of old, hence the name "Alchemilla".

PARTS USED Fresh flowering stems are used as foliage, filler or the whole plant as a potted flower.

CULTIVATION Propagation is usually from seed. Plants are often pruned back hard after flowering for the next production cycle, or else treated as annuals. They prefer well-drained, light soils and full sun or partial shade. Plants self-seed and are drought tolerant. They are invasive weeds in certain countries.

PROPERTIES Vase life is average (6–8 days). The foliage and flowers are fairly sensitive to ethylene.

QUALITY CRITERIA Select stems with 75–100% of the flowers open. Check that leaves are green and healthy and not bleached or pale due to excessive sun exposure.

CARE & HANDLING Recut the stems and place them in a floral preservative. Remove leaves below the water line. Water tends to "stick" to the leaves, so take care that unsightly marks are not left. Storage is not recommended, but if this is necessary then the stems can be held for 2–3 days at 2–4°C (36–39°F) and a relative humidity of 90–95%. The flowers can also be dried.

Alchemilla mollis (Buser) Rothm.   family: Rosaceae

vrouwenmantel (Dutch); *manteau de Notre-Dame* (French); *Weicher Frauenmantel* (German); *alchemilla* (Italian); *pie de leon* (Spanish)

Allium giganteum

ornamental onion • giant onion • florist allium

Allium gigantium

Allium christophii

DESCRIPTION A true bulb with fleshy basal leaves and a thick, hollow flowering stalk of up to 2 m (about 6′) high. The star-shaped, purple or white flowers are borne in large, dense spherical umbels of up to 150 mm (6″) in diameter. There are very few cultivars of florist alliums. Species such as *A. neapolitanum* and *A. christophii* are also used as cut flowers.

ORIGIN & HISTORY Himalayas (*A. giganteum*) or Mediterranean Europe (*A. neapolitanum*). There are around 750 species, many of which make useful florist flowers.

PARTS USED Leafless flowering heads are used as cut flowers.

CULTIVATION Plants are normally field-grown. Most allium bulb species need a cold cycle to induce flowering (or to improve uniformity) and do not grow well in warmer climates. In the wild this cold period would occur during winter months. However, like all commercially viable bulbous cut flowers, allium bulbs are artificially vernalised in cold-rooms by breeders, bulb growers or suppliers. Bulbs are prone to viruses and new, clean stock (especially for *A. giganteum*) can be relatively expensive.

PROPERTIES Vase life is average (7–10 days). An "onion smell" (present in all species) is most noticeable when stems are cut or crushed but once in a vase the scent usually does not persist for long. Flowers are fairly sensitive to ethylene.

QUALITY CRITERIA Look for strong, straight stems with well-formed flowering heads. Purchase stems with only 30–50% of the florets open. The rest opens easily in any normal preservative. Flowers that are shipped too open are prone to damage during handling and transit. Flower and stem colour should be uniform and true.

CARE & HANDLING Unpack and fluff out flattened heads by holding them upside down in between the palms of the hands and spinning them to and fro. Recut the stems and leave to stand overnight in a preservative at room temperature, before cool storage or use. Flowers are suitable for drying. Hang upside down in a cool, airy place to dry.

Allium giganteum Reg.   family: Alliaceae

sierui (Dutch); *ail d' ornament, ail de géant de l'Himalaya* (French); *Riesen-Lauch* (German); *aglio* (Italian); *ajo* (Spanish)

Alpinia purpurata

torch ginger • ginger lily • red ginger

Alpinia purpurata dark red form

Alpinia purpurata 'Eileen McDonald'

DESCRIPTION A ginger-like plant with stems that grow from a rhizome below the ground, reaching a height of 3 m (10′) or more. The broad, hairless leaves are arranged in two ranks and are up to 0.3 m (1′) long. The cone-like, cylindrical flower clusters are erect or nodding and have numerous overlapping reddish purple bracts that hide the small white flowers. Famous cultivars include 'Eileen McDonald' (with candy pink bracts), 'Pink Princess' (with rose pink bracts) and 'Tahitian Ginger' (with very large, dark red bracts).

ORIGIN & HISTORY The plant originated from the south-eastern Pacific region and has become a popular florist flower in recent years.

PARTS USED The fresh flower heads are used as cut flowers and fillers or the whole plant may be used as potted flower.

CULTIVATION Plants require high temperatures and humid conditions, as well as deep, rich soils. They need copious amounts of water during the active growing season. After flowering, watering is reduced and the growing medium allowed to dry out to encourage the formation of new rhizomes. Plants are very sensitive to frost.

PROPERTIES Vase life is very good (10–14 days), with some cultivars having an even better vase life of up to 21 days. Flowers and foliage have a strong ginger scent.

QUALITY CRITERIA Select stems with well-coloured and well-developed bracts and no true flowers having emerged. Make sure flowers are free of black spots and pests. Check for chill damage such as grey or blue colouration (off colour).

CARE & HANDLING Recut the stems by about 50–75 mm (2–3″). Place them in a floral preservative. Hydrate wilted flowers in an acidic solution (pH 3.5) for 1–2 hours, or submerge them in clean water at room temperature for 30–60 minutes. Do not store *Alpinia* flowers at below 10°C (50°F) as cold damage will result. They can be stored for 4–5 days at 15°C (59°F) and a high relative humidity (90–95%).

Alpinia purpurata (Vieill.) Schum.

family: Zingiberaceae

alpinie (French); *Roter Ingwer* (German); *ginger rojo* (Spanish)

Alstroemeria cultivars

Inca lily • Peruvian lily

Alstroemeria 'Atlanta'

Alstroemeria 'Fuego'

Alstroemeria 'King'

DESCRIPTION Bulbous perennials with soft, fleshy and dark green stems and leaves arising from rhizomes. Flowers are trumpet-shaped and orchid-like. The inner petals are characteristically streaked or speckled. The array of colours is vast, from soft pastels, to dark and bright colours to bicolours. Commercial cultivars are hybrids derived from *A. aurea* and other species.

ORIGIN & HISTORY South America (named after the Swedish botanist Von Alstroemer). Alstroemerias have become one of the biggest selling florist flowers worldwide.

PARTS USED The whole plant is used as a potted flower or the leafy flowering stems as cut flowers.

CULTIVATION Potted flowers and cut flowers are grown in greenhouses and under shade cloth. Plants are lifted and divided every few years. Flowering is mainly temperature-induced (5–13°C; 41–55°F). However, newer cultivars are less sensitive to temperature. Soil temperatures above 21°C (70°F) inhibit continual flowering. Long days (14–16 hours) result in faster flowering.

Flowers are not cut but are pulled out of the rhizome, which stimulates renewed flowering in the next cycle.

PROPERTIES Vase life is average to good (7–14 days), although individual flowers may begin to die sooner (these can simply be removed). Flower stems are soft and break very easily. There is no noticeable fragrance. The pollen does not stain clothing. Leaves tend to yellow easily and petals drop off. Flowers are ethylene sensitive.

QUALITY CRITERIA The main limiting factor is premature yellowing of leaves. Select strong, straight stems with deep green leaves having 1–2 flowers opening and most buds showing good colour.

CARE & HANDLING Recut and hydrate the flowers as soon as possible. Remove any foliage that will end up below the water line. Use a preservative with an anti-ethylene agent and bactericide. Clean water and sterilised buckets are essential as flowers are susceptible to stem block.

Alstroemeria cultivars   family: Alstroemeriaceae

incalelie (Dutch); *alstroemère, lis des Incas* (French); *Inkalilie* (German); *peregrina de Lima* (Spanish)

Amaranthus caudatus

love-lies-bleeding • cat's tail • velvet flower • tassle flower

Amaranthus caudatus red form

Amaranthus caudatus brown form

DESCRIPTION A robust annual herb of up to 1.5 m (5') high with green, reddish or purple stems and leaves. The tassel-like flower clusters are drooping and bright red. This is one of several species of *Amaranthus* grown for decoration and as green vegetables. These include *A. cruentus* (purple amaranth, red amaranth or prince's feather), *A. hypochondriacus* (prince's feather) and *A. tricolor* (Joseph's coat, tampala or Chinese spinach). Some cultivars of *A. caudatus* are known, including a bright green, long-lasting form known as 'Viridis' or 'Green Thumb'. Several other garden cultivars with coloured leaves and brightly coloured flower clusters have been developed from the other species listed.

ORIGIN & HISTORY The plant originated as a cultigen and is known from Peru, Africa and India.

PARTS USED The fresh or dried flower tassels are used.

CULTIVATION *Amaranthus* species are short-day plants. They initially need at least 16 hours day length after which "short" days of 8–10 hours are needed to initiate flowering. Most cultivars need to be supported as the plants fall over easily if overhead watering is used. Reducing growing temperatures to around 13°C (55°F) a week or so prior to harvesting helps to enhance flower colour.

PROPERTIES Vase life is poor to slightly above average (5–8 days). The flowers are not ethylene sensitive.

QUALITY CRITERIA Look for strong stems with 50–75% of the flowers open and with no lesions or soft spots where they may buckle. Ensure that the flower racemes are well formed and have good colour.

CARE & HANDLING Recut the stems and place them in water as soon as possible. Use a preservative with a bactericide and a carbohydrate to assist in flower opening. Flowers can be stored for 2–3 days at a temperature of 2–5°C (36–41°F). Flowers can be dried by hanging them upside down and allowing them to air-dry slowly. However, accelerating the drying process with some heat will result in better preservation of flower colour.

Amaranthus caudatus L.

family: Amaranthaceae

kattestaart (Dutch); *amaranto* (French); *Gartenfuchsschwanz* (German); *amaranto* (Italian); *amaranto* (Spanish)

Amaryllis belladonna

belladonna lily • Cape belladonna • Jersey lily

Amaryllis belladonna

DESCRIPTION A deciduous bulb (dormant in summer) with strap-shaped leaves which flowers in late summer prior to its foliage appearing during the winter. The large trumpet-shaped flowers are arranged in an umbel, on a leafless purple-green stem. They are usually pink, rarely white or purple. There are several described cultivars, including 'Barberton', 'Capetown' and 'Jagersfontein' (all dark rose), 'Johannesburg', 'Kimberley' and 'Spectabilis' (all pink with lighter centre), 'Purpurea' (purple) and 'Hathor' (white). Do not confuse this plant with hippeastrums (which are often referred to as "amaryllis").

ORIGIN & HISTORY South-western Cape, South Africa. A beautiful lily-like flower that is underdeveloped as a florist flower despite its long history in cultivation. It is however, occasionally seen in florists and is always received with enthusiasm. The plant is more popular as a minor garden bulb.

PARTS USED Flowering stems are used as cut flowers.

CULTIVATION Plants do not like to be moved and will often not flower for several seasons after being moved. They prefer sandy loam soils with good drainage and full sun to partial shade, depending on the region. To prevent the hollow stems from splitting and rolling outwards, growers often pulse them overnight or ideally for 24 hours in a sucrose solution.

PROPERTIES Vase life is average to good (7–10 days). The flowers are sweetly scented.

QUALITY CRITERIA Select stems with the buds fully coloured but not yet open. Look for straight, sturdy stems with a good number of evenly spaced buds. Make sure that the buds as well as stems are free of damage and marks.

CARE & HANDLING Recut and place the stems in a preservative overnight at room temperature. Use a preservative with sugar to facilitate bud opening. Display the flowers at room temperature or store them for 2–3 days at 9–10°C (48–50°F). Avoid low temperatures (below 9°C) which may cause discolouration.

Amaryllis belladonna L.   family: Amaryllidaceae

belladonnalelie (Dutch); *amaryllis belle-dame* (French); *Belladonnenlilie* (German)

Ammi majus

lace flower • false Queen Anne's lace • false bishop's weed

Ammi majus 'Graceland'

Ammi visnaga 'Cassablanca'

DESCRIPTION A biennial or perennial herb with compound, feathery leaves and large, umbels of tiny white flowers. The plant dies down every year but sprouts again in the new season. Two of the six species of *Ammi* are grown for the florist trade, namely *A. majus* and *A. visnaga*. Some cultivars have been developed but they are similar to the wild types.

ORIGIN & HISTORY Europe, Asia and North Africa. Flowers look very similar to those of Queen Anne's lace, hence the common name.

PARTS USED Leafy flowering stems are used as cut flowers or fillers.

CULTIVATION Plants are mainly cultivated in large, open fields as annuals, although greenhouse production does occur. Growth retardants are sometimes used to produce thicker, stronger stems.

PROPERTIES The vase life of *A. majus* is average to good (7–10 days), while that of *A. visnaga* is better (10–16 days). Colour is limited to white. A slight scent (for some people unpleasant) is

noticeable. Sap from the stems or flowers contain phototoxic compounds that may cause skin irritation.

QUALITY CRITERIA Select stems with at least 60% of the florets on the umbel open. Florets continue to open over a 3–4 day period. Flowering stems harvested too early (with less than 50% of the florets open) do not take up water properly and tend to wilt easily. Selected flowering stems should have no hint of shed pollen, because once the flowers start to shed pollen they decline rapidly. Make sure the flower heads are dry and select stems that are sturdy and straight with no lesions or soft spots where they may buckle.

CARE & HANDLING Recut the stems and place them in water as soon as possible. Remove the lower leaves and if possible use a preservative with a bactericide and a carbohydrate to assist in flower opening. Flowers may be air-dried for 2–3 weeks in a dark, well-ventilated dry place. Darkness is necessary to ensure that the stems stay green and the flowers stay white and do not turn brown.

Ammi majus L.

family: Apiaceae (Umbelliferae)

dille-wit, kantbloem (Dutch); *ammi* (French); *Bischofskraut, Knorpelmöhre* (German); *ameo bastardo* (Spanish)

Ammobium alatum

winged everlasting

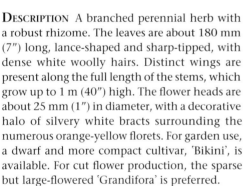

Ammobium alatum flower head

Ammobium alatum plant

Ammobium alatum leaves and flower heads

DESCRIPTION A branched perennial herb with a robust rhizome. The leaves are about 180 mm (7") long, lance-shaped and sharp-tipped, with dense white woolly hairs. Distinct wings are present along the full length of the stems, which grow up to 1 m (40") high. The flower heads are about 25 mm (1") in diameter, with a decorative halo of silvery white bracts surrounding the numerous orange-yellow florets. For garden use, a dwarf and more compact cultivar, 'Bikini', is available. For cut flower production, the sparse but large-flowered 'Grandifora' is preferred.

ORIGIN & HISTORY Australia. The plant has become a popular garden subject and cut flower.

PARTS USED The fresh or dried flower heads are used in much the same way as *Helichrysum* species (everlasting flowers), mainly as fillers.

CULTIVATION Plants prefer sunny to partially shady conditions, with warm days and cool nights. Soils should be deep and well drained and they should not be allowed to dry out completely. Plants are susceptible to disease during conditions of temperature stress combined with high humidity. They are often grown as an annual in cold climates. Flower heads are harvested for drying as soon as they have opened.

PROPERTIES The vase life of fresh flower heads is average to fairly good (7–10 days). They are not sensitive to ethylene.

QUALITY CRITERIA Select stems with 80–100% of the flower heads open. Make sure the stems are free of marks and damage. Check that the flower heads are free of browning and that none of them have started to deteriorate.

CARE & HANDLING Recut fresh flower heads and place in a preservative with a bactericide and sugar. Handle with care as stems snap fairly easily. Stems can pollute the water, so be careful when holding or storing together with pollutant-sensitive flowers. Flower heads are excellent for drying and retain colour very well. Hang small, loose bunches upside down in a shady, cool place.

Ammobium alatum R. Br.   family: Asteraceae

immortelle de sables (French); *Papierknöpfche, Sandimmortelle* (German)

Ananas comosus

pineapple • decorative pineapple

Ananas comosus inflorescences

Ananas comosus fruits

DESCRIPTION A perennial herb with a basal rosette of oblong, rigid leaves. The leaf margins are distinctly spiny. Flowers are borne in a dense cluster on the branch end, surrounded by numerous bracts. The whole structure becomes fleshy (resulting in the familiar pineapple "fruit", which is in fact a compound fruit or syncarp). Numerous cultivars are used for fruit production but the decorative foliage of the cultivar 'Porteanus' (with yellow stripes along the middle) makes it popular in flower arrangements. The leaves of 'Variegatus' are similarly yellow striped, sometimes with red marks.

ORIGIN & HISTORY The pineapple is a cultigen that originated from South America (Brazil). It has become an important commercial fruit crop but some decorative forms are used in the florist trade.

PARTS USED The leaves and fruit are used fresh as decorations in bouquets and arrangements.

CULTIVATION Propagation is normally by means of vegetative cuttings, which results in a reduction of the time needed for the plants to reach the fruiting stage. Application of iron as a micronutrient is necessary in soils of low pH (5.6–7.0). Plants thrive in climates that are uniformly warm and leaves are damaged by low temperatures. Plants are productive for 3–5 years, after which they are normally replaced.

PROPERTIES Vase life is average to good (8–14 days). The flowers and fruits are not sensitive to ethylene.

QUALITY CRITERIA Select straight stems with well-formed fruit heads. Check that heads and stems are free of damage and disease. Make sure that the tips of leaves and bracts have not dried out or deteriorated and show no chill damage.

CARE & HANDLING Handle with care – the leaf margins are spiny. Stems are normally short, so recut them by a minimal length. Immediately place them in water with a bactericide. Flowering stems can be stored for 4–5 days at 8–10°C (46–50°F) and a relative humidity of 80–90%. Storage at 5°C (41°F) and lower will cause chill damage.

Ananas comosus (L.) Merr. (=*A. sativus*)   family: Bromeliaceae

ananas (French); *Ananas* (German); *ananasso* (Italian); *piña* (Spanish)

Anemone coronaria
windflower • poppy anemone

Anemone mixed colours

Anemone 'St Brigid Mixed'

DESCRIPTION Perennial herbs of up to 0.3 m (1') high with tuberous rhizomes and finely dissected basal leaves. Solitary flowers (about 70 mm or nearly 3" in diameter) are borne on the stem tips. The sepals are brightly coloured (pink, purple, blue, red, white or bicoloured). True petals are absent. The collective name for single, poppy-shaped types with coloured sepals and black anthers is the De Caen group. The St Brigid group includes several semi-double cultivars. Both groups are popular as cut flowers. There are numerous cultivars of related species such as Japanese anemones (*A.* ×*hybrida*) – much taller plants of up to 1.5 m (5') and Chinese anemones (*A. hupehensis*) – up to 0.6 m (2') high. The daisy-flowered anemones (*A. nemorosa*) are another popular group.

ORIGIN & HISTORY Southern Europe and the Mediterranean region. Anemones have a long history of use as garden plants.

PARTS USED The flowers as cut flowers.

CULTIVATION Flowers open during the day and close again at night. Ideally they should be harvested the morning after the flowers have opened and closed for the first time. This is seldom practical and growers generally harvest flowers once "petals" have started to separate from the centre and before they have fully opened.

PROPERTIES Vase life is poor to average (3–7 days). Flowers will continue to grow and twist even after they have been harvested. Anemones are ethylene sensitive.

QUALITY CRITERIA Select stems with tight flowers, standing at least 20–30 mm (1") above the collar of the foliage. Anemones are disease-prone, so ensure that they are damage and disease free.

CARE & HANDLING Flowers tend to wilt quite easily, so hydrate them as soon as possible. Use a preservative containing an anti-ethylene agent. Storage is not recommended, but if necessary only store for 1–2 days at 3–4°C (37–39°F) with good ventilation. Flowers can be dried.

Anemone coronaria L.   family: Ranunculaceae

anemoon (Dutch); *anémone* (French); *Anemone, Windröschen* (German); *anémona* (Spanish)

Anethum graveolens
dill

Anethum graveolens plants

Anethum graveolens inflorescence

DESCRIPTION This is a slender, erect annual herb (up to 0.6 m or 2′) with attractive feathery leaves that are divided into numerous thin segments. The flower heads are typical umbels borne at the tips of the hollow stems. Small yellow flowers are followed by the familiar dill "seeds" which are actually small dry fruits. They are flattened and winged along their margins. There are no special cultivars for use in the flower industry.

ORIGIN & HISTORY Probably south-western Asia. The exact origin of dill is not certain, as it has been cultivated in Egypt, Asia and Europe since ancient times.

PARTS USED The fresh flowering stems with their fluffy and feathery appearance are used as foliage and filler.

CULTIVATION Plants are produced from seed and require a well-drained, slightly acidic (pH 5.6–6.2) medium. In outdoor production seeds are sown directly and once seedlings have established, they are thinned out. Established plants grow rapidly and flower freely. Dill has a tendency to bolt (flower and seed prematurely) under dry conditions. It is similar to fennel, but has a hollow and not a solid stem. If planted near fennel they are said to cross-pollinate and produce off-flavours in seeds. The use of growth regulators on dill is prohibited, even when grown as florist filler, because it is a food crop.

PROPERTIES Vase life is poor to average (4–8 days). The whole plant is aromatic and edible. Flowers are highly scented. Dill is sensitive to ethylene.

QUALITY CRITERIA Select straight, sturdy stems with numerous, full flower heads. Look for stems with 50–75% of the florets on the main umbel open.

CARE & HANDLING Recut stems and place in a preservative containing an anti-ethylene agent, bactericide and a sugar (to help florets to open fully). Dill flowers do not store well. Flower heads can be successfully dried.

Anethum graveolens L.   family: Apiaceae (Umbelliferae)

dille (Dutch); *aneth* (French); *Dill* (German); *aneto* (Italian); *eneldo* (Spanish)

Angelonia angustifolia
summer snapdragon • summer orchid

Angelonia 'Angel Face'

Angelonia 'Angel Mist'

DESCRIPTION A perennial herb with lance-shaped, toothed leaves borne on stems of up about 0.4 m (16") high. The attractive flowers have a 2-lobed upper lip and a 3-lobed lower lip but no spur or tube. Cultivars are selected by stem length (for pots or cut flowers). A number of colours are available, including pink, purple and white, purple, deep mauve, violet, lavender, blue and white. Two well-known cultivars are 'Alba' (white) and 'Blue Pacific' (an indigo blue and white bicolour). *Angelonia salicariifolia* is sometimes also used. It is a perennial of up to 0.7 m (28") high with glandular leaves and opaline-mauve or white flowers. Species with spotted flowers (e.g. *A. gardneri* and *A. integerrima*) are occasionally seen in gardens.

ORIGIN & HISTORY Central America (Mexico and the West Indies). Other species originate from wet areas in Brazil. Summer snapdragon is relatively new to the florist industry.

PARTS USED Flowering stems are used as cut flowers or the whole plant as potted flower.

CULTIVATION Angelonias are easily grown from cuttings. Low light levels and over-fertilising result in flowering stems becoming weak and floppy. Plants grow best under warm conditions – day temperatures of 24–32°C (75–90°F) and night temperatures of 18–21°C (65–70°F). Even higher temperatures can be tolerated as long as plants receive adequate water.

PROPERTIES Vase life of cut flowers is good (8–10 days). The shelf life of potted flowers is also very good. Plants can be cut back by 50% and will flower again in 2 to 3 weeks. Watch out for botrytis. Some people might find the sticky leaves unpleasant.

QUALITY CRITERIA Look for strong, straight stems with no or only a few lateral branches and leaves with a uniform green colour.

CARE & HANDLING Recut stems and remove lower leaves. Place in a preservative with a bactericide and sugar. Keep potting medium moist to prevent flower and bud fall. Good ventilation and bright light are important.

Angelonia angustifolia Benth.

family: Plantaginaceae (Scrophulariaceae)

angelonia (Dutch, French, Italian, Spanish); *Angelonia* (German)

Anigozanthos flavidus

kangaroo paw • tall kangaroo paw • Australian sword lily

Anigozanthos yellow

Anigozanthos red

DESCRIPTION An evergreen perennial clump with narrow, hairless leaves. The tubular and curved flowers have a felt-like outer surface. They are typically arranged in two ranks and are borne on stems of up to 3 m (10′) high. Flower colour is often dull yellow or red but new cultivars have more vibrant colours.

ORIGIN & HISTORY Native to Australia. Kangaroo paws have become popular garden plants and florist flowers in recent years.

PARTS USED Flowering stems: cut flowers; whole plants: potted flowers.

CULTIVATION Slightly acidic, well-drained sandy soils are best. Frost damages buds and high temperatures cause fading of flower colour. New plants are planted in spring or autumn to avoid high summer temperatures. Plants achieve full production in the second or third year – thereafter yields increase but quality decreases. Therefore plants are severely pruned back or replaced, while species such as *A. manglesii* are best cultivated as annuals or biennials.

PROPERTIES Vase life is average to good (7–14 days). Flowers are ethylene sensitive. Presently many of the yellow colours tend to look washed out or dirty. Vibrant yellows are, however, available. Excessive heat can cause flower colour to fade. They are also fairly sensitive to wilting.

QUALITY CRITERIA Select stems with 1–4 open florets and vibrant (not faded) colours. Limp flowers and flowers with brown tips are indicative of water stress, so avoid purchasing them. Stem lengths can vary considerably (0.6–1.5 m) but make sure bunches are of uniform length. Flowers and leaves should be free of blackening (ink disease).

CARE & HANDLING Recut at least 50 mm (2″) off the stems and place in a preservative containing an anti-ethylene agent at room temperature for at least 5 hours to rehydrate. Use a bactericide to prevent stem blockages. Flowers can be stored for 3–4 days at 2–4°C (36–39°F). Flowers dry well.

Anigozanthos flavidus DC.   family: Haemodoraceae

kangeroepootje (Dutch); *plante kangourou* (French); *Känguruhpfote* (German); *zampa di canguro* (Italian)

Anthemis tinctoria

dyer's chamomile • yellow chamomile

Anthemis tinctoria plant

Anthemis tinctoria flower head

DESCRIPTION A perennial herb with finely dissected, hairy or woolly leaves. The flower heads are about 30 mm (1¼") in diameter and occur in various shades of gold, yellow or white. Cultivars differ mainly in growth form and in the colour of the ray and disc florets. Well-known examples include 'Alba' (yellow ray florets and white disc florets), 'Beauty of Grallagh' (uniformly bright gold), 'E.C. Buxton' (uniformly pale yellow) and 'Sauce Hollandaise' (pale yellow changing to creamy white). *Anthemis punctata* is also commonly cultivated – the subspecies *cupaniana* (sometimes listed as 'Cupaniana') has silvery grey foliage and white ray florets.

ORIGIN & HISTORY The plant is native to Europe (Caucasia) and the Near East (Iran). It has a long history of use as a source of dye but has more recently become an important cut flower.

PARTS USED Flowering stems: cut flowers or dried flowers. Whole plant: potted flower.

CULTIVATION Chamomile can be cultivated from seed, cuttings or divisions. Plants prefer full sun, but moderate temperatures and slightly acidic soils (pH 6.1–7.5). They are quite drought tolerant and prefer not to be over-watered. High humidity may affect quality negatively and plants are usually cut back heavily after flowering.

PROPERTIES Vase life is average to fairly good (7–10 days). Leaves are fragrant when crushed. Chamomile is not sensitive to ethylene.

QUALITY CRITERIA Select stems with flower heads 75% to fully opened. Look for well-branched stems full of flower heads, none of which should have started to deteriorate. Check flowers and foliage for botrytis infections.

CARE & HANDLING Recut stems and place in a preservative containing a sugar and bactericide. Remove any foliage below the water line. Stems are stored for 2–4 days at 2–4°C (36–39°F) if necessary. Flower heads can be air-dried, but allow them to first open fully.

Anthemis tinctoria L.   family: Asteraceae

gele kamille (Dutch); *camomille des teinturiers* (French); *Färber-Hundskamille* (German); *camomila* (Spanish)

Anthurium andraeanum
flamingo flower • anthurium • painted tongue

Anthurium 'Tropical'

Anthurium 'White Champion'

DESCRIPTION Evergreen perennial with large leaves. The heart-shaped "flower" is actually a bract with a cylindrical spadix. The flower often gives the impression of being made of plastic or wax. There are four main groups: (1) *A. andraeanum* cultivars – typically large flowers (good cut flowers), available in white, pink, red, red-orange and green; (2) Andreacola types (*A. andraeacola* and dwarf hybrids) – smaller flowers with heart-shaped leaves used for potted flowers; (3) *A. scherzerianum* hybrids – potted flowers, with lance-shaped leaves and the spadix curled; (4) Foliage anthuriums.

ORIGIN & HISTORY Central America (Colombia and Ecuador). Since the 1980s anthuriums have become popular as potted flowers.

PARTS USED Inflorescences: cut flowers; leaves: cut greens; whole plants: potted flowers.

CULTIVATION Plants are cultivated in greenhouses or under shade cloth (mainly the Netherlands and the United States). Only mature flowers are harvested (shipped in boxes to avoid damage to the protruding spadix).

PROPERTIES Colours range from white and soft pastels to striking deep reds and bicolours. Flowers are popular for their unusual shape and texture. They have no fragrance. Ideal for large arrangements. Tolerant of heat but not cold.

QUALITY CRITERIA Vase life is very good (14–25 days). Leaves also have good vase life (10–20 days). Look for flowers void of bruising or blackened edges (cold damage).

CARE & HANDLING Unpack boxes carefully to avoid damage. Immerse the entire flower upside down in room temperature water 21–24°C (70–75°F) for 30–60 minutes. Afterwards, recut stems and place in clean, fresh water. There is no real need to use a preservative as flowers are very long lasting. Do not refrigerate or store at temperatures below 15°C (59°F) to avoid blackening. Pot plants: Display in bright light but not direct sunlight. They need high humidity, so mist regularly but avoid spraying the flowers.

Anthurium andraeanum Linden ex André   family: Araceae

lakanthurium (Dutch); *Flamingoblume* (German); *anturio* (Italian); *anturio* (Spanish)

Antirrhinum majus

snapdragon

Antirrhinum majus 'Connexion Rose'

Antirrhinum majus 'Rocket'

DESCRIPTION Perennial herbs with erect stems of up to 2 m (6½′) high bearing leaves of variable shape and size. The attractive, tubular, two-lipped flowers are about 38 mm (1½″) long and hairy outside. Cultivar groups differ mainly in the size of the plants. There are numerous dwarf forms (used in gardens) but as cut flowers the intermediate types (Monarch Series, 'Pixie') and especially the taller types (Rocket and Penstemon types) are commercially grown. Flower colour in modern cultivars range from white to various shades of yellow, orange, peach, pink, red and purple.

ORIGIN & HISTORY Mediterranean region. Snapdragons are old favourite garden plants and florist flowers.

PARTS USED Flowering stems are used as cut flowers.

CULTIVATION Snapdragons are similar in their requirements to other cold-loving plants, such as larkspurs and delphiniums. Plants are produced from seeds. Low light intensities result in blind shoots and reduced stem quality and yields.

PROPERTIES Vase life is poor to average (5–7 days). Flowers are geotropic (respond to gravity) as well as phototropic (bend towards light). They are sensitive to botrytis and ethylene.

QUALITY CRITERIA Select stems with the bottom 30–50% of flowers open and buds on the tip showing colour. Choose sturdy, straight stems with a good spike length. Check flowers and leaves carefully for disease and damage.

CARE & HANDLING Use a preservative with an anti-ethylene agent and a sugar. The sugar ensures that all buds will open and improves bud colour and vase life. Do not store below 0°C (32°F) as chill damage will occur. Always store or display upright and in bright light to prevent bending of tips. To prevent tips from bending towards the light once in an arrangement, simply break them off. If necessary store for only 2–3 days at 4–6°C (39–43°F) and a relative humidity of 75–85%.

Antirrhinum majus L.   family: Plantaginaceae (Scrophulariaceae)

leeuwebek (Dutch); *muflier* (French); *Löwenmaul* (German); *bocca di leone* (Italian); *boca de dragón* (Spanish)

Aphelandra squarrosa
zebra plant • saffron spike

Aphelandra squarrosa plant

Aphelandra squarrosa flowers

DESCRIPTION An evergreen shrub with tough, glossy leaves of up to 0.3 m (1') long. The leaves are decorated with white or silver markings along the veins, hence the name "zebra plant". The attractive flowers are arranged in 4-sided spikes with overlapping, highly ornate bracts. The waxy yellow bracts are maroon-tinted and enclose the tubular, two-lipped, yellow flowers. Cultivars differ in growth form, size and colour pattern of the leaf and flower colour. Examples include 'Citrina' (citron yellow flowers), 'Dania' (large, white-veined leaves), 'Leopoldii' (dark green and white leaves, dark red bracts and pale yellow flowers), 'Fritz Prinsler' (narrow, variegated leaves, green-tinted bracts and bright yellow flowers) and 'Saffron Spike Zebra' (orange bracts and pale yellow flowers).

ORIGIN & HISTORY South America (tropical Brazil). The plant was a great favourite with the Victorians who grew it in their conservatories.

PARTS USED Whole plants are used as attractive potted flowers.

CULTIVATION Plants are mostly produced in glasshouses under warm, moist conditions.

PROPERTIES The bracts and flower clusters remain attractive for about 6 weeks. There is no fragrance.

QUALITY CRITERIA Select plants that are compact and not too tall or spindly. Make sure leaves are damage-free and well formed, as they are part of the whole attractive display of the plant and not just the yellow spike.

CARE & HANDLING For good results place in bright natural light (but not in direct sunlight) and avoid draughts (this can cause leaf drop). Water regularly (but avoid "wet feet") and spray often with tepid water during hot weather. Plants can be cut back after flowering to promote new growth (remove the dead flower along with 2–3 pairs of leaves). Cut away to just above the remaining leaves. Temperature: minimum (13°C; 55°F); maximum (21°C; 70°F).

Aphelandra squarrosa Nees.　　　　　　　　　　　　　　　　family: Acanthaceae

zebraplantbromelia (Dutch); *plante zébre* (French); *Glanzkölbchen* (German); *afelandra* (Italian); *afelandra* (Spanish)

Aquilegia vulgaris

columbine

Aquilegia 'Songbird Robin'

Aquilegia 'Songbird Nightingale'

DESCRIPTION A perennial herb with compound leaves and distinctive, spurred flowers. A large number of species, hybrids and cultivars are grown, differing in flower colour, flower size and growth form. They are mostly derived from *A. vulgaris* (spur short, strongly hooked), *A. caerulea* (spur long, straight or curving), *A. chrysantha* (spur long, curving outward) and *A. flabellata* (spur short, curved).

ORIGIN & HISTORY Europe (*A. vulgaris*), North America (*A. caerulea*, *A. chrysantha*) and Asia (*A. flabellata*). Columbine species and hybrids have become popular bedding plants and potted plants. Individual florets resemble doves in side view, hence the name "columbine".

PARTS USED Whole plants are used as potted flowers.

CULTIVATION Cultivation from seed takes a long time, so most growers tend to purchase ready seedlings or bare-root transplants. Columbine can be forced to flower all year round by cold treatment: up to 8–10 weeks at 5°C (41°F),

followed by 16–20°C (61–68°F). Lowering the night temperature by a few degrees (when flower buds become visible) results in more compact plants with a better shelf life.

PROPERTIES Potted plants will flower for several weeks provided dead flowers are continually removed. They are sensitive to ethylene.

QUALITY CRITERIA Look for compact plants with sturdy stems that are full of buds. Ensure that leaf colour is good and uniform and free from marks or blotching.

CARE & HANDLING Continually groom the plant by removing dead flowers and leaves. This not only maintains the attractive appearance of the plant but prevents a build-up of ethylene. Display pots in bright light but not in full sunlight and in a cool area. Make sure ventilation is good but avoid cold draughts. Do not over-water the plants but rather allow the medium to dry out slightly before watering again. Potted plants should not be displayed with ethylene producing items such as ripening fruits.

Aquilegia vulgaris L.   family: Ranunculaceae

akelei (Dutch); *ancolie* (French); *Akelei* (German); *aguileña* (Spanish)

Argyranthemum frutescens
marguerite

Argyranthemum frutescens 'Cherry Red'

Argyranthemum frutescens pink

Argyranthemum frutescens yellow

DESCRIPTION A subshrub of 1 m (40") high, with aromatic, dissected leaves and single or double flower heads. The wild form has white ray florets surrounding yellow disc florets but modern cultivars often have pompom-like double heads in a range of colours (mainly white, pink or yellow). Only a few cultivars are used in the florist trade. Breeding and selection has focused on the bedding plant industry and not on florists.

ORIGIN & HISTORY Canary Islands. The common name is derived from Margaret of Anjou (wife of Henry VI) because she used daisies on her banner.

PARTS USED Flowering stems (as cut flowers) and whole plants (as potted flowers).

CULTIVATION Marguerites are grown from cuttings in well-drained, slightly acidic soil (pH 6.0–6.5) at day/night temperatures of around 18–24°C (65–75°F) / 7–13°C (45–55°F). The best quality potted flowers and cut flowers are produced at lower temperatures but this takes longer. Plants require high light intensity levels and flower faster under long days.

PROPERTIES Vase life is poor to average (3–8 days). Foliage wilts and deteriorates faster than the actual flowers. They are not ethylene sensitive.

QUALITY CRITERIA Purchase stems with flower heads 75% to fully open. Leaves may appear wilted but not the flower heads. Ensure that leaves are not pale, blotchy or chlorotic. Potted flowers should be compact, well branched and full of blooms.

CARE & HANDLING Unpack, recut and hydrate as soon as possible. Remove leaves below the water line. Place stems in a preservative with a bactericide and sugar. Removal of foliage discourages water loss and wilting. Flowers can be stored for 2–3 days at 0–4°C (32–39°F) and a relative humidity of 90%. Display potted flowers in a bright area, but not in direct sunlight and preferably at a cool to moderate temperature. Allow to dry out slightly before watering again.

Argyranthemum frutescens (L.) Sch. Bip. (=*Chrysanthemum frutescens* L.)   family: Asteraceae

magriet (Dutch); *anthémis* (French); *Strauchmargerite* (German); *manzanilla loca* (Spanish)

Artemisia annua

sweet wormwood • Chinese wormwood • sweet Annie

Artemisia annua plant

Artemisia annua flower heads

DESCRIPTION An erect annual herb up to 2 m (6½′) in height, with feathery leaves and minute, cream-coloured flower heads. Various foliage forms of the perennial plant known as white sage or western mugwort (*Artemisia ludoviciana*) are used in a similar way. Cultivars vary in growth form, leaf shape and leaf colour. Some are less scented than the wild type or even scentless.

ORIGIN & HISTORY Europe and Africa (sweet Annie), North America (white sage). Plants are harvested for their foliage and stems and not their flowers, which tend to be rather insignificant. Most product is dried, although some is sold fresh for use as florist fillers.

PARTS USED Stems are used for foliage, potpourri and wreaths.

CULTIVATION Growers often prefer to buy transplants because seeds are very small. White sage, on the other hand, is usually propagated by means of cuttings and/or plant divisions. Plants are susceptible to a number of fungal diseases, including mildew and botrytis.

PROPERTIES Vase life is poor to average (5–7 days). Foliage of all *Artemisia* species has an aroma that is not usually found pleasant. However, the scent of sweet Annie is much more pleasant, hence the name. It can cause allergies in some people.

QUALITY CRITERIA Select fresh cut stems that are not flowering. Once it flowers the stems tend to go brown when dried or becomes messy if used as filler. For material to be dried, select undamaged, disease-free stems with buds that have elongated into an egg shape. If cut too early, the dried quality will be poor.

CARE & HANDLING Recut fresh stems and place in a preservative. Remove foliage that will end up below the water line. Cold storage of fresh stems is not recommended. The flowering stems dry well when cut at the correct stage. Hang small bunches upside down in a cool, well-ventilated area. The fragrance remains after drying.

Artemisia annua L.   family: Asteraceae

qing hao (Chinese); *zoete alsem, someralsem* (Dutch); *absinthe chinoise* (French); *Einjäriger Beifuß* (German); *ajenjo anual* (Spanish)

Asclepias tuberosa
milkweed • butterfly weed

Asclepias curassavica 'Silky'

Asclepias physocarpa

Asclepias tuberosa

DESCRIPTION A tuberous perennial (up to 1 m or 40"), with erect branches and minutely hairy leaves. The flowers are about 10 mm (nearly ½") long and have bright yellow, orange or red petals. A popular seed race of *A. tuberosa* is "Gay Butterflies Mixed" (0.6 m or 2' high, multicoloured). Two cultivars are 'Orange Flame' (bright orange, scented) and 'Vermillion' (red). Another United States species used by florists is the swamp milkweed, with pink and white or rosy-pink flowers (*A. incarnata*). The weedy South American *A. curassavica* (blood flower) usually has bright red flowers. In the case of the South African swan plant (*A. physocarpa*), the bladdery and softly spiny fruits are the main attraction.

ORIGIN & HISTORY Eastern and southern United States (*A. tuberosa*). Milkweeds have become popular florist flowers in recent years.

PARTS USED Fresh or dried flowers are used as cut flowers, or the fresh or dried fruits in the case of *A. physocarpa*.

CULTIVATION Plants prefer dry production conditions and tolerate full sun and high temperatures, although low percentage shading is also used. Milkweed benefits from a cold dormant period and flowering is accelerated under long day conditions.

PROPERTIES Vase life is average to good (7–10 days). The milky sap is not excessive and is normally removed during post-harvest handling at the grower. Flowers are ethylene sensitive.

QUALITY CRITERIA Purchase blooms with at least 50–60% of the florets open. Flowers do not open fully if harvested too early (less than 50% of buds open). Ensure that ornamental fruits are green and not damaged or splitting.

CARE & HANDLING Recut the stems and place in warm water for a few minutes to stop sap flow (if any). Place in a preservative containing an anti-ethylene agent and a sugar. Store for 3–5 days in water at 4–6°C (39–43°F) if necessary. Flowers and fruits can be successfully dried.

Asclepias tuberosa L.   family: Apocynaceae (Asclepiadaceae)

zijdenbloem, knolzijdeplant (Dutch); *asclépiade tubéreuse* (French); *Knollige Schwalbenwurz* (German); *esculapia* (Italian); *asclepias* (Spanish)

Asparagus asparagoides
string smilax • smilax asparagus • greenbrier

Asparagus asparagoides

DESCRIPTION The plant is a twining and creeping perennial of up to 3 m (10') in length. It has bright green, hairless cladophylls (leaf-like structures that closely resemble leaves). These are broad (up to 18 mm or ¾" wide), leathery and have the tips gracefully curved backwards. Inconspicuous white flowers are followed by small red berries. There are very few cultivars. 'Myrtifolius' has a compact growth form and slightly smaller "leaves" (cladophylls) of up to 18 mm (¾") long.

ORIGIN & HISTORY South Africa (naturalised in southern Europe). The smilax asparagus has long been a popular garden plant.

PARTS USED Stems with leaves are used as garlands around wedding cakes and for table decorations. They are not suitable for use as a foliage or filler in arrangements or bouquets because they do not last very long.

CULTIVATION String smilax is cultivated to grow around a string. The stems are then harvested with string and all and are carefully packed in a moist plastic bag to ensure freshness.

PROPERTIES Vase life is very poor (1–3 days). The main attraction is the fresh green colour, gracefully curved shape of the "leaves" and the slender, pliable stems that can be wrapped around other objects.

QUALITY CRITERIA Make sure the bag containing foliage is full. Check length of string on the bag. Select foliage with a medium green colour. Make sure packages contain moisture.

CARE & HANDLING Refrigerate unopened bags at 5–10°C (41–50°F) and at a relative humidity of 90–95%. Do not unpack the stems from the bags until they are to be displayed and then only place them at the last moment to retain freshness for as long as possible. Do not attempt to remove the string. If the foliage needs to be stored for periods longer than a week, then open the bag in the cooler and spray with mist every two days.

Asparagus asparagoides (L.) Druce   family: Asparagaceae

sierasperge (Dutch); *Stechwinden Spargel* (German)

Asparagus densiflorus

sprenger fern • asparagus fern

Asparagus densiflorus 'Myriocladus'

Asparagus densiflorus 'Meyersii'

Asparagus densiflorus 'Sprengeri'

DESCRIPTION A somewhat woody plant with erect or trailing, ridged and slightly spiny stems of up to 1 m (40") long. The leaf-like cladophylls are narrow, up to 18 mm (¾") long, and occur in clusters of 1–3. The three main cultivars are *A. densiflorus* 'Sprengeri' (sprenger fern), *A. densiflorus* 'Myriocladus' (ming fern) and *A. densiflorus* 'Meyersii' (Meyer's fern or foxtail fern, previously a separate species, *A. meyeri*).

ORIGIN & HISTORY Africa (South Africa). Sprenger fern is probably the most common ornamental asparagus used in the garden industry and as container plant. This cultivar, along with a few others, is also very popular in the florist industry.

PARTS USED Foliage is used as cut greens. Whole plants are used as potted plants or for hanging baskets.

CULTIVATION Plants are usually propagated by means of seed. Some growers germinate their own seed while others prefer to purchase young plants. Plants do best in a disease-free, well-drained growing medium that is slightly acidic (pH 5.5–6.2). Moderate light levels are best with temperatures ranging from 16–21°C (61–70°F), although higher temperatures are tolerated. Plants grown for cut foliage remain productive for many years. 'Sprengeri' flowers in late summer and forms red berries.

PROPERTIES Vase life is sometimes below average to good (5–10 days). Sudden, rapid loss of leaves (defoliation) may be caused by air-borne fluoride pollution.

QUALITY CRITERIA Select stems that are full and not too spindly. Make sure leaves are a good green colour and not pale or yellowish. Choose young stems, as they are less spiny than the older ones.

CARE & HANDLING Recut stems and place in a preservative. Remove foliage that will be below the water line. Stems can be kept in the cooler at 2–4°C (36–39°F) at a very high humidity (90–95%). Display pots in a bright area. Poor light can cause "leaves" to yellow and fall off.

Asparagus densiflorus (Kunth) Jessop (=*A. sprengeri*, =*A. meyeri*)   family: Asparagaceae

sierasperge (Dutch); *Zier-Spargel* (German)

Asparagus setaceus
asparagus fern • lace fern • plumosa

Asparagus setaceus

Asparagus falcatus

Asparagus virgatus

DESCRIPTION A woody, wiry, leafless climber. What appear to be leaves are modified stems – arranged in a single plane, forming a flat, leaf-like spray resembling a fern frond. *Asparagus* species are commonly called "ferns" but they are not ferns (related to the edible asparagus). Examples of cultivars are 'Cupressoides', 'Nanus', 'Robustus' and 'Pyramidalis'. Last-mentioned has feathery but wiry stems and is sometimes erroneously listed as a species (*A. pyramidalis*). Other species used by florists include *A. falcatus* (with broad, sickle-shaped "leaves") and *A. virgatus* (broom fern – erect and feathery).

ORIGIN & HISTORY *A. setaceus* (previously known as *A. plumosus*) is native to South Africa and is an old favourite amongst florists.

PARTS USED Foliage is used as cut greens (especially for buttonholes). Whole plants are used as potted plants or for hanging baskets.

CULTIVATION Plants grow best in well-drained, slightly acidic soils (pH 5.5–6.2) under medium light intensities and adequate fertilisation. Yellowing and "leaf" loss may result from too low levels of nutrition, poor light or airborne fluoride pollution. Plants cultivated for cut foliage can remain productive for many years.

PROPERTIES Vase life of *A. setaceus* is sometimes below average to fairly good (5–10 days); in the cultivar 'Pyramidalis' (tree fern, tiki) it is average to usually good (7–12 days).

QUALITY CRITERIA Select sturdy stems that are long, well-branched and healthy green in colour. *A. setaceus* stems often tend to be short and bushy, but 'Pyramidalis' usually has long, straight single stems.

CARE & HANDLING Leave the foliage in boxes or bags with the tops open and store in a cooler at about 5°C (41°F) and a high relative humidity of 90–95%. Stems can be recut and placed in a preservative solution. Display pots in a bright area. Most asparagus types have small, sharp thorns so handle carefully or use gloves.

Asparagus setaceus (Kunth) Jessop (=*A. plumosus*)   family: Asparagaceae
sierasperge (Dutch); *Farn-Spargel, Feder-Spargel* (German)

Aspidistra elatior
cast-iron plant • bar room plant • aspidistra

Aspidistra plant

Aspidistra leaf

DESCRIPTION The plant is a tough perennial herb with large, broadly lance-shaped leaves arising one by one from a thick underground rhizome to form a dense clump. The leaves are glossy green, leathery and often variegated (streaked or speckled with white marks). Small, 8-lobed, cream-coloured and purple-spotted flowers are borne at ground level. Cultivars have been described on leaf size and colour. 'Green Leaf' has very large (up to 0.5 m or 20" long), uniformly glossy green leaves. 'Milky Way' has relatively short (to 0.15 m or 6"), dark green leaves speckled with small white spots. Medium-sized (about 0.3 m or 12"), variously cream- or white-streaked leaves are encountered with cultivars such as 'Variegata', 'Variegata Ashei' and 'Variegata Exotica'.

ORIGIN & HISTORY Asia (China), naturalised in Japan. A popular houseplant, especially in the 19th century and once considered "a symbol of middle class respectability".

PARTS USED The fresh leaves are used as foliage (for arrangements, handties, underlining and wedding work).

CULTIVATION Plants are easy to cultivate and will survive extreme conditions (low light, irregular watering). However, for commercial production of leaves, good light, irrigation and fertilisation are essential.

PROPERTIES Vase life is very good (2–3 weeks).

QUALITY CRITERIA Leaves should have a uniform green and glossy appearance with no obvious blemishes, yellowing or dry margins. Make sure leaves are free of brown spots and that the tip is fresh and green. Select leaves with leaf stalks that are not too short.

CARE & HANDLING Recut leaf stalks by less than 10 mm (½") and place in water with only a germicide. Alternatively, hold or store leaves at 2–5°C (36–41°F) in a loosely wrapped plastic bag. Mist them regularly to keep fresh or maintain a high percentage relative humidity (90–95%).

Aspidistra elatior Blume   family: Asparagaceae (Convallariaceae)

aspidistra, plantes des concierges (French); *Schildnarbe* (German); *aspidistra* (Spanish)

Asplenium nidus

bird's nest fern

Asplenium nidus

DESCRIPTION This fern has simple (undivided) fronds of about 0.2 m (8") long that form a distinctive rosette. The fronds are leathery, hairless and bright green, with a prominent midrib. In its natural habitat, the bird's nest fern is an epiphyte that grows on tree trunks. The "nest" formed by the leaf rosette serves to collect fallen leaves and other debris that eventually decompose and form a source of nutrients for the plant. There appears to be no cultivars of this species.

ORIGIN & HISTORY Tropical regions of the Old World (Africa and Asia). The bird's nest fern has been cultivated as a houseplant for centuries.

PARTS USED The mature fronds as foliage, or the whole plant as a pot plant.

CULTIVATION Bird's nest fern prefers a well-drained, slightly acidic growing medium. Plants require shade, as strong direct sunlight will cause bleaching of the fronds. A growing environment of high air humidity and a temperature range of 15–20°C (59–68°F) is required, along with regular feeding to obtain high quality plants and cut foliage.

PROPERTIES Vase life is average to good (7–12 days). Plants are sensitive to ethylene.

QUALITY CRITERIA Select cut fronds that have a good, uniform green colour, with no yellowing. Make sure leaves are free of brown spots or dead tips. Pot plants should be well established, balanced in shape and have a good volume of healthy leaves.

CARE & HANDLING When fronds are used as foliage, recut less than 10 mm (½") off the leaf stalk and place in water with only a germicide. Alternatively, store or hold in clear plastic bags at 4–5°C (39–41°F). Mist occasionally or ensure a high percentage relative humidity (90–95%). Do not store longer than 4–5 days. Display pots in a well-lit area (not direct sunlight), at room temperature and out of any direct draughts. Keep potting medium moist.

Asplenium nidus L.   family: Aspleniaceae

nestvaren (Dutch); *Vogel-Nestfarn* (German); *asplenio* (Italian); *nido de ave* (Spanish)

Aster ericoides

michaelmas daisy • aster

Aster novi-belgii 'Monte Casino'

Aster ericoides 'Blue Moon'

Aster novae-angliae

DESCRIPTION An erect, perennial herb (up to 1 m or 40"), with slender stems that are much-branched above, bearing numerous small flower heads of 10 mm (about ½") in diameter. The best-known cultivar until recently has been 'Monte Casino'. Hybrids involve mainly *A. ericoides* (heath aster), *A. novi-belgii* (New York aster, michaelmas daisy) and *A. novae-angliae* (New England aster). Nowadays breeding is focused on *A. ericoides*. (For summer asters or Chinese asters see *Callistephus*).

ORIGIN & HISTORY North America. The name comes from Old English aster (Latin: star) and starwort (wort = "medicinal root"). Asters were laid on the graves of French soldiers to symbolise the wish that things had turned out differently. Aster is one of the top florist flower groups today.

PARTS USED Flowering stems are used as cut flowers and whole plants as potted flowers.

CULTIVATION Year-round flowering is induced by artificial lighting and heating. A period of long days (>16 hours) stimulates stem elongation, followed by a period of relatively short days (12–14 hours) to induce flowering.

PROPERTIES Vase life is slightly poor to above average (5–10 days). New England asters tend to have a shorter vase life than New York asters. Flower heads open from top to bottom (unlike most other plants). They are not particularly sensitive to ethylene.

QUALITY CRITERIA Select stems with 20–30% of the heads open. For large-flowered types, select stems with all florets at the branch tips fully open and the other buds showing colour. Avoid stems with brown or dry florets. Select potted flowers with 25–40% of flower heads open.

CARE & HANDLING Recut and place in a preservative containing a germicide and a sugar. Remove foliage below the water line. Storage is not recommended, but if necessary, store at 4°C (39°F) for 3–4 days. Flowers do not dry well.

Aster ericoides L.   family: Asteraceae

herfstaster (Dutch); *aster d' automne* (French); *Erika-Aster, Myrten-Aster* (German); *astro* (Italian)

Astilbe arendsii
false goat's beard • spirea

Astilbe ×arendsii white

Astilbe ×arendsii lilac

DESCRIPTION A perennial herb with rhizomes and compound, jointed leaves. Numerous small flowers in many colours, ranging from white, purple to red, are borne on widely branched panicles. The foliage also varies in colour, from green to bronze. Most of the popular cultivars are derived from the already hybridised *A. ×arendsii*. Other popular species include *A. chinensis*, *A. ×hybrida*, *A. japonica* and *A. simplicifolia*.

ORIGIN & HISTORY *Astilbe* species are indigenous to North America and Europe. *A. ×arendsii* is of hybrid (garden) origin.

PARTS USED Flowering stems are used as cut flowers and whole plants as potted flowers.

CULTIVATION Plants require a cold, dormant period (differs between cultivars). This improves uniformity of flowering as well as quality and colour of flowers. Floral abortion can occur at high temperatures. The best temperatures for production are generally 15–24°C. Dry spells or inadequate moisture causes quality to deteriorate rapidly. Under ideal conditions plants can stay

productive for 3–5 years before they need to be replaced.

PROPERTIES Vase life is poor to average (3–7 days). *Astilbe* is sensitive to ethylene. Some cultivars have a sweet fragrance.

QUALITY CRITERIA Select plumes with 50–75% of the flowers open and the upper (closed) flowers showing full colour. Stems harvested and sold with panicles less than 50% open do not develop and open properly, even when placed in a preservative. Actual vase life is also reduced as flowers wilt prematurely without opening. Leaves age more rapidly than the flowers, so make sure the leaves are in a good condition. Purchase flowers that have been pre-treated by the grower.

CARE & HANDLING Use a preservative containing an anti-ethylene agent. Storage is not recommended. Flowers are suitable for drying, but keep them upright during the drying process. Keep the medium of potted flowers moist but not soggy; do not allow it to dry out. Display pots in a shady area at an ideal temperature of 18–21°C (64–70°F).

Astilbe ×arendsii Arends

family: Saxifragaceae

spirea (Dutch); *Garten-Astilbe, Prachtspiere* (German); *piuma d'argento* (Italian)

Astrantia major

masterwort

Astrantia major pale pink

Astrantia major pale pink

Astrantia major 'Rubra'

DESCRIPTION A perennial herb with palmately lobed leaves and tiny florets grouped in clusters (umbels), each surrounded by showy, papery bracts. These clusters resemble flowers. The florets are stalked (sterile) or subsessile (fertile). Several cultivars have been developed, presenting an array of colours. Examples include 'Alba' (white), 'Margery Fish' or 'Shaggy' (bracts large, shaggy, pink-white) and 'Rosensymphonie' (silver-rose). Some cultivars are eye-catching with different colours forming a halo between the actual flowers and the collar of bracts.

ORIGIN & HISTORY Europe. Masterwort (greater masterwort) is not that well known as a cut flower in many countries. However, it is always readily accepted when available.

PARTS USED Stems with flowering heads are used as cut flowers.

CULTIVATION Plants are productive for 3–5 years before they need to be replaced. First year yields are not as good as from the second year onwards. Constant moisture is important if production is to be a success. Plants prefer cooler growing conditions and do not do well in warm weather. Stage of harvest is quite critical, which is when the uppermost flowers are open. If harvested too early, flowers will not open and the whole flowering stem will wilt prematurely. On the other hand, if harvested too late then vase life will suffer.

PROPERTIES Vase life is poor to nearly average (3–6 days).

QUALITY CRITERIA The vase life is poor so make sure that you do not purchase flowers that are too open (old) as they will then only last a few days. Also do not purchase flowers that are too closed, as they will fail to open and wilt prematurely. Select stems with only the uppermost flowers open.

CARE & HANDLING Recut and hydrate the stems immediately, using a preservative. Storage is not recommended. Flowers can be dried – silica gel is better than air-drying because the flowers dry better and shrink less.

Astrantia major L.

family: Apiaceae (Umbelliferae)

groot sterrenscherm (Dutch); *astrance, radiaire* (French); *Sterndolde* (German); *astrancia* (Spanish)

Atriplex hortensis
garden orache • orach • mountain spinach

Atriplex hortensis cultivars

DESCRIPTION An erect annual herb growing up to 2.5 m (8′) high. It has variously coloured, triangular or spear-shaped leaves and spikes of inconspicuous flowers. A few cultivars are available, with the plume types having been selected for use as ornamentals. Leaf cultivars include 'Cupreatorosea' (coppery red stems and leaves) and 'Rosea' (leaves with the stalks and veins darker red).

ORIGIN & HISTORY Western Asia, but the plant has become a naturalised weed through much of Europe and North America. The colourful leaves, with or without the flowering stem, are often used by florists as a filler, although the plant is much better known as a vegetable and is more often used as such. The taste is similar to that of spinach, but with a less succulent texture.

PARTS USED Leafy stems (with or without flowers) are used as filler.

CULTIVATION Orach grows easily and is tolerant of salty and alkaline conditions. It prefers well-drained, sandy soils. Quality and yields are best in full sun (which realises best leaf colour) and cool temperatures. During a period of long days the plant bolts, producing an erect stalk with numerous tiny petal-less, wind-pollinated flowers. These have flattened, papery, husk-like bracts.

PROPERTIES Vase life is poor to average (4–8 days). Leaves are edible, but not necessarily those of the ornamental plume types. Orach is not ethylene sensitive.

QUALITY CRITERIA Look for straight, sturdy and well-branched cut stems (plume types). Make sure that leaves are healthy and stems in general are free of pests and diseases. Select younger stems that are not too woody.

CARE & HANDLING Recut stems and remove leaves below the water line. Place in a general floral preservative. Storage is not recommended, but if necessary store stems for only 2–3 days at 0–2°C (32–36°F) and a high relative humidity (90–95%).

Atriplex hortensis L.   family: Amaranthaceae (Chenopodiaceae)

tuinmelde (Dutch); *arroche rouge des jardins* (French); *Garten-Melde* (German); *armuella de huerta* (Spanish)

Bambusa vulgaris

common bamboo

Bambusa vulgaris stems

Bambusa multiplex

DESCRIPTION This exceptionally fast-growing bamboo (bamboos are woody grasses) varies in height (about 6–24 m or 20–80'). The canes are 50–250 mm (2–10") in diameter, hollow inside and have prominent nodes. Leaves are up to 100 mm (4") long and up to 38 mm (1½") wide, with a sheathing base that is typically brown and hairy. Various green and variegated forms are available, but the exact species is not always clear as they are all very similar. *Bambusa vulgaris* 'Vittata' has the culms, sheaths and sometimes the leaves striped with green and yellow. Canes are typically available in various thicknesses and colours, including brown, black and pale yellow.

ORIGIN & HISTORY Probably Asia. The plant is a cultigen of unknown origin. It has been cultivated since ancient times so that the natural distribution area has become obscure. Bamboos have a diversity of uses (construction, water pipes, pulp for paper and especially as edible shoots for canning). Several species have become popular garden ornamentals (e.g. *B. multiplex*).

PARTS USED The culms and leaves are used as foliage or as decorative ornaments for arrangements.

CULTIVATION Bamboos are exceptionally easy to cultivate in warm climates and are typical multi-purpose crops. Rhizomes are simply divided and planted in a suitable place. Regular watering is essential. Exceptionally fast growth rates have been recorded (nearly 1 m per day or more than 0.5 mm per minute). Growers simply harvest stems at various ages of maturity, colour or thickness depending on market demands.

PROPERTIES The canes are very durable and strong and can literally last for years.

QUALITY CRITERIA There are no widely used quality criteria for bamboo. However, make sure that selected canes are free of general damage and pests (especially insects that bore into the wood).

CARE & HANDLING Do not recut or place canes in water, including the green types. Simply store or display canes dry and at any temperature.

Bambusa vulgaris Schrader ex Wendl.

family: Poaceae

yin zhu (Chinese); *bamboe* (Dutch); *bambou commun, bambou ordinaire* (French); *Gemeiner Bambus* (German); *daisan chiku* (Japanese); *bambú común* (Spanish)

Banksia ashbyi
banksia • Ashby's banksia

Banksia ashbyi

DESCRIPTION An evergreen, woody perennial (up to 8 m or about 27'). The narrow leaves are up to 250 mm (10") long, with serrate margins. The bright orange flower spikes are about 200 mm (8") long. Some species are more suitable as cut flowers, others as cut foliage, while some are suitable as both. A number of species and cultivars are commercially cultivated and new ones are often released. Colours are mainly red, yellow and orange and the flower heads vary considerably in shape and size.

ORIGIN & HISTORY Australia. *Banksia* is a large genus of approximately 75 species, named after the naturalist Sir Joseph Banks. Nearly all have potential as florist flowers or greens, but presently those with cylindrical and terminal flower heads are the most popular.

PARTS USED Flower spikes: cut flowers; foliage: cut greens.

CULTIVATION Most members of the protea family can be grown from seed or cuttings, but selected forms are only propagated from cuttings (clonal material) to maintain favourable characteristics. However, banksias are still widely propagated from seed. Like most Proteaceae, banksias are intolerant of soils with high phosphorus concentrations and do best in light, sandy soils that are acidic. Continued pruning is necessary to remove shoots that will not flower and to encourage development of new shoots.

PROPERTIES Vase life is good to very good (10–18 days). Stems have the tendency to be a bit short.

QUALITY CRITERIA Select flower spikes with the first styles beginning to, or having just, unfolded. Look for young, straight stems with well-formed spikes. Make sure the foliage is free of marks, disease and general damage.

CARE & HANDLING Recut the stems and place them in a preservative solution containing a germicide and sugar. Remove leaves that will end up below the water line. Flowers can be stored for 7–10 days at 2–4°C (36–39°F). Longer storage will reduce vase life by about 30%. Banksias dry well.

Banksia ashbyi Bak. f.   family: Proteaceae

banksia (Dutch, French, Italian, Spanish); *Banksia* (German)

Baptisia australis
blue false indigo

Baptisia australis plants

Baptisia australis flowers

DESCRIPTION An upright or spreading perennial herb (up to 1.5 m or 5′) with compound (trifoliate), somewhat greyish leaves and short clusters of mauve and partly purple or blue flowers borne at the branch ends. At present no named cultivars of *B. australis* have been commercialised. However, hybrids between *B. australis* and *B. alba* are used.

ORIGIN & HISTORY North America. The name *Baptisia* comes from the Greek word "bapto" (to dip) in reference to extracts that were used for dyes. The dye was a substitute for the real indigo dye which was obtained from *Indigofera*, hence the name "false". Since the 1700s blue false indigo has been used in the United States to supplement dye supplies from the West Indies. It is a minor florist flower, but is readily accepted when available. The plant is also occasionally used as a garden ornamental.

PARTS USED Flowering stems are used as cut flowers, while leaves are used as cut greens and foliage. Stems with seed pods are also used as foliage.

CULTIVATION Plants come into full production in year 3 or 4 and are productive for at least 4–6 years. They are quite drought tolerant and can survive some neglect. Allow plants to establish properly by not harvesting foliage in the first year and only moderately in the second year.

PROPERTIES Vase life is slightly poor to average (5–7 days).

QUALITY CRITERIA Select stems with approximately 30% of the flowers open and the rest of the buds showing colour. Do not purchase stems with more than 60% of the flowers open, as these will have a poor vase life. Make sure foliage is clean and free of disease or damage. Look for dark pods that are brown to black. If the foliage is desired as part of the stem, then look for slightly lighter coloured pods, which will have fresher, longer lasting leaves.

CARE & HANDLING Recut and hydrate flowers as soon as possible. Use a general preservative. Storage is not recommended.

Baptisia australis (L.) R. Br.   family: Fabaceae

lupin indigo (French); *Blaue Färberhülse, Indigolupine* (German)

99

Begonia cultivars

begonia • elatior begonia • winter-flowering begonia

Begonia (Hiemalis Group) red

Begonia (Tuberhybrida Group) 'Pendula'

Begonia (Hiemalis Group) pink

Wax leaf begonia (Semperflorens-cultorum Group)

DESCRIPTION Herbs with fibrous roots and asymmetrical, green to bronze leaves. The fleshy flowers are single or double and white, pink, yellow, orange or red. There are three main groups: Hiemalis (Elatior) – grown from cuttings for the florist trade; Tuberhybrida – angel wing begonias (large-flowered, double begonias used as potted flowers and in the garden industry); Bedding plant begonias – wax leaf begonias (Semperflorens-cultorum Group) used predominantly in the garden industry. The main cultivars and hybrids in the florist trade are from the Hiemalis Group (also known as the Elatior Group, derived from *B. socotrana* and the *B.* Tuberhybrida Group).

ORIGIN & HISTORY *Begonia* cultivars originated as garden hybrids. The genus is pantropical in distribution and is named after Michel Begon (1638–1710) a French amateur botanist.

PARTS USED Whole plants, as potted flowers.

CULTIVATION Most cultivars are propagated vegetatively and grown in small rooting containers within the retail pots. Potted flowers are produced year-round – flowering can be programmed. Irrigation and fertilisation is done via ebb-and-flood, capillary mats or drip tube systems to keep leaves and flowers dry at all times and thus avoid diseases.

PROPERTIES Some cultivars are susceptible to mildew or bud drop. Flowers appear delicate but are very hardy. They are sensitive to ethylene. Plants transport well.

QUALITY CRITERIA Look for mildew, reddening or darkening of leaves, cupping of leaf margins, brittle leaves, yellow spots, stem collapse or leaf-scorch – all signs of poor cultivation.

CARE & HANDLING Provide bright, natural light and adequate ventilation. Begonias are sensitive to ethylene, which can cause flower drop. Regularly remove dead flowers and check for signs of mildew (a fungal infection). Steady, warm temperatures and high humidity will ensure a longer flowering time. Temperature: minimum (13°C; 55°F); maximum (21°C; 70°F) for winter flowering types. Keep moist but do not over-water.

Begonia cultivars   family: Begoniaceae

begonia (Dutch); *bégonia* (French); *Begonie, Schiefblatt* (German)

Berzelia lanuginosa
berzelia • Cape greens • lanuginosa

Berzelia lanuginosa

Berzelia galpinii

DESCRIPTION This *Berzelia* is an erect woody shrub of up to 4 m (about 13′) high with small ericoid leaves, giving the stems a feathery appearance. The small white flowers are densely arranged into small rounded flower heads. These are borne in small clusters at the branch tips. *Berzelia lanuginosa* is one of the most common plants in the Western Cape Province of South Africa, where it is usually found in wet places. There are as yet no cultivars, but this and other species are commonly distinguished by the second parts of their species name (the so-called specific epithet), such as *lanuginosa, paleacea, galpinii* and *squarrosa*. They differ in the size and colour of the flower heads.

ORIGIN & HISTORY Africa (the fynbos region of the Western Cape Province of South Africa). Stems have been harvested for a long time as one of the main ingredients of the traditional Cape greens (fillers that are commonly used, especially in combination with other fynbos plants such as proteas, cone-bushes, pincushions and ericas).

PARTS USED The leafy flowering stems are used as greens and fillers, usually in mixed bunches.

CULTIVATION *Berzelia* species are not cultivated to any extent but are wild-harvested from natural stands. The plant is exceptionally common.

PROPERTIES Vase life is good (10–14 days). The lime-green foliage is popular for flower arrangements, especially for colour and texture.

QUALITY CRITERIA Cut greens are usually available in mixed bunches and seldom on their own in straight bunches. However, still check quality where possible. Select stems that are long, straight and not too woody. (Stems are often short, crooked and woody.) Make sure that foliage is free of pests and general damage, as most product is wild-harvested.

CARE & HANDLING Recut stems and place in a preservative containing a germicide and low sugar concentration (no anti-ethylene agent). Foliage can be stored for 4–6 days in moisture-retentive boxes or a preservative at 4°C (39°F) and a percentage relative humidity of 90–95%. *Berzelias* are excellent for drying.

Berzelia lanuginosa (L.) Brongn.   family: Bruniaceae

berzelia (French); *Berzelia* (German); *berzelia* (Italian); *berzelia* (Spanish)

Bougainvillea buttiana

bougainvillea

Bougainvillea ×buttiana lilac

Bougainvillea ×buttiana red

Bougainvillea ×buttiana orange

DESCRIPTION A perennial, usually thorny, climbing shrub or vine, with colourful papery bracts surrounding the inconspicuous flowers. Few species or hybrids are suited to the florist trade – most are bred for the garden industry. *B. ×buttiana* is a hybrid between *B. glabra* and *B. peruviana*. At present some of the well-known potted hybrids include 'Mrs Butt' and 'Crimson Lake'. 'Alexandra', a popular cultivar in the florist industry, is derived from *B. glabra*. Other well-known hybrid cultivars include 'Vera Deep Purple' and 'Barbara Karst'.

ORIGIN & HISTORY South America. The genus is named after L.A. de Bougainville, a French navigator (1729–1811). It was first described and classified in 1789, yet it was already discovered 20 years earlier in Brazil.

PARTS USED Flowering stems with leaves are used as cut flowers or fillers, while whole plants are used as potted flowers.

CULTIVATION Bougainvilleas need hot, sunny conditions – new growth and flowering is retarded by cool conditions.

PROPERTIES The main attraction is the clusters of long-lasting, colourful leafy bracts that surround the small white flowers (often loosely referred as "flowers" because the bracts are mistaken for petals). There is no fragrance. Bougainvilleas are sensitive to ethylene, which will cause flower and leaf drop.

QUALITY CRITERIA Select well-formed, compact plants that have numerous, evenly distributed "flowers". Do not purchase plants that are too vegetative, with strong, green growth but hardly any flowering stems. Ensure that the main stem is not too woody and that it has many short side shoots. Check that leaves are bright green and not too pale or yellowish.

CARE & HANDLING Display pots in bright light. Potted plants tolerate direct sunlight (if not too fierce) but take care to avoid direct midday sun through a glass window. Water the pot freely in summer and sparingly during other seasons. Plants rarely flower for a second season if kept indoors. Display at a temperature of above 13°C (55°F). Keep the potting medium moist but not too wet.

Bougainvillea ×buttiana Holttum & Standl.   family: Nyctaginaceae

bougainvillée (French); *Bougainvillee* (German); *buganvillea* (Italian); *buganvilla* (Spanish)

Bouvardia longiflora
bouvardia

Bouvardia longiflora red

Bouvardia longiflora white

DESCRIPTION A perennial woody shrub with toothed or lobed leaves and sheathing stipules. The attractive tubular flowers each have four petals and are usually borne in rounded clusters. Various colour forms are known, including red, pink, white and orange. An added attraction is the strong, sweet frangrance of the flowers.

ORIGIN & HISTORY Mexico. Several species of *Bouvardia* are old favourite garden shrubs.

PARTS USED Flowering leafy stems are used as cut flowers, or the whole plant as a potted flower.

CULTIVATION Bouvardias prefer well-drained, slightly acidic soils and bright light. Cut flowers are difficult to handle and wilt or lose quality easily. Growers typically place stems in water containing a preservative immediately after harvesting, while still in the field and normally leave them in there for a number of hours.

PROPERTIES The vase life of cut flowers is average to fairly good (6–12 days). Potted flowers should remain flowering for 2–4 weeks. Flowers have a pleasant fragrance. They are sensitive to ethylene and also to polluted water.

QUALITY CRITERIA Look for cut stems and potted flowers with tight clusters of buds, showing good colour and with only 1–2 having opened. Stems should be sturdy and straight, with dark green leaves free of brown tips. Potted plants should be compact and dense.

CARE & HANDLING Flowers tend to wilt prematurely, so unpack and hydrate as soon as possible. Recut stems, remove leaves below the water line and hydrate in warm water (38–40°C; 100–105°F), preferably acidified to pH 3.5. Use a preservative with bactericide and a low percentage carbohydrate to assist in opening of buds. Storage is not recommended, but if absolutely necessary store for 4–5 days at 2–4°C (36–39°F) and 95% relative humidity. Cut flowers last longer if all newly developing side shoots and flowers outside of the main flower umbel are removed. Unpack potted flowers immediately and display in a bright, cool area. Keep moist, but do not over-water.

Bouvardia longiflora (Cav.) Humb., Bonpl. & Kunth — family: Rubiaceae

bouvardia (Dutch); *bouvardie* (French); *Bouvardie* (German); *buvardia* (Italian)

Brassica oleracea

ornamental cabbage • ornamental kale

Brassica oleracea (purple)

Brassica oleracea (variegated)

DESCRIPTION A perennial herb with dense heads of frilly, colourful leaves borne on a sturdy, unbranched stem. Flowering cabbage looks like brightly coloured cabbages that have not really formed a solid head, while flowering kale has wavy leaves, generally with two distinct colours. Cultivars used in the florist industry are available in numerous colours – cream, green, pink, purple, red and white. The plants are usually replaced once they start flowering.

ORIGIN & HISTORY Garden origin. The original wild cabbage is from western Europe. Ornamental cabbage is related to kale (the Acephala Group of vegetable cabbages). In horticulture, ornamental brassicas were first used as bedding plants. Fairly recently they have become popular in the floral trade, especially in bouquets.

PARTS USED Cabbage heads are used as colourful ornamental fillers. Whole plants are grown as potted ornamentals.

CULTIVATION Planting density affects the size of the head, with smaller heads obtained under denser plantings and vice versa. During the early stages of cultivation lower leaves are regularly removed. To obtain good colouring, the almost mature plants need night temperatures that are moderately low (10–13°C; 50–55°F) for 3–4 weeks.

PROPERTIES Most heads have a distinct "cabbage" fragrance. The leaves are soft, brittle and often damaged during handling. They are not ethylene sensitive.

QUALITY CRITERIA Stems are naturally short, but look for sturdy, straight stems. Make sure heads are compact and symmetrical with bright colours (dull colouring is often a sign of poor quality or inferior cultivars). Check that leaves have no physical or pest damage or any disease-related yellowing.

CARE & HANDLING Treat and handle as a florist flower, not as a vegetable. Recut stems and place in water with a bactericide. Display pots in a cool, bright area. Keep potting medium moist but do not over-water. Store cut stems for 2–3 days at 0–2°C (32–36°F).

Brassica oleracea L.   family: Brassicaceae

sierkool (Dutch); *Zier-Kool* (German)

Browallia speciosa
browallia • bush violet • sapphire flower

Browallia 'Blue Bells'

DESCRIPTION A shrubby perennial plant of up to 1.5 m (3'). Numerous cultivars are available and these vary in colour and compactness and also tend to have larger flowers than the original wild species. Cultivars include 'Blue Bells improved' (violet-blue), 'Major' (blue-purple; known as sapphire flower), 'Marine Bells' (indigo-blue), 'Powder Blue' (lilac) and 'White Bells' (= 'Weissglocken') (pure white). Some are more suited to the garden industry, while other, more compact ones are ideal for pots and hanging baskets. A second species, *B. viscosa*, is occasionally seen in gardens. It has viscid hairs and blue or white flowers.

ORIGIN & HISTORY Colombia. Browallias are generally known as bush violets. This species, together with *B. americana* and *B. viscosa* are popular garden shrubs.

PARTS USED Whole plants are used in hanging baskets or in pots as potted flowers.

CULTIVATION Plants are typically grown and treated as annuals and discarded once they deteriorate. Performance is best under cool growing conditions of 15–18°C (59–64°F) and long days are required to initiate flowering. During cultivation growing tips are pinched out periodically to encourage and maintain bushiness of the plants. Growth regulators are usually used to get compact, low-growing plants.

PROPERTIES Flowers last a long time in warm climates, but are not really suited for outdoors in cold climates. They are sensitive to ethylene.

QUALITY CRITERIA Make sure that plants have a good volume of flowers and buds. Over-feeding during cultivation results in plants having lots of leaves and few or no flowers. Select compact, well-branched plants in full flower. Check that the leaves are free of marks and damage.

CARE & HANDLING Display in a cool area (10–15°C; 50–59°F) as plants flower for longer if the temperature is not too high. Place containers in bright light but not direct sunlight, and protect from draughts. Deadhead regularly. Keep potting medium moist, but do not over-water.

Browallia speciosa Hook.   family: Solanaceae

browalia (French); *Saphir-Veilchenstrauch* (German)

Brunia nodiflora

spray brunia

Brunia nodiflora

Brunia albiflora

DESCRIPTION A branched shrub of about 1 m (40") high. The leaves are very small (3 mm or ¼" long), lance-shaped to awn-shaped and distinctly overlapping each other, creating a scale-like appearance. The rounded flower heads are relatively large (12 mm or ½" in diameter) and the individual florets are cream-coloured. There are as yet no cultivars available but several different species are used. White brunia (*B. albiflora*) is a tall plant of 3 m (10') high with longer leaves (12 mm or ½") and white flowers in large flower heads of 15 mm (1¼") in diameter. *Brunia laevis* (silver brunia) has silvery flower heads borne on thin, scale-like stems.

ORIGIN & HISTORY South Africa (fynbos region of the Western Cape Province). *Brunia* species have commonly been included in "Cape greens", together with other fynbos plants such as conebushes (*Leucadendron* species), Cape myrtles (*Phylica* species) and Cape heaths (*Erica* species).

PARTS USED Flowering stems are used as cut greens and fillers.

CULTIVATION Material is almost exclusively wild-harvested in the mountains.

PROPERTIES Vase life is very good (10–15 days). The rounded, pom pom appearance of the flower heads and the scaly stems are the main attractions of these plants.

QUALITY CRITERIA Cut foliage is usually available in mixed bunches and seldom on their own in straight bunches. However, still check quality where possible. Select stems that are as long as possible, straight and not too woody. (Stems are naturally short and often crooked.) Make sure that foliage is free of pests and general damage, as most product is wild-harvested. The flower heads should ideally be fully developed and well coloured.

CARE & HANDLING Recut the stems by only 10 mm (½") and place them in a preservative with a germicide and a low sugar concentration. Foliage can be stored for 4–7 days in moisture-retentive boxes or in a preservative solution at 4°C (39°F) and a relative humidity of 95%. Brunias are excellent for drying.

Brunia nodiflora L.

family: Bruniaceae

stompie (Afrikaans); *brunia* (Dutch, French, Italian, Spanish); *Brunia* (German)

Buddleja davidii
butterfly bush • summer lilac

Buddleja davidii 'Empire Blue'

Buddleja cultivars

DESCRIPTION A deciduous shrub (3 m or 10′ high) with large, dark green leaves that are silver-felted below. The flowers are 10 mm or ½″ long and are borne in clusters – they are usually pale violet to purple with an orange eye. A few dozen cultivars have been bred but availability is not always easy. Of these cultivars only a few are really suitable to the florist trade.

ORIGIN & HISTORY China and Japan. Availability is presently quite seasonal as the plant is not really forced for year-round production. Butterfly bush has more importance as a garden plant and is marginal as a cut flower for florists. The flowers are fragrant and attract butterflies to the garden (hence the common name).

PARTS USED Flowering stems with leaves are used as cut flowers.

CULTIVATION Plants grow rapidly and vigorously, but luckily flowers are borne on new growth and growers can therefore cut back the bushes to the ground after the flowering season is over. In some climates plants die back naturally each year. Seeds germinate easily and plants are also multiplied by means of cuttings. Yields per plant depend on cultivar, winter conditions and the severity of harvesting in the previous season.

PROPERTIES The vase life is poor (2–3 days). Florets have a strong, sweet fragrance. White flowers decline more quickly than other colours, with yellow flowers seeming to last the best. Flowers are sensitive to ethylene.

QUALITY CRITERIA Select stems with 50–60% of florets open, but make sure that the basal ones have not yet started to fade. Ensure that leaves are healthy and free of damage and/or disease.

CARE & HANDLING Recut stems and place in a preservative solution. Make sure the stems hydrate properly (this is very important) – flowers can persist for 7–10 days if properly treated. Store the stems for 1–2 days at 3–4°C (38–39°F) if necessary. Flowers can be dried and retain their scent after drying. Remove large leaves and hang upside down in a well-ventilated area.

Buddleja davidii Franch.

family: Scrophulariaceae (Buddlejaceae)

vlinderstruik (Dutch); *arbre aux-papillons, lilas d'eté* (French); *Sommerflieder* (German); *buddleja* (Spanish)

Bulbinella latifolia
cat's tail

Bulbinella latifolia var. *dolomitica*

Bulbinella latifolia var. *latifolia*

DESCRIPTION A perennial with a rosette of fibrous leaves growing from a compact rhizome. The long flowering stalk bears an elongated cluster of small flowers. Flowering occurs naturally in late winter and early spring. *Bulbinella nutans* is a similar species that produces higher yields (1–5 stems per rhizome), compared to 1–2 stems per rhizome in *B. latifolia*. Colours are predominantly bright orange or yellow (rarely white or cream). *Bulbinella* is sometimes confused with *Bulbine* because the flower clusters are superfically similar. *Bulbine* species are easily distinguised as they are succulent plants with characteristic hairy stamens on the short-lived flowers.

ORIGIN & HISTORY Mainly Africa (South Africa). There are 22 species of *Bulbinella*, predominantly from the winter rainfall region of the Cape. Strangely, six species occur in New Zealand.

PARTS USED Flowering stems are used as florist flowers.

CULTIVATION Growers purchase rhizomes ("bulbs") that are certified virus-free by suppliers to ensure quality flowers. Rhizomes are then held at 17–20°C (63–68°F) until they are planted, which for outdoor production is in autumn. Plants need a well-drained, sandy soil and good watering during spring and winter, but should be kept fairly dry during summer (resting phase). Rhizomes can be lifted, processed and replanted again in late summer.

PROPERTIES Vase life is average to fairly good (7–10 days). Flowers are fragrant and not sensitive to ethylene.

QUALITY CRITERIA Choose stems that are straight and sturdy and have long flower spikes (racemes). Several of the lower florets should show good colour but must preferably still be closed. Check that stems are free from bruises or soft spots.

CARE & HANDLING Recut stems and place in a preservative containing a bactericide and with a low sugar content. Handle stems carefully to avoid bending or bruising. Flowers can be stored for 3–4 days upright in water containing a bactericide at 2–4°C (36–39°F).

Bulbinella latifolia Kunth   family: Asphodelaceae

bulbinella (Dutch, French, Italian, Spanish); *Bulbinella* (German)

Bupleurum rotundifolium

thoroughwax • hare's ear

Bupleurum rotundifolium 'Griffithii'

Bupleurum rotundifolium 'Griffithii'

DESCRIPTION An annual or short-lived perennial herb easily recognised by the distinctive and attractive leaves. They are rounded in shape, stem-clasping (sessile, without stalks), greenish-blue and about 25–50 mm long (1–2"). The leaves are flushed with red when young and are prominently veined. Small yellow flowers are borne in umbels of 25 mm (1") in diameter, surrounded by small yellow-green bracts. Cultivars of *B. rotundifolium* are sometimes listed as *B. griffithii*. 'Green Gold' is a cultivar with light green leaves.

ORIGIN & HISTORY Europe (naturalised in the United States). The genus name comes from the Greek *boupleurs* (oxen rib). The leaves surround the stems (they are perfoliate), hence the common name derived from "throw-wax" (through-grow).

PARTS USED The leafy flowering stems are used as decorative fillers.

CULTIVATION Propagation is from seed, which is sometimes sown directly and then thinned out once seedlings have emerged and established themselves. Ideal production temperatures are 18–20°C (64–68°F). *Bupleurum* is seen as an inexpensive crop in many countries and is therefore usually grown outdoors under full sun conditions. Plants can become heavy and fall over, so growers will often use a layer or two of support netting.

PROPERTIES Vase life is average to above average (7–10 days). It is not ethylene sensitive.

QUALITY CRITERIA Select cut stems with 80–90% of flowers open. Stems should be well branched, stiff and have a good volume and spread of flowers. Leaf colour should be a deep uniform green, not pale or blotchy.

CARE & HANDLING Foliage tangles easily, so do not simply pull stems apart. First hold upside down and shake gently to loosen, otherwise leaves and flowers may be pulled off and damaged. Recut stems and place in an all-purpose floral preservative. Make sure short stems do not have the leaves below the water line. Stems can be stored for 3–4 days at 1–4°C (34–39°F) and 90–95% relative humidity. For drying purposes make sure the stems are still young and fresh.

Bupleurum rotundifolium L.   family: Apiaceae (Umbelliferae)

hazenoor (Dutch); *buplèvre à feuilles rondes, oreille-de-lièvre* (French); *Durchwachsenes Hasenohr, Rundblättriges Hasenohr* (German); *haloche* (Spanish)

Buxus sempervirens

boxwood • common box

Buxus sempervirens 'Faulkner'

Buxus sempervirens 'Faulkner'

DESCRIPTION An evergreen shrub or small tree with small, bright green, glossy and hairless leaves and inconspicuous yellow flowers (male and female ones separate). Numerous cultivars have been developed, differing mainly in growth habit and foliage colour (bright green, bluish green or variously variegated).

ORIGIN & HISTORY Southern Europe, western Asia and North Africa. Box has been used as a hedge plant for centuries (especially the famous formal knot gardens of Europe). The cut foliage is always readily accepted and used in the florist trade.

PARTS USED Leafy stems are used as florist greens and fillers.

CULTIVATION Propagation is normally by means of rooted cuttings. Plants do well in full sun to partial shade, but newly planted young plants need to be protected from harsh midday sun. Boxwoods have shallow root systems and excessive digging around the shrubs should be avoided. Plants benefit from being mulched and respond very well to regular pruning.

PROPERTIES Vase life is average to good (7–14 days). Flowers are not showy but fragrant. Contact with the plant sap can cause skin irritation in some people. The foliage is not sensitive to ethylene.

QUALITY CRITERIA Select stems with clean, undamaged and disease-free leaves. Make sure leaves have a lush, uniform colour and not a blotchy or yellowish appearance. Select stems that are well formed and branched and not too large or woody. Look for stems with mature leaves, but make sure none are showing signs of ageing.

CARE & HANDLING Recut stems by 25–50 mm (1–2"). Carefully remove foliage that will be below the water level. Avoid contact with the sap or preferably use gloves. Place in a preservative containing a bactericide. Stems can be stored for 4–5 days in water or packaging at 2–4°C (36–39°F) and at a high relative humidity (90–95%).

Buxus sempervirens L.   family: Buxaceae

buis commun (French); *Europäischer Buchsbaum, Gewöhnlicher Buchsbaum* (German)

Calathea makoyana

calathea • peacock plant • cathedral windows

Calathea makoyana

DESCRIPTION A perennial herb with a branched stem and oblong leaves which are beautifully decorated with dark and light green blotches and with the undersides a deep maroon colour. The flowers are relatively small and are borne on short stems near the ground. There are numerous cultivars of several species, including *C. lancifolia* (rattlesnake plant), *C. majestica*, *C. picturata* and *C. zebrina*.

ORIGIN & HISTORY Brazil. More than 60 species of *Calathea* are regularly grown as foliage plants. The tubers of *C. allouia* are eaten like potatoes in the West Indies.

PARTS USED The leaves of certain cultivars are used as cut greens, while other cultivars are used as pot plants.

CULTIVATION Plants prefer a well-drained soil and partial shade (full sun causes bleaching and damage). Although soils must not become waterlogged, they need to be kept moist. Plants are sensitive to frost and active growth only occurs at temperatures of 15°C (60°F) and above.

PROPERTIES Vase life is very good (20–25 days). Leaf patterns are incredibly varied and ornate, with brightly coloured spots and lines.

QUALITY CRITERIA Look for flat leaves that do not have brown marks on the edges or tips and are not curling. Make sure the leaves are free of pests and diseases, as well as general handling damage. Where possible, select leaves with long stalks. Pot plants must have mature, well-marked and coloured leaves. The plant itself should be compact and branched.

CARE & HANDLING Recut stems and place in water with a bactericide. There is no need to use a full preservative. Make sure that only the stem and not the blade of the leaf is in the water. Wipe leaves clean with a damp cloth prior to use. Leaves can be stored for 7–10 days in a preservative at 5°C (41°F) and 90–95% relative humidity. Alternatively store the leaves in their packaging or water retentive boxes in the cooler for 1 week.

Calathea lancifolia Boom (=*C. insignis*)   family: Marantaceae

pauwenplant (Dutch); *galanga* (French); *Pfauen-Korbmaranthe* (German); *calathea* (Spanish)

Calceolaria herbeohybrida

slipper flower • florists' calceolaria • pocketbook plant

Calceolaria 'Sunset Orange'

DESCRIPTION A small, compact, biennial herb with hairy leaves and very distinctive, slipper-like flowers. The lower lip of the flower is modified into a large pouch, and the yellow to red flowers are often beautifully decorated with spots and blotches. Numerous cultivars and seed races are usually sold as mixed-colour seedling strains (such as 'Multiflora Nana') or as hybrids (including Anytime, Confetti, Pocket and Tiger Spotted Hybrids). There are more than 300 species and several are grown in gardens. Amongst the most popular are the somewhat shrubby *C. fruticohybrida* group of hybrids with relatively small flowers.

ORIGIN & HISTORY *Calceolaria* is mainly from tropical America. *C. ×herbeohybrida* is a complex hybrid involving *C. crenatiflora*, *C. corymbosa* and *C. cana* (all three of them Chilean species).

PARTS USED The whole flowering plant is used as a potted flower.

CULTIVATION Plants are propagated from seed and cultivated under controlled conditions in greenhouses. Cool temperatures are essential,

as are regular feeding and watering. Many of the new cultivars will flower regardless of cold treatment and day length. Plants are sensitive to several fungal diseases.

PROPERTIES Plants remain in flower for 2–3 months. The flowers have no scent and are sensitive to ethylene and botrytis.

QUALITY CRITERIA Select compact, well-formed plants with even growth, dense masses of buds and only 4–8 flowers open. Make sure that the leaves are not deformed and have an even green colour. Flowers and leaves must be free of blemishes and healthy, with no signs of botrytis or bud drop.

CARE & HANDLING Flowers are easily damaged, so handle with care. If in boxes, unpack immediately. Display pots in bright light but avoid direct sunlight. Good air-circulation is important, as the plants are very susceptible to fungal diseases. Keep plants uniformly moist, but not wet. Do not get water on the flowers or leaves. Continually remove dead leaves and blooms. Do not keep plants in the dark, which will result in bud drop.

Calceolaria ×herbeohybrida Voss   family: Calceolariaceae (Scrophulariaceae)

pantoffelplantje (Dutch); *calcéolaire* (French); *Pantoffelblume* (German); *pantofolina* (Italian)

Calendula officinalis
common marigold • pot marigold

Calendula 'Indian Prince'

Calendula single

Calendula double

DESCRIPTION An annual or short-lived perennial herb (about 0.6 m or 2' high) with large, glandular leaves and attractive yellow, orange or bronze flower heads of up to 75 mm (3") in diameter. Like sunflowers, calendula flower heads follow the sun. There are numerous seed races and named cultivars. The flower head shapes vary from pompoms and double-flowered types to single and open disc shape types.

ORIGIN AND HISTORY Mediterranean region, but the exact origin is unknown. Marigold is associated with healing, religion and grief. Very early Christians called it Mary's Gold, and placed it by the statues of the Virgin Mary. In ancient India it is a sacred flower used to adorn holy statues. Calendulas were very popular in the early 1900s.

PARTS USED Flowering stems: cut flowers; whole plants: potted flowers.

CULTIVATION Propagation is from seed, although most growers buy seedlings. Plants need cool temperatures (12–15°C; 54–59°F), low humidity levels and good light to produce high quality flowers. In open fields, sowing or planting has to be after the frost period, yet early enough to allow harvesting before temperatures and/or humidity becomes too high. In greenhouses, calendulas are produced all year round.

PROPERTIES Vase life is usually poor (5–7 days). Marigolds are not sensitive to ethylene.

QUALITY CRITERIA Select flower heads that are 90–100% open, but make sure they have not started to decline, with no signs of pests or diseases. Stems must be sturdy and free of any bruising or soft spots, where they will buckle.

CARE & HANDLING Cut stems wilt easily, so recut and place in a preservative with a bactericide as soon as possible. Remove any leaves at the bottom of the stems. If flowers look wilted, first allow to stand 1–2 hours at room temperature in a hydrating solution. Keep in a cool area. Flowers can be held for 1–2 days at 0–2°C (32–36°F) at 90–95% relative humidity.

Calendula officinalis L.   family: Asteraceae

goudsbloem (Dutch); *souci des jardins* (French); *Ringelblume* (German); *calendola* (Italian); *caléndula* (Spanish)

Callicarpa dichotoma

beautyberry

Callicarpa japonica

Callicarpa americana

Callicarpa dichotoma

Callicarpa bodinieri

DESCRIPTION A woody shrub (to 1.2 m or 4′) with broad simple leaves, small pink flowers and bright lilac-violet, bead-like fruits of 3 mm (1/8″) in diameter. A few of the various species and closely related cultivars are grown in different parts of the world. The Chinese *C. bodinieri* (Bodinier beautyberry) is popular in Europe, while *C. dichotoma* and *C. americana* are commonly grown in the United States. Other species that are occasionally cultivated include *C. japonica*, *C. longifolia*, *C. macrophylla*, *C. nudiflora* and *C. pedunculata*.

ORIGIN & HISTORY China and Japan. *C. americana* is indigenous to tropical areas of Central and North America. These plants have become popular garden shrubs on account of their brilliantly coloured violet berries.

PARTS USED Fruiting stems are used as cut foliage.

CULTIVATION Plants are mainly field cultivated. Fruits are borne on new wood, so growers normally cut their plants back hard to within 0.3 m (1′) of the ground after harvesting. Excessive fertilisation during active growth results in less fruit.

PROPERTIES Vase life of fruit is good (10–14 days). Stems do not transport well over long distances.

QUALITY CRITERIA Select stems with all fruit fully coloured. If terminal fruits are still green they will not colour fully. Inevitably some ripe fruit will fall off during harvesting, but check to ensure that stems purchased have not lost significant amounts of fruit, due to poor handling or too late harvesting.

CARE & HANDLING Handle carefully as fruits drop off easily. Leaves are usually removed at the grower. Remaining leaves can be removed as follows: (1) Recut stems, place in a preservative for 2 hours, then allow to stand dry for 2 days to make leaf removal easier; or (2) Store in a preservative in a dark cooler at 0–2°C (32–36°F) for 1–3 days, to loosen leaves and at the same time limit fruit loss. Once all leaves are removed, stems can be used or stored in water at 0–2°C (32–36°F).

Callicarpa dichotoma (Lour.) K. Koch

family: Lamiaceae (Verbenaceae)

schoonvrucht (Dutch); *callicarpa* (French); *Purpur-Schönfrucht* (German)

Callistemon speciosus
bottlebrush • Albany bottlebrush

Callistemon speciosus

Callistemon citrinus

DESCRIPTION A medium-sized shrub with erect, stiff branches. The leaves are narrow and spreading, with conspicuously veined surfaces and sharp, thorn-like tips. Dense spikes of bright red filaments (with golden anthers) are borne near the branch tips. Different flower colours (including white) are available but there are no well-known named cultivars. The crimson bottlebrush (*C. citrinus*) has similar dark red filaments but the anthers are dark-coloured.

ORIGIN & HISTORY Australia. Bottlebrushes are popular garden shrubs and are increasingly popular as florist flowers.

PARTS USED Flowering branches are used as fillers or cut flowers. Leafy stems without flowers are used as cut greens.

CULTIVATION Propagation is usually from cuttings, taken from semi-ripe wood in summer (rarely from seeds). Bottlebrushes do best in full sun. They like well-drained soil, preferably sandy loam, but are quite adaptable. However, heavy soils and soggy ground are unsuitable. Plants are drought tolerant once established.

PROPERTIES Vase life of flowers is good (7–10 days) and vase life of foliage is very good (14–18 days). Flowers may cause allergies in some people. They do not have a strong scent and are not ethylene sensitive.

QUALITY CRITERIA Select stems with flowers that are fully mature, but make sure that they have not started to deteriorate. Select well-branched, straight stems that are still young and not too woody. Check foliage for disease and general damage. Flower spikes should be well developed, brightly coloured and not damaged.

CARE & HANDLING Recut stems by 50–100 mm (2–4") and place in a preservative with a low sugar content and a bactericide. Storage of flowers is not recommended. If necessary, store only for 2–3 days at 4–6°C (39–43°F) in a preservative. Foliage can be stored for 7–10 days at the same conditions if necessary.

Callistemon speciosus (Sims) DC.   family: Myrtaceae

lampenpoetser (Dutch); *callistemon, rince-bouteille* (French); *Albany Zylinderputzer* (German); *calistemo* (Spanish)

Callistephus chinensis

China aster • summer aster

Callistephus chinensis double purple

Callistephus chinensis single pink

Callistephus chinensis mixed

DESCRIPTION An erect annual (0.8 m or about 2½" high) with broad, toothed leaves and large flower heads of up to 120 mm (nearly 5") in diameter. The yellow disc florets are surrounded by a halo of white to mauve ray florets. There is only one species but hundreds of cultivars, with many colours in single and double-flowered forms. China aster should not be confused with aster (*Aster ericoides*).

ORIGIN & HISTORY China. The Greek name *Callistephus* means "beautiful Chinese crown". China asters have been cultivated in China for 2000 years and were introduced to Europe in 1728.

PARTS USED Flower heads with leaves are used as cut flowers and whole plants as potted flowers.

CULTIVATION Propagation is mainly from seed. Flowers develop most rapidly when grown under a period of long days, followed by a period of short days. Temperature is an important production factor and best results are achieved between 13°C (55°F) and 30°C (86°F).

PROPERTIES Vase life is slightly poor to average (5–8 days). Flowers do not transport well over long distances. They are ethylene sensitive.

QUALITY CRITERIA Purchase pre-treated flower heads, as they will last much longer. The foliage declines faster than the flowers (turning yellow and black), so make sure that it is fresh and healthy. Ensure that flowering stems are sturdy and straight and that there is no "neck droop". Select stems with about 30% of the flower heads open.

CARE & HANDLING Recut the stems and hydrate with citric acid or a solution that acidifies the water (pH 3–3.5). Strip away leaves below the water line and place the stems in a preservative solution with an anti-ethylene agent as this significantly increases vase life. Storage is not recommended. The flower heads can be dried. First allow them to open fully, then hang upside down in a well-ventilated place, in small bunches with their leaves on. Drying with a desiccant such as silica gel is also successful.

Callistephus chinensis (L.) Nees

family: Asteraceae

Chinese aster (Dutch); *reine-marguerite* (French); *Sommeraster* (German); *astro cinese* (Italian); *reina margarita* (Spanish)

Calluna vulgaris
heather • Scots heather • Scotch heather • ling

Calluna vulgaris

DESCRIPTION An evergreen shrub up to 0.6 m (2') high with minute, scale-like leaves. Small flowers of 4 mm (⅓") long are borne along the stem tips. The single species of *Calluna* differs from *Erica* species in the calyx that completely conceals the corolla. There are more than 1 000 cultivars with green, silver, golden or reddish leaves and a range of flower colours (white, yellow, lavender, pink and red).

ORIGIN & HISTORY Europe and the Mediterranean region (naturalised in North America). Traditional uses include "hops" for "heather ale", traditional medicine, yellow dye for wool and garden ornamental.

PARTS USED Whole plants are cultivated as potted flowers. White- and pink-flowered cultivars are sometimes grown in the same pot to give an interesting colour contrast. Flowering stems are used as fillers for bouquets.

CULTIVATION Propagation is primarily by means of stem cuttings, to ensure that new plants are true to type. Heather prefers well-drained, slightly acidic soils and full sun to partial shade. It is common in heaths and moorlands and flowering foliage is also wild-harvested.

PROPERTIES Vase life of cut stems is average to good (7–14 days). Flowers are fragrant. Potted flowers remain in bloom for several weeks. They are not ethylene sensitive.

QUALITY CRITERIA Select well-branched cut stems with 30–50% of the flowers open. Potted flowers should be compact, with a few flowers opening but with many buds showing colour. Look out for bud or leaf drop, blemishes or disease.

CARE & HANDLING Recut stems and place in a floral preservative or bactericide. Remove leaves and flowers below the water line. Ensure good air-circulation to prevent the development of mould on the flowers. Heather is suitable for drying – spray the dried stems with a fixative to avoid flower shattering. Display pots in a bright, cool area. Do not over-water but keep uniformly moist.

Calluna vulgaris (L.) Hull   family: Ericaceae

heide (Dutch); *bruyère commune, callune* (French); *Besenheide, Heidekraut* (German); *erica* (Italian); *bereza* (Spanish)

Camellia japonica
camel(l)ia • common camellia • japonica

Camellia japonica double red

Camellia japonica single red

Camellia japonica pink

DESCRIPTION An evergreen shrub or tree of up to 15 m (50′) high with simple, leathery and markedly glossy leaves. The large flowers are single, semi-double and double (resemble roses) and vary from 50 to 150 mm (2″ to 6″) in diameter. Colours range from white to pink or red, often with striking colour patterns, spots and streaks. There are more than 2 000 cultivars. Another popular species is *C. sasanqua* from Japan.

ORIGIN & HISTORY Japan, Korea and China. The plants are highly prized, not only in Japan (where they are viewed as a symbol of elegance and aristocracy) but also in most other countries of the world. More than 40 species and hybrids are commonly grown as garden shrubs.

PARTS USED Flowers are used as cut flowers and the foliage as cut greens.

CULTIVATION Plants grow well in semi-shade to full shade, although for some cultivars too much shade will result in spindly, poor flowering plants. Camellias are able to be cultivated in a range of soil types, as long as they are fairly acidic (pH5–6.5). They do not like alkaline soils. Flower size is reduced where plants are subject to too much cold.

PROPERTIES Vase life is poor to average (5–7 days). Flowers are sensitive to ethylene.

QUALITY CRITERIA Select stems with a good volume of dark green leaves that are free of any damage or disease. Also check that leaves have no sunburn (yellow or bronze colour). Preferably look for stems that are not too large or woody. Select flowers that are 75–100% open. Do not purchase flowers that are too closed or that have marks on the petals and general damage.

CARE & HANDLING On arrival immediately recut stems and place in a preservative containing an anti-ethylene agent. Remove any leaves that are below the water line. Storage of flowers is not recommended, but if necessary they can be stored for 3–4 days at 1–4°C (34–39°F) and a high relative humidity.

Camellia japonica L.   family: Theaceae

camelia (Dutch); *camélia du Japon* (French); *Japanische Kamelie* (German); *camelia* (Italian, Spanish)

Campanula persicifolia
bellflower • peach-bells • willow bell

Campanula pyramidalis

Campanula persicifolia

Campanula medium

DESCRIPTION A perennial herb of up to 0.75 m (30") with nodding flowers borne in slender terminal clusters. The typically bell-shaped flowers are single or double and are white to blue or purple. There are numerous cultivars but the colour range is fairly limited. Several species are cultivated – some tend to be more suitable as potted flowers than cut flowers, and vice versa.

ORIGIN & HISTORY Europe, North Africa and northern and western Asia. *Campanula* (Latin: bell) is an old favourite garden plant and more than 120 species are regularly planted as garden ornamentals and florist flowers.

PARTS USED Flowers are used as cut flowers and whole plants as potted flowers or for hanging baskets.

CULTIVATION Plants benefit from a period of cold. Warm temperatures and high levels of nitrogen result in tall spindly plants. In cut flower production, plants are harvested for at least 3 years before they are lifted and divided.

PROPERTIES Vase life of cut flowers is average to good (7–10 days). Most species are ethylene sensitive, causing flowers to shrivel up.

QUALITY CRITERIA Cut flowers: *C. glomerata* (clustered bellflower) – select stems with flowers still in bud and only 2–3 flowers in the cluster open; *C. pyramidalis* (chimney bells), *C. persicifolia* (bellflower) and *C. medium* (Canterbury bells) – select stems with top two-thirds of flowers still in bud. Check that flowers and plants are free of pests and diseases. Potted flowers: select well-budded plants with only 1–3 open flowers.

CARE & HANDLING Cut flowers: Recut and place in a preservative containing an anti-ethylene agent and a sugar. Do not hydrate flowers in warm water, as this is detrimental to bellflowers. Store in a preservative at 2°C (36°F). Flowers do not dry well. Display pots in a bright cool area. Keep potting medium moist, as flowers may invert if medium dries out.

Campanula persicifolia L.   family: Campanulaceae

klokjesbloem (Dutch); *campanule, campanule à feuilles de pêcher* (French); *Glockenblume, Pfirsichblättrige Glockenblume* (German)

Cannomois virgata

rekoala • bell reed

Cannomois virgata male plant

Cannomois virgata stems and fruits

DESCRIPTION The plant is a robust tuft with erect, much-branched green stems of up to 3 m (10′) or more. Leaves are highly reduced to brown, scale-like structures. Male and female flowers occur on separate plants. The bell-like fruits are borne only on female plants. There are as yet no named cultivars.

ORIGIN & HISTORY South Africa (a typical element of the fynbos vegetation of the Cape). The bell reed is one of several so-called restios (from the family Restionaceae) that are well known as thatch plants. They are becoming increasingly popular as garden plants and florist greens. The dark brown, chaff-like flowers can be very decorative.

PARTS USED The fresh or dried stems (with or without the bell-like fruits) are used as fillers or decorations. Especially popular are the young stems, which are sharply pointed and javelin-like before they unfold.

CULTIVATION Most of the harvesting of bell reed is still done in the wild. However, plants grow easily under ideal conditions. They prefer wet, fairly waterlogged sandy soils that dry out from time to time and that are acidic, but rich in nutrients. Plants prefer full sun conditions and remain productive for many years.

PROPERTIES Vase life is good (8–10 days), although seed pods may open a few days prior. The stems have no fragrance and are not sensitive to ethylene.

QUALITY CRITERIA Select reeds with stems that are long and supple. Make sure that there is a good volume and spread of fruits on the culms and that the colour of the stems is a uniform green and not pale or yellowish.

CARE & HANDLING Recut stems and place in clean water with a bactericide. There is no need to use a floral preservative. Although the reeds look hardy, use as soon as possible as seed pods open and stems lose their appeal. If necessary, stems can be held for 3–4 days in a cooler at 0–2°C (32–36°F). Do not store in the dark. Stems can be dried – tie into small loose bunches and hang upside down in a dark, well-ventilated area.

Cannomois virgata (Rottb.) Steud.

family: Restionaceae

cannomois (Dutch, French, Italian, Spanish); *Cannomois* (German)

Capsicum annuum

ornamental pepper

Capsicum annuum

Capsicum annuum

Capsicum annuum

DESCRIPTION An annual herb with bright green, hairless leaves, inconspicuous white flowers and green fruits of various shapes that ripen to different shades of yellow, orange, red or purple. All fruits go through a series of colours when ripening, but the difference between cultivars is often the shape of the fruit as well as the final colour (deep red, bright orange, yellow or purple). Some cultivars display the entire range of colours at once. Three main groups of *C. annuum* are grown as potted "flowers". The cherry peppers (Cerasiforme group) have small, rounded, nodding fruit, while the more commonly cultivated cone peppers (Conioides group) have erect, cone-shaped fruits in a multitude of colour forms. The third group is the red cone peppers (Fasciculatum group) with erect, slender red fruits borne in clusters.

ORIGIN & HISTORY Tropical America (including Mexico and the Caribbean region). Peppers are an ancient crop, better known as salad and spice plants. Cultivars of *C. annuum* and *C. frutescens* are widely grown for their pungent fruits used in chilli sauces.

PARTS USED Whole plants are used as potted novelties (sought for their coloured fruits and not the flowers).

CULTIVATION Growers need to produce compact plants for pots therefore height control is an important part of production. Plant height is managed by growing naturally compact cultivars or by regulating feeding, watering and high night temperatures. Keep in mind that in many countries chemical growth regulators may not be used on peppers, as they are a food crop.

PROPERTIES Fruits remain attractive for several weeks. They are edible.

QUALITY CRITERIA Select plants that are free of disease, marks and general damage. Purchase plants that are well formed and have an abundance of fruits. Ensure that fruit drop has not occurred.

CARE & HANDLING Displaying pots in cool, humid conditions and partial shade will extend shelf life. Hot, dry air causes fruits to drop off prematurely. Mist regularly and keep potting medium moist.

Capsicum annuum L.   family: Solanaceae

sierpeper (Dutch); *piment d'ornement* (French); *Zier-Paprika* (German); *peperoncino ornamentale* (Italian)

Carthamus tinctorius

safflower

Carthamus tinctorius 'White Grenade'

Carthamus tinctorius 'Orange Grenade'

Carthamus tinctorius 'Yellow Grenade'

DESCRIPTION An erect annual herb with dark green, toothed and spiny leaves. The attractive yellow, red or orange flower heads are surrounded by bristly bracts. A few cultivars are available as florist flowers, varying slightly in shape and size. Colours are predominantly yellow and orange, with a few white or cream-coloured. Popular cultivars include 'Lasting White' (florets creamy white) and 'Orange Ball' (florets bright orange).

ORIGIN & HISTORY The origin is unknown (the earliest archaeological records are from the Near East). Safflower is an ancient medicinal plant and important oil crop. The flowers are a source of yellow or red dye used to colour butter and various other products. It is used as an adulterant of saffron. Safflower has become a popular florist flower in recent years.

PARTS USED Flower heads are used as cut flowers.

CULTIVATION Cultivation usually takes place in open fields under full sun or in greenhouses. Plants are generally propagated from seed that can easily be sown directly. In outdoor production this is done in early spring. Plants need to be grown in well-drained soils, especially in warmer climates where root rot can be problematic.

PROPERTIES Vase life is average (6–8 days). Foliage deteriorates much faster than the flower heads. Safflower is slightly difficult to work with because of the sharp spines on the flower heads and leaves.

QUALITY CRITERIA Purchase stems with the majority of buds beginning to open and the orange or yellow colour of the florets clearly visible. Avoid stems with too many green buds as many will fail to open. Check that stems are free of pests, disease and damage.

CARE & HANDLING Recut the stems and place them in a preservative. Storage is not recommended, but if necessary store for only 2–3 days at 2–4°C (36–39°F). Flowers can be very successfully air-dried upside down in a cool place.

Carthamus tinctorius L.   family: Asteraceae

saffloer (Dutch); *carthame* (French); *Färber-Distel* (German); *cartamo* (Italian); *cártamo* (Spanish)

Caryopteris clandonensis
blue beard • blue spiraea

Caryopteris ×clandonensis

Caryopteris ×clandonensis flowers

DESCRIPTION A shrub of up to 1.5 m (5′) with hairy leaves and numerous small flowers (usually bright blue) borne in clusters at the branch ends. There are several cultivars with flowers in different shades of blue and with variously coloured foliage. Examples are 'Kew Blue' (leaves silvery, flowers Cambridge blue to lavender-blue) and 'Worcester Gold' (leaves gold, flowers blue).

ORIGIN & HISTORY The plant is of garden origin. *C. ×clandonensis* is a hybrid between *C. incana* (from China and Japan) and *C. mongholica* (from Mongolia and northern China). Both these species are also popular garden shrubs.

PARTS USED The flowering stems are used as cut flowers.

CULTIVATION Plants are propagated from cuttings or from seed. Excessive heat tends to reduce the intensity of flower and leaf colour. In climates with hot summers and high light intensities, flowers are grown under shade cloth to improve stem length and to reduce the brittleness of stems. Temperatures below 13°C (55°F) or above 29°C (85°F) slow down growth and reduce flowering. The shrubs usually die back in winter. Most flower production is in open fields with very little presently taking place in greenhouses.

PROPERTIES Vase life is average to fairly good (6–10 days).

QUALITY CRITERIA Look for stems with buds showing colour or with the lower-most whorl of flowers open. Select young, straight, sturdy stems with evenly spaced flower whorls. Make sure the leaves are undamaged and unmarked, with a healthy green colour.

CARE & HANDLING Recut stems and hydrate in acidified water (preferably pH 3.5) for 1–3 hours at room temperature (warm water can be used although not necessary). Place in a preservative. Flowers can be stored for 3–4 days at 2–4°C (36–39°F). Flowering stems can be air-dried by hanging them upside down in a warm, well-ventilated area for about 7–10 days.

Caryopteris ×clandonensis Rehder

family: Lamiaceae (Verbenaceae)

blauwe spirea (Dutch); *caryoptéris* (French); *Clandon-Bartblume* (German); *carióptera* (Italian); *barba azul* (Spanish)

Catharanthus roseus
Madagascar periwinkle • rose periwinkle

Catharanthus roseus 'Sun Storm Apricot'

Catharanthus roseus 'Pacifica' mix

Catharanthus roseus 'Sun Storm Violet Eye'

DESCRIPTION This is an erect perennial herb of up to 0.6 m (2½') with glossy green leaves and colourful flowers, often with a prominent "eye". Sometimes referred to as "impatiens for the sun", Madagascar periwinkles have grown in popularity with the continued release of more cold-tolerant cultivars with a wider range of colours (white and pink to red). Well-known cultivars include 'Cooler', 'Pacifica', 'Stardust' and 'Mediterranean'.

ORIGIN & HISTORY Madagascar. The plant has become a pantropical weed and is a source of alkaloids for treating leukaemia and Hodgkin's disease.

PARTS USED Whole plants are used as potted flowers.

CULTIVATION Propagation of plants is predominantly by means of seed and occasionally by means of cuttings. A very well-drained, acidic (pH 5.5–6.3) soil or growing medium is necessary. Plants are cultivated at warm temperatures (18–24°C; 64–75°F). Growers

typically treat the plants with growth regulators to keep them short and compact.

PROPERTIES Plants remain in flower for many weeks. They are prone to fungal diseases in the soil that attack the roots and cause the death of the plant. Plants are also sensitive to ethylene.

QUALITY CRITERIA Make sure the specimen does not have stunted or uneven growth, which is often a result of too low production temperatures and/or high soil pH levels. Well-formed, compact plants, full of well-dispersed blooms are signs of quality. Leaves need to be a uniform green colour (not yellowish) and free of damage and blemishes.

CARE & HANDLING Unpack the pots immediately if they were packed in closed shipping containers. Water well and display in full sun and warm air temperatures. Avoid cold temperatures (<18°C; <64°F) and draughts. Do not over-water plants but keep them uniformly moist. Preferably do not get the leaves wet (or water early so that they are dry by nightfall).

Catharanthus roseus (L.) G. Don.

family: Apocynaceae

roze maagdenpalm (Dutch); *pervenche de Madagascar* (French); *Rosafarbenes Zimmerimmergrün* (German); *vinca (Italian); vinca rosea* (Spanish)

Cattleya cultivars
cattleya orchid

Cattleya cultivar (pink)

Cattleya cultivar (light pink)

DESCRIPTION Cattleyas are mostly epiphytes with cylindrical pseudobulbs bearing 1 (unifoliate cattleyas) or 2 (bifoliate cattleyas) leaves that are thick and leathery. Flowers are typically large and showy, and are often borne in relatively few-flowered clusters. The lip is mostly tubular and markedly frilly around the mouth.

ORIGIN & HISTORY Tropical America. There are over 50 species and thousands of hybrids and cultivars. Cattleyas are the most familiar and most highly prized of the orchids used for bouquets and buttonholes.

PARTS USED Flowers are used as cut flowers and whole plants as potted flowers.

CULTIVATION One of the most debated issues of orchid production is growing medium and subsequently just about every grower uses a different medium mix. Cattleyas require unimpeded drainage and coarse bark mixtures. They grow well in plastic or terracotta pots, which must be allowed to dry out completely between waterings.

PROPERTIES The vase life of the flower is poor to below average (4–5 days) so that potted specimens have become popular. Most cultivars have a very pleasant fragrance. They are sensitive to ethylene.

QUALITY CRITERIA Select spikes with fully opened blooms, but check that they are not showing any signs of ageing. Make sure petals do not have marks or bruises. Spikes and individual flowers should be sold with the stem placed in a water vial. Potted flowers should have 1–4 flowers open.

CARE & HANDLING Unpack immediately and check that the vials are full of water. Handle flowers as little as possible – bruising leads to browning of the petals. Store at a temperature of 13–15°C (55–60°F), as flowers are sensitive to lower temperatures. Avoid getting water on the petals as this can cause marks or spots. Display potted flowers in a bright cool area, out of cold draughts. Plants prefer high humidity, but do not over-water. Do not store pots in the dark.

Cattleya cultivars   family: Orchidaceae

cattleya (Dutch, French, Italian, Spanish); *Cattleya* (German)

125

Cedrus deodara

cedar • deodar

Cedrus deodara foliage

Cedrus deodara male cones

Cedrus deodara tree

DESCRIPTION Large evergreen trees with long shoots and short shoots – the latter bearing numerous short, often greyish green needles in a spiral arrangement. The branches are usually spreading in tiers, with the tips nodding. The cones have thin scales and break apart at maturity. There are two species – *C. deodara* and *C. libani* (cedar of Lebanon). Numerous cultivars of both species have been developed, differing in cold tolerance, growth form, branching pattern, leaf length and foliage colour. Pines differ from cedars in their few-needled short shoots and the persistent cone scales.

ORIGIN & HISTORY North Africa, Eastern Mediterranean and western Himalayas. Cedars are well-known timber trees and were once used to build Solomon's temple. They are also popular ornamentals and the foliage is generally known as Christmas greens.

PARTS USED Leafy branches are used as cut greens. Young or small trees are sold as pot plants or Christmas trees.

CULTIVATION Trees are grown from cuttings or seed in open fields. Some cultivars can tolerate freezing temperatures. When cultivated in warm climates, the trees are often plagued by fungal and bacterial diseases, which cause the leaves and young shoots to die.

PROPERTIES Vase life is very good (21–28 days). Leaves have a slight, clean (resinous) scent. Working with stems can leave the hands sticky, but the gum seldom causes allergic reactions.

QUALITY CRITERIA Select stems with leaves in full colour. Dropping of needles (leaves) is an indication of dry or old stems or incorrect handling. Make sure leaf tips have not yellowed. Select stems that are fairly young and not too woody.

CARE & HANDLING Recut stems and place in clean water with a bactericide. Remove leaves below the water line. Store separate from cut flowers to avoid ethylene damage. Stems can be stored in water (or kept in original boxes or bags) for 7–10 days at 2–4°C (36–39°F) and a relative humidity of 95%.

Cedrus deodara (Roxb.) G. Don   family: Pinaceae

Himalaya ceder (Dutch); *cèdre de l'himalaya* (French); *Himalaya-Zeder* (German); *cedro* (Italian); *cedro del himalaya* (Spanish)

Celosia argentea
cockscomb • celosia • red fox

Celosia argentea 'Bombay Orange'

Celosia argentea 'Flamingo Feather'

DESCRIPTION An erect annual (up to 2 m or just over 6') with strongly coloured flowering heads or plumes. The leaves and stems are soft and break easily. Most florist cultivars are derived from *C. argentea* (= *C. cristata*). There are four main cultivar groups: Cristata (crested forms) – common cockscomb; Plumosa (plume forms) – long feathery plumes; Spicata (spired forms) – wheat celosia, with long, slender flower spires; Childsii (globose forms) – rounded flower heads.

ORIGIN & HISTORY Tropics of Asia, Africa and America. The name *Celosia* comes from the Greek *keleous*, which means burning, in reference to their brilliant colours.

PARTS USED Flowering stems are used as cut flowers and whole plants are especially popular as potted flowers.

CULTIVATION Cultivars bred for indoor production usually do not do well in outdoor production. Plants that become water-stressed often flower prematurely. Foliage needs to be dry before nightfall to prevent disease. Low temperatures and low light intensities result in flat stems and flower combs that shatter.

PROPERTIES Vase life is average to good (7–14 days). Vase life of crested forms is better than that of plume forms. There is no fragrance. Foliage deteriorates much faster than the flower.

QUALITY CRITERIA Choose flowers with well-formed heads or plumes. In the case of crested forms, the flowers should all be fully open, while 80–100% should be open on plume forms.

Look for vibrant colour. Select flowers with bright green leaves (even if they are going to be removed), as healthy leaves indicate quality.

CARE & HANDLING Remove lower leaves before placing stems in water. Use a preservative as this will assist in foliage lasting longer and retaining colour. Cut flowers can be stored for a few days at 4–5°C (39–41°F). Remove wilted leaves prior to use. Cut flowers can be dried. Remove foliage and hang upside down in small bunches.

Celosia argentea L. (=*C. cristata*)   family: Amaranthaceae

hanekam (Dutch); *crête-de-coq* (French); *Hahnenkamm* (German); *cresta di gallo* (Italian)

Centaurea cyanus

cornflower • bachelor's button

Centaurea cyanus flower head

Centaurea cyanus 'Florence Blue Improved'

Centaurea cyanus 'Florence' mix

DESCRIPTION Annual to biennial herb (up to 0.9 m or 3′) with narrow, lance-shaped leaves and flower heads of about 12 mm (½″) in diameter. The heads are bright violet-blue (the inner florets violet, the outer ones dark blue) but there are pure blue, purple, red, pink and white colour forms. Well-known cultivars include the tall, large-flowered 'Blue Diadem' and the 'Florence' series. The yellow globe cornflower (*C. macrocephala*) is also used as a cut flower.

ORIGIN & HISTORY Europe and Asia. The genus was named after the Centaurs, Greek mythological creatures that were half-man, half-horse. Cornflower was formerly a weed of wheat cultivation but has become popular as a colourful garden plant.

PARTS USED Cut stems with flower heads are used as florist flowers.

CULTIVATION Cornflower is a long-day plant, meaning that flowering is induced by periods of long days. Growers force plants to flower out of season by supplying supplementary lighting to artificially lengthen the days. Cultivation is done in greenhouses and in open fields. Flowers do best in full sun as shading reduces flowering and quality.

PROPERTIES Vase life is poor to slightly above average (4–8 days). Flower heads last longer than the foliage. Cornflower is one of the few truly blue florist flowers available. There is no noticeable fragrance.

QUALITY CRITERIA Select single-stemmed flower heads that are 30–50% open. Select sprays with only 50% of the flower heads open. *C. macrocephala* – select when 50–75% open – when the yellow tuft of florets has almost entirely emerged.

CARE & HANDLING Recut and place in a general preservative. If necessary, flower heads can be stored for 2–3 days at 2–5°C (36–41°F) and 90% relative humidity, but storage is not recommended. Fully double forms are most suited to drying. Hang stems upside down (with foliage) in a warm, dark and well-ventilated area.

Centaurea cyanus L.

family: Asteraceae

korenbloem (Dutch); *bleuet* (French); *Kornblume* (German); *fiordaliso* (Italian); *aciano* (Spanish)

Centranthus ruber

red valerian • wallflower • Jupiter's beard

Centranthus ruber plants

Centranthus ruber red

Centranthus ruber white

DESCRIPTION A short-lived perennial herb growing to a height of 0.5 m (20"). It has lance-shaped, hairless leaves and numerous small, usually red flowers borne in clusters on long stalks. Only a few cultivars or selections are available as florist flowers, mainly pink, white or shades of red. These include cultivars such as 'Alba' (white) and 'Coccineus' (red).

ORIGIN & HISTORY Mediterranean region and Europe. Wild and naturalised plants often grow in limestone areas. Valerian is not a major florist flower and its availability is usually limited and erratic. However, when available, it makes a nice filler and break from the norm.

PARTS USED Flowering stems are used as filler.

CULTIVATION Propagation is most often from seed and sometimes, but seldom, from cuttings. Seed is usually purchased and grown in a mixture of colours, so that growers harvest and sell bunches of mixed colours. Valerian prefers a moderate climate, with limited fluctuations in temperature. Low or high temperatures negatively affect flower quality and yields. Plants prefer poor, alkaline soil – too much feeding results in tall, spindly stems. The period from sowing to flowering is roughly 4 months.

PROPERTIES Vase life is poor to average (4–7 days). Some cultivars are slightly scented, but not all.

QUALITY CRITERIA Select stems with only the first few flowers fully open. Select stems that are well branched and that have large terminal clusters of flowers. Most production is in open fields so check to make sure that the flowers are free of pests, disease and damage.

CARE & HANDLING Recut stems and immediately place in a preservative. If foliage is wilted, first hydrate in a hydrating solution at room temperature for 2–3 hours. Storage is not recommended, but flowers can be stored in a preservative at 4°C (39°F) for 3–4 days.

Centranthus ruber (L.) DC.   family: Caprifoliaceae (Valerianaceae)

rode valerian, rode spoorbloem (Dutch); *lilas d'Espagne, valériane rouge* (French); *Rote Spornblume* (German); *valeriana roja* (Spanish)

Cerinthe major
honeywort

Cerinthe major 'Kiwi Blue'

DESCRIPTION An annual herb growing to a height of about 0.6 m (2'). It bears waxy, fleshy leaves on short stalks and clusters of tubular nodding flowers surrounded by large bracts. The bracts are typically tinged with purple and the flowers are purple to dark red. There are no well-known named cultivars.

ORIGIN & HISTORY Mediterranean region of southern Europe and northern Africa. The plant has become a popular cultivated ornamental in Europe but is relatively unknown in most other parts of the world.

PARTS USED Flowering stems are used as florist filler. The whole plant is sometimes available as a potted flower.

CULTIVATION Propagation is from seed. Plants prefer full sun conditions and can tolerate heat, but require regular watering. The soil needs to be fertile and loose to ensure high quality plants and large volumes of flowers. As the plant matures, the coloured bracts around the flowers change colour. Plants are sensitive to frost.

PROPERTIES Vase life of cut stems is slightly poor to average (5–8 days). The colourful bracts outlast the small flowers. Honeywort is not sensitive to ethylene.

QUALITY CRITERIA Select stems that are well branched and full of buds and open flowers. Stems tend to be floppy and not as sturdy as one might want in a filler. Check that stems are free of disease and general damage, especially to the fleshy, waxy leaves. In the case of pots, make sure that the plants are fairly compact, even though they will naturally cascade over the edge of the pot.

CARE & HANDLING Recut stems and immediately place in a preservative. Allow to hydrate for 2–3 hours at room temperature before using or holding in the cooler. Handle with care as the fleshy leaves and stems can easily break or be damaged. Only store for 2–3 days at 2–4°C (36–39°F) and a relative humidity of 90–95%. Display pots in bright light and keep medium moist.

Cerinthe major L.   family: Boraginaceae

cerinthe (Dutch); *mélinet* (French); *Große Wachsblume* (German)

Chamaedorea elegans
parlour palm • bella palm

Chamaedorea elegans 'Bella'

Chamaerops humilis leaf

DESCRIPTION A small palm of up to 2 m high (about 6½') with slender stems of 20 mm (little over ¾") in diameter. A few spreading, pinnate leaves are borne near the stem tip. They are bright green and fern-like in appearance. The leaf segments (11–20 per side) are about 180 × 18 mm (7 × ¾"). The most famous cultivar is 'Bella', a compact plant with relatively short leaves, a conspicuous short crownshaft and golden-yellow inflorescences. *Chamaerops humilis* (fan palm) has similar leaves and is also used as a cut green. Various other species are occasionally used in the same way, especially for large flower arrangements.

ORIGIN & HISTORY Central America (Mexico and Guatemala). The parlour palm, and especially the cultivar 'Bella' is one of the most popular of all palms grown as houseplants.

PARTS USED Green leaves are used as cut greens or fillers, especially in large bouquets or arrangements.

CULTIVATION Most material is wild-harvested. Some commercial cultivation takes place and then propagation is from seed or cuttings. The plants do not tolerate wet feet but should be regularly watered. They are slow growing.

PROPERTIES Vase life is poor to average (5–8 days) and not as long as would be expected from similar cut greens.

QUALITY CRITERIA Select only fully mature leaves. Look for clean, unmarked and undamaged leaves with good, uniform colour. Make sure that there is no scale or spots on the individual leaf segments (pinnae), and that the tips have not dried out.

CARE & HANDLING Unpack as soon as possible, as the leaves are susceptible to mildew if stored in closed boxes. Recut and place in clean water with a bactericide. Make sure that the bottom leaf segments are not standing in the water. There is no need for a floral preservative. Allow stems to hydrate at room temperature for 2–3 hours prior to storing in a cooler. Display leaves in a well-ventilated area (not in a direct draught) or hold at 2–4°C (36–39°F).

Chamaedorea elegans Mart.   family: Arecaceae (Palmae)

kamerpalm (Dutch); *palmier de montagne* (French); *Mexikanische Bergpalme, Zierliche Pergpalme* (German); *neanthe bella* (Italian); *chamedorea eregansu* (Japanese); *chamadorea, palmilla* (Spanish)

Chamelaucium uncinatum

Geraldton waxflower • Geraldton wax

Chamelaucium uncinatum pink

Chamelaucium uncinatum white

DESCRIPTION An evergreen shrub with narrow, lemon-scented leaves of which the tips are hooked. The small flowers are short-stalked and occur in various shades of red, purple, pink to white, depending on the cultivar. *C. uncinatum* has also been hybridised with *C. megalopetalum*, a similar species but with larger flowers.

ORIGIN & HISTORY South-western Australia. The plants are named after Geraldton, the town in Australia where the flower originated. There are about 21 species, all of which are endemic to Australia.

PARTS USED Flowering stems are used as filler and whole plants as potted flowers.

CULTIVATION The species is not suitable for humid, tropical regions or regions experiencing frost. It prefers sandy soils that are slightly acidic to neutral, with good drainage and full sun to partial shade. Established plants can tolerate extended periods of dryness. Once a year shrubs are pruned back by about one third.

PROPERTIES Vase life is average to good (7–14 days). Some cultivars and species are ethylene sensitive (which causes flower fall) while others are not. It is therefore best to treat Geraldton waxflower as ethylene sensitive. They are highly susceptible to botrytis. The flowers have a faint sandalwood fragrance. As stems age they tend to shed their leaves.

QUALITY CRITERIA Select branches with approximately 30% of the flowers open. Flowers that are still closed should have good colour and be well developed. Avoid stems that are too woody as this inhibits good water uptake.

CARE & HANDLING Recut the stems by removing about 50–100 mm (2–4") and strip away the lower foliage. Use a preservative containing a bactericide and an anti-ethylene agent. Let flowers stand in preservative at room temperature for 6–8 hours to hydrate before using or storing at 4–10°C (39–50°F). Warm temperatures stimulate flowers to open – cool conditions slow down bud opening.

Chamelaucium uncinatum Schauer

family: Myrtaceae

"*Geraldton waxflower*" (Dutch, French); "*Geraldton Waxflower*" (German); *fior di cera* (Italian); *flor de cera* (Spanish)

Chrysanthemum morifolium

florist chrysanthemum • dendranthema • "cut mums"

Chrysanthemum ×morifolium 'Anastasia White'

Chrysanthemum ×morifolium 'Biarritz'

Chrysanthemum ×morifolium 'Yoko Ono'

DESCRIPTION A perennial herb with lobed, aromatic leaves and colourful flower heads in a multitude of sizes, shapes and colours. Large, single-headed types are spectacular as novelties but the well-known spray types are by far the most important as commercial cut flowers. There are thousands of cultivars that have been classified into 10 groups – including single or fully double types, globular pompom blooms and so-called quill, reflexed, spider and spoon types (based on the length, width and orientation of the ligulate florets).

ORIGIN & HISTORY China. Chrysanthemums had already been cultivated in Chinese gardens for more than 2 500 years before they were first exhibited in Europe (England) in 1795. Today they are amongst the most popular of all florist flowers.

PARTS USED Stems with flower heads are used as cut flowers.

CULTIVATION Flowering can be precisely timed to the day by carefully manipulating the day length. Plants are first grown for 2–3 weeks under long day conditions, after which blackout screens are used to simulate short days, to force flowering.

PROPERTIES Vase life of cut flowers is very good (10–14 days) depending on cultivar. Chrysanthemums are not ethylene sensitive.

QUALITY CRITERIA Make sure the foliage colour is lively and uniform and that stems are thick and strong. In the case of spray chrysanthemums, make sure that there are a sufficient number of flower heads per stem. Stem weight is an important quality criterion – the heavier the stem, the more flowers and/or the sturdier the stem. Purchase sprays with 50–75% of the flower heads open.

CARE & HANDLING Recut the stem bases and remove all foliage that will end up below the water line. Hydrate them for at least 2 hours. Use a suitable cut flower food, which will help the flower heads to open fully and keep the leaves turgid and fresh. The flower heads can be stored for a few days at 2–3°C (36–37°F), but ensure that high humidity and good air-circulation is maintained.

Chrysanthemum ×morifolium Ramat. (=*Dendranthema ×grandiflora*) family: Asteraceae

krisant (Dutch); *chrysanthème* (French); *Garten-Chrysantheme* (German); *crisantemo* (Italian); *kiku* (Japanese); *crisantemo* (Spanish)

Chrysanthemum morifolium

potted chrysanthemum • potted dendranthema • "pot mums"

Chrysanthemum ×morifolium white

Chrysanthemum ×morifolium yellow

DESCRIPTION An aromatic perennial herb with glandular, distinctly lobed leaves and colourful flower heads. Many cultivars are available in a wide range of colours. New types have been bred that do not require disbudding.

ORIGIN & HISTORY China (probably of ancient hybrid origin). Potted flowers have become a very large industry in recent years.

PARTS USED The whole flowering plant is used as potted flower.

CULTIVATION Unrooted cuttings are dipped in growth hormone and planted directly into the final pot or are rooted in a moist, well-drained potting medium that is acidic (pH 5.8–6.2). Flowering of pot mums, like cut mums, can be precisely timed. Flowering is initiated by short days (in most cultivars, 12 hours or less), during which time the dark period must be completely dark. Irrigation and nutrition are important for producing high quality plants with a good shelf life. Drip tubes or ebb-and-flow flood systems are often used.

PROPERTIES Vase life of potted flowers is very good but varies between cultivars (15–21 days). They are not sensitive to ethylene. Pot mums do not make good garden plants and are usually frost-sensitive.

QUALITY CRITERIA Plants should be well branched, compact and full of blooms – not too leafy with few blooms, or lanky. The whole pot should look balanced and be uniform with regard to stage of flowering, shape and height. Make sure there are no yellowing leaves, damaged buds, blemishes or diseases. Select pots with 25–30% of flower heads open – if too immature, many buds will not open to their full potential.

CARE & HANDLING Unpack immediately and water well if the medium is dry. Display pots in bright light (but not direct sunlight) and moderate temperatures (18–24°C; 64–75°F). Ensure good ventilation (but avoid direct draughts). Pots can be stored for a few days at 2–4°C (36–39°F) and a low humidity. Allow the medium to dry out slightly between waterings and keep moist but not wet.

Chrysanthemum ×morifolium Ramat. (=*Dendranthema ×grandiflora*)   family: Asteraceae

potkrisant (Dutch); *chrysanthème* (French); *Garten-Chrysantheme* (German); *crisantemo* (Italian); *kiku* (Japanese); *crisantemo* (Spanish)

Chrysanthemum parthenium

feverfew

Chrysanthemum parthenium 'Spring Spirit'

Chrysanthemum parthenium 'Magic Lime Green'

Chrysanthemum parthenium 'Rotary'

DESCRIPTION An erect perennial herb (to 0.5 m, 20") with aromatic, lobed leaves and clusters of attractive flower heads borne at the branch tips. The heads have yellow disc florets surrounded by white ray florets. There are several cultivars with flower heads ranging from white to yellow. 'Aureum' has gold-tinted leaves and single flower heads. Double-flowered (pompom) types include 'Sissinghurst' (white) and 'Snowball' (cream-coloured). Cultivars also differ in growing habit and temperature regimes.

ORIGIN & HISTORY South-eastern Europe and Asia Minor. In many books, feverfew is listed under the alternative name, *Tanacetum parthenium*. The name "feverfew" is perhaps derived from the feathery leaves ("featherfew"). It is commonly grown in herb gardens and has become famous as a migraine prophylactic.

PARTS USED Flower heads are used as cut flowers, while whole plants are produced in containers as potted flowers.

CULTIVATION Feverfew is propagated from seeds, which are not covered and germinated at a temperature of 21°C (70°F). However, most growers purchase seedlings in plug form from suppliers. It is a long-day plant and flowering is initiated under daylight periods of 16 hours or longer. Uniform irrigation is important as dry spots result in short plants that flower prematurely. The best quality is achieved at day / night temperatures of 16–18°C (60–65°F) / 13–16°C (55–60°F) and a soil pH of 6.0–7.2.

PROPERTIES Vase life is average to good (7–14 days). Foliage wilts and deteriorates faster than the flower heads. Feverfew is not sensitive to ethylene.

QUALITY CRITERIA Select stems with only about 25% flower heads open. Select tight bunches. Leaves may appear wilted but not the flower heads. Select long, straight stems.

CARE & HANDLING Recut stems and hydrate. Remove any leaves that are below the water line. Afterwards place in a preservative containing a bactericide and sugar.

Chrysanthemum parthenium L. (=*Tanacetum parthenium*)   family: Asteraceae

moederkruid (Dutch); *grande camomille* (French); *Mutterkraut* (German); *partenio* (Italian); *matricaria* (Spanish)

Cirsium japonicum
thistle • Japanese thistle • tiger thistle

Cirsium japonicum mixed colours

DESCRIPTION A biennial or perennial of 0.6 m (2') high with spiny flower heads of 50 mm (2") in diameter. A few cultivars are available but the colour range is fairly limited to shades of pink, red, lavender and purple. Well-known examples are 'Pink Beauty' (pale pink) and 'Rose Beauty' (carmine).

ORIGIN & HISTORY Japan. About 20 species of thistle are occasionally cultivated, including the bull thistle (*C. vulgare*). Some have edible stems and roots and others have become troublesome weeds. Although thistles are a pleasant alternative to the everyday fillers used by florists, they are not readily grown or bred for the cut flower industry.

PARTS USED Flower heads are used as cut flowers.

CULTIVATION Germination of seed is erratic, so most growers purchase plugs from suppliers or first produce seedlings themselves and do not sow seed direct. Production lasts about 2–3 years, but after every 2 years plants can be lifted, divided and replanted to rejuvenate them.

PROPERTIES Vase life is poor to slightly below average (3–6 days). The prickly leaves can result in irritation if handled without gloves.

QUALITY CRITERIA Select fully opened flower heads but make sure that they have not started to fade. Heads harvested and sold too closed will not open well or last well. Most flowers are field-grown so check to make sure that leaves and flower heads are free of marks, damage and disease. Select sturdy stems, with well-formed flower heads showing bright colour. Make sure leaves have a uniform green colour.

CARE & HANDLING Recut and place in water with a general all-purpose preservative. Remove leaves below the water line. Flowers should not be stored, but if necessary can be held temporarily at 3–5°C (37–41°F). Flower heads can be dried by hanging them upside down in a well-ventilated area. Drying flower heads will sometimes shatter.

Cirsium japonicum DC.   family: Asteraceae

vederdistel (Dutch); *cirse du Japon* (French); *Japanische Kratzdistel* (German); *no-azami* (Japanese)

Clarkia amoena

godetia • satin flower

Clarkia amoena 'Grace Zartrosa mit Lachsschein'   *Clarkia amoena* pink

DESCRIPTION An annual herb of up to 1 m (about 3') high and wide with large, funnel-shaped flowers. All commercial cultivars are derived from *C. amoena* and *C. unguiculata* (=*C. elegans*). Cultivars can be broadly grouped into single- and double-flowered types. Many colours and bicolours are available, in shades of lavender, red, pink or white.

ORIGIN & HISTORY California (United States). *Godetia* nowadays comprises a subgenus of *Clarkia*. It was named after Captain William Clark (1770–1838). Godetia has been transformed from a unique and uncommon garden plant into a well-known florist flower.

PARTS USED Flowers are used as cut flowers and whole plants as potted flowers.

CULTIVATION Godetias require much less feeding than most other florist flowers. If over-fed, the flower stems become soft and crooked. They perform best under cool growing conditions and as temperatures rise, stem length and quality decreases.

PROPERTIES Vase life is sometimes slightly poor but generally good (5–10 days). Individual flowers may last only 5–6 days but buds continually open. The flowers are ethylene sensitive.

QUALITY CRITERIA Select sturdy, straight cut stems with 3–6 open flowers. Do not purchase stems with all the flowers still in bud stage, as not all of them will open properly.

CARE & HANDLING Remove all foliage that will be below the water line. Hydrate in a solution of warm water and commercial floral preservative for 2 hours before display or usage. Use a preservative with an anti-ethylene agent, but no sugar (it causes leaf burn). There is no need to cut stems under water if properly treated. Storage is not recommended. Cold temperatures can cause godetia blossoms to turn bluish or transparent. Display potted flowers in a bright but cool area. Keep medium moist. Flowers can be dried. Strip foliage and hang upside down in a warm, dark, well-ventilated area.

Clarkia amoena (Lehm.) A. Nelson & MacBryde (=*C. grandiflora*)   family: Onagraceae

zomerazalea (Dutch); *clarkia* (French); *Atlasblume* (German); *flor de setim, godetia* (Italian); *godetia* (Spanish)

Clivia miniata

clivia • bush lily • flame lily

Clivia miniata orange

Clivia miniata yellow

DESCRIPTION An evergreen plant with fleshy, strap-like leaves and thick, fleshy roots growing from short rhizomes. Umbels of trumpet-shaped flowers appear mainly in spring. The flowers are normally bright orange, but modern cultivars are available in a range of red, orange and yellow colours. Cultivars with variegated leaves are continuously being developed, especially in Japan and China. *C. miniata* is the showiest of the six known species and is most often found in gardens and florists.

ORIGIN & HISTORY South Africa. Clivia is an old favourite garden plant in warm parts of the world and a popular houseplant in cold regions. New cultivars have become fashionable in recent years.

PARTS USED Whole plants are used as potted flowers.

CULTIVATION Plants like bright early morning and late afternoon sunlight, but shade during the heat of the day. During their active growing season in spring to autumn (fall),

day/night temperatures need to be kept above 10/21°C (50/70°F).

PROPERTIES Flowering lasts 4–6 weeks. With or without flowers, clivias are very showy and can survive for many years. The flowers have no fragrance.

QUALITY CRITERIA Select plants with dark green, shiny leaves. Make sure flowers and leaves are free of damage or marks. Look for plants with sturdy flowering stems and compact flower heads, with at least 10 flowers. Flowers should only be about 50% open.

CARE & HANDLING Display in good light but avoid direct sunlight. Keep potting medium moist at all times. Do not mist, although leaves can be occasionally sponged to remove dust. Remove old flowering stalks by cutting them back as low as possible. Temperature: minimum (10°C; 50°F). Avoid warm winter temperatures. Clivias require careful watering for regular blooming. Water moderately from spring to autumn, but sparingly in winter (when it is usually dormant and not flowering).

Clivia miniata (Lindl.) Bosse

family: Amaryllidaceae

clivia (Dutch, French, Italian, Spanish); *Zimmer-Clivie, Riemenblatt* (German)

Cocos nucifera

coconut palm

Leaves before and after unfolding

Young leaves

DESCRIPTION The plant is a large palm of up to 30 m (100') high with a slender, curving and often basally swollen trunk. Several dwarf forms of about 8 m (27') high have been developed. Leaves are about 6 m (20') long and pinnate, with numerous single-folded segments arranged in a flat plane. The fruit is the familiar coconut that contains a solid white endosperm with liquid (coconut milk) in the centre. Several cultivars have been developed, with emphasis on a dwarf growth form. These include 'Dwarf Golden Malay', 'Dwarf Green', 'Dwarf Samoan' and 'Niño'.

ORIGIN & HISTORY Asia (West Pacific region or Indian Ocean Islands). Coconut palms have been widely cultivated since ancient times in all tropical regions of the world.

PARTS USED The young fronds before they unfold are used as florist greens.

CULTIVATION Coconut palms are easily propagated from seeds and are widely cultivated in all tropical regions of the world. Large scale, commercial cultivation is mainly for the fruits and seldom specifically for harvesting as florist greens.

PROPERTIES The pleated young leaves or the stripped buds of variegated forms (known as "coco strips") are used in arrangements and decorative work.

QUALITY CRITERIA Leaves should be a healthy green colour and not pale or yellowish. Make sure that selected leaves show no signs of brown margins or blemishes. Choose young leaves that are still quite tightly folded and have not opened too much.

CARE & HANDLING Place the leaves in clean water with a bactericide, after recutting. Alternatively, the leaves can be loosely wrapped in plastic and kept in a cool place 5°C (41°F) and high humidity. If unpacked and displayed at room temperature, then regular misting is essential and the leaves should be used as soon as possible. Leaves may also be stored for 4–5 days at 2–4°C (36–39°F) and a relative humidity of 95%.

Cocos nucifera L.   family: Arecaceae (Palmae)

kokospalm (Dutch); cocotier (French); Kokospalme (German); palma del cocco (Italian); koko yashi (Japanese); cocotero (Spanish)

Codiaeum variegatum

croton

Codiaeum variegatum leaves

Codiaeum variegatum (pots)

DESCRIPTION A shrub of up to 1.8 m (6′) high with simple to lobed and often brightly coloured leaves (variegated with white, yellow and red). The flowers are small and white. The cultivated forms of croton are derived from *C. variegatum* var. *pictum*. There are numerous named cultivars, including 'Excellent' (green, yellow and red), 'Evening Embers' (bluish black, green and red) and 'Sunrise' (green and orange-red).

ORIGIN & HISTORY Asia (Moluccas). People of the western Pacific region have selected decorative forms for ornamental plants over a long period. In 19th century Europe, crotons were very fashionable as houseplants.

PARTS USED The leaves are used as cut foliage, or the whole plant as a pot plant.

CULTIVATION Crotons require warm, humid conditions if they are to grow well and produce high quality leaves. They are sensitive to frost and plants will eventually die if kept at temperatures below 8°C (46°F). Cultivating them outside of controlled greenhouses or the tropics is difficult and quality is usually inferior.

PROPERTIES Cut leaves last well (10–14 days). They are not sensitive to ethylene. The milky sap that exudes from cut foliage can cause skin irritation in some people.

QUALITY CRITERIA Look for mature cut leaves that have vibrant colours. Make sure leaves are free of physical damage, burnt tips or edges. Select pot plants that are mature, well established and have good quality and coloured leaves.

CARE & HANDLING Cut leaves are usually short, but still recut and place in water containing a bactericide. Cut leaves can be stored in moisture-retentive boxes for 7–10 days at 2–4°C (36–39°F). Display pots in bright light, but not in direct sunlight or cold draught. The better the light, the brighter the foliage colours will be. Water regularly and do not allow potting soil (medium) to dry out.

Codiaeum variegatum (L.) Blume (=*Croton pictum*)   family: Euphorbiaceae

croton (Dutch); *croton* (French); *Wunderstrauch, Kroton* (German); *croton* (Italian); *croton* (Spanish)

Consolida ajacis
larkspur • rocket larkspur

Consolida ajacis 'Red Caroline'

Consolida ajacis white

DESCRIPTION An annual herb with deeply dissected leaves and erect clusters of usually bright blue but sometimes pink or white flowers. *Consolida* is closely related to *Delphinium* (perennial) but has the upper two petals fused. Most florist larkspur cultivars are derived from *Consolida ajacis*, *C. hispanica* (=*C. orientalis*) and occasionally *C. regalis*. The differences between the species are slight. There are a fair number of cultivars and hybrids, offering a wide range of colours.

ORIGIN & HISTORY Western Mediterranean to Central Asia. Flowers were used to decorate mummies in ancient Egypt. *Consolida* has long been considered to be merely an annual delphinium and therefore included in the genus *Delphinium*.

PARTS USED The flowering stems are used as cut flowers.

CULTIVATION Larkspurs require a period of cold for development and flower initiation. Growth and flowering are reduced at temperatures above 21°C

(70°F). Flower production under long days (>16 hours) results in higher yields and longer stems.

PROPERTIES Vase life can be poor to slightly above average (5–8 days). Flowers are very sensitive to ethylene.

QUALITY CRITERIA Select stems with up to 30% of the flowers open. Only purchase flowers pre-treated with STS or some other anti-ethylene agent. Make sure flowers are free of damage and disease as many are field-grown.

CARE & HANDLING Recut the stems and place them in a preservative with a sugar and anti-ethylene agent. Also make sure the preservative contains a bactericide as flowers cause water to deteriorate quickly, resulting in slimy stems. Keep the stems upright or else they well bend towards the light (geotropic response). The flowers can be stored upright for 1–2 days at 3–5°C (37–41°F). They are excellent for drying. Quick drying is best for retaining colour. Foliage does not need to be removed and flowers can be air-dried or dried with silica gel or other desiccants.

Consolida ajacis (L.) Schur. (=*C. ambigua*)   family: Ranunculaceae

ridderspoor (Dutch); *dauphinelle, pied d' alouette* (French); *Garten-Rittersporn* (German); *speronella* (Italian); *delfinio* (Spanish)

Convallaria majalis
lily-of-the-valley • Jacob's ladder

Convallaria majalis

DESCRIPTION A perennial herb with spreading fleshy rhizomes bearing numerous broad, hairless leaves. The small, white, bell-shaped and fragrant flowers are followed by small, red, fleshy fruits. Very few cultivars or hybrids are available. The pure species and one or two similar cultivars are grown for the florist industry and are still the most popular. Colours are limited to white and pink, with single and double flowering forms available.

ORIGIN & HISTORY Temperate regions of Europe and Asia (naturalised in North America). The plant is a traditional heart stimulant. It is an old favourite garden perennial that has become increasingly popular as a cut flower, especially for wedding bouquets.

PARTS USED Leaves and flowers are used as cut flowers, while whole plants are used as potted flowers.

CULTIVATION Lily-of-the-valley needs cool conditions to grow well and produce high quality flowers. Growing temperatures need to be kept in the region of 18–22°C (64–72°F). Cut flowers and potted flowers are produced in greenhouses, but flowers can also be grown outdoors under partial shade. Plants also need loose, well-drained soils – heavy soils that tend to become waterlogged will lead to diseases and rotting of the rhizomes.

PROPERTIES Vase life is poor (3–6 days). Flowers have a pleasant fragrance. They are ethylene sensitive. Warning: all parts of the plant are very poisonous.

QUALITY CRITERIA Select stems with 3–4 of the basal flowers open. Check to make sure that flowers are not browning or dried out. Ensure that the foliage has a uniform green colour, with no brown or dead tips.

CARE & HANDLING Recut and place in a preservative containing an ethylene agent. Flowers are prone to wilting if exposed to heat or if there is a lack of adequate ventilation. Flowers are suitable for drying. Hang upside down in small bunches in a cool, airy place.

Convallaria majalis L.   family: Asparagaceae (Convallariaceae)

lelietjes der dalen (Dutch); *muguet de mai* (French); *Maiglöckchen* (German); *mughetto* (Italian); *muguete* (Spanish)

Cordyline terminalis

ti leaves

Cordyline terminalis (ti leaves)

Cordyline australis 'Red Sensation'

DESCRIPTION A shrub of up to 4 m high with erect, sparsely branched stems bearing attractive, narrowly lance-shaped leaves. Small white flowers are borne in branched clusters. The colourful leaves are 0.3–0.6 m (1-2′) long and 50–125 mm (2–5″) wide. There are many new cultivars with colourful leaves – solid green or various shades of yellow, bronze, red and pink. The so-called New Zealand cabbage tree (*C. australis*) is a popular garden plant but also used as a source of foliage.

ORIGIN & HISTORY East Asia, Australia, New Zealand, Polynesia and Hawaii. Ti leaves have numerous traditional uses, not only in medicine and magic, but also in everyday life (clothing and wrapping of food). The roots are edible. Plants are commonly grown outdoors (often in pots) and have in recent years become an important source of florist foliage.

PARTS USED Leaves are used as cut foliage.

CULTIVATION Propagation is usually from cuttings and by division. Plants prefer to be cultivated in rich soils and under warm temperatures and high humidity conditions.

PROPERTIES Vase life is sometimes average but most often good (7–14 days), depending on the age of the leaves when purchased. Leaves can be curled, tied or stapled into many interesting shapes and bows in design work.

QUALITY CRITERIA Select fully mature leaves. Make sure that leaves are unblemished and are free of browning on the tips or edges. Also see that there is no yellowing (a sign of poor quality). Leaves must have vivid colours and be clean.

CARE & HANDLING Recut the stems or leaf bases and place them in a suitable preservative containing a bactericide. Preferably use the foliage as soon as possible. However, leaves can be stored in moisture retentive boxes at 7–10°C (45–50°F) for 14 days, or in water at 2–4°C (36–39°F) and 90–95% relative humidity. Wipe leaves clean prior to use. Leaves do not dry well.

Cordyline terminalis (L.) Kunth (=*C. fruticosa*)   family: Asparagaceae (Agavaceae, Dracaenaceae)

ti-plant (Dutch); *cordyline* (French); *Keulenlilie, Kolbenbaum* (German); *caña de indio* (Spanish)

Coreopsis grandiflora
tickseed

Coreopsis grandiflora 'Sunfire'

Coreopsis grandiflora 'Early Sunrise'

Coreopsis grandiflora 'Sunray'

DESCRIPTION An erect annual or short-lived perennial of 0.6 m (2′) high with irregularly divided leaves and large yellow flower heads of up to 120 mm (nearly 5″) in diameter (usually with 8 yellow ray florets and numerous orange disc florets). There are many cultivars, such as 'Badengold' (single) and 'Early Sunrise' (semi-double).

ORIGIN & HISTORY Central and south-eastern United States. Several species of *Coreopsis* have become popular garden plants.

PARTS USED Fresh flower heads are used as cut flowers or filler for bouquets.

CULTIVATION Nearly all commercial production is in open fields. Plants require approximately 3 weeks of long days to initiate flowering after which photoperiod (day length) is unimportant. Plants are productive for 3–5 years and are usually lifted and separated after 2–3 years. Flowering is mostly during the summer months. Most cultivars benefit from being planted in early autumn (fall) and are less productive in their first year. However, a few cultivars flower well in their first year if planted in the early spring.

PROPERTIES Vase life is below average to average (5–10 days), with some cultivars lasting much longer. Botrytis and mildew can sometimes be a problem. Flower heads are not sensitive to ethylene.

QUALITY CRITERIA Select sturdy, straight stems with most of the flower heads 75% to fully open. Check to ensure that they are free of damage and disease. Although leaves are not that aesthetically important, still check to make sure those present are healthy and bright green, as this is often an indication of overall flower quality and vase life.

CARE & HANDLING Use a general preservative with a bactericide to keep the water clean, but not with an anti-ethylene agent. Storage is not recommended, but if necessary only store for 1–2 days at a temperature of 2–5°C (36–41°F) and a relative humidity of 90–95%.

Coreopsis grandiflora T. Hogg ex Sweet   family: Asteraceae

meisjesogen (Dutch); *coréopsis à grandes fleurs* (French); *Großblumiges Mädchenauge* (German); *coreopsis* (Italian)

Cornus alba

dogwood • Siberian dogwood

Cornus alba flowers

DESCRIPTION A suckering shrub of about 3 m (10′) high with branches that turn bright red during autumn and winter. The leaves are bright green above and greyish below. There are many cultivated species and several cultivars. The best-known cultivar of *C. alba* is 'Sibirica'(= 'Splendens'), a plant with bright red stems. The eastern flowering dogwood (*C. florida*) is a source of cut flowers (small flowers but large, colourful bracts).

ORIGIN & HISTORY Central and eastern Asia (*C. alba*) or eastern North America (*C. florida*). Stems were once used as "dogs" (skewers), hence the name dogwood.

PARTS USED Leafless (bare) stems are used as fillers. Flowering stems are used as cut flowers.

CULTIVATION Plants are grown from seed or cuttings. Stems, especially the standard bare stems, are harvested only in winter when they have a bright red or yellow colour. A period of cold is required to bring out the colouration in the stems for which they are sought. A large portion of harvesting is done in the wild and product availability is usually localised and sporadic.

PROPERTIES Vase life of bare stems is very good (2–3 months), during which time colour may fade. Vase life of flowers is poor to average (5–7 days).

QUALITY CRITERIA Purchase long, straight stems that are still young and flexible. Selected stems should have a clean, bright colouration. Flowering stems should also be straight and with flowers starting to open to 50% open. Make sure flowers and buds have not been broken off.

CARE & HANDLING Recut the stems by 50–100 mm (2–4″). Place bare, woody stems in clean water with only a bactericide. Flowering stems should be placed in a floral preservative which also contains a low sugar concentrate. Bare stems need not be stored. Flowering stems should be used as soon as possible or held in a cooler at 4–5°C (39–41°F) and 90–95% relative humidity.

Cornus alba L.   family: Cornaceae

witte kornoelje (Dutch); *cornouiller blanc* (French); *Tatarischer Hartriegel* (German); *cornolio albo* (Italian); *cornejo* (Spanish)

Cortaderia selloana

pampas grass

Cortaderia selloana White

Cortaderia selloana 'Rosea'

DESCRIPTION A large grass forming a rounded tuft of up to 3 m (10') in height. The slender leaves have razor-sharp edges that can cause nasty cuts. Although the distinctive flowering plumes are usually white, they are also available in a light pink colour (the cultivar 'Rosea'). *Cortaderia jubata* is sometimes also used.

ORIGIN & HISTORY South America (Argentina, Brazil, Uruguay). It is a popular garden ornamental grass (often a feature on lawns) that has become naturalised and invasive in Spain, France and South Africa. Florists regularly use the large, decorative and fluffy plumes in fresh and dried arrangements and decorative work.

PARTS USED The long flowering stems are used as fillers and accents, especially in large arrangements.

CULTIVATION Propagation is by means of seed or division. Plants grow fast and although fairly adaptable to various conditions, do best in full sun and deep, well-drained soils.

Flowering occurs naturally in late summer and autumn (fall).

PROPERTIES Flowering stems are long-lasting and remain attractive as they age and dry, keeping their shape and colour (sometimes browning). Fluff from plumes comes loose easily (especially when dry) and can cause allergic reactions. The flowers are not sensitive to ethylene.

QUALITY CRITERIA There is no general quality standard for pampas grass. Look for long, straight, sturdy stems with full, well-developed plumes. Select size and thickness of stems as required. Stems that are too large usually need to be supported in arrangements and often cause space problems when used in vases with other flowers.

CARE & HANDLING Store or display the plumes dry, in a cool, ventilated area. There is no need to cut the stems or to use preservatives or water. Plumes can be sprayed with a glue or other fixative to prevent shattering. Flowering stems dry very well, but the plumes eventually start to fall apart. Simply stand them up straight to air-dry in a cool, well-ventilated area.

Cortaderia selloana (Schult. & Schult. f.) Asch. & Graebn. (=*Gynerium argenteum*)   family: Poaceae

pampasgras (Dutch); *herbe de la pampa* (French); *Pampasgras* (German); *carrizo de las pampas* (Spanish)

Corylus avellana

corkscrew hazel • hazel • cob

Corylus avellana leaves

Corylus avellana tree

Corylus avellana stems

DESCRIPTION The plant is usually a multistemmed shrub of about 6 m (20′) high. It has rounded, hairy and toothed leaves. The flowers and fruits are borne in small clusters surrounded by toothed bracts. The ripe fruits are the familiar hazel nuts. Several cultivars are known, including 'Aurea' (with yellow-green leaves) and 'Contorta' (also known as corkscrew hazel or Harry Lauder's walking stick) which has remarkably twisted branches that make it popular as florist filler.

ORIGIN & HISTORY Europe and Asia. Corkscrew hazel is a mutant that originated in Frocester, England in 1863. Hazel is a traditional food item in Europe and is also important in European mythology. The stems, for example, are traditionally used as water-divining rods. *Corylus* is the Greek name for a hazel bush.

PARTS USED The long catkins on bare branches are used as fillers. Branches with flowers still in bud are also used as fillers.

CULTIVATION Propagation is mostly from seed or rooted cuttings. A period of cold is required in winter. Hazel nuts do well in most soil types. The production of high quality cut flowers and fillers requires regular irrigation and pest control.

PROPERTIES Plants are either male or female. Stems last very long but the vase life of catkins is average (7–8 days). They are not ethylene sensitive.

QUALITY CRITERIA Look for well-branched stems full of buds or catkins. Make sure that the catkins are of good size and are free of disease and damage. Do not purchase any stems with catkins showing pollen.

CARE & HANDLING Recut the stems by a fair amount (50–100 mm; 2–4″) and place them in clean water with a bactericide. There is no need to use a preservative. Display or hold stems in a cool, well-ventilated area, but not in a direct draught. Use promptly as pollen can develop. Long storage is not recommended – store for a few days in water at 2–3°C (36–38°F).

Corylus avellana L.   family: Betulaceae

hazelaar (Dutch); *coudrier, noisetier tortueux* (French); *Gewöhnliche Hasel, Haselnuss* (German); *nocciola* (Italian); *heezeru nattsu* (Japanese); *avellana* (Spanish)

Cosmos bipinnatus
cosmos • garden cosmos • cosmea

Cosmos bipinnatus mixed

Cosmos bipinnatus 'Purity Superior'

Cosmos sulphureus

DESCRIPTION An erect, annual herb (up to 2 m or 6½') with finely divided, feathery leaves and striking pink, white or purplish red flower heads (they look like single dahlias). Many hybrids, cultivars and seed races are available, including single and semi-double forms in a wide range of colours. *Cosmos sulphureus* (sulphur cosmos) is sometimes seen in florists, but its short growth form makes it much more suitable as a bedding plant.

ORIGIN & HISTORY Mexico and southern United States. Although better known as a garden flower, cosmos is seasonally seen in florists. The plant is naturalised in Madagascar and South Africa and can be seen along roadsides at the start of autumn (fall). The flower has a poor vase life once picked, which negatively affects its use as a florist flower, especially if transport over long distances is involved.

PARTS USED The stems with flower heads are used as cut flowers.

CULTIVATION Cosmos is known as a quantitative short-day plant – although it flowers more rapidly under short days, it eventually flowers regardless of day length. Flowers grow best at temperatures above 15°C (60°F) and flowering and growth are inhibited at temperatures below 13°C (55°F). Cosmos is propagated from seed and cultivated in greenhouses and in open fields. Support netting is necessary, especially in open fields if grown in a windy climate.

PROPERTIES Vase life is poor (4–6 days). It is not sensitive to ethylene.

QUALITY CRITERIA Purchase flower heads that are still in bud but showing full colour (they will open). If purchased when fully open, vase life is already half spent.

CARE & HANDLING Recut stems and hydrate immediately. Place in a preservative. Storage is not recommended, but if necessary only store for 2–3 days at a temperature of 2–4°C (36–39°F). The flower heads can be successfully dried using silica gel or borax.

Cosmos bipinnatus Cav.   family: Asteraceae

cosmos (Dutch, French, Italian, Spanish); *Fiederblättriges Schmuckkörbchen, Kosmee* (German)

Cotinus coggygria

smoke tree • smokebush • wig tree • Venetian sumach

Cotinus coggygria

DESCRIPTION The plant is a shrub of 3 m (10') or more with simple, rounded leaves that are typically red or purple-coloured in spring and autumn (fall). Sterile parts of the inflorescences elongate and become hair-like, giving a distinctive (smoky) appearance to the flowering branches. Several cultivars are available, including the popular 'Purpureus' (purple leaves and pink inflorescences) and 'Red Beauty' (purple to dark red).

ORIGIN & HISTORY Southern Europe to China. Smoke trees have become popular garden plants.

PARTS USED The leafy, branched stems are used as florist greens in pedestals, arrangements and hand-ties.

CULTIVATION Trees are propagated from seed or cuttings. If cultivated specifically for florist greens, then trees are regularly cut back and kept short to force plants to produce numerous young and well-branched stems. Smoke tree is quite localised in its availability.

PROPERTIES Cut stems have a good vase life of 10–14 days. They are available in various shades of dark brown and/or red. The leaves and hairy flowers have no distinctive fragrance.

QUALITY CRITERIA Look for well-branched stems that are long and straight. Choose younger stems that are not too woody and make sure that leaves are fresh, evenly spaced on stems and are brightly coloured. Pay special attention to young leaves and stem tips and make sure they have not dried out. Leaves need to be free of physical damage.

CARE & HANDLING Recut stems and place in clean water with a bactericide and a surfactant to help with water uptake. There is no need to use a full preservative but it will do no harm. Remove leaves that are below the water line. Display stems in a cool area, but out of direct draughts. Stems can be stored for 7 days at 2–4°C (36–39°F) and a high relative humidity (90–95%). They are not suitable for air-drying.

Cotinus coggygria Scop.   family: Anacardiaceae

pruikenboom (Dutch); *arbre à perruque* (French); *Europäischer Perückenstrauch* (German); *sommacco selvatico* (Italian); *árbol de las pelucas* (Spanish)

Craspedia globosa

drumsticks

Craspedia globosa stems

Craspedia globosa flower heads

DESCRIPTION A perennial herb of up to 1.5 m (5′) high with white-woolly leaves and stems. The 4–6 small yellow flower heads are grouped together into characteristic globose, ball-shaped clusters (up to 25 mm or 1″) in diameter. These are borne on slender, unbranched stems (hence the highly descriptive name "drumsticks"). Billy buttons or bachelor's buttons (*C. uniflora*) is a closely related species with larger flower clusters (38 mm or 1½″), each with more (5–10) flower heads. Some botanists consider *Pycnosorus* to be the correct genus for *Craspedia* species.

ORIGIN & HISTORY Australia (*C. globosa*) or Australia, Tasmania and New Zealand (*C. uniflora*). Eight closely similar species are cultivated as ornamentals.

PARTS USED The leafless stem with its globose cluster of flower heads is used as cut flower or filler.

CULTIVATION *Craspedia* species are mainly grown from seed. They prefer well-drained soil but are not drought tolerant. Plants do well in full sun provided that temperatures are not excessively hot. High humidity usually results in disease problems.

PROPERTIES Vase life is good (8–14 days). The flower heads have no distinctive or sweet fragrance. They are not sensitive to ethylene.

QUALITY CRITERIA Look for straight, sturdy stems with proportionally large, well-formed flower clusters. Make they are free of damage and black marks and that the colour is vivid. Check stems and leaves for signs of disease.

CARE & HANDLING Rinse the stems in plain water to remove any dirt. Recut and place in a floral preservative with a bactericide. Handle with care as the stems can buckle and break, even though they are generally strong and wiry. First allow the flower heads to stand in preservative at room temperature for 1–2 hours before storing. Flower heads can be stored for 4–7 days at 1–4°C (34–39°F). They are excellent for drying – hang small, loose bunches upside down in a well-ventilated area.

Craspedia globosa Benth.   family: Asteraceae

gele ballen (Dutch); *baguette de tambour* (French); *Trommelschlägel* (German)

Crinum japonicum

Japanese crinum

Crinum japonicum

Crinum japonicum

DESCRIPTION The plant is a true bulb with channelled, strap-shaped leaves and an apical cluster of trumpet-shaped flowers, borne on a long, smooth flowering stalk. Stems can be up to 1 m (40") tall. Flower colour in *C. japonicum* is limited to white. Several species and cultivars are available (evergreen or deciduous, short or tall flower stalks and winter or summer flowering). *C. bulbispermum* is one of the more showy species and has pink and whitish flowers.

ORIGIN & HISTORY Japan (*C. japonicum*). The species is usually considered to be merely a variety of *C. asiaticum*. There are approximately 120 species, mainly from the warm to temperate regions of the Americas, Europe (Caucasia) and Africa. At least 45 species are cultivated for their attractive lily-like flowers.

PARTS USED The leafless flowering stalk is used as a cut flower.

CULTIVATION The plants are usually grown from bulbs and are popular in certain regions as garden plants. Bulbs are not always available or suitable for commercial production because they need to be very large in order to flower successfully. Like many bulbous plants, crinums prefer well-drained, slightly acidic soils and good light, but moderate temperatures.

PROPERTIES Vase life is average to good (8–12 days) with new flowers opening all the time. Flowers are sensitive to ethylene.

QUALITY CRITERIA Select tall, sturdy stems with a tight cluster of buds. Choose stems with a few swollen buds showing good colour, but still closed or at most only 1–2 flowers open or opening. Make sure that the flowering stalk is a good uniform green colour and has no soft spots or damage, where it could buckle.

CARE & HANDLING Recut stems by at least 50–100 mm (2–4") and place in a floral preservative. Support stems so that they do not fall out of buckets and get damaged. Remove any dead flowers. Stems can be stored for 4–5 days at 2–4°C (36–39°F) and a high relative humidity (90–95%).

Crinum japonicum (Bak.) Hannibal (=*C. asiaticum* var. *japonicum*) family: Amaryllidaceae

haaklelie (Dutch); *crinum* (French); *Hakenlilie* (German); *hamayu, hama yū* (Japanese)

Crocosmia crocosmiiflora

montbretia

Crocosmia ×crocosmiiflora flower

Crocosmia ×crocosmiiflora stems

Crocosmia aurea

DESCRIPTION A deciduous, summer flowering corm plant with strap-shaped leaves arranged in a flat fan. The star-shaped flowers are typically reddish, orange or yellow. *C. ×crocosmiiflora* is the best-known hybrid amongst florists. It is a cross between *C. aurea* (with beautiful flowers) and *C. pottsii* (with vigorous growth). Several species, hybrids and cultivars are available.

ORIGIN & HISTORY South Africa (all 7–9 species). *C. ×crocosmiiflora* was developed in France in 1880. Montbretia has become naturalised in many parts of the world, most notably in the south-west of Ireland. *Crocosmia* species are sometimes called "falling stars" – a very appropriate name when considering the bright orange flowers that seem to be falling from the arching stems.

PARTS USED Flowering stems are used as cut flowers.

CULTIVATION A single flowering stem is produced per corm per season. After flowering, the mature corm produces several new corms. These often do not flower (or give blind stems) in their first year and will only produce high quality flowers in their second year of cultivation.

PROPERTIES Vase life is average to good (7–14 days). Flowers open from the bottom upwards. They are sensitive to ethylene.

QUALITY CRITERIA Select cut stems with 1–2 flowers open. Stems with all the flowers closed can still be purchased, but the buds must show colour and they must be treated with a preservative to assist in flower opening. Petals bruise easily, so check for damage. For pods (berries), select stems with ripe fruit, bright colour and free of damage.

CARE & HANDLING Recut and place the stems in a suitable preservative solution. Flowering stems and fruiting stems should be handled similarly. Flower buds and fruits are quite fragile, so handle them with care. Store the flowers for 3–5 days at 1–2°C (34–36°F) but only if necessary. Montbretia is suitable for drying – air-dry with good ventilation to retain colour.

Crocosmia ×crocosmiiflora (Burb. & Dean) N.E. Br.   family: Iridaceae

montbretia (Dutch, French, Italian, Spanish); *Garten-Montbretie* (German)

Crocus vernus

crocus • Dutch crocus

Crocus vernus plants

Crocus vernus flowers

DESCRIPTION A corm plant with a single, stalkless flower of up to 150 mm (6") long, emerging from below the ground. The flower is funnel-shaped, with a narrow tube broadening into six lobes arranged in two overlapping whorls. There are three stamens and the orange-coloured style is divided into three branches. Many cultivars are available, with a range of vivid, clean colours, including white, lilac, mauve and purple. The distinctive darker-coloured veination patterns on the flowers often add to their decorative value.

ORIGIN & HISTORY Central and southern Europe (*C. vernus*). The 80 species originate from Central and South Europe, North Africa, the Middle East and Central Asia. The stigmas of *C. sativus* have been harvested since ancient times for saffron. There are numerous cultivated ornamentals, including winter- and autumn-flowering species.

PARTS USED The whole plant is used as a potted flower. Flowers are rarely used as cut flowers because the stems are usually too short.

CULTIVATION The modern Dutch cultivars that dominate the florist industry require cold, wet winter conditions and cool, moist summer conditions to grow well and produce good quality flowers. They are therefore seldom, if ever, cultivated in the tropical and warmer areas of the world.

PROPERTIES Vase life of the flowers is average to good (6–10 days). Flowers have a very pleasant fragrance. They are sensitive to ethylene.

QUALITY CRITERIA Select plants with buds still closed, but showing good colour. Check that leaves have a healthy green colour and are not blotchy, yellowish or that leaf tips or edges are not discoloured or burnt.

CARE & HANDLING Flowers can be stored in moisture-retentive boxes, or in plastic bags, at 1–2°C (34–36°F) for 1–2 weeks. Display potted flowers in a bright, cool area (13–18°C; 55–64°F), but not in a draught. Keep potting medium or soil moist. Do not pour water directly onto the plant as this can promote decay and shorten the overall vase life.

Crocus vernus (L.) Hill   family: Iridaceae

krokus (Dutch); *crocus* (French); *Frühlings-Krokus, Holländischer Krokus* (German); *croco* (Italian); *crocus* (Spanish)

153

Cucurbita pepo
ornamental gourd

Cucurbita pepo fruits

Cucurbita pepo fruits

DESCRIPTION A leafy and bristly annual plant with large, shield-shaped, markedly lobed leaves arising from an erect or trailing stem. Male and female flowers occur on the same plant. They are large, yellow and trumpet-shaped. Cultivars are of three basic types: edible pumpkin (round or flat), vegetable marrow or zucchini (oblong) and summer squashes (variously shaped and including ornamental types). Ornamental summer squashes are available in a remarkable range of shapes and colour forms.

ORIGIN & HISTORY Mexico and Central America. It is one of the world's most ancient crop plants. Ornamental gourds have become popular in recent years and are used as decorations in autumn (fall).

PARTS USED The dried, ornate fruit is used as a novelty in various ways by florists and retailers.

CULTIVATION Plants grow best in well-drained soils and warm, full sun conditions. Gourds are frost-sensitive annuals that prefer a slightly acidic

soil (pH 5.5–5.9). Plants need to be fed well until fruit is formed. They are usually planted outdoors in spring and harvested in summer and autumn. The fruits are normally dried outside in the full sun.

PROPERTIES Ornamental gourds are not edible. They are robust and durable with a very long shelf life. They typically do not have any fragrance and are not sensitive to ethylene.

QUALITY CRITERIA Inspect gourds for damage by insects that bore into them. Make sure that they are properly dried and not still soft or have soft spots. Check for general damage and select gourds with good, healthy colouration.

CARE & HANDLING There are no specific care or handling procedures for ornamental gourds. They should not be put in water or stored in a very humid place (including tightly closed boxes or plastic packaging). Simply store or display them dry. Hot or cold temperatures will not affect the lasting quality of the gourds.

Cucurbita pepo L.   family: Cucurbitaceae

sierkalebas (Dutch); *potiron, courgette* (French); *Gartenkürbis* (German); *zucca* (Italian); *pepo kabotcha* (Japanese); *calabaza comúne* (Spanish)

Curcuma petiolata

queen lily

Curcuma petiolata

Curcuma petiolata

DESCRIPTION A perennial herb of up to 0.6 m (2′) with large, long-stalked hairless leaves arising from a rhizome below the ground. The leafy stems each produce a spike of large, showy, concave or hooded green bracts that are usually tinted with violet (but white, pink, scarlet or orange in some cultivars). The small yellow flowers are rather inconspicuous. Other species and cultivars used as florist flowers include *C. alismatifolia* 'Gagnepain' (grown as a cut flower) and *C. parviflora* 'White Angel' or 'Siam Silver' (for pot plants).

ORIGIN & HISTORY Malaysia (*C. petiolata*). Some 40 species occur in forest habitats in southern Asia (Myanmar, Thailand and India). Turmeric (*C. longa*), Indian arrowroot (*C. angustifolia*), mango ginger (*C. amada*) and zedoary (*C. zedoaria*) are well-known examples of species that are used as commercial sources of spice.

PARTS USED Flowering stems are sometimes used as cut flowers but more often the whole plant is grown as an attractive and long-lasting potted flower.

CULTIVATION Plants are propagated from rhizomes. Each rhizome may produce three or more consecutive inflorescences. The rhizomes are stored dry for two to three months at 20–25°C before forcing (at 20/18°C, day/night). Plants reach the flowering stage in about 3 months. The post-production longevity is very good.

PROPERTIES Vase life of the flowering stems is good (12–14 days). The stems are generally a bit short for use as a cut flower – only 0.3–0.6 m (1–2′) long. Therefore the plant is more popular as potted flower than cut flower.

QUALITY CRITERIA Look for long, straight stems with well-coloured flower spikes. Bracts should still be tight with no actual flowers having emerged. Check that bract tips have not discoloured or dried out.

CARE & HANDLING Recut stems and place in a floral preservative. Display potted flowers in a bright area out of any cold draughts. Do not over-water, but keep potting medium moist.

Curcuma petiolata Roxb.   family: Zingiberaceae

curcuma (Dutch, French, Italian, Spanish,); *Curcuma* (German)

Cycas revoluta

cycas • sago cycas

Cycas revoluta tree

Cycas revoluta leaf

DESCRIPTION A palm-like cycad with a short, thick stem bearing a crown of slender pinnate leaves of about 0.9–1.5 m (3–5′) long. Each leaflet is narrowly linear, glossy green in colour and has a distinct, sunken midrib and rolled in margins. The distinctive cone scales (modified leaves) are densely hairy and leaf-like, with a row of seeds along the margins. There are several cultivars or clones, including dwarf, variegated and cristate forms. The normal green form is most commonly used as a source of cut foliage.

ORIGIN & HISTORY Southern Japan. Although the leaves are very popular amongst florists and flower retailers, the plant is mainly used in gardens and outdoor containers (rarely also as indoor pot plant).

PARTS USED The leaves resemble "palm fronds" and are used as cut greens, especially for large arrangements, baskets or bouquets.

CULTIVATION Plants are grown from seed or suckers (young plants arising from the base of the parent plant). Cycads grow relatively slowly and prefer well-drained soils and full sun conditions. They are often attacked by scale insects that may spoil the appearance of the leaves.

PROPERTIES Leaves are available in various sizes and lengths and have a very good vase life (2–4 months). Leaves are not as prickly, or difficult to work with, as many true palm leaves. They have no distinct fragrance and are not sensitive to ethylene.

QUALITY CRITERIA Select the desired size and length of frond but make sure that the colour is a vibrant, uniform dark green and not pale or yellowish. Especially check that the fronds are free of white, dry specks that can be present over the entire leaf surface.

CARE & HANDLING Unpack fronds (if in packaging or boxes) and display or hold in a dry, cool place. There is no need to recut stems or place in water with a preservative. The leaves do not dry well.

Cycas revoluta Thunb.   family: Zamiaceae

cycas (Dutch); *cycas du Japon* (French); *Japanischer Sagopalmfarn* (German); *palma a sagù* (Italian); *sotetsu* (Japanese); *cicas revoluta, palma sagú* (Spanish)

Cyclamen persicum
cyclamen • florist cyclamen • Persian violet

Cyclamen persicum plant

DESCRIPTION A tuberous perennial herb with a rosette of long-stalked leaves arising from a fleshy tuber at ground level. The solitary flowers are nodding and have five twisted and strongly reflexed petals. A multitude of hybrids and cultivars are used in the florist trade. The petals are ruffled or frilled and white to pink, purple, salmon or red. The foliage is attractive – from plain green to green with white or silver marbled or zoned patterns. Several other species are grown in gardens, including *C. coum*, *C. hederifolium* and *C. repandum*.

ORIGIN & HISTORY South-eastern Europe, Tunisia and the Aegean region (not Iran, despite the name "persicum"). Cyclamen is derived from the Greek *kyklos* (circular) and describes the form of the individual petals.

PARTS USED Whole plants are used as potted flowers.

CULTIVATION Cyclamens are relatively difficult to grow and have a long production time. Plants prefer bright light but cool temperatures. Growers normally provide light shade during the hottest times of the year.

PROPERTIES Plants and flowers are very poisonous so be cautious. The original wild forms had scented flowers but modern cultivars often have no noticeable scent. The flowers are ethylene sensitive.

QUALITY CRITERIA Select plants with at least 2–4 open flowers, but not fewer or too many more. Make sure the foliage is not yellowing or pale. Check that no leaves or flowers have dropped off (usually a sign of disease and/or poor cultivation practices). Purchase plants in paper sleeves (botrytis develops easier in plastic sleeves with their higher humidity and sometimes only shows a few days later).

CARE & HANDLING Display the pots in bright light but keep slightly shaded. Plants do not like any abrupt change to their environment. High temperatures will shorten the flowering period; draughts can result in leaf drop. Do not over-water and preferably use lime-free, tepid water. Regularly remove dead flowers and stalks.

Cyclamen persicum Mill.   family: Primulaceae

cyclaam (Dutch); *cyclamen, pain de pourceau* (French); *Zimmer-Alpenveilchen* (German); *ciclamino* (Italian); *ciclamen* (Spanish)

Cymbidium cultivars
cymbidium • cymbidium orchid

Cymbidium cultivar (yellow)

Cymbidium cultivar (brown)

DESCRIPTION Terrestrial or usually epiphytic orchids with fleshy pseudobulbs bearing tough, strap-shaped leaves. The flower spikes are upright to arching (or pendulous in epiphytic species) and bear only a few to over 20 flowers. The tens of thousands of cultivars are loosely grouped by their flower size: miniature (under 60 mm or 2½"); intermediate (60–90 mm or 2½–3½") and standard (over 90 mm or 3½"). Cymbidiums are available in all colours except blue.

ORIGIN & HISTORY Tropical Asia to Australia. Cymbidiums have been cultivated in China and Japan for centuries and now form the basis of a large industry in temperate regions.

PARTS USED Flowers: cut flowers; whole plants: potted flowers.

CULTIVATION Plants require warm temperatures, high light intensities and good humidity levels to produce strong growth and to flower well. Standard cultivars require a 6–8 week cold period (7–10°C; 45–50°F) to initiate

flowering. Miniatures can initiate flowering at higher temperatures (16°C; 60°F).

PROPERTIES Vase life of cut flowers is average to good (7–14 days). Vase life of potted flowers is very good (2–5 weeks). Cymbidiums have no scent and are sensitive to ethylene.

QUALITY CRITERIA Select spikes with fully opened blooms, but check that they are not showing any signs of ageing. Make sure none of the pollinia have been damaged, as pollinated flowers deteriorate quickly. Make sure petals do not have marks or bruises. Select potted flowers with 1–4 open flowers.

CARE & HANDLING On arrival check that flower vials are filled with water. Cut off stem ends that have turned black. Handle the flowers as little as possible to avoid bruising the petals. Store at a temperature of 10–13°C (50–55°F), as flowers are sensitive to lower temperatures. Avoid water on the petals as this can leave marks. Display potted flowers in a bright cool area, out of cold draughts. Keep the growth medium moist but do not overwater.

Cymbidium cultivars

family: Orchidaceae

cymbidium (Dutch, French, Italian, Spanish); *Kahnorchis* (German)

Cynara cardunculus
cardoon • wild artichoke

Cynara cardunculus blue

Cynara cardunculus purple

Cynara scolymus (ornamental artichoke)

DESCRIPTION An erect and spiny, thistle-like perennial herb of up to 1.2 m (4') high with large, pinnately compound leaves. The bright purple flower heads are about 60 mm (2½") in diameter and have sharp spines on the tips of the bracts. There are a few cultivars, including 'Porto Spineless' (blue with no spines) and 'Brittany Blue' (blue, edible). The closely related globe artichoke or French artichoke (*C. scolymus*) has large, edible flower heads. It can also be used as a florist flower.

ORIGIN & HISTORY Southern Europe. Cardoon is an old Victorian favourite, once grown as a leaf vegetable and considered to be an aphrodisiac. It is now a popular garden plant, florist flower or ornamental.

PARTS USED The grey-green leaves are used as cut foliage and the flower heads as a novelty or ornamental flower in arrangements.

CULTIVATION Plants are cultivated from suckers rather than seed. They prefer well-drained, rich soils, although they are fairly tolerable of most soil types. Full sun and moderate to warm growing conditions are also needed to produce high quality foliage and flower heads.

PROPERTIES Vase life is poor to average (5–8 days). Flower heads are not sensitive to ethylene.

QUALITY CRITERIA Select straight, sturdy stems with well-formed flower heads. Flower heads must be mature, with the spiny involucre bracts still closed but starting to open. Cut foliage must have a bright grey-green colour and not be pale or yellowish. Check that flower heads and foliage are free of any blemishes.

CARE & HANDLING Recut stems and place in clean water with a bactericide. Display in a cool, bright place, or hold in the cooler at 4°C (39°F) and a high relative humidity. Flower heads and foliage can be stored for 4–5 days at 1–2°C (34–36°F) and a high relative humidity (90–95%). Flower heads can be successfully dried.

Cynara cardunculus L.   family: Asteraceae

kardoen (Dutch); *cardon* (French); *Wilde Artischocke* (German); *cardo* (Italian); *kardo* (Spanish)

Cyperus papyrus

papyrus • Egyptian paper plant

Cyperus papyrus

Cyperus textilis

DESCRIPTION A tall sedge of up to 5 m (16′) high with bluntly triangular stems arising from fleshy rhizomes. The stem is topped with a compound umbel of 100–200 thin, wiry rays. True leaves are absent. The related *C. textilis* is a smaller plant with thin stems bearing rosettes of leaves at the tips. It is also used to some extent as a foliage and filler.

ORIGIN & HISTORY Tropical Africa and the lower Nile Valley. It is the source of papyrus (the original paper) in ancient Egypt, made by pressing and drying thin strips of stem pith laid side by side. Papyrus is one of several species of sedges that have become popular as garden plants.

PARTS USED Stems with grassy tufts are used as fillers.

CULTIVATION Plants grow very easily from divided rhizomes. They prefer rich soils and unlimited water. Plants do not mind becoming waterlogged and will actually do better in such conditions compared to drought conditions.

In many areas of the world, stems are wild-harvested along river banks or marshlands.

PROPERTIES Vase life is very good (21–28 days). Stems are not sensitive to ethylene and do not have any significant fragrance.

QUALITY CRITERIA Select mature, sturdy, straight stems with full heads ("brushes"). Make sure that the tufts have full, green colour, with no browning or other blemishes. The colour must not be pale or yellowing. Check that stems have no soft or damaged spots where they may buckle or break.

CARE & HANDLING Recut stems by at least 50–100 mm (2–4″) and place in clean water with a bactericide. There is no need to use a full preservative. Display in a cool, ventilated area out of any direct draughts. There is no reason to store stems as they already last very well. However, stems can be kept in the cooler along with other flowers at temperatures anywhere between 2–6°C (36–43°F) and a relative humidity of 90–95%.

Cyperus papyrus L.   family: Cyperaceae

papirus (Dutch); *souchet du Nil* (French); *Papyrus-Zypergras* (German); *papiro* (Italian); *papirusu* (Japanese); *papiro* (Spanish)

Cytisus scoparius

common broom • Scotch broom

Cytisus scoparius plant

Cytisus scoparius flowers and pods

DESCRIPTION A branched shrub of up to 2 m (6½') high. It has ridged stems, small trifoliolate leaves, usually bright yellow flowers and oblong, flat fruits that turn black when they mature. There are more than 80 hybrids and cultivars, differing in growth habit and flower colour. Hybrids mostly involve the white-flowered *C. multiflorus* and *C. ×dallimorei* (flowers partly purple). Examples of cultivars are 'Burkwoodii' (red and gold), 'Cornish Cream' (off-white), 'Donard Gem' (pink flushed red), 'Golden Sunlight' (yellow) and 'Windlesham Ruby' (ruby red).

ORIGIN & HISTORY Central, southern and eastern Europe. It has become a popular garden plant but also a noxious weed in parts of the world.

PARTS USED The long thin stems (either leafless or with leaves) are used as cut greens. Whole plants are popular as potted flowers.

CULTIVATION Grown mainly from seed, Scotch broom is very tolerant of a wide range of soil types. It grows aggressively and can spread rapidly. It is not drought tolerant and prefers warm to moderate growing temperatures.

PROPERTIES Vase life can be a bit variable, from average to very good (7–21 days). Flowers are not sensitive to ethylene. The flexible stems are excellent for floral design work because they can be gently bent and shaped into curves or straight lines.

QUALITY CRITERIA Select fresh, young stems with a dark green colour that is even and not blotchy, pale or yellowish. The freshness of the stems can be tested by breaking a piece of stem and checking that the centre is white. Stems can vary in length, so choose as desired.

CARE & HANDLING Recut the stems (20–30 mm; 1") and place them in clean water with a bactericide. There is no need to use a full floral preservative. Stems can be displayed in a cool area, or held in a cooler at 2–4°C (36–39°F) and a relative humidity of 90–95% until needed.

Cytisus scoparius (L.) Link.   family: Fabaceae

gewone brem (Dutch); *genêt à balais* (French); *Besenginster* (German); *ginestra scopareccia* (Italian); *escoba, escobón* (Spanish)

Dahlia hortensis

dahlia

Dahlia cultivars

DESCRIPTION Stout, erect herbaceous plants with hollow, woody stems arising from tuberous roots. The flower heads appear naturally from midsummer to early winter. There are thousands of modern hybrids and cultivars but not all are suitable as florist flowers. Double flower heads are most common.

ORIGIN & HISTORY Central America (Mexico to Colombia). *Dahlia* ×*hortensis* is believed to be a garden hybrid between *D. coccinea* and *D. pinnata*. Dahlias were exceptionally popular in the 1830s and 1840s.

PARTS USED Flower heads are used as cut flowers and whole plants as potted flowers.

CULTIVATION Dahlias grow easily in most soils as long as they receive regular, deep watering. Tubers that are dug up, cleaned and stored each year last much longer than those left in the ground. A cold period is needed to break dormancy, followed later on by long days to initiate flowering. Better yields and higher quality flowers are realised under cooler growing conditions.

PROPERTIES Vase life of cut flowers is poor to fairly good (5–10 days). Open flowers on pot plants last about 9 days. Flowers do not ship particularly well and tend to be sold more on local markets. A vast array of shapes, sizes and colours are available. There is no fragrance.

QUALITY CRITERIA Select flower heads that are opening with good colour showing. Those harvested and sold too tightly closed will fail to open properly. Check leaves for diseases, especially powdery mildew. Select pot plants with flowers still in bud, but showing good colour.

CARE & HANDLING Cut flowers: Use a preservative (to assist bud opening as well as protect against ethylene). Store, only if absolutely necessary, at 3–4°C (37–39°F) and 80% relative humidity. Pot plants: Display under cool temperatures (10–21°C; 50–70°F) and bright light conditions. Keep pots moist and continually remove dead flowers to encourage subsequent flowering.

Dahlia ×*hortensis* Guillaumin   family: Asteraceae

dahlia (Dutch); *dahlia* (French); *Dahlie* (German); *dalia* (Italian); *dalia* (Spanish)

Daucus carota

wild carrot • Queen Anne's lace

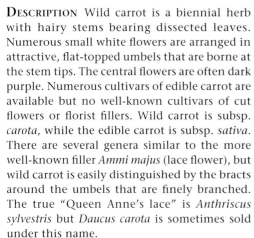

Daucus carota plant

Daucus carota flower head

DESCRIPTION Wild carrot is a biennial herb with hairy stems bearing dissected leaves. Numerous small white flowers are arranged in attractive, flat-topped umbels that are borne at the stem tips. The central flowers are often dark purple. Numerous cultivars of edible carrot are available but no well-known cultivars of cut flowers or florist fillers. Wild carrot is subsp. *carota*, while the edible carrot is subsp. *sativa*. There are several genera similar to the more well-known filler *Ammi majus* (lace flower), but wild carrot is easily distinguished by the bracts around the umbels that are finely branched. The true "Queen Anne's lace" is *Anthriscus sylvestris* but *Daucus carota* is sometimes sold under this name.

ORIGIN & HISTORY Europe to central Asia. Wild carrot has become popular as a commercial florist flower in recent years.

PARTS USED Leafy flowering stems are used as fillers.

CULTIVATION Plants are easily grown from seed and are mostly produced in open fields. Two years are necessary for the plant to come into full production. Plants prefer a loose, deep and well-drained soil.

PROPERTIES Vase life is poor (3–5 days). Foliage or flowers are fairly sensitive to ethylene.

QUALITY CRITERIA Select flowers with tight heads and vivid colour, free of browning or bruises. Check that the foliage is a good uniform colour and not pale or yellowish and free of marks and general damage.

CARE & HANDLING Handle flowers as little as possible, as touching causes bruising of the petals which leads to browning. Recut stems and place in a floral preservative or a bactericide with a low sugar concentration. Cut stems should not be stored, but used as soon as possible due to poor vase life. Stems can be held in a preservative in the cooler, prior to use, at 2–4°C (36–39°F) and at a high relative humidity (90–95%). Flowers can be dried.

Daucus carota L.   family: Apiaceae (Umbelliferae)

wilde wortel (Dutch); *carotte sauvage* (French); *Wilde Möhre* (German); *carota selvatica* (Italian); *zanahoria silvestre* (Spanish)

Delphinium elatum

delphinium

Delphinium elatum 'Blue Shadow'

Delphinium elatum 'Sydney Blue'

DESCRIPTION Short-lived perennial with deeply dissected leaves and blue flowers in long, dense racemes of up to 2 m. Racemes are more lax in *D. grandiflorum*. There are two main groups of hybrids used as florist flowers: Elatum hybrids – dense racemes of double flowers (the classical delphiniums); and Belladonna hybrids – sparse racemes of single- to semi-double flowers. Cultivars in the florist trade are mostly derived from *D. ×belladonna*, *D. grandiflorum* and *D. elatum*. The floriculture and horticulture industries continue to interchange the names and plants of delphiniums (*Delphinium*) and larkspurs (*Consolida*) even though there are many differences between the two.

ORIGIN & HISTORY Europe and Asia. *Delphinium* is from the Greek *delphis*, meaning dolphin. The flower resembles the bottle-like nose of a dolphin. Delphiniums were traditionally used to make blue dye or ink.

PARTS USED Flowering stems as cut flowers.

CULTIVATION Delphiniums generally do best under cool night and day temperatures. Above 21°C (70°F) flower size and yields are reduced. Long days speed up flowering and increase stem length.

PROPERTIES Vase life can be poor to slightly above average (5–8 days). Flowers are very sensitive to ethylene.

QUALITY CRITERIA Select stems with half the flowers open or opening. Only purchase flowers from sources you know have pre-treated them with STS or some other anti-ethylene agent.

CARE & HANDLING Recut stems and place in a preservative with a sugar and anti-ethylene agent. Also make sure the preservative contains a bactericide as delphiniums cause plain water to go off quickly and the stems get slimy as a result. Keep stems upright or else they will bend (geotropic response). Flowers can be stored upright for 1–2 days at 3–5°C (37–41°F). They can be dried, but not as easily as larkspurs.

Delphinium elatum L.

family: Ranunculaceae

ridderspoor (Dutch); *pied d' alouette* (French); *Rittersporn* (German); *speronella* (Italian); *delfinio* (Spanish)

Dendrobium cultivars
dendrobium orchid

Dendrobium cultivars

Dendrobium flower

DESCRIPTION A perennial herb with cane-like pseudobulbs of 1 m (40″) long and up to 20 flowers arranged in clusters of 0.4 m (16″) long. Flowers are 50–70 mm (about 2–3″) in diameter, often with a tubular, pointed lip. Colours range from white to mauve, pink and purple. The main cultivars and hybrids found in florists are related to *D. bigibbum* subsp. *phalaenopsis* – so-called phalaenopsis types because the flowers strongly resemble those of the genus *Phalaenopsis* (moth orchid).

ORIGIN & HISTORY New Guinea and Australia. *Dendrobium* is the largest genus in the orchid family, with thousands of variable forms.

PARTS USED Flowering stems are used as florist flowers and whole plants as potted flowers.

CULTIVATION Nearly all commercially grown plants are cultivated from tissue culture. Because orchids are protected under international laws, permits are required by growers to import plant material. Flowering is induced by shorter day lengths but many hybrids flower freely year-round.

PROPERTIES Flowers of pot plants can last 6–10 weeks. They are sensitive to ethylene.

QUALITY CRITERIA Purchase sprays with buds developed and open. Potted flowers should have 3–4 open buds (winter) or 1–2 open buds (summer). Look for turgid flowers that are free of brown spots, spotting and discolouration. Tubes with cut flowers should be full of solution. Avoid plants or stems with florets that are transparent, have dry patches or lost buds.

CARE & HANDLING Immediately unpack and recut stems and place in a preservative containing a bactericide, low sugar content and anti-ethylene agent. Flowers are chill sensitive, so do not hold or store below 13°C (55°F). Keep humidity at 80–90%. Do not display potted flowers below 16°C (61°F). Keep out of cold draughts and do not over-water. Do not store pots in the dark, as light is needed for buds to open properly.

Dendrobium cultivars

family: Orchidaceae

dendrobium (Dutch, French, Italian, Spanish); *Dendrobium* (German)

Dianthus barbatus

sweet william • pinks

Dianthus barbatus 'Dynasty Pink Magic'

DESCRIPTION A short-lived perennial plant of up to 0.6 m (2') high. The flowers have no stalks and are borne in dense heads. They are usually reddish purple with paler spots. Most of the many hybrids of *D. barbatus* have been bred for the bedding and pot plant industries, so that their flower stems are far too short for the cut flower market. However, a few cultivars, most of which do not need a cold treatment during cultivation, are found in florists.

ORIGIN & HISTORY Indigenous to southern Europe. Pinks are old favourite garden plants and a large number of cultivars have been developed.

PARTS USED Flowers are used as cut flowers and the whole plants as potted flowers.

CULTIVATION Plants require a cold period at a temperature of approximately 4°C (39°F) to flower properly. The actual length of cold treatment differs from cultivar to cultivar. Even after cold treatment plants need to be grown in a cool environment if good quality flowers are to be obtained.

PROPERTIES Vase life is poor to average (3–8 days). Fungal infection can be a problem, which commonly occurs if foliage and flowers are harvested when wet. Flowers are ethylene sensitive.

QUALITY CRITERIA Select cut stems with 10–30% of the flowers in the head open. Purchase stems that are straight, as they cannot be wired straight. Select pots with very few open flowers, because flowers do not last well. Some growers even sell with flowers still green and attach a colour tag to indicate the flower colour of the cultivar. Ensure that leaves are free of damage and are of a good colour.

CARE & HANDLING Unpack cut flowers and pots and aerate, to reduce the possibility of fungal infections. Use a preservative with an anti-ethylene agent. Flowers can be stored for a few days at 1–2°C (34–36°F). Flowering pots require cool temperatures and good light. Keep medium moist but do not over-water.

Dianthus barbatus L.   family: Caryophyllaceae

dizendschoon (Dutch); *oeillet de poètes* (French); *Bart-Nelke* (German); *garofano del poeta* (Italian); *minutisa* (Spanish)

Dianthus caryophyllus

carnation

Dianthus caryophyllus 'Leila'

Dianthus caryophyllus 'Alta'

Dianthus caryophyllus 'Late'

DESCRIPTION Perennial herb (to 0.8 m or about 2½') with narrow, glaucous leaves and stiff flowering stems. Many cultivars are available with a vast range of colours, petal shapes and flower sizes – they are grown as standard, spray or potted carnations.

ORIGIN & HISTORY Near East. It is said to have been first cultivated by the Moors in Valencia in 1460 and became a major florist flower, first in Europe in the 17th and 18th centuries and later all over the world.

PARTS USED Flowers (cut flowers) and the whole plant (potted flowers).

CULTIVATION Carnations are grown from cuttings and prefer cool climates. High temperatures and low light lead to low quality, poor yields and weak stems. Plants are very susceptible to fungal and viral diseases. Two main "types" cultivated are spray carnations (where the terminal bud is broken off) and standard carnations (where the side buds are removed – disbudded).

PROPERTIES Vase life is average to good (7–18 days), depending on the cultivar. Spray carnations tend to last better. Flowers can be colour-dyed. Some types have a pleasant fragrance. They are very sensitive to ethylene, which causes petal browning, buds failing to open and flower shrivelling (sleepiness). Stems snap easily.

QUALITY CRITERIA Standard carnations – look for tight, solid buds that are half open. Spray carnations – look for stems with only one to three buds open. Watch out for split calyx and broken stems. Only purchase flowers that have been pre-treated with anti-ethylene agents.

CARE & HANDLING Carnations are often packed and shipped dry. If so, recut and hydrate immediately in warm water (35°C; 96°F) with the pH lowered to 3.5 or in a hydrating solution, for at least 4 hours at room temperature. If necessary, flowers can be stored for 4–5 days at a relative humidity of 90–95% and a temperature of 1–2°C (34–36°F).

Dianthus caryophyllus L.   family: Caryophyllaceae

anjer (Dutch); *oeillet* (French); *Garten-Nelke* (German); *garofano* (Italian); *clavel* (Spanish)

Dianthus caryophyllus
pot carnation

Pot carnation – salmon

Pot carnations – mixed colours

DESCRIPTION A short-lived perennial herb with erect, brittle stems and single or double flowers in a multitude of colours. Amongst the more than 30 000 carnation cultivars recorded are compact types that have been developed for use as potted flowers. Some are fragrant (e.g. 'Sari'), but most are not.

ORIGIN & HISTORY Near East. Potted carnations have become important florist flowers since cultivation techniques had been perfected and appropriate cultivars developed.

PARTS USED Whole flowering plants are used as potted flowers.

CULTIVATION Their upright growth pattern allows for plants to be grown tight in a pot. Overhead irrigation (and over-irrigating) is avoided because carnations are very susceptible to diseases. Occasional irrigation with clean water prevents the build-up of salts. Plants are pinched to encourage branching. Temperature, light, nutrition and soil aeration are important factors in growing high-quality plants. There is no need to use growth regulators.

PROPERTIES Under good conditions (bright light and cool temperatures) flowering continues for 4–8 weeks. Carnations are highly sensitive to ethylene and to many diseases.

QUALITY CRITERIA Plants should be compact, with even growth and healthy green foliage. Look for pots with a few flowers open and a number of coloured buds. Only purchase disease-free plants that have been treated with ethylene inhibitors.

CARE & HANDLING If packaged in closed boxes unpack immediately. Handle with care as stems snap easily. Check if medium is dry and if so water thoroughly. Display pots in bright light and under cool conditions. Make sure ventilation is good and keep away from sources of ethylene. Allow potting medium to dry out slightly between waterings. Pots can be stored for a few days at 2–5°C (36–41°F) and low humidity (50–70%).

Dianthus caryophyllus L.   family: Caryophyllaceae

pot anjer (Dutch); *oeillet* (French); *Garten-Nelke* (German); *garofano* (Italian); *clavel* (Spanish)

Dieffenbachia seguine

dumb cane

Dieffenbachia seguine

Dieffenbachia seguine 'Vesuvius'

Dieffenbachia amoena

DESCRIPTION An erect perennial herb with stout fleshy stems and simple, bright green leaves, usually decorated with white or yellow spots or streaks. *D. seguine is* by far the most popular species and a large number of cultivars have been developed. Pot plant cultivars include 'Camilla' and 'Compacta' (both pale yellow and green variegated) and 'Green Magic' (solid dark green). A narrow-leaved form (with numerous cultivars) is widely known as *D. maculata* but this species has now been included in *D. seguine*. Another popular species is *D. amoena*.

ORIGIN & HISTORY Central America. Chewing a piece of dumb cane will lead to death in children and pets (it makes speech impossible because of swelling of the mouth and tongue). The plants were fashionable as houseplants in the 19th century.

PARTS USED Whole plants are used as pot plants and the leaves as cut greens (florist greens).

CULTIVATION Plants are grown from cuttings but nowadays more often from tissue culture – the latter grow more uniformly and are free of certain diseases and viruses that can totally destroy the crop.

PROPERTIES Vase life of cut foliage is very good (10–21 days), but can differ between cultivars. Pot plants can keep for several years. The leaf sap is poisonous – wash the hands after working with cut foliage. There is no fragrance. Ethylene can cause leaves to yellow prematurely.

QUALITY CRITERIA Select fully mature cut foliage or pot plants. Make sure colours are clear and vivid. Avoid small, poorly coloured leaves, burnt tips or edges and yellowed leaves (especially check the bottom leaves of pot plants).

CARE & HANDLING Recut the leaf stalks and place them in clean water with a bactericide. Check that the leaf blades are above the water level. Cut foliage can be stored for 7 days at 2–4°C (36–39°F) and a relative humidity of 90–95%. Display pot plants in dispersed light or semi-shade. Water them regularly. Plants can be stored for up to 2 weeks in the dark at 15°C (59°F) and a relative humidity of 90–95%. Chill damage can occur at below 14°C (57°F).

Dieffenbachia seguine (Jacq.) Schott (=*D. maculata*)   family: Araceae

dieffenbachia (Dutch, French, Italian); *Dieffenbachie* (German); *difembaquia* (Spanish)

Digitalis purpurea
foxglove

Digitalis purpurea (wild form)

Digitalis purpurea 'Foxy'

DESCRIPTION A biennial herb which forms a basal rosette of leaves in the first year and only flowers in the second year. It forms a slender raceme of up to 1.8 m (6′) with distinctive purple flowers, each with decorative spots. Most of the commercial cultivars are also biennial but some flower in their first year and are treated as annuals. A range of colours and inflorescence sizes are found, including 'Alba' (white), 'Apricot' (apricot), 'Gelbelanze' (gold) and 'Giant Shirley'(large, pink). Not all cultivars are suitable for cut flower production.

ORIGIN & HISTORY Europe. Foxglove is the source of heart glycosides (especially digitalis) used since 1785 to treat a weak heart. Foxglove signifies insincerity in the language of flowers.

PARTS USED Flowering stems are used as cut flowers.

CULTIVATION Cultivation is mainly from seed. Most growers purchase seedlings in plug form from suppliers. Plants require a period of cold if even flowering and good yields are to be obtained. In field production plants are usually planted in late autumn (fall), allowing them to establish before the onset of the cold winter. Flowers are then harvested in the summer. In greenhouse production, seedlings are given approximately an 8-week cold period at temperatures of 13–18°C (55–64°F), after which they are transplanted. Flowering occurs within 12 weeks.

PROPERTIES The vase life is poor to average (5–7 days).

QUALITY CRITERIA Select stems with 30–50% of the flowers open. Look for stems with densely packed flowers. Make sure flowers and leaves are free of damage, marks or disease.

CARE & HANDLING Immediately recut and rehydrate flowers. Remove foliage below water line and place in a preservative with a sugar to help more flowers to open fully. Keep or display in a cool, bright area. If necessary, store for 2–3 days at 5–6°C (41–43°F).

Digitalis purpurea L.   family: Plantaginaceae (Scrophulariaceae)

vingerhoedkruid (Dutch); *digitale* (French); *Fingerhut* (German); *digitale rossa* (Italian); *digitalis, dedalera* (Spanish)

Dracaena fragrans

fragrant dracaena

Dracaena fragrans

Dracaena sanderiana

DESCRIPTION A shrub or small tree that may reach a height of 15 m (50′) or more. Glossy pale green leaves of up to 1 m (40″) long and 0.1 m (4″) wide are borne in rosettes. The small yellow flowers occur in large numbers in pendulous clusters and are very fragrant (hence the scientific name). Cultivars include 'Massangeana' (also known as corn plant), which has recurved leaves that are striped with yellow or cream along the middle. 'Lindenii' has the leaf margins striped with white. Twisted bamboo or lucky bamboo (*D. sanderiana* and other species) has become popular as a novelty in arrangements.

ORIGIN & HISTORY Africa (Sierra Leone to Malawi). Fragrant dracaena survives under low light conditions and for this reason has become a popular houseplant.

PARTS USED The leaves as cut foliage. Whole plants are also used as pot plants and indoor plants.

CULTIVATION The plants are easily cultivated from seeds or cuttings. Since decorative leaf forms are grown, clonal cuttings are the preferred method of propagation. Production usually occurs in open fields in tropical or subtropical climates. The best leaf yields are achieved under high light intensities.

PROPERTIES Vase life of cut foliage is good (10–14 days). Unlike the flowers, the leaves have no fragrance. Ethylene can cause leaves to yellow prematurely.

QUALITY CRITERIA Select fully mature cut leaves and well-developed pot plants. Look for foliage that has a lively green (or variegated) colour, free of brown or dead tips and margins. Make sure leaves have no handling damage.

CARE & HANDLING Recut stems and place in clean water with a bactericide. If displayed or held at room temperature, occasionally mist leaves, as low humidity causes severe necrosis along leaf margins. Leaves can be stored for 7 days at 4–5°C (39–41°F) and a high relative humidity (90–95%). Preferably use foliage as soon as possible.

Dracaena fragrans (L.) Ker-Gawl.

family: Asparagaceae (Agavaceae, Dracaenaceae)

drakeboom (Dutch); *dragonnier, pléoméle* (French); *Drachenbaum* (German); *dracaena, dracena* (Italian); *dracena* (Spanish)

Dryopteris erythrosora

Japanese shield fern • Baker fern

Dryopteris erythrosora plants

Dryopteris erythrosora leaves

DESCRIPTION This fern has thick rhizomes with brown to black scales. The fronds are bipinnate, oblong in shape, 0.3–0.7 m (12–28") long and up to 0.3 m (12") wide. There are 8–12 pairs of main leaflets, each of which is again divided into several narrow and toothed smaller lobes or leaflets. There are no special cultivars used in the florist industry.

ORIGIN & HISTORY Indigenous to East Asia. The Japanese shield fern is also known as the copper shield fern and has become a popular garden plant. It is sometimes sold as leather leaf fern (or as an alternative or substitute) but the true leather leaf is *Rumohra adiantiformis*.

PARTS USED Leaves (often called fronds) are used as cut foliage.

CULTIVATION Production of Baker ferns is mainly done in shaded beds but leaves are also wild-harvested to some extent. Plants do best in loose, rich soils that are well drained and have a high organic matter content. Every few years growers lift, separate and replant plants.

PROPERTIES Vase life is average to good (7–14 days). Leaves have no fragrance and are not sensitive to ethylene.

QUALITY CRITERIA Select mature, stiff, well-formed fronds that have a uniform green colour and sturdy leaf stalks. Check that the leaf tips are not dry, browning or curling. The undersides of the fronds should be free of any spores.

CARE & HANDLING Stems can be placed in a bactericide and displayed in a cool area, but need to be misted daily to prevent the tips from drying. Stems can also be held until needed at 1–4°C (34–39°F) in their boxes, or covered with the plastic wrapping to maintain moisture and a high relative humidity. Store boxes flat to prevent fronds from curling. Alternatively, recut stems and store in a preservative at a temperature of 2–4°C (36–39°F) and a relative humidity of 95%.

Dryopteris erythrosora (Eaton) Kuntze   family: Dryopteridaceae

rode sluiervaren, Japanse schildvaren (Dutch); *fougère à indusies rouges* (French); *Rotschleier-Wurmfarn* (German)

Echinacea purpurea

purple coneflower • echinacea

Echinacea purpurea plants

Echinacea purpurea flower heads and cones

DESCRIPTION A perennial herb (up to 1 m or 40") with branched stems, bristly leaves and large purple flower heads on relatively short stems. A number of cultivars are available as florist flowers. Many are very similar but there is considerable variation in colour (pure white, purple, reddish or partly orange).

ORIGIN & HISTORY Southern and central United States. As florist flower it is better known for the interesting "cone" left after the ligulate florets ("petals") have been removed than as a fresh cut flower. *Echinacea* species are important medicinal plants.

PARTS USED Flower heads are used as cut flowers or fillers.

CULTIVATION Long days of 12–16 hours are needed for flowering. Stem lengths and yields are greatly increased when plants are provided with at least 6 weeks of cold treatment at approximately 4°C (39°F). Flowers are harvested when the "petals" start to expand. If sold as a cone or disk flower only, then harvesting is delayed slightly to allow the cone to achieve better colour and to make removal of the "petals" easier. Most production occurs in open fields, where plants are productive for 3–5 years.

PROPERTIES The vase life of the fresh cut flower is poor to average (4–7 days). Dried cones can last indefinitely. The "petals" tend to droop naturally, giving it a slightly wilted look that dissuades buyers.

QUALITY CRITERIA Select fresh flower heads with petals not fully open. Select cones that are well formed and have good colour. Make sure stems are straight and sturdy.

CARE & HANDLING Recut the stems of fresh flower heads and place them in a preservative immediately. Fresh cones can also be used by simply removing the "petals". However, still treat them as fresh cut flowers. Storage of fresh flowers is not recommended. Flower heads are excellent for drying. Remove "petals", if necessary, and hang upside down in an airy place.

Echinacea purpurea (L.) Moench   family: Asteraceae

rode zonnehoed (Dutch); *échinacée, rudbeckie poupre* (French); *Purpur-Sonnenhut* (German); *rudbeckia rossa, echinacea* (Italian); *equinácea* (Spanish)

Echinops bannaticus
globe thistle

Echinops bannaticus flowering stems

Echinops bannaticus flower heads

DESCRIPTION A sturdy perennial herb (up to 1 m or 40") with large, spiny leaves. The rounded (globose) grey-blue flower heads each comprises numerous small florets surrounded by short spiny bracts. Very few cultivars exist (e.g. 'Blue Globe' and 'Blue Ball') – they tend to have more intense blue-coloured globes than the wild form of the species. Some cultivars of the closely related *E. ritro* are also available, such as 'Blue Glow' and 'Veitch's Blue'.

ORIGIN & HISTORY Southern Europe. Globe thistles have become popular garden (border) plants.

PARTS USED Flower heads are used as cut flowers and fillers.

CULTIVATION Plants require a period of cold to flower uniformly, reduce leaf yellowing, give good colour and yields. After the cold period plants flower faster under long days of more than 16 hours. Growers use interrupted lighting (night-break lighting) to simulate long days. All that is needed is 2–3 hours with 40 W incandescent lights. Plants stay productive for 3–5 years.

PROPERTIES Vase life is average to good (6–10 days). Vase life of foliage is poor (4–5 days). Flower heads are difficult to handle with bare hands. If harvested too early, they fail to open. Foliage deteriorates much quicker than the flowers.

QUALITY CRITERIA Select stems with globes 75% to fully coloured, but before the individual florets have opened. Make sure the foliage, although fairly insignificant to the aesthetic value of the thistle, is healthy and not yellowing. Select sturdy, straight stems with good sized "globes".

CARE & HANDLING Recut stems and place in a preservative. Refrigeration at 4°C (39°F) intensifies the colour (can be stored at this temperature for 5–8 days). Flower heads are excellent for drying – hang small bunches upside down and do not remove leaves. If stems were harvested with open florets then the heads will shatter when dried.

Echinops bannaticus Rochel ex Schräd. (=*E. ritro*)

family: Asteraceae

kogeldistel (Dutch); *boule azurée* (French); *Kugeldistel* (German); *cardo globoso* (Italian); *cardo* (Spanish)

Equisetum hyemale
rough horsetail • Dutch rush • snake grass

Equisetum hyemale stems

Equisetum arvense

DESCRIPTION Horsetails are fern allies that produce fertile fronds with small, brown, spore-bearing cones in early spring. In summer, the distinctive sterile fronds emerge. These are about 1.5 m (5′) high and have no, or few, side branches. The ridges on the stems have prominent bands of silica, hence the name "rough horsetail". Common horsetail (*E. arvense*) and other species have 5–7 side branches arranged in whorls at each node. Leaves are highly reduced and form collars at each node. No cultivars are yet known, but several species are used in the florist industry. These include common horsetail (*E. arvense*), marsh horsetail (*E. palustre*) and swamp horsetail (*E. fluviatile*).

ORIGIN & HISTORY Europe, Asia and North America. The name comes from the Latin words *equis* meaning horse and *seta* meaning bristle. There are 15–25 different species, all with their own characteristic stems.

PARTS USED The sterile stems are used as fillers in design work and arrangements.

CULTIVATION Horsetails are commonly cultivated in gardens and are also grown on a small scale for foliage production, but most of the material used is wild-harvested.

PROPERTIES Vase life is average to good (7–10 days). Stems are fairly strong, but are hollow and can damage or buckle if handled roughly.

QUALITY CRITERIA Select stems with a healthy, green colour and well-defined dark nodules (nodes). Look for straight, sturdy stems with no obvious blemishes or dry tips.

CARE & HANDLING Recut and place in a bactericide, in a cool area. Stems can be held in the cooler, until needed, by keeping them in their boxes or plastic wraps (to maintain a high humidity) at 4–5°C (39–41°F). Alternatively, hold in a bactericide at 4–5°C (39–41°F) and a relative humidity of 90–95%. Cut off any dry or yellowing tips prior to use. Stems can be dried.

Equisetum hyemale L. family: Equisetaceae

hollepijp (Dutch); *prêle de hiver* (French); *Winter-Schachtelhalm* (German); *equiseto invernale* (Italian); *cola de caballo* (Spanish)

Eremurus stenophyllus

foxtail lily • desert candle

Eremurus stenophyllus

Eremurus robustus

DESCRIPTION A rhizomatous plant producing dense tufts or rosettes of numerous narrow, grass-like leaves at ground level. The flowering stalks are erect, up to 1.5 m (5') high, with dense racemes of yellow flowers that turn brown when they age. The stamens are orange. *Eremurus himalaicus*, a tall white-flowering species is a parent of many cultivars. *E. stenophyllus* and its cultivars have flowers in shades of yellow, while cultivars of *E. ×isabellinus* have long racemes in shades of yellow, pink, white and copper. The latter is believed to be a hybrid between *E. stenophyllus* and the pink-flowered *E. olgae*. *Eremurus robustus* is also sometimes used as cut flower.

ORIGIN & HISTORY The species is indigenous to Asia (from Iran to the Himalayas). About 45 species are native to the drier regions of central and western Asia and several of them have become popular garden plants.

PARTS USED Flower spikes are used as cut flowers.

CULTIVATION Cold is necessary to initiate flowering. The plants require rich, well-drained soil and regular watering.

PROPERTIES The vase life is good (10–14 days). The flowers have no fragrance. They are ethylene sensitive.

QUALITY CRITERIA Select flowers with the top 50–75% of the flowers still closed. If too open they will not last very long and if too closed the flower spike will not open fully. Check to see that buds have formed all the way to the tip of the flower spike. Select spikes with straight, sturdy, undamaged stems and that are also free of damaged flowers. Make sure no flowers have turned brown. Ideally purchase only pre-treated flowers.

CARE & HANDLING Recut the stems and place them in a preservative solution with a sugar and an anti-ethylene agent. Avoid getting the flower spike itself wet. Flowers do not store well, but if necessary store them at 2°C (36°F) for 3–4 days to prevent flowers from opening further. Keep flowers upright, as they will bend upward if laid flat.

Eremurus stenophyllus (Boiss. & Buhse) Baker (=*E. bungei*)　　　　　　　　family: Asphodelaceae

naald van Cleopatra (Dutch); *aiguille de Cléopâtre* (French); *Kleopatranadel, Steppenkerze* (German); *candelabro del desierto* (Spanish)

Erica coriifolia
Cape heather

Erica coriifolia

Erica perspicua (Prince of Wales heath)

Erica fastigiata (Four Sisters)

DESCRIPTION A shrub with small, leathery, needle-shaped leaves closely clustered along the stems. Attractive pink flowers are borne in rounded clusters on the stem tips. They are urn-shaped and about 9 mm (about ⅓") long, with prominent sepals that are almost as long as the petals. In addition to *E. coriifolia* and *E. perspicua*, other popular cut flower species include *E. fastigiata* (Four Sisters), *E. nutans*, *E. melanthera*, *E. leucanthera* and *E. bicolor*. Some species are grown as potted flowers.

ORIGIN & HISTORY *Erica coriifolia* is widely distributed in the fynbos region of South Africa. It has long been a popular and colourful component of fynbos greens. These greens often include an assortment of several *Erica* species.

PARTS USED The flowering stems are used as foliage and fillers in arrangements, mixed bunches and bouquets. Whole plants are sometimes used as potted flowers.

CULTIVATION Most of the material sold is wild-harvested. Potted flowers require slightly acidic, well-drained soil.

PROPERTIES Vase life is average to good (7–14 days). Flowers are not sensitive to ethylene. Many of the types do not have a scent.

QUALITY CRITERIA Select stems or bunches with half of the florets open. The corolla (petals) tends to turn brown but the calyx (sepals) remains fresh for a long time. Therefore, look for stems with no brown-tipped flowers, as this is an indication of good quality. Look for straight, well-branched stems that have a good length. Stems sometimes tend to be short and/or crooked.

CARE & HANDLING Recut stems and place them in a preservative solution with a bactericide and a low sugar concentration. Remove any foliage that may be below the water line. Foliage can be stored in moisture-retentive boxes at 4°C (39°F) (or in water and a relative humidity of 95%) for one week. Flowers are excellent for drying.

Erica coriifolia L.   family: Ericaceae

dopheide (Dutch); *bruyère* (French); *Erika, Heide* (German); *erica* (Italian); *brezo roseo* (Spanish)

Eryngium planum

sea holly

Eryngium planum 'Silver Salentino'

Eryngium planum

Eryngium alpinum 'Blue Star'

DESCRIPTION A perennial herb of up to 0.7 m (28″) high with leathery and spiny leaves. The cone-shaped flower heads and surrounding bracts are deep blue or purple. *E. planum* is more economical to freight, while *E. alpinum* has much more striking and larger flower cones (but more difficult to germinate). These two species and their cultivars make up the bulk of sea holly found in florist's shops. Sea holly and blue flowers are synonymous, but white flowered cultivars are also available.

ORIGIN & HISTORY Europe to central Asia. Roots of some species were used as tonics and to make sweets. Plants are sometimes seen in gardens.

PARTS USED Flowering stems are used as cut flowers and unusual filler.

CULTIVATION Seed germination is poor at best and drops significantly within 6 months if seeds are not sown immediately. Many growers prefer to purchase young plants in plug form from professional suppliers. Sea holly is a long-lived perennial that prefers cooler climates and production over a period of 3–5 years is easily achievable. Plants need a period of cold to really produce good quality, deep blue flowers. Flowers are harvested when the entire flowering head and the bracts turn blue.

PROPERTIES Vase life is average to good (7–14 days). Life of foliage is about 50% less than that of the flowers.

QUALITY CRITERIA Select stems with flower heads in bud stage, but with well-formed and open coloured bracts. Bracts and flowers should have good colour. Look for sturdy, straight stems. Leaves damage easily and often have signs of disease, so check them carefully.

CARE & HANDLING Recut stems and place in a general preservative. Cooling for a day or two at 4°C (39°F) intensifies the colour. Flowers can be stored for up to one week at 3–4°C (37–39°F). Drying in silica gel or similar desiccant preserves flower colour better than simply air-drying.

Eryngium planum L.   family: Apiaceae (Umbelliferae)

zilverdistel (Dutch); *panicaut à feuilles mutiques* (French); *Flachblättriger Mannstreu* (German); *eringio* (Italian); *cardo corredor* (Spanish)

Etlingera elatior

torch ginger

Etlingera elatior flowers

DESCRIPTION A ginger relative with cane-like stems (to 5 m or 16′), large leaves and long flowering stalks. The spectacular, torch-like inflorescence is up to 0.3 m (1′) in diameter. It has numerous pinkish red, thick and waxy bracts forming a cone-like structure, with small flowers between the bracts. Each flower has a bright red, tubular lip with a white or yellow margin. Of the more than 50 species of *Etlingera*, only *E. elatior* is cultivated to any extent. *Zingiber* cultivars tend to be more popular as they have a better vase life. Cultivars with average to good vase life (6–10 days) include 'Thai White' (light pink, torch form) and 'Hintze Red' (red, tulip form).

ORIGIN & HISTORY Malaysia. Flowers are traditionally used in curries. Torch ginger has become popular for large arrangements. The old name *Phaeomeria magnifica* is still sometimes used.

PARTS USED The flowering stem is used as cut flower.

CULTIVATION Torch gingers are relatively easy to cultivate (from rhizomes) if conditions are fairly humid and minimum temperatures are above 15°C (59°F). A rich, moist but well-drained soil is needed, along with full sun to partial shade. Good soil aeration is important to ensure healthy growth and ultimately good quality cut flowers.

PROPERTIES The vase life is generally considered poor – it can be anything from 3–10 days, depending on cultivar, the stage of harvest and quality. Flowers are fragrant. They are not sensitive to ethylene.

QUALITY CRITERIA Select long stems and well-formed flower heads with closed buds (known as candlesticks) or bracts just starting to open. They should show no discolouration and be free of any blemishes or damage.

CARE & HANDLING Recut the stems and place in a floral preservative. Use promptly, as the vase life is short. Hold flowers at 13–15°C (55–59°F) and a high relative humidity (95%). Storage is not recommended.

Etlingera elatior (Jack) R.M. Sm. (=*Phaeomeria magnifica*) family: Zingiberaceae

sceptre de l'empereur, gingembre aromatique (French); *Malayischer Fackelingwer* (German); *boca de dragon, bastón del emperador* (Spanish)

Eucalyptus cinerea

florist gum • Argyle apple • pennygum

Eucalyptus cinerea (natural colour)

Eucalyptus cinerea (dyed foliage)

DESCRIPTION A large tree (15 m or 50′), easily distinguished from other species by the red stringy bark combined with the opposite, stalkless, rounded, silver leaves. Inconspicuous flowers are borne in small clusters along the nodes. Only a few cultivars are available as florist foliage, differing slightly in leaf shape, size and colour.

ORIGIN & HISTORY Australia. The foliage is an old favourite amongst florists.

PARTS USED Branches with leaves are used as foliage.

CULTIVATION *Eucalyptus* species are very easy to grow and tolerate drought and poor soil. Seedlings are usually obtained from suppliers and planted densely. Harvesting from cultivated trees gives a more uniform and better quality than wild-harvested material. Trees are cut back completely after the main harvesting season to encourage new growth of young, high quality stems.

PROPERTIES Vase life can be anything from good to very good (10–25 days), depending on the care of harvesting and handling. Leaves and stems have a pleasant, distinct fragrance but leaves a sticky (but non-irritant) gum on the hands. Foliage is not ethylene sensitive (except when not hydrated properly).

QUALITY CRITERIA Select well-branched leafy stems that are not too woody. Harvesting in the heat of the day or lack of proper hydration causes the soft stem tips to wilt. Ensure that the tips are fresh and firm and that the leaves are not damaged.

CARE & HANDLING Recut 30–50 mm (1–2″) and hydrate in acidified water (pH 3–3.5). Store in own water (not with other flowers) as it often releases a sticky sap. There is no need to use a preservative in the water apart from a bactericide if properly hydrated. Pinch off or cut off the top 20–30 mm (1″) or so of each tip, which tends to wilt and dry out much faster than the rest of the stem. This will make the stems look fresh for longer but will not affect their general appearance. They can be dyed or dried.

Eucalyptus cinerea F. Muell. ex Benth.

family: Myrtaceae

eucalyptus (Dutch, French); *Blaugummibaum* (German); *eucalipto* (Spanish)

Eucharis grandiflora

Amazon lily • Eucharist lily

Eucharis ×grandiflora

Eucharis ×grandiflora flowers

Hymenocallis littoralis

DESCRIPTION An evergreen bulbous plant with glossy green leaves narrowing to a long stalk. The flowering stalks are up to 0.5 m (20") high and bear attractive, narcissus-like flowers of about 70 mm (nearly 3") in diameter. The flowers are white, cream-coloured or partly yellow. There are no well-known named cultivars. Amazon lily is sometimes confused with the similar-looking *Hymenocallis littoralis* (sacred lily of the Incas).

ORIGIN & HISTORY South America (Colombia). The genus name is derived from Greek and means "graceful" or "pleasing". The plant is a sterile hybrid, possibly resulting from a cross between the Peruvian *E. amazonica*, the Colombian *E. sanderi* and *E. moorei* from Ecuador and Peru.

PARTS USED The flowering stems are used as cut flowers and corsages. Whole flowering plants are sold as potted flowers.

CULTIVATION The plant requires rich, well-drained soil and regular watering. High humidity and warm growing conditions result in high quality flowers.

PROPERTIES The vase life of cut flowers is average to good (6–10 days). The attractive flowers are strongly scented and are also ethylene sensitive. Potted flowers can flower over a period of 1–2 months.

QUALITY CRITERIA Select cut flowers and potted flowers with buds showing good colour and swollen, but still closed, or only 1 flower open. Look for sturdy stems that are not damaged or have soft spots where they can buckle. Make sure that the leaves of the potted flowers are a healthy, uniform green with no marks or dry tips.

CARE & HANDLING Recut the stems and place them in a preservative with a low sugar concentration and some anti-ethylene agent. Display or hold flowers in a cool, bright area. The flowers can be stored for 5–7 days in moisture-retentive boxes, or in a preservative solution, at 7–10°C (45–50°F) and 90–95% relative humidity. Display potted flowers in a bright, high humidity environment, away from any cold draughts. Keep moist.

Eucharis ×grandiflora Planchon & Linden   family: Amaryllidaceae

amazonelelie (Dutch); *lis du Brésil* (French); *Amazonaslilie, Herzkelch* (German); *eucharis* (Italian); *lirio del Amazonas* (Spanish)

Eucomis comosa

pineapple lily

Eucomis comosa

Eucomis autumnalis

DESCRIPTION A deciduous, bulbous plant, with a basal rosette of broad, soft leaves. The greenish, pale cream or purple star-shaped flowers are tightly arranged on a tall flowering stem, which ends in a tuft of bracts, giving it the look of a pineapple. Flowering occurs naturally in summer, except in one species (*E. regia*). Most of the commercial pineapple lilies are hybrids derived from *E. comosa*, *E. autumnalis* and *E. bicolor*. The perianth lobes of *E. bicolor* have beautiful purple margins. 'Alba', a cultivar of this species, has uniformly greenish white flowers. Different cultivars have different length stems, from 0.1–1 m (4–40") tall.

ORIGIN & HISTORY Tropical southern Africa (mainly South Africa but extending into Malawi). There are around 15 species. Pineapple lilies have a long history of cultivation and are also important in African traditional medicine.

PARTS USED Flower stems are used as cut flowers.

CULTIVATION Plants can easily be grown from seed. They prefer a well-drained, rich soil and full sun growing conditions, provided temperatures are not too hot.

PROPERTIES Vase life is average to good (7–10 days). Stems often tend to be short. Some species or cultivars are sweetly scented, but others have an unpleasant odour.

QUALITY CRITERIA Select straight, sturdy stems with well-formed spikes having a large number of densely spaced flowers. Make sure the flowers and stem are free of marks or damage. Check that the crown of bracts does not have brown or dead tips. Select stems with only ¼ to ½ of the flowers open.

CARE & HANDLING Recut the stems and place them in a floral preservative. A bactericide is also needed to keep the water clean. Stems can be top-heavy, so ensure that they do not topple and damage (use tall buckets or preferably use some form of support). Stems can be stored for 5–7 days at 2–4°C (36–39°F) and a relative humidity of 90–95%.

Eucomis comosa (Houtt.) H.R. Wehrh.　　　　　　　　　　family: Asparagaceae (Hyacinthaceae)

ananasplant, kuiflelie (Dutch); *eucomis* (French, Italian, Spanish); *Scopflilie* (German)

Eupatorium purpureum

Joe Pye weed • gravel root

Eupatorium purpureum

Eupatorium perfoliatum

DESCRIPTION A robust, erect perennial herb of up to 3 m (10') high, with simple, oblong leaves borne in threes along the stems. The small flower heads vary from greenish yellow to pink or purple. They are grouped in large clusters towards the stem tips. Cultivated forms closely resemble the wild species. The cultivar 'Atropurpureum' however, has purple leaves. The European hemp agrimony (*E. cannabinum*) has similar flower heads but deeply dissected leaves like those of *Cannabis*. A well-known species is boneset or thoroughwort (*E. perfoliatum*) from the south-eastern United States. Cultivars of *E. cannabinum*, such as 'Plenum' and the white-flowered *E. perfoliatum* are also available.

ORIGIN & HISTORY *E. purpureum* is indigenous to the eastern parts of the United States. It is a traditional medicine used to treat various ailments of the urinary tract but has also become a popular garden plant and cut flower.

PARTS USED The flowering stems are used as cut flowers or fillers.

CULTIVATION Propagation is by seed or by dividing the clumps in autumn (fall). The ideal growing conditions are a moist soil and partial shade. Plants are cut back to ground level after harvesting, to promote new growth.

PROPERTIES Vase life is poor to average (4–7 days). Leaves have a vanilla fragrance if crushed. Flowers are ethylene sensitive.

QUALITY CRITERIA Select long, straight, sturdy stems with full flower heads. Look for cut stems with approximately 50% of flowers open. Leaves need to have a good, uniform colour. Make sure leaves and flower heads are free of blemishes and general damage.

CARE & HANDLING Recut the stems by at least 50–100 mm (2–4"). If the leaves are limp then first hydrate at room temperature for 2–3 hours. Place in a floral preservative. Long storage is not recommended, but rather use the flowers promptly. If necessary hold them for 3–4 days at 2–3°C (36–37°F) and 95% relative humidity.

Eupatorium purpureum L.   family: Asteraceae

purper leverkruid (Dutch); *eupatoire pourpre* (French); *Purpur-Wasserdost* (German); *eupatorio* (Spanish)

Euphorbia fulgens
scarlet plume • sun spurge

Euphorbia fulgens

DESCRIPTION A shrub of about 2 m (6½') high with arching branches and dark green, elliptic leaves. All parts of the plant exudes a milky latex when broken. The flower clusters (cyathea) each have six large, rounded petal-like processes, so that the whole structure closely resembles a flower. Several cultivars and colour forms are available, with red, orange pink and yellow "flowers". The leaves are dark green, blue-green or purple.

ORIGIN & HISTORY Mexico. *E. fulgens* has become a popular ornamental plant and several colour forms have been selected.

PARTS USED Flowering stems are used as cut flowers or fillers.

CULTIVATION Sun spurge is a common florist flower that is produced in greenhouses. They are short-day plants – flower initiation requires a period of days with 12-hour photoperiods or less. Time of harvest can be predicted quite accurately when cultivated under a flower-forcing programme of 12-hour short days at 20°C (68°F).

PROPERTIES Vase life is average to good (7–10 days). Flowers are sensitive to ethylene.

QUALITY CRITERIA Look for flowering stems showing colour all along the stem. The centres should be unopened and green. Select stems with about 30–50% of the flowers along the stem open. Select long sprays. The leaves are prone to falling off as they age, prior to flower senescence. Purchase flowers that have been pre-treated with an anti-ethylene agent.

CARE & HANDLING Cut 30–50 mm (1–2") off the stem and use a preservative containing a bactericide and an anti-ethylene agent, as flowers are prone to premature wilting. Stems can be dipped in warm water at 27–32°C (80–90°F) to stop the flow of sap that occurs after cutting. Be careful, as sap causes skin and eye irritation in some people. Remove foliage below the water level. Storage is not recommended, but if need be, store for only 2–3 days at 10°C (50°F). *E. fulgens* is sensitive to temperatures below 9°C (48°F).

Euphorbia fulgens Karw. ex Klotsch   family: Euphorbiaceae

wolfsmelk (Dutch); *Korallenröschen, Leuchtende Wolfsmilch* (German); *euforbia* (Italian)

Euphorbia marginata

snow-on-the-mountain

Euphorbia marginata 'Kilimanjaro'

DESCRIPTION An annual with variegated or entirely white upper foliage. The small, inconspicuous flowers are surrounded by large, white bracts. There are several cultivars, differing mainly in the distinctiveness of green and white variegation. Some cultivars have pure white bracts.

ORIGIN & HISTORY North America. It has become a popular florist green.

PARTS USED Leaves with small flowers are used as cut foliage.

CULTIVATION Snow-on-the-mountain is a short day plant – flowers are initiated under short day-length conditions, while long days result in vegetative growth. A "short" day of less than 14 hours initiates flowering. Cultivation from seed can be difficult, with erratic germination. Plants produce larger flowers and thicker stems below 24°C (75°F). Higher temperatures result in lower yields of spindly and sparse cut foliage. Cultivation is in open fields as well as greenhouses.

PROPERTIES The vase life is average to good (7–10 days). The foliage ages more quickly than the flowers and bracts. Therefore, many florists prefer to remove the foliage from the stems prior to using them in bouquets or arrangements. The milky sap that exudes from the plant can cause severe skin and eye irritation.

QUALITY CRITERIA Select foliage with bracts that are fully coloured, but before the actual flowers are fully opened (yellow stamens of open flowers are clearly visible). Look for well-branched, thick stems and compact, well-coloured bracts. Make sure the true foliage on the stems is fresh and damage-free.

CARE & HANDLING Cut the stems by at least 30–50 mm (1–2") – avoid the irritant sap (or use gloves). Stems can be dipped in warm water 27–32°C (80–90°F) to stop the sap that leaks after cutting. Flowers are prone to premature wilting so use a preservative solution. Storage is not recommended, but if absolutely necessary store only for 2–3 days at 6–10°C (43–50°F). Remove foliage that will end up below the water level.

Euphorbia marginata Pursh

family: Euphorbiaceae

sneeuw op den berge (Dutch); *euphorbe marginé* (French); *Schnee auf dem Berge* (German); *euforbia* (Italian); *euforbia blanca* (Spanish)

Euphorbia pulcherrima
poinsettia • Christmas rose

Euphorbia pulcherrima white

Euphorbia pulcherrima red

Euphorbia pulcherrima bicoloured

DESCRIPTION A perennial shrub (up to 5 m or 16') with lobed leaves. The real focus is the brightly coloured bracts, which surround the tiny, fairly insignificant yellow flowers. Potted plants are specially bred to have a short, compact growth form. Available cultivars have white, pink or red leaf bracts but red is always the most popular colour over Christmas time.

ORIGIN & HISTORY Mexico. Plants were first brought to the United States in 1928 by Dr Joel Roberts-Poinsett, the US ambassador to Mexico.

PARTS USED Plants are used as potted "flowers".

CULTIVATION The demand for poinsettia is huge over the Christmas season and tapers off significantly during the rest of the year. Therefore, production mainly focuses on that time of year. Although compact plant hybrids are used, growers still apply growth-retarding chemicals to further stunt and compact growth.

PROPERTIES A plant should remain attractive for about 4–6 weeks. New cultivars are less prone to leaf drop than older ones. The plants are sensitive to ethylene.

QUALITY CRITERIA Select compact plants with well-formed and brightly coloured "flowers" (bracts), free of damage or disease. Also make sure that the leaves have a bright green, uniform colour. Only purchase plants with pollen showing on some of the true flowers. Premature plants will have a reduced lifespan.

CARE & HANDLING Unpack as soon as possible, as darkness causes leaf drop. Remove sleeves – because of ethylene sensitivity, the leaves and bracts may droop. Unsleeved plants will "bounce back", but the longer they are sleeved the longer they will take to recover. Place in maximum natural light, but out of direct sunlight or draughts. Do not over-water but allow potting medium to dry out slightly. Preferably use tepid water and do not let plants stand in the water. Temperature: minimum (10°C; 50°F); maximum (21°C; 70°F).

Euphorbia pulcherrima Willd. ex Klotzsch

family: Euphorbiaceae

kerstster (Dutch); *rose de noël* (French); *Weihnachtsstern* (German); *stella di natale* (Italian); *flor de pascua* (Spanish)

Eustoma grandiflorum

lisianthus • prairie gentian • Texas bluebell

Eustoma 'Pico Blue'

Eustoma 'Mariachi' pink

Eustoma 'Mariachi' white

DESCRIPTION Annual or perennial herbs with fleshy, grey leaves and attractive petals with a satiny sheen. Many new cultivars are being developed with multiple short stems (potted flowers) or long stems (cut flowers). Cut flower cultivars can be single- or double-flowering, and spring, summer or winter flowering.

ORIGIN & HISTORY United States and Mexico. It is now one of the top-selling florist flowers in the world.

PARTS USED Flowering stems: cut flowers; whole plants: potted flowers.

CULTIVATION Eustoma is difficult to grow – growers often say it gets all the known diseases and then a few more. Production is primarily from seedlings. Moisture is critical when plants are in flower. Potted flowers are kept compact by maintaining higher night than day temperatures, or by spraying chemical growth regulators. It is important to harvest cut flowers when the blooms are dry. Flowers are normally harvested when two blooms are opening on the stem. The first flower is often pinched out and thrown away, thereby inducing the others to open more readily.

PROPERTIES Vase life is average to fairly good (7–10 days). Flowers are sensitive to botrytis. There is no noticeable scent.

QUALITY CRITERIA Select stems with at least one flower open, another 75% to fully open and the third starting to open and showing colour. Check for bruising or signs of diseases on petals and foliage.

CARE & HANDLING Recut stems and keep flowers upright in a sucrose floral preservative, to avoid bending. Store at 2–5°C (36–41°F), in a well-lit cooler. Provide good air-circulation and protect the flowers from high humidity. Lisianthus produces measurable levels of ethylene so do not store with ethylene-sensitive flowers. Display potted flowers in a lightly shaded, cool area. The ideal is 20–21°C (68–70°F) in the day and 16–18°C (61–64°F) at night. Do not allow flowering plants to dry out.

Eustoma grandiflorum (Raf.) Shinn. (=*E. russellianum*)   family: Gentianaceae

lisianthus (Dutch); *gentiane de la prairie* (French); *Bauchblume, Großblütiger Prärieenzian* (German); *lisianthus* (Italian)

Foeniculum vulgare

fennel

Foeniculum vulgare green

Foeniculum vulgare plants

Foeniculum vulgare purple

DESCRIPTION The plant is an aromatic, biennial or perennial herb with soft, hollow stems (up to 2 m or 6½′ high). The feathery leaves are compound (3–4-pinnate) with numerous filiform segments. Leaf bases are typically broad and form sheaths around the stem. There are up to 40 rays in each of the typical umbels. Bracts and bracteoles (involucre and involucel) are absent and the flowers are yellow. In the edible Florence fennel (var. *azoricum*), the leaf bases are massively swollen and overlapping to form a bulbous structure. Cultivars have been developed for culinary or medicinal use but very few for the cut flower industry. 'Purpurascens' (bronze fennel) is an attractive form with red-tinted stems and leaves that turn bronze-green over time.

ORIGIN & HISTORY Europe and the Mediterranean area. Plants have become naturalised in many temperate parts of the world. Fennel has a long history of use as a medicine, culinary herb and spice. In the language of flowers, fennel is associated with strength.

PARTS USED The flowering stems are used as foliage and filler, if and when available.

CULTIVATION Fennel is exceptionally easy to cultivate. Plants are propagated from seed and for good quality cut stems, deep, rich soils and sunny conditions, as well as adequate watering are required. Plants also thrive on chalky soils.

PROPERTIES Vase life is fairly poor (5–6 days). Flowers and foliage have a distinctive, anise scent. There is no ethylene-sensitivity. The foliage is edible.

QUALITY CRITERIA Look for full, well-branched stems or bunches, with bright green and not pale foliage. Flower heads should be 50–75% open and not yet gone to seed.

CARE & HANDLING Stems and foliage are relatively soft, so handle with care. Recut and place in a bactericide. Use promptly or hold in a cooler at 4–5°C (39–41°F) and a high relative humidity (90%+).

Foeniculum vulgare Mill.

family: Apiaceae (Umbelliferae)

venkel (Dutch); *fenouil* (French); *Fenchel* (German); *finocchio* (Italian); *fenneru* (Japanese); *hinojo* (Spanish)

Forsythia intermedia

golden bell

Forsythia ×intermedia

DESCRIPTION Deciduous shrub (up to 3 m or 10') with erect and spreading golden green stems bearing simple or 3-lobed, toothed leaves in opposite pairs. The dark yellow flowers are 25 mm (1") long, each with four oblong petals fused at the base to form a short tube. They are borne in clusters and arise from each of the scaly buds along the stems. Leaves are formed after flowering. A large number of cultivars have been developed, mainly for use as garden plants. 'Spectabilis', is one of the most sought after cultivars for the florist trade. 'Lynwood' is a large-flowered mutation derived from 'Spectabilis'. 'Charming' is a cultivar with variegated foliage.

ORIGIN & HISTORY China. *Forsythia intermedia* is a hybrid between *F. suspensa* and *F. viridissima*, both Chinese species. The plant was named after William Forsyth of the Chelsea Physic Garden (1737–1804).

PARTS USED The flowering stems are used as florist fillers.

CULTIVATION *Forsythia* is a quick-growing shrub that prefers full sun conditions. Correct harvesting and pruning is important to maintain a high level of production. Cut stems are harvested from 2-year-old shoots, and old wood pruned out after flowering.

PROPERTIES Vase life can vary from poor to fairly good (4–10 days).

QUALITY CRITERIA Select branches that are still in the bud stage. Make sure that the stems are young, straight and full of well-formed buds, clustered along the length of the stem. Check that stems and buds are free of blemishes.

CARE & HANDLING Recut stems and place in a floral preservative and hold at 5°C (41°F) for 4–5 hours before using. Buds can be forced to open by placing in a warm floral preservative (38–44°C; 100–110°F) and held at room temperature in low light or darkness. Stems can be stored wet at 5°C (41°F) and a relative humidity of 90–95%, for 3–4 days.

Forsythia ×intermedia Zab.   family: Oleaceae

forsythia (Dutch); *forsythia de Paris* (French); *Garten-Forsythie, Goldglöckchen* (German); *forsizia di zabel* (Italian); *forsitia* (Spanish)

Freesia hybrida

freesia

Freesia ×hybrida red

Freesia ×hybrida mixed colours

Freesia ×hybrida yellow

DESCRIPTION A deciduous plant growing from a cone-shaped corm. The leaves are arranged in a fan. The inflorescence is a spike, with several sessile flowers all directed to one side. The flowers are tubular and very fragrant in the original species. Florist freesias are complex hybrids involving several species (*F. alba*, *F. corymbosa*, *F. refracta* and *F. leichtlinii*). Many single- or double-flowered cultivars and hybrids with good keeping qualities are available – either as cut flowers or potted flowers. There is a wide range of colours.

ORIGIN & HISTORY South Africa. This beautiful flower has become one of the most popular florist flowers in modern times.

PARTS USED Flowering stems are used as cut flowers and whole plants as potted flowers.

CULTIVATION Growers buy corms from specialists. Corms require a dry storage period at very warm temperatures, followed by cool, moist pre-cooling and growing conditions. Single-flowered cultivars are normally cut with at least 4 viable flowers per stem, while double-flowered cultivars should have at least 4 viable flowers.

PROPERTIES Vase life is average (7–10 days). Some cultivars have a strong, pleasant fragrance. Freesias are ethylene sensitive – the buds more so than the open flowers.

QUALITY CRITERIA Select stems with no less than 7 buds per spike. Choose long, straight stems with only the first 1–2 flowers open. Potted freesias should have all the flowers still closed and the first 1–3 flowers showing colour, or only 1 flower open.

CARE & HANDLING Recut and place flowers in a preservative containing a sugar and an ethylene inhibitor. The sugar will ensure that most of the flowers open. Do not use fluorinated water. Little or no storage is recommended. If absolutely necessary, only store for 2–3 days at 2–4°C (36–39°F). Display pots in a cool, bright area away from sources of ethylene.

Freesia ×hybrida L.H. Bail.   family: Iridaceae

fresia (Dutch); *freesia* (French); *Freesie* (German); *fresia* (Italian); *fresia* (Spanish)

Fritillaria imperialis

crown imperial

Fritillaria imperialis orange

Fritillaria imperialis plants

DESCRIPTION A bulbous, perennial herb, about 0.6–0.9 m (2–3′) high. The lance-shaped leaves are borne in 3–4 whorls, each with 4–8 leaves. Attractive yellow, orange or red bell-shaped flowers are borne at the top of a sturdy stem, topped by a crown of green bracts. Cultivars with variegated leaves or different flower colours are available, including 'Maxima Lutea' (yellow), 'Aurora' (orange) and 'Rubra' (red). The leaves are edged with white in 'Argenteovariegata' and golden yellow in 'Aureomarginata'. 'Crown on Crown' is unusual in having a double crown of flowers, one above the other. Several other species such as the snake's head fritillary (*F. meleagris*) and the imposing Persian fritillary (*F. persica*) are cultivated.

ORIGIN & HISTORY Western Asia (southern Turkey, Iran, Kashmir, northern India). It was once a medicinal plant, a source of edible starch and a favourite subject of Dutch master painters.

PARTS USED The flowering stems are used as cut flowers; whole flowering plants as potted flowers.

CULTIVATION *Fritillaria* grows naturally at high altitudes, and even under normal cultivation requires cold winters and cool summers to produce high quality flowers.

PROPERTIES Vase life of individual flowers is poor (4–6 days). Potted flowers may flower for 2–3 weeks. Flowers have a musky scent and are sensitive to ethylene.

QUALITY CRITERIA Select cut stems with the buds swollen and showing colour, but still closed (or with only 1–2 flowers opening). Flowers of potted plants should also be closed but showing colour. Leaf tips should not be brown or dry.

CARE & HANDLING Recut the stems and place them in a floral preservative with a bactericide and anti-ethylene agent. Cut stems can be held in a cooler at 1–2°C (34–36°F) and high humidity (90–95%). Display potted flowers in a cool, bright area. Keep medium moist.

Fritillaria imperialis L.　　　　　　　　　　　　　family: Liliaceae

keizerskroon (Dutch); *couronne impériale* (French); *Kaiserkrone* (German); *corona imperiale* (Italian); *corona imperial* (Spanish)

Fuchsia cultivars

fuchsia

Fuchsia red

Fuchsia pink and white

Fuchsia purple and white

DESCRIPTION Fuchsias range from tall shrubby plants of up to 3 m (10′) to trailing and pendulous forms. The leaves are simple and borne in opposite pairs. The flowers each have a bright red (rarely white or pink), tubular calyx with four flaring or reflexed lobes and four or more overlapping petals in a wide range of colours, from white to red or purple. Trailing fuchsias are popular for hanging baskets. Several cultivars are available, including double (e.g. 'Humbolt Holiday'), semi-double (e.g. 'La Campanella') or single (e.g. 'Marinka') flower types. Upright fuchsias include 'White Eyes' and 'June Bride'.

ORIGIN & HISTORY Fuchsias are indigenous to Central and South America, New Zealand and Tahiti. As a popular garden subject, hundreds of hybrids and cultivars have been developed so that the limits between some species have become obscured.

PARTS USED Whole flowering plants are used as potted flowers and for hanging baskets.

CULTIVATION Fuchsias require an acidic soil (pH 5–5.5) and regular feeding. Plants are initially grown under low light conditions to promote vegetative growth and later under high light intensities to promote flowering.

PROPERTIES Flowering continues for several months. Poor light and ethylene will cause flowers to drop off. Most cultivars have no noticeable fragrance.

QUALITY CRITERIA Plants are ready to be sold when they start flowering. Look for plants that are full of buds and well branched. Check that buds have not been damaged or broken off and that leaves are free of marks.

CARE & HANDLING Unpack the containers and water the plants well. Display in full sun, provided temperatures are not too hot (but in the range of 21–24°C or 70–75°F), and shade them from the hot, midday sun. Water regularly and keep moist to prevent wilting. Plants can be stored for a few days at 3°C (37°F).

Fuchsia cultivars

family: Onagraceae

fuchsia (Dutch, French, Italian); *Fuchsie* (German); *fucsia* (Spanish)

Gaillardia grandiflora

blanket flower

Gaillardia aristata

Gaillardia ×grandiflora

Gaillardia ×grandiflora

DESCRIPTION A perennial herb of 0.3 –0.9 m (1–3') high with simple, oblong and hairy leaves borne directly on the stems. The attractive bicoloured flower heads are about 100 mm (4") in diameter and typically have a dark reddish brown to reddish purple centre and a contrasting halo of bright yellow. Some forms, however, are pure yellow or pure red. Various cultivars and seed races are derived from G. ×grandiflora. They differ in the height of the plants and in the colour patterns of the flower heads. Amongst the many cultivars are 'Goblin', which has a broad yellow halo and 'Wirral Flame', with only the tips of the ray florets yellow. Double forms are derived chiefly from G. pulchella, an annual species of less than 0.5 m (20") high.

ORIGIN & HISTORY North America. Gaillardia ×grandiflora originated as a garden hybrid between G. aristata and G. pulchella, both North American species. They have become popular garden plants in many parts of the world.

PARTS USED Flowering stems are used as cut flowers or fillers. Whole plants are popular as container plants and for hanging baskets.

CULTIVATION Gaillardias are grown from seeds or cuttings. They require full sun conditions and succeed in any moderately fertile, well-drained soil. Plants perform well even in poor soils and are very tolerant of drought, heat or windy conditions.

PROPERTIES Vase life is average (5–7 days). The flower heads are not sensitive to ethylene.

QUALITY CRITERIA Select flower heads that are fully opened, or sprays with at least 50% of the buds open and the rest showing good colour. Look for stems that are sturdy and straight or well branched and full of buds.

CARE & HANDLING Use a floral preservative. Storage is not recommended – preferably use cut flowers as soon as possible. If absolutely necessary, store for a maximum of 3–4 days at 4°C (39°F) and a high relative humidity (95%).

Gaillardia ×grandiflora Van Houtte   family: Asteraceae

kokardebloem (Dutch); gaillarde (French); Kokardenblume (German); gaillardia (Italian); gailardia (Spanish)

Galanthus nivalis

snowdrop

Galanthus nivalis

DESCRIPTION A small bulbous plant with strap-shaped leaves and attractive white flowers that typically hang down (nodding). The inner three lobes are shorter than the outer three and are decorated with green marks. Snowflakes (*Leucojum* species) are very similar but the perianth lobes are all of the same length. Cultivars such as 'Scharlokii' have two flowers per stem, while 'Ophelia, 'Flore Pleno' and 'Lady Elphinstone' have double flowers. A cultivar variously known as 'S. Arnott', 'Sam Arnott' or 'Arnott's Seedling' has large, strongly scented flowers. A few other species (e.g. *G. caucasicus* and *G. plicatus*) and various hybrids are also commonly cultivated.

ORIGIN & HISTORY Europe. Snowdrops have become very popular garden plants and millions of bulbs are sold each year.

PARTS USED Flowering stems are used as cut flowers, while whole plants are cultivated as potted flowers.

CULTIVATION Plants require a rich, moist soil and full sun to partial shade. Snowdrops do best in soils that are not too sandy that can either be slightly acidic or alkaline. Cool to moderate growing temperatures result in good quality flowers.

PROPERTIES Snowdrops are one of the first flowers to announce the impending arrival of spring – they flower in late winter when other plants are still dormant. Vase life is poor to average (4–8 days). Flowers are sensitive to ethylene.

QUALITY CRITERIA Select stems with buds closed, but swollen and well coloured. Potted flowers should be compact, well formed and full of coloured buds. Make sure that the leaves have a lively colour and that the tips are not browned or dry.

CARE & HANDLING Recut stems (albeit by only 10–20 mm or about ½") and place in a floral preservative. Flowers can be held in a cooler at 1–2°C (34–36°F) until used. Display potted flowers in a bright, cool area (not in direct sunlight) and keep moist.

Galanthus nivalis L.   family: Amaryllidaceae

gewoon sneeuwklokje (Dutch); *perce-neige, galanthe des neiges* (French); *Gemeines Schneeglöckchen* (German); *bucaneve, foraneve* (Italian); *campanilla blanca* (Spanish)

Galax urseolata

beetle weed • wand plant

Galax urseolata (green)

Galax urseolata (bronze)

DESCRIPTION A tufted perennial herb with thick, creeping rhizomes. The rounded to heart-shaped leaves are borne on slender stalks and have toothed margins. They are glossy green and turn a rich bronze colour with time. Small white flowers of about 40 mm (1½") in diameter occur in spike-like clusters of up to 0.3 m (1') high. There is only one species and it appears that no distinct cultivars have yet been developed.

ORIGIN & HISTORY South-eastern United States. The plants are commonly grown in gardens as a ground cover. There are numerous common names, including wandflower, galaxy and coltsfoot. It is sometimes called *Galax aphylla* but this is not the correct name.

PARTS USED Leaves are used as florist greens, particularly for bridal and funeral work, as well as in many modern and underlining designs.

CULTIVATION Propagation can be by means of seed, rhizomes or division. Most plants are grown for the garden industry and not for the commercial florist flower industry. The leaves are a green colour in spring and summer and turn dark red, bronze or a mottled colour in autumn (fall) and winter.

PROPERTIES Vase life is average to good (7–14 days). Leaves have no noticeable fragrance and are not sensitive to ethylene.

QUALITY CRITERIA Select well-formed leaves with good round shapes, free of any blemishes or damage. Make sure that the colour of the leaves is vibrant and uniform. Check that the leaf stalks are long and sturdy enough to carry the weight of the leaf blade.

CARE & HANDLING Recut the leaf stalks and place them in clear water with a bactericide. There is no need to use a full floral preservative. Cut leaves can be stored in water for 5–7 days at a temperature of 2–5°C (36–41°F) and a relative humidity of 95%. Alternatively, leaves can be stored in moisture-retentive boxes or plastic bags at the same temperatures and relative humidity.

Galax urceolata (Poir.) Brummit (=*G. aphylla*)   family: Diapensiaceae

galax (Dutch, French, Italian, Spanish); *Bronzeblatt* (German)

Gardenia augusta

Cape jasmine • gardenia

Gardenia augusta

DESCRIPTION An evergreen woody shrub or tree of up to 12 m (40′) high. The leaves are glossy green and borne in opposite pairs. The rose-like, white or ivory-coloured flowers are intensely fragrant. Not many cultivars are available as florist flowers and colour is restricted to white or ivory. Some cultivars are taller with larger flowers, while others produce a greater abundance of smaller flowers.

ORIGIN & HISTORY China, Japan and Taiwan. In China, the flowers are traditionally used to flavour tea.

PARTS USED Flowering stems: cut flowers. Whole plants: potted flowers.

CULTIVATION Gardenias are propagated from cuttings, which take between 12–18 months to reach flowering size. Short days enhance flower induction and cool night temperatures of 16–17°C (61–63°F) are needed for flower development. Growers treat plants with a growth inhibitor which keeps them compact and also increases the number of flowers per plant.

PROPERTIES Vase life is poor (2–4 days). Cut flowers and pots do not ship well over long distances due to poor vase life and sensitive petals (they bruise easily). Flowers are very sweetly scented. They are sensitive to ethylene.

QUALITY CRITERIA Purchase cut stems with the flowers almost open to fully open, but make sure that they have not started to decline. Select flowers with vivid colour, free of browning. Leaves should have a deep and uniform green colour. Select potted flowers with buds still closed but swollen.

CARE & HANDLING Handle flowers by the stems only and do not touch the petals, as this causes bruising and browning. Store immediately at 1–2°C (34–36°F) and at a high humidity. Wrap loosely in plastic bags to maintain high humidity or refrigerate in the original packaging. Flowers can be stored at 5°C (41°F) for a short period after arranging. Display potted flowers in a cool (preferably 18°C; 64°F) and high light intensity area. Keep moist.

Gardenia augusta (L.) Merril. (=*G. jasminoides*)　　　　　　　　　　family: Rubiaceae

Kaapse jasmijn (Dutch); *jasmin du Cap* (French); *Kap-gardenie* (German); *jazmín del cabo* (Spanish)

Gaultheria shallon

lemon leaf • salal • shallon

Gaultheria shallon

DESCRIPTION A small woody shrub of up to 0.6 m (2′) high with broad leaves that have toothed and bristly margins. The small flowers are urn-shaped, about 5 mm (less than ¼″) in diameter, with a white corolla that may be tinged with pink. The small fruits are 10 mm (about ½″) in diameter and turn from red to partially black when they mature. A few cultivars are known. Hybrids between *G. sallon* and *G. mucronata* (*G. ×wisleyensis*) have given rise to several cultivars such as 'Wisley Pearl' (purple-red fruits), 'Pink Pixie' (pink-tinged flowers and purple-red fruits) and 'Ruby' (white flowers and ruby red fruits).

ORIGIN & HISTORY North America (naturalised in the United Kingdom). *Gaultheria* species have become popular garden shrubs. The most famous species is *G. procumbens* (checkerberry), the original source of wintergreen (the characteristic smell is due to methyl salicylate). Equally well known amongst gardeners is *G. mucronata*, a popular shrub with numerous garden forms bearing white flowers that are often speckled and tinted with pink or red.

PARTS USED Flowering and/or fruiting branches are occasionally used as florist fillers. However, it is mainly the leafy stems that are used as cut foliage.

CULTIVATION Plants are grown from cuttings, divisions or seeds. They do best under cool, bright conditions in deep soils.

PROPERTIES Vase life can vary considerably, from average to very good (7–28 days). Foliage has a pleasant fragrance.

QUALITY CRITERIA Make sure leaf colour is a uniform, dark green colour and not pale or yellowish. Select young stems with mature, evenly spaced leaves that are not damaged or marked.

CARE & HANDLING Recut stems and place in clean water with a bactericide. Remove any leaves that may be below the water line. Stems can be stored for at least 10–14 days at 0–2°C (32–36°F) and 90–95% relative humidity.

Gaultheria shallon Pursh.

family: Ericaceae

gaultheria (Dutch); *palommier* (French); *Hohe Rebhuhnbeere, Shallon-Scheinbeere* (German); *gaulteria* (Italian, Spanish)

Genista canariensis

florist's genista • Canary Island broom

Genista canariensis

DESCRIPTION Evergreen shrub of up to 2 m (6½') with trifoliate, hairy leaves and clusters of 5–12 flowers on the tips of lateral branches. The flowers are 12 mm (½") long and bright yellow, with a strong pleasant fragrance. The fruits are oblong, hairy pods of about 25 mm (1") long. Garden cultivars differ mainly in growth form (e.g. low spreading plants used as ground covers). There are as yet no well-known cultivars that are specifically used in the cut flower industry.

ORIGIN & HISTORY Africa (Canary Isles). Florist's genista is one of several species cultivated as garden ornamentals and occasionally harvested as cut flowers. These include Mt Etna broom (*G. aetnensis*, from the slopes of Mt Etna), the spiny Spanish gorse (*G. hispanica*) and the dyer's greenweed (*G. tinctoria*, indigenous to Europe and Asia). Last-mentioned species is a traditional dye plant, the flower extracts of which were mixed with woad (the blue dye from *Isatis tinctoria*) to obtain "Kendal green".

PARTS USED The flowering stems are used as cut flowers and florist fillers.

CULTIVATION Propagation is from seed. Plants prefer full sun conditions but moderate temperatures. Soils need to be well drained and slightly acidic or alkaline.

PROPERTIES The vase life is average to good (7–10 days). Flowers are fragrant. They are sensitive to ethylene.

QUALITY CRITERIA Select stems with several basal flowers open. The stems should be long, with many terminal branches and healthy foliage. Check that branches have a good volume of buds and flowers. Top grade cut stems are from the terminal branches, while secondary grade stems are from woodier parts of the plant.

CARE & HANDLING Use a floral preservative with an anti-ethylene agent. Flowers can be stored for 4–6 days at 1–3°C (34–37°F) and 90–95% relative humidity. Flowers can be dyed a variety of colours.

Genista canariensis L. (=*Cytisus canariensis*)   family: Fabaceae

brem (Dutch); *genêt* (French); *Ginster* (German); *ginestra* (Italian)

Gerbera jamesonii
gerbera • Barberton daisy • Transvaal daisy

Gerbera 'Tamara'

Gerbera 'Serena'

Gerbera pots (mixed)

DESCRIPTION A perennial herb with a rosette of toothed leaves near the base of the plant and characteristic, solitary, broad and flat flower heads borne on long slender stalks. There are many cultivars with new ones continually being introduced. Two main groups are the large-flowering types (known as "gerberas") and small-flowering types (known as "minis", "gerbera minis" or "germinis"). Colours are numerous and vibrant.

ORIGIN & HISTORY South Africa (eastern subtropical regions). Most breeding and hybridisation have taken place in the Netherlands. Gerbera has become one of the most popular of all florist flowers.

PARTS USED The whole plant: potted flower. Flower heads (without leaves): cut flowers.

CULTIVATION Pot plants and cut flowers are grown in greenhouses and under shade cloth. Cut flowers are widely grown using hydroponic techniques. Growers typically replace plants after two years of production. Flowers are harvested by pulling and not cutting, thereby inducing further flowering.

PROPERTIES Vase life is slightly poor to good (5–10 days), depending on cultivar. Flowers have no noticeable fragrance. The hollow stems are easily damaged.

QUALITY CRITERIA The main limiting factor is the soft hollow stems that bend easily, preventing water uptake. Select cut flowers that are fully open, with straight, strong stems. Make sure leaves of potted flowers are free of any black marks, disease and general damage. Choose pots with at least one open flower head.

CARE & HANDLING Hydrate flower heads as soon as possible. They can be stored dry at 2°C (36°F) in moisture-retentive boxes for two days or in a preservative at 4°C (39°F) for 4–7 days and at a relative humidity of 90–95%. Hygiene is essential (use clean water and sterilised buckets) to prevent stem block and botrytis infection. Display pots in bright, indirect light and water moderately.

Gerbera jamesonii Bolus ex Adlam
family: Asteraceae

gerbera (Dutch); *gerbéra* (French); *Gerbera, Barberton-Gerbera* (German), *gerbera* (Italian, Spanish)

Gladiolus cultivars
sword lily • "glad"

Gladiolus hybrids

Gladiolus 'Spic and Span'

DESCRIPTION A mostly deciduous corm plant, with narrow leaves and long spikes of attractive flowers. Most of the large-flowered, tall-stemmed hybrids have been bred from summer-growing South African species. There are over 30 000 cultivars derived from 8 species, with a vast array of colours and bicolours.

ORIGIN & HISTORY Southern Africa. Some species are found throughout the rest of Africa, Madagascar, southern Europe, the Middle East and western Asia. The Latin *gladius* means "sword" (the leaves are sword-like). In the 18th century, gladioli were exported in large quantities from South Africa to Europe.

PARTS USED The flower spikes are used as cut flowers.

CULTIVATION In commercial production, corms are planted either in greenhouses, under low percentage shade cloth and in open fields. "Standard glads" produce a single flowering stem per corm, while "miniature glads" produce several. The corm dies after flowering and a new, larger one is formed directly above the old one, along with numerous cormlets.

PROPERTIES Vase life is average to fairly good (7–10 days). Gladiolus flowers are susceptible to viruses. Flowers of some cultivars are fragrant. They are not sensitive to ethylene but very sensitive to fluoride (>0,25 g/l) in the water.

QUALITY CRITERIA Select spikes with only 1–2 of the bottom flowers starting to open but not nearly fully open, with a further 3–4 buds showing colour. Purchase only straight, sturdy stems with healthy green leaves (not yellowish or blotchy) and free of marks and damage.

CARE & HANDLING Recut stems and place in a preservative containing a bactericide and a sugar. The sugar will ensure that all the flowers along the spike open. Flowers can be stored at 2°C (36°F) and a relative humidity of 95% for 5–8 days. Store upright and in good light because the tips will bend towards the light (phototropic).

Gladiolus cultivars
family: Iridaceae

gladiool (Dutch); *glaïeul* (French); *Gladiole, Siegwurz* (German); *gladiolo* (Italian); *gladiolo* (Spanish)

Gloriosa superba

flame lily • glory lily

Gloriosa superba 'Rothschildiana'

Gloriosa superba yellow

DESCRIPTION A deciduous, climbing plant with a fleshy corm. The narrow leaves have tendrils on their tips, which anchor the stems as they climb up trees or bushes to an average height of 2 m (6½'). Plants flower naturally in summer and are dormant in winter. The flowers are spectacular and graceful, ranging from greenish yellow to bright red in colour. The flame lily is a variable species and several named selections are known, including 'Rothschildiana' (a large red and yellow form), 'Carsonii' (flowers purple red), 'Simplex' (deep orange and yellow, not crisped) and 'Verschuurii' (crimson with yellow, undulate margins).

ORIGIN & HISTORY Africa and Asia. There is only one species, with a wide natural distribution range in southern, central and eastern Africa, and further eastwards to Asia. The corms are poisonous and have been used for suicide in India. They contain colchicine and other alkaloids.

PARTS USED Flowering, leafy stems are used as cut flowers.

CULTIVATION Propagation is by means of corms or seeds. Flowers are cultivated in greenhouses and under shade cloth. Plants need well-drained and damp (but not wet) soils, to prevent diseases and rotting of the corms. Due to their climbing nature the plants need to be staked or supported with netting to prevent damage.

PROPERTIES Vase life is poor (4–5 days per bloom). All parts of the plant are extremely poisonous. Flowers are ethylene sensitive.

QUALITY CRITERIA Select single stems with fully opened flowers. On branched stems, select ones with 1–2 open flowers.

CARE & HANDLING Place stems in a preservative solution with a sugar to ensure that most of the buds will open. Do not store single flowers, but use them promptly. Branched stems can be stored at 3–4°C (37–39°F) and 95% relative humidity. The pollen will stain clothing – so either pull off the anthers, or seal them with a spray to prevent staining.

Gloriosa superba L. (=*G. rothschildiana*)   family: Colchicaceae

klimmende lelie (Dutch); *gloriosa, superbe de Malabar* (French); *Ruhmeskrone* (German); *giglio rampicante* (Italian)

Gomphrena globosa

globe amaranth • bachelor's button

Gomphrena globosa 'Pink Pinheads'

Gomphrena globosa purple and white

Gomphrena globosa 'QIS Red'

DESCRIPTION The plant is an annual herb (0.6 m or 2' high) with hairy stems and leaves. Solitary flower spikes are borne at the stem tips. They are white, pink, purple or red. Several seed races and numerous cultivars are bred for the florist trade (bigger flowers, sturdier stems, better shapes, brighter colours and better yields). Many of the recent cultivars are derived from hybrids between *G. globosa* and *G. haageana*.

ORIGIN & HISTORY Old World tropics, but widely cultivated (e.g. Central America) for the edible leaves. Nowadays the main interest is the dried flower market.

PARTS USED Flowering stems are used as cut flowers.

CULTIVATION Plants flower when they mature and when they form additional nodes. The number of nodes is, however, influenced by light intensity and temperature. Plants grow and flower more rapidly at temperatures above 21°C (70°F) and slow down significantly as temperatures consistently fall below 18°C (65°F).

Globe amaranths are cultivated in open fields, seldom in greenhouses.

PROPERTIES The vase life is slightly poor to average (5–8 days). Flower heads are sometimes prone to shattering and the plants are susceptible to fungi and viruses.

QUALITY CRITERIA Select stems with flowers in full colour and closed or only beginning to open. Most flowers are field-grown so check carefully for disease and damage. Make sure leaves have good uniform colour and are not pale or blotchy.

CARE & HANDLING Recut the stems and place them in a general preservative. Remove any foliage that will end up below the water line. Storage of fresh flowers is not recommended, but if absolutely necessary, store for only 2–3 days at 3–4°C (37–39°F). Flowers are excellent for drying. First allow them to open fully and then hang them upside down in small bunches to air-dry. Foliage can be left on the stems. Dry in a well-ventilated area with low humidity to avoid flowers becoming mouldy.

Gomphrena globosa L.   family: Amaranthaceae

kogelamarant (Dutch); *amarantine* (French); *Kugel-Amarant* (German)

Goniolimon tataricum

statice • tartarian statice • German statice

Goniolimon tataricum flowering stems

Goniolimon tataricum flowers

DESCRIPTION A small perennial herb (0.3 m or 1') with a woody base and large leaves. The dense flower spikes are maroon, lavender, mauve or blue. Very few cultivars are available as florist flowers and it would seem more attention is given to breeding and selecting of *Limonium* hybrids (which are similar in appearance and use). *Goniolimon* species are similar to *Limonium* species but the styles are hairy and the stigmas are capitate.

ORIGIN & HISTORY South-eastern Europe to southern Russia. German statice is also a common name used for *Limonium* species. The popularity of *Goniolimon* as a filler and dried flower has declined steadily over the last few years.

PARTS USED Flowering stems are used as filler.

CULTIVATION Most cultivation takes place in open fields, where plants remain productive for at least three years. A cold period is necessary for good flower quality and yields. Hot summers, however, have no serious effect on flower quality but colour intensity is not as good. Long days tend to accelerate flowering even though statice is not a long-day plant.

PROPERTIES Vase life is average to good (7–10 days). Flowers have a fairly unpleasant scent.

QUALITY CRITERIA Select stems where the bracts are fully unfolded to within 25 mm (1") of the tip, that is, with approximately 80–90% of the flowers open. Do not purchase stems with 100% open flowers as these may discolour or have a short vase life. Stems harvested too early (30% or less flowers open) will not open and display well. Make sure stems are well branched, have good length and open flowers have not started to decline.

CARE & HANDLING Recut the stems and place them in a preservative solution containing a sugar and bactericide. Remove any foliage that will end up below the water line and preferably replace the water every few days. Statice is ideally suitable for drying. Hang the stems upside down in small bunches in a well-ventilated, cool area. Once dried, the flowers should last for up to two years.

Goniolimon tataricum (L.) Boiss. (=*Limonium tataricum*)   family: Plumbaginaceae

statice de Tartarie (French); *Statice* (German)

Grevillea whiteana

spider flower • honeycomb

Grevillea 'Misty Pink'

Grevillea 'Moonlight'

Grevillea whiteana flowers

DESCRIPTION This is a tall shrub or small tree of 5 m (16') or more. The compound, silvery leaves are very large (150 mm or 6" long), with long, narrow segments. The cream-coloured flowers are spider-like in appearance and are borne in cylindrical clusters of more than 100 mm (4") long. A large number of species have become popular garden shrubs and some of them are also used to varying degrees as cut flowers and fillers. There are very few cultivars, but the well-known *Grevillea* 'Honeycomb' has honey-coloured flowers. Other species often harvested for their flowers include *G. concinna* (red), *G. longistyla* (red) and *G. leucopteris* (pale yellow). *G. baileyana* has glossy, green leaves harvested as cut greens.

ORIGIN & HISTORY Eastern Australia. The spectacular racemes have become popular as rather unusual cut flowers.

PARTS USED Flowering stems used as fillers and leaves as cut greens.

CULTIVATION Plants do best in airy, full sun conditions. Soils should be fairly light, free-draining and acidic. Plants are sensitive to heavy frost. Many flowers are still wild-harvested.

PROPERTIES Vase life is average to good (7–14 days), depending on flower quality and stage of harvest. Flowers are sensitive to ethylene.

QUALITY CRITERIA Look for well-branched, long, straight stems full of flowers. Flowers must be mature with styles starting to appear. Check that no flowers have started to deteriorate. Stems should be young, not too woody and all leaves healthy and free of blemishes.

CARE & HANDLING Immediately recut stems and hydrate in a hydrating solution at a low pH (3–3.5), for 2–4 hours at room temperature. Afterwards transfer stems into a floral preservative and display in a cool place, or hold in the cooler at 4–6°C (39–43°F). Stems can be stored in a preservative for 5–7 days at 1–2°C (34–36°F) and a relative humidity of 90–95%.

Grevillea whiteana McGillivray

family: Proteaceae

grevillea (Dutch); *grévillée* (French); *Grevillee* (German); *grevillea* (Italian, Spanish)

Guzmania lingulata

scarlet star • bromeliad

Guzmania lingulata red

Guzmania lingulata yellow

DESCRIPTION An epiphyte with overlapping leaves forming a rosette. The leaves form a natural container in which rainwater is collected. The flower bracts are brightly coloured – red, pink or orange. Improvements in tissue culture techniques have resulted in many (20–30+) new hybrids being released every year.

ORIGIN & HISTORY Rainforests of Central and South America. It is named after the 18th century Spanish naturalist and plant collector Anastasio Guzman. *Guzmania* plants naturally grow in trees but are not parasites.

PARTS USED Whole plants are used as potted flowers.

CULTIVATION Bromeliads are propagated from seed, tissue culture and cuttings. However, this is done by specialists and growers typically purchase young plants. Good ventilation and ample space are essential. Overcrowding results in stretched leaves, reduced flower size and low quality. Although naturally epiphytic, the plants adapt well to a variety of planting mediums, as long as they are slightly acidic.

PROPERTIES Coloured "flowers" (bracts) last several months but the actual flowers (small, yellow) will fade much quicker. Every year new growth is produced at soil level from which new flowers will appear. Bromeliads are sensitive to botrytis.

QUALITY CRITERIA Select plants with well-formed, good length flowering spikes. Choose plants with healthy, light green coloured leaves and brightly coloured bracts. Make sure the leaves and bracts are free of damage and marks.

CARE & HANDLING Place in maximum natural light, but shaded from direct sunlight. Do not over-water, as the vase life of the flower and plant will suffer. Keep the potting medium on the dry side. Use soft, tepid water and keep the central "vase" of the plant filled. Mist plants occasionally as they do best in a high humidity environment. Temperatures between a minimum of 16°C (61°F) and a maximum of 27°C (81°F) are ideal.

Guzmania lingulata (L.) Mez.

family: Bromeliaceae

bromelia (Dutch); *guzmania* (French); *Guzmanie* (German)

Gymnocalycium mihanovichii
chin cactus • plaid cactus

Gymnocalycium mihanovichii

DESCRIPTION The chin cactus is small and ball-shaped, with prominent ribs (often decorated with cross-banding) and rather short, thin spines (but some forms are totally devoid of spines). The brightly coloured forms sold by florists completely lack chlorophyll and will not survive if they are not grafted onto green cactus rootstocks (rooted stem sections of *Hylocereus trigonus* are mostly used). There is a wide range of colours available, including dark green, red, yellow, orange, grey and even black. The cultivar 'Red Top' is also commonly known as 'Ruby Ball' or 'Hibotan'.

ORIGIN & HISTORY Paraguay. The exact origin of the brightly coloured mutant forms is not well documented. It is thought to have originated from a greenhouse in Canada or from Japan or Korea in the mid 1900s.

PARTS USED Whole plants are used as potted "flowers".

CULTIVATION Plants are propagated by means of seed or stem cuttings. Growers have to work very

hygienically as grafted cactuses are susceptible to viral infections.

PROPERTIES Potted plants can last for many years. They can have sharp thorns and should be handled with care. Plants can tolerate cold days and nights, but not when the temperate drops below freezing (–1°C; 30°F). Flowers only open fully in bright light and can bloom for several months.

QUALITY CRITERIA There are no definite quality criteria but make sure the plants are well developed and well rooted (not loose in the pot). Avoid plants that are soft or wilted and not fully turgid. The base stem (on which the coloured stems are grafted) must be of a uniform green colour. Plants must be free of marks, blemishes and general damage.

CARE & HANDLING Display these cacti in light shade to filtered sun but avoid strong direct sunlight. If exposed to full sun, the colour will fade and the tender plant bodies will be scorched. Water regularly in summer, but keep the roots quite dry during winter or during cold periods.

Gymnocalycium mihanovichii (Fric & Guerke) Britt. & Rose   family: Cactaceae

Gymnocalycium mihanovichii (Dutch, French, Italian, Spanish); *Spinnenkaktus* (German)

Gypsophila paniculata
baby's breath • gypsophila • "gyp"

Gypsophila 'Million Stars'

Gypsophila 'Million Stars'

Gypsophila 'Perfecta'

DESCRIPTION A perennial herb with a fleshy taproot, narrow grey leaves and intricately branched, sparse clusters of minute white flowers. Flowering occurs naturally from late spring to late summer. Only a few of the numerous cultivars account for more than 90% of "gyp" found in florists. 'Perfecta' and 'Million Stars' are presently setting the world standard.

ORIGIN & HISTORY Central Europe to central Asia. *Gypsophila* means "gypsum loving" and refers to the preferred soil type. Baby's breath has become exceptionally popular as filler for bridal bouquets.

PARTS USED Flowering stems are used as cut flowers and whole plants as potted flowers.

CULTIVATION Flowering is inhibited by short days. In temperate regions gypsophilas are grown as perennials and in cold regions under glass as annuals. Plants prefer full sun and well-drained soils. Stems for export are harvested with 25–30% of flowers open. They are then placed in a preservative (STS and 5–7% sugar), followed by a few days in a well-lit opening room at 26–27°C (79–81°F). When 50% of the flowers are open, the stems are dry-packed and shipped.

PROPERTIES Vase life is poor to average (5–7 days). "Gyp" is sensitive to ethylene (flowers shrivel), bacterial contamination in the vase water and botrytis during cool storage.

QUALITY CRITERIA Select stems with 30–50% of the flowers open. Look for heavy bunches with sturdy, well-branched stems and evenly spaced flowers. Check that none of the flowers have browned, dried out or shrivelled.

CARE & HANDLING Recut the stems and place them in a preservative with a sugar (to assist in bud-opening) and an anti-ethylene agent. Stems tangle easily and hooked flowers are pulled off if not carefully handled. Hold upside down and shake lightly to loosen and separate the stems. Stems can be stored for 3–4 days in water at 1–2°C (34–36°F). Flowers dry well, but first make sure that 80–90% of them are open.

Gypsophila paniculata L.   family: Caryophyllaceae

gipskruid (Dutch); *gypsophile* (French); *Schleierkraut* (German); *gissofila* (Italian); *gisofila* (Spanish)

Hakea victoria
pincushion tree

Hakea victoria foliage

Hakea multilineata flowers

DESCRIPTION The plant is an erect to bushy shrub of about 3 m (10′) high. The leaves are 120 mm (nearly 5″) in diameter and green or variegated. They are at first silvery in colour and then change to orange and red. The small flowers (8 mm or ⅓″ long) are cream-coloured to pink and are borne in clusters. Flowering occurs in late winter to spring. As yet there appears to be no registered cultivars and there is still a fair amount of wild-harvesting. *Hakea coriacea* (pink spike hakea) and *H. multilineata* are also commonly used as florist fillers (they have red-pink "cushions" with white needles).

ORIGIN & HISTORY Western Australia. Plants are becoming popular as garden shrubs. Considerable efforts in research and marketing are underway to commercialise the production and to improve availability.

PARTS USED The leafy flowering branches are used as cut foliage or fillers.

CULTIVATION Plants require a free-draining soil because without adequate aeration at the root zone rootlets will often die off, creating a favourable environment for soil-borne fungal diseases. Plants are drought and heat tolerant and generally dislike sheltered, humid conditions, but prefer good air-circulation.

PROPERTIES Vase life is average to usually good (7–18 days). Flowers are not sensitive to ethylene.

QUALITY CRITERIA Look for well-branched stems full of flowers. Flowers need to be mature and fully developed but make sure that no flowers have started to deteriorate. Leaves need to be a bright green colour, clean and free of damage or disease.

CARE & HANDLING Recut stems and remove leaves below the water line. Place in a full floral preservative (with a sugar) and leave to hydrate at room temperature for 3–4 hours before using or storing. Cut stems can be stored at 1–3°C (34–37°F) for 5–7 days (relative humidity 90–95%). Flowers can be dried.

Hakea victoria J. Drumm.   family: Proteaceae

hakea (Dutch, Italian, Spanish); *arbre-aux-oursins*, hakea (French); *Hakea, Nadelkissen* (German)

Hedera helix

ivy • common ivy • English ivy

Hedera helix (green)

Hedera helix (variegated)

DESCRIPTION A climber (vine) with creeping stems that cling to objects by means of aerial climbing roots. Lower leaves are 3-lobed to 5-lobed and much smaller than the leaves found on flowering stems. Small yellowish flowers are borne in rounded umbels, followed by purple berries of about 9 mm (⅓") in diameter. A large number of leaf forms and named cultivars are available, ranging from the ordinary green (wild) form to a diversity of shapes and variegated types (with white, silver, yellow or purple colour patterns).

ORIGIN & HISTORY Ivy has a wide natural distribution in Europe and Asia. It is used in herbal medicine as an expectorant. Ivy is traditionally associated with fidelity in the language of flowers.

PARTS USED The leafy stems are used as foliage and are very popular in wedding work and on pedestals. Flowers or fruits may be present (then called "berried ivy").

CULTIVATION Plants are easily propagated from cuttings. The leaf form of the parent plant is maintained when cuttings are taken from upper branches. To produce high quality foliage, regular irrigation and rich, well-drained soils are required.

PROPERTIES Vase life can be quite variable, from poor to good (5–10 days), depending on quality and cultivar.

QUALITY CRITERIA Select fully mature leaves. Look for clean leaves without damage or marks, especially browned tips or edges. Leaves need to be evenly spaced along the length of the stem and have good colour and markings, if variegated.

CARE & HANDLING Recut stems and place in a floral preservative. Remove leaves that will be below the water line. Preferably do not keep vines longer than 1 m (40"), but cut into smaller pieces (unless for a specific reason). Mist the stems, wrap them loosely in plastic bags and store at 2–4°C (36–39°F) or store in preservative at the same temperature and a high relative humidity (95%). Stems can be stored for 7–10 days.

Hedera helix L.   family: Araliaceae

klimop (Dutch); *lierre grimpant, lierre commun* (French); *Efeu* (German); *edera* (Italian); *hiedra* (Spanish)

Hedychium coronarium

white ginger lily • butterfly lily • garland flower

Hedychium coronarium

Hedychium gardnerianum

Hedychium coccineum flowers

DESCRIPTION This ginger relative is a robust perennial herb of up to 3 m (10') high, with thick rhizomes and large hairless leaves. The fragrant flowers are borne in multi-flowered clusters. Each flower has a long tube of 70 mm (nearly 3") long, ending in a broad, 2-lobed lip of 50 mm (2") in diameter. A few cultivars have been developed, including 'F.W. Moore' (a hybrid between *H. coronarium* and *H. coccineum*). It has large, very showy amber yellow flowers with orange-yellow blotches.

ORIGIN & HISTORY India. Several ginger lilies are grown as ornamental plants. Some have became troublesome weeds, such as the yellow ginger lily (*H. gardnerianum*) – yellow flowers with bright red styles. *H. coccineum* is similar to *H. coronarium* but has red to orange flowers. *Abir*, a scented powder used in Hindu ceremonies, is made from the rhizome of the Indian *H. spicatum*.

PARTS USED The flowering stems are used as cut flowers and the leaves as cut greens.

CULTIVATION Plants require rich, well-drained soils and regular watering. Warm, high light intensity (full sun to partial shade) conditions are preferred. Plants die down during winter, but emerge again in spring.

PROPERTIES Plants can flower over a period of 5–6 weeks, but the individual flowers do not last very long once harvested. The vase life of individual flowers is very poor (1–2 days). The flowers are fragrant.

QUALITY CRITERIA Flower clusters must be well formed but buds still closed, with the first few just starting to open and showing colour. Flower heads and leaves must be free of any blemishes. Avoid stems with flowers that have fully opened.

CARE & HANDLING Recut the stems and immediately hydrate them at room temperature. Do not store but use cut flowers promptly. Leaves can be placed in a bactericide and held at 4–6°C (39–43°F) and 95% relative humidity until needed.

Hedychium coronarium J.G. Koenig   family: Zingiberaceae

hedychium (Dutch); *hédychium* (French); *Kranzblume, Schmetterlingsingwer* (German); *edichio blanco, jengibre blanco* (Spanish)

Helenium autumnale

sneezeweed • sneezewort • autumn sunspray

Helenium autumnale

DESCRIPTION The plant is a perennial herb of 0.6–1.5 m (2–5′) high (depending on the cultivar) with lance-shaped leaves and attractive yellow to copper-coloured daisy-like flower heads. Each flower head has a prominent cone-shaped disc in the middle, surrounded by large ray florets that gradually become reflexed. Numerous cultivars are available, many of them dwarf types intended for use in gardens as herbaceous borders. Amongst the taller types are the copper-red 'Moerheim Beauty', the yellow 'Sonnenwunder' and the brown and gold 'Goldrausch'.

ORIGIN & HISTORY North America (Canada and the United States). Almost all garden sneezeweeds are derived from one species, *H. autumnale*. Amongst the 40 species of *Helenium*, some are notorious weeds, while others are poisonous to farm animals.

PARTS USED The flowering stems are used as cut flowers or fillers. Whole plants are grown as potted flowers or container plants.

CULTIVATION Plants are easily propagated from seeds or by division of the clumps in autumn or spring. Well-drained soil and regular irrigation is essential. The stems of the taller cultivars have to be supported.

PROPERTIES Vase life is average to good (7–10 days). The main attraction of sneezeweed flower heads is their rich yellow and copper colours. Flowers are not ethylene sensitive.

QUALITY CRITERIA Select stems with several to most of the flower heads open. No flowers should have started to deteriorate. Stems need to be well branched. Check that flower petals (ligulate florets) are free of blemishes. Foliage must also be healthy and clean.

CARE & HANDLING Recut stems and remove foliage below the water line. Put in a preservative with a bactericide and sugar and leave to hydrate at room temperature for 2–3 hours prior to use or storage. Flower heads can be stored for 5–6 days at 2–3°C (36–37°F) (relative humidity of 90–95%).

Helenium autumnale L.   family: Asteraceae

zonnekruid (Dutch); *hélénie* (French); *Gewöhnliche Sonnenbraut* (German); *elenio* (Italian); *helenio* (Spanish)

Helianthus annuus

sunflower

Helianthus annuus 'Double Shine'

Helianthus annuus 'Sunrich Orange'

Helianthus annuus 'Prado Red'

DESCRIPTION The common sunflower is an erect annual herb with a sturdy stem bearing a single, large flower head. Each flower head has numerous disc florets surrounded by bright yellow ray florets. The ordinary single type is still preferred above double forms. However, the pompom or "teddy bear" types have become popular. Red and light yellow (lemon) coloured cultivars do not stay true to colour when grown in warm, outdoor climates. Another popular group is the multi-flowering stems with small flower heads (e.g. 'Sonja').

ORIGIN & HISTORY Western parts of the United States. Since the 16th century, sunflower has been an important food item and oil crop. Only recently, sunflowers have also become a popular cut flower.

PARTS USED Flower heads are used as cut flowers and whole plants as pot plants.

CULTIVATION Plants are grown in greenhouses as well as in open fields. All F$_1$ hybrids are grown from seed. Sunflowers need good light and warmth (above 12°C; 54°F) to grow and produce well. A critical factor in production is spacing. If spaced too far apart, stems become too thick and tall. However, dense planting increases the risk of rust and powdery mildew.

PROPERTIES Vase life ranges from slightly below average to fairly good (5–10 days). New cultivars are pollen-free and quite different to the familiar type of sunflower grown for oil.

QUALITY CRITERIA Flower heads are usually heavy, so select straight, sturdy stems with the flowers in bud stage but showing colour. Make sure leaves are free of damage and have a bright green colour (not pale, which is often a sign of poor nutrition). In the case of pot plants, stems should not be too tall or spindly and flowers not more than half open.

CARE & HANDLING Recut stems and place in clean water with an all-purpose preservative, which also assists flower opening. Store at 5–10°C (41–50°F). Flower heads air-dry well.

Helianthus annuus L (=*H. giganteus* L.)   family Asteraceae

zonnebloem (Dutch); *soleil, tournesol* (French); *Sonnenblume* (German); *corona del sole, girasole* (Italian); *himawari, koujitsuki* (Japanese); *girasol* (Spanish)

Helichrysum bracteatum
strawflower • everlasting

Helichrysum bracteatum bronze

Helichrysum bracteatum pink

DESCRIPTION An annual or perennial herb (up to 1.5 m or 5'). The flower heads are surrounded by dry, stiff, papery bracts in a multitude of colours. Cultivar selection has focused on tall flower heads with limited side branching, as well as on colour and drying properties. There are many cultivars and species that are used as dried flowers.

ORIGIN & HISTORY Australia. The strawflower is sometimes placed in the genus *Bracteantha*. Rosemary strawflower (*H. rosmarinifolium*) is now *Ozothamnus rosmarinifolius*. Strawflowers are important in the dried flower market.

PARTS USED Flower heads are used as dried flowers and to a lesser extent as fresh cut flowers.

CULTIVATION Long days result in faster flowering but flowering occurs regardless of day length. Growth is influenced by light intensity and temperature. For optimum quality and yields, temperatures need to be above 13°C (55°F). Optimum production temperatures are 21–24°C (70–75°F). Soils need to have good drainage.

Heavy rainfalls and high temperatures often lead to disease.

PROPERTIES The vase life of fresh cut flowers is often disappointing, although average to fairly good when compared to many other florist flowers (5–10 days). The flower heads have no disernable fragrance.

QUALITY CRITERIA Select heads that are opening, with the centres visible. Heads intended for drying should not be too open, as open bracts turn backwards in the drying process. Check that stems and leaves are free of spots.

CARE & HANDLING Recut and place fresh flowers in a preservative. Storage is not recommended. If absolutely necessary for a day or two, then store at 3–5°C (37–41°F). Flower heads dry very well and keep for a long time. Remove leaves and hang upside down in tight bunches in a warm, but well-ventilated area. Just the flower head can be dried – leave only 15–25 mm (½–1") of stem attached (for wiring).

Helichrysum bracteatum (Vent.) Andrews (=*Bracteantha bracteatum*)   family: Asteraceae

strobloem (Dutch); *immortelle* (French); *Garten-Strohblume* (German)

Heliconia bihai

macaw flower • balisier • firebird • lobster claws

Heliconia bihai

Heliconia aurantiaca

DESCRIPTION A banana-like plant with erect stems of up to 5 m (about 16') tall and leaves of up to 2 m (6½') long. The erect flowering stalks are about 1 m (40") long and comprise 3 to 15 large, colourful bracts that are arranged side by side on a strongly flexuous (zigzag) stalk. The relationship between the wild form of *H. bihai* (which is rarely cultivated) and numerous cultivars ascribed to it is not clear. Cultivars differ in colour patterns and in the degree to which the stem (rachis) is twisted or spiralled. Cultivars include 'Arawak' (bracts red, yellow and green), 'Chocolate Dancer' (bracts chocolate red with yellow edges) and 'Jade Forest' (bracts jade green). The similar-looking *H. aurantiaca* is also used.

ORIGIN & HISTORY Central and South America. A very large number of cultivars and colour forms have been described but their origin is not always certain.

PARTS USED The flowering stems are used as cut flowers or fillers and for design work. The leaves are used as cut greens.

CULTIVATION Heliconias require tropical growing conditions if quality flowers are to be produced, that is, consistently warm temperatures, high humidity, good watering and high light intensities.

PROPERTIES Vase life is normally good (7–21 days). Flowers are easily damaged by careless handling and are also very sensitive to chill damage. They are not sensitive to ethylene.

QUALITY CRITERIA Select sturdy stems with mature, well-formed and well-coloured bracts. Bracts must be closed with no actual flowers having emerged or visible. Check that stems and flowers are free of black marks and other damage.

CARE & HANDLING Recut the stems and loosen the bunches to ensure good air-movement. Hydrate them at room temperature for a few hours before using. Flowers can be stored in a bactericide for 8–10 days at 12°C (54°F) and under a high relative humidity (95%). Do not store at temperatures below 12°C (54°F).

Heliconia bihai (L.) L.

family: Heliconiaceae

grote kreeftsklauw (Dutch); *balisier* (French); *Scharlachrote Hummerschere* (German); *bijao* (Spanish)

Heliconia psittacorum

parrot's flower • parakeet flower

Heliconia psittacorum bicolour

Heliconia psittacorum red

Heliconia psittacorum yellow

Description A relatively small plant (about 1.5 m or 5′) with oblong to linear leaves. The flowering stalks are erect and slender, with 2–7 waxy, often narrow, non-overlapping, upcurved bracts. They range in colour from red and pink to orange, yellow or green. A multitude of cultivars, differing mainly in the colour of the bracts, have been developed. Cultivars with sturdy stems derive from a hybrid of this species with *H. spathocircinata*. Known cultivars include 'Rubra' (orange-red bracts) and 'Sassy' (yellow with red tips).

Origin & history South America (eastern Brazil to the Lesser Antilles). Parrot's flowers have become popular as garden plants in tropical regions (especially Indonesia, Malaysia, Singapore and in parts of tropical Africa).

Parts used Flowering stems: cut flowers. Leaves: cut greens.

Cultivation Heliconias require well drained, rich but loose soils. They also need warm temperatures and high light intensity. Plants thrive under conditions of regular watering and high humidity.

Properties Vase life is average to good (7–14 days), depending on the cultivar. Stems do not develop further once they are harvested. Flowers are prone to cold damage and physical damage. They are not ethylene sensitive.

Quality criteria Select stems with fully developed bracts and clean, bright colours. Bracts must still be closed with no flowers emerging. Look for long, straight flowering stems, free of damage and black spots, which are often the result of cold damage due to incorrect post-harvest handling.

Care & handling Recut stems by at least 20–50 mm (1–2″) and loosen bunches to improve air-movement. Hydrate stems for a few hours in acidic water (pH 3–3.5), as proper water uptake is critical. Use a preservative containing a bactericide, to ensure uninterrupted water uptake and reduce microbial growth. Heliconias are tropical plants, so store flowers above 10°C (50°F), ideally at 13–14°C (55–57°F).

Heliconia psittacorum L. f.   family: Heliconiaceae

papegaaienbanaan (Dutch); *héliconia bec de perroquet, héliconia perroquet* (French); *Papageien-Hummerschere* (German); *platanillo* (Spanish)

Heliconia rostrata

hanging lobster claws • beaked heliconia

Heliconia rostrata inflorescence

Heliconia rostrata flowers

DESCRIPTION The plant is leafy and banana-like with slender stems of about 2 m (6½') high. Leaves vary in length from 0.6 to 1.2 m (2–4'). The inflorescences are highly characteristic and spectacular – typically hanging (pendulous), with a markedly flexuous (zigzag) axis. The large bracts of about 150 mm (6") long are laterally flattened and resemble enormous lobster claws. They are arranged side by side in two ranks along the axis and are not overlapping when mature. The colour pattern is particularly striking. The flowers themselves are yellowish green. Unlike other heliconias (with countless cultivars), only the wild form of this species is cultivated.

ORIGIN & HISTORY South America (Peru to Argentina). The hanging lobster claw is widely cultivated all over the world for its spectacular flowers.

PARTS USED The flowering stems are used as cut flowers.

CULTIVATION High temperatures, adequate moisture and high humidity are essential. Plants cannot be grown successfully in cool or temperate climates, let alone areas that experience frost. Cultivation is in open fields, with and without partial shading.

PROPERTIES Vase life is average to very good (7–21 days). Flowers are sensitive to chill damage as well as handling damage. They are not sensitive to ethylene.

QUALITY CRITERIA Select sturdy stems with well-formed, evenly spaced flower bracts. Bracts must be mature, vividly coloured and almost ready to open. Check that flowers (coloured bracts) and stems are free of black spots and other blemishes or damage.

CARE & HANDLING Unpack and check flowers for any damage that may have occured during transport. Handle with utmost care and recut the stems and hydrate them for 2–4 hours at room temperature before using or storing. Do not store below 13°C (55°F). Store or hold at 13–16°C (55–61°F) and a high relative humidity (95%).

Heliconia rostrata Ruiz. & Pav.

family: Heliconiaceae

snavelheliconia (Dutch); *héliconia rostré* (French); *Hängende Hummerschere* (German); *patujú* (Spanish)

Heliopsis helianthoides

heliopsis • ox-eye

Heliopsis helianthoides

DESCRIPTION The plant is a perennial herb of up to 1.5 m (5') high with a bushy growth form, lance-shaped leaves and numerous flower heads borne at the stem tips. The flower heads are about 75 mm (3") in diameter and are borne on long stems. Both the ray florets and disc florets are various shades of yellow. The heads may be single, semi-double or double. A large number of long-stemmed cultivars are available to the florist industry. Examples are the bright golden, fully double 'Sonneschild', the deep gold 'Zinniiflora' and the semi-double, orange-flowered 'Hohlspiegel'. The 1.5 m (5') tall 'Mars' (dark gold) and the massive 'Jupiter' (orange-yellow) are examples of single-flowered cultivars.

ORIGIN & HISTORY North America (Canada and the United States). The plant is well known in the United States as *H. scabra* but this hairy form is now considered to be merely a subspecies of *H. helianthoides*. Modern tall cultivars have become popular as cut flowers.

PARTS USED The flowering stems are used as cut flowers or fillers.

CULTIVATION Plants are easily cultivated from seed or by division of the roots. Heliopsis is tolerant of most soil types as long as it is fairly well draining. For the best results, warm temperatures and full sun conditions are necessary.

PROPERTIES Vase life is average (6–8 days).

QUALITY CRITERIA Look for flower heads that are 75% to fully open, but make sure they have not started to deteriorate and are free of any blemishes or pests. Stems should be well branched and full of buds. Leaves should be of a uniform green colour and damage-free.

CARE & HANDLING Recut stems and place in a preservative and allow to hydrate for a few hours at room temperature before using or storing. Remove leaves that are below the water line. Flower heads can be stored at 1–2°C (34–36°F) for 4–5 days and at 90–95% relative humidity.

Heliopsis helianthoides (L.) Sweet (=*H. scabra*)   family: Asteraceae

zone-oog (Dutch); *héliopsis* (French); *Sonnenauge* (German); *heliopsis* (Italian, Spanish)

Helleborus orientalis

lenten rose

Helleborus niger (pink)

Helleborus orientalis flowers

Helleborus niger (green)

DESCRIPTION A perennial herb with underground rhizomes, long-stalked, segmented leaves and flowers in groups of up to 4 on stems of 0.3 m (1') high. The flowers are saucer-shaped, 70 mm (nearly 3") in diameter and typically nodding or facing outwards. The colour varies and includes shades of white, cream, purple and green. *H. orientalis* is used more as a cut flower and the similar-looking Christmas rose (*H. niger*) more as a potted flower (it has shorter flowering stems). Numerous species, hybrids and cultivars are known.

ORIGIN & HISTORY Greece and Turkey. This species and *H. niger* are well-known garden plants but are not extensively used as florist flowers.

PARTS USED Flowering stems are used as cut flowers and whole plants as potted flowers.

CULTIVATION Seeds are difficult to germinate and require specialised care. Flowers are only harvested from the second year on, but once established the plants flower for many years.

Cold temperatures are beneficial for growth and flowering and appear to be necessary to break flower dormancy. Most flowers are field-grown and are not produced in greenhouses.

PROPERTIES Vase life is good (10–14 days). Flowers are not ethylene sensitive.

QUALITY CRITERIA Select flowers that are 50–75% open (stamens should be visible). Make sure leaves of cut flowers are free of disease and damage as most are field-grown. Select potted flowers with only 2–5 flowers partially open and showing stamens.

CARE & HANDLING Recut the stems and place them in a general preservative solution. Flowers can be stored for quite a few days at 5–6°C (41–43°F), but then do so in a preservative. Display pots in good light (not direct sunlight) and preferably in a cool, draught-free area. Keep the potting medium moist but not wet. Flowers can be dried. Hang them upside down in small bunches in a cool, airy place or use silica gel or a similar desiccant.

Helleborus orientalis Lam.

family: Ranunculaceae

kerstroos (Dutch); *hellebore d'Orient* (French); *Orientalische Nieswurz* (German); *rosa di natale* (Italian)

Hesperis matronalis

sweet rocket • damask flower • damask violet

Hesperis matronalis

DESCRIPTION This is a biennial or perennial herb of up to 1 m (40") high with hairy, glandular leaves and clusters of white to purple flowers. Each flower has four white to lilac petals of about 20 mm long surrounding four long and two short stamens. Garden forms may have double flowers. Several cultivars are available, including 'Alba' (white, single flowers), 'Alba Plena' (white, double), 'Lilacina Flore Plena' (lilac, double), 'Nana Candidissima' (dwarf, white), 'Purpurea' (purple, single) and 'Purpurea Plena' (purple, double).

ORIGIN & HISTORY Europe to Asia. The plant is a popular garden ornamental that is extensively used for borders and containers. It is occasionally grown as a cut flower and potted flower.

PARTS USED The leafy, flowering stems are used as florist flowers or fillers. The whole plant is used as a potted flower or container plant.

CULTIVATION The flowers are normally grown from seed. Plants do best in full sun conditions and free-draining soils. They can be cut back after flowering and will flower again the next season. However, commercial growers usually treat plants as annuals.

PROPERTIES Vase life can be a bit variable, from fairly poor to fairly good (5–10 days). Flowers are scented. If harvested too mature then flowers tend to drop their petals and vase life is poor. They are not sensitive to ethylene.

QUALITY CRITERIA Select flowering stems with 25–30% of flowers opened or opening. Look for sturdy, straight stems with full flower heads. Check that buds, leaves and stems are free of any blemishes.

CARE & HANDLING Recut the stems and hydrate them at room temperature for 2–3 hours prior to use or storage. Place the flowers in a floral preservative with a bactericide. Storage is not recommended, but rather use promptly. Flowers can be held at 4–6°C (39–43°F) and a relative humidity of 90–95% until used.

Hesperis matronalis L.
family: Brassicaceae

damastbloem (Dutch); *julienne des dames* (French); *Nachtviole, Gewöhnliche Nachtviole* (German); *violacciocca antoniana* (Italian); *juliana* (Spanish)

Heuchera sanguinea
coral bells • alum root

Heuchera sanguinea 'Fire Fly'

DESCRIPTION A perennial, evergreen or semi-evergreen herb with lobed, hairy and conspicuously veined leaves. The flowers are typically small pink or red bells that are borne in branched clusters. Each flower is about 12 mm (½") long and bright red in the wild form (but variously white or pink in cultivated forms). Several cultivars are available, many of them also derived from *H. ×bizoides* (which in turn is thought to be a hybrid between *H. sanguinea*, *H. americana* and *H. micrantha*). These include 'Alba' and 'Virginalis' (both with white flowers), 'Grandiflora' (vigorous, with large flowers), 'Maxima' (wine red flowers) and 'Oxfordii' (dark red). 'Variegata' has variegated leaves. Cultivars with dark bronze-coloured foliage are also available.

ORIGIN & HISTORY North America (south-western parts of the United States and Mexico). The plant is a popular ground cover and garden plant, the flowers of which are occasionally used by florists.

PARTS USED The flowering stems are used as cut flowers or fillers.

CULTIVATION Coral bells are propagated by means of seeds or by division, although results from seed are variable. Plants prefer full sun to partial shade conditions, and are fairly tolerant of different soils types, so long as they are well drained.

PROPERTIES Vase life is average (6–8 days). Flowers are sensitive to ethylene.

QUALITY CRITERIA Flowering stems need to be long, straight and sturdy enough to carry the flowers. Select stems with 30–50% of the flowers open. Make sure that no flowers have deteriorated and that all flowers and stems are free of any blemishes.

CARE & HANDLING Recut the stem ends and place in a full floral preservative with a low sugar concentrate to help more buds to open fully. Flowers can be stored for a few days (3–4) at 1–2°C (34–36°F) and a high relative humidity (95%). Handle with care as the bells tend to hook onto one another and break off.

Heuchera sanguinea Engelm.   family: Saxifragaceae

purperklokje (Dutch); *heuchera sanguin* (French); *Blut-Purpurglöckchen* (German); *campane di corallo* (Italian); *coralito, flor de coral, campanas de coral* (Spanish)

Hibiscus rosa-sinensis

hibiscus • Chinese hibiscus

Hibiscus rosa-sinensis 'Luna Red'

Hibiscus rosa-sinensis 'Salmon'

Hibiscus rosa-sinensis red

DESCRIPTION A woody shrub (up to 5 m or 16') with large, glossy leaves. The flowers are characteristically red but variously coloured or double in modern cultivars. There are many cultivars and colours (lavender, orange, peach, pink, red and white). Some are more tolerant of low light levels and more compact, thus requiring less or no growth regulators during production.

ORIGIN & HISTORY Unknown in the wild. It is possibly an ancient hybrid between several species and is widely cultivated. Flowers are used for shining shoes in India.

PARTS USED Flowers: florist flowers. Foliage: cut greens. Whole plants: potted flowers.

CULTIVATION Hibiscus plants like heat and humidity and grow best in full sun. Production temperatures need to be kept high (24–29°C; 75–84°F) during the day and around 18–21°C (64–70°F) at night. For year-round production in greenhouses, growers provide supplementary lighting to artificially extend daylight hours.

The growing medium should be well drained and slightly acidic (pH 6–6.5). Plant height is usually controlled by means of growth regulator chemicals.

PROPERTIES Vase life of individual flowers is very poor (1 day). They are sensitive to ethylene.

QUALITY CRITERIA Purchase pots with 2–4 flowers open. Select compact plants, with dark green leaves and numerous buds. Check that leaves are free of spots and yellowing. For cut greens, select well-branched young stems (not too woody) with deep green foliage showing no blemishes.

CARE & HANDLING Unpack and unsleeve potted flowers immediately. Water if medium is dry and do not allow to dry out, as this will result in bud drop. Display in bright light to ensure that buds continue to open. Avoid ethylene-forming agents. Do not display at temperatures below 10°C (50°F) or above 27°C (80°F). Cut greens should be recut and placed in a bactericide.

Hibiscus rosa-sinensis L.   family: Malvaceae

Chinese roos (Dutch); *rose de Chine* (French); *Chinesischer Roseneibisch* (German); *ibisco* (Italian); *fusou, haibisukasu* (Japanese); *rosa de China* (Spanish)

Hippeastrum cultivars

amaryllis

Hippeastrum 'Intokazi'

Hippeastrum single bicolour

DESCRIPTION A bulbous, tropical plant with fleshy, sheath-like leaves and a strong, straight flowering stem. The large, trumpet or open-faced flowers are borne in a cluster at the top of the stem. Bulb size and cultivar determine the number of flowering stalks per plant (usually 2 to 6). Most cultivars produce 4 flowers per stalk. Extensive hybridisation has resulted in large blooms (up to 220 mm or nearly 9"), more flowers per stem and more stems per plant. Colours range from white to pink, red, orange, salmon and also red with white stripes.

ORIGIN & HISTORY Tropical America. Cultivated plants are complicated hybrids of tropical American species. Amaryllis is primarily grown as a potted flower.

PARTS USED Leafless flowering heads are used as cut flowers and whole plants as potted flowers.

CULTIVATION In cut flower production, stems are cut as close to the bulb as possible, without removing any leaves as well. The minimum stem length allowed on many markets is 300 mm (12"). Grading is by the number of buds per stem and stem length. To prevent the hollow stems from splitting and rolling outwards, growers often pulse them overnight or ideally for 24 hours in a sucrose solution.

PROPERTIES Vase life of cut flowers is average to good (7–10 days). The blooms on potted flowers last from 14 to 21 days. Flower buds initially point upwards, but begin to turn down at right angles to the stem as they mature.

QUALITY CRITERIA Select stems with closed buds, just beginning to open and showing colour. High quality stems have numerous buds. Avoid flowers with bruises or blemishes.

CARE & HANDLING Handle blooms carefully as they bruise easily. Store at about 10°C (50°F), as cooler temperatures may cause discolouration. Unpack potted flowers immediately and display in a bright, cool area. Irrigate with tepid water.

Hippeastrum cultivars   family: Amaryllidaceae

amaryllis (Dutch); *amaryllis de rouen* (French); *Amaryllis der Gärtner, Ritterstern* (German); *amarillide* (Italian); *amarilis* (Spanish)

Hosta sieboldiana

plaintain lily

Hosta sieboldiana leaves and flowers

Hosta undulata 'Univitta'

Hosta sieboldiana 'Golden Anniversary'

DESCRIPTION Clump-forming perennial herbs with underground rhizomes and large, often heavily textured and puckered leaves. Clusters of bell-shaped, white or lilac flowers are borne on slender stalks of up to 0.6 m (2') high. There are many cultivars, some of hybrid or unknown origin. Those specifically assigned to *H. sieboldiana* include 'Alba' (also known as 'Golden Sunburst') and 'Semperaurea' which both have golden leaves, 'Bressingham Blue' (broad, blue-green leaves and white flowers), 'Krossa Regal' (blue-grey ribbed leaves and pale lilac flowers on tall stems) and 'Green Sheen' (green, shiny leaves and pale lavender flowers). *Hosta crispula* and *H. undulata* are also sources of florist greens.

ORIGIN & HISTORY Asia (Japan, China and Korea). Plants have been cultivated and hybridised in Japan since ancient times.

PARTS USED The medium-sized, single leaves are used as cut greens and are popular for use in arrangements, baskets and on pedestals.

CULTIVATION *Hosta* species are typically cultivated from cuttings or by division. The plants thrive in a rich, moist soil and prefer partial shade (not full sun). Plants are usually lifted and divided in spring, just as new growth is starting.

PROPERTIES Vase life is average to good (6–10 days). Leaves have no noticeable fragrance. They are not sensitive to ethylene.

QUALITY CRITERIA Look for well-formed, fully mature leaves that are still young and fresh. The leaf colour needs to be clean and distinct, with no browned tips or edges and no physical damage to the leaf blade. Make sure the leaf stalks are sturdy.

CARE & HANDLING Recut the leaf stalks and put them into clean water with a floral preservative. Make sure that the blades of the leaves are not touching the water. Display in a cool, bright place or hold in the cooler. Store the leaves at 2–4°C (36–39°F) and 90–95% relative humidity.

Hosta sieboldiana (Hook.) Engl. & Prantl   family: Hostaceae

hartlelie (Dutch); *funkia, hosta bleu* (French); *Blaublatt-Funkie* (German); *hosta* (Italian); *giboshi* (Japanese); *hosta* (Spanish)

Hyacinthus orientalis

hyacinth • common hyacinth

Hyacinthus orientalis blue

Hyacinthus orientalis mixed colours

DESCRIPTION A true bulb with narrow leaves and small waxy flowers arranged in a dense cluster. They are blue, violet, pink, cream or white in colour and exceptionally fragrant. The plant grows and flowers in winter and is dormant in summer. Many hybrids and cultivars are available, including 'Amethyst' (lilac), 'Appleblossom' (pale pink), 'Ostara' (purple-blue) and 'Multiflora White' (white). Deep red and yellow cultivars are difficult to cultivate in warm climates.

ORIGIN & HISTORY Turkey, Syria and Lebanon (already cultivated in Austria around 1560). The flower symbolises peace and power or simplicity.

PARTS USED Flowers: cut flowers. Whole plant: potted flower.

CULTIVATION Cut flowers are cultivated from smaller bulbs (to avoid stems being too heavy) and are cut off with part of the bulb left attached (to improve water uptake and vase life). Unlike most other bulbs, the colour of the bulb agrees with flower colour.

PROPERTIES Vase life of cut flowers is poor (4–7 days) and the stems are naturally short (therefore ideal as a potted flower). Flowers have a very sweet fragrance and are often chosen for this reason.

QUALITY CRITERIA Look for straight, well-formed flower spikes. Select stems with the basal flowers open and the upper 75% still in bud. Make sure stems and leaves are deep green and not yellowing.

CARE & HANDLING Do not cut off the ends of the stems, as the remaining bulb base is vital to vase life. Place upright in shallow water with a preservative and change water every 2 days. Store in own container for at least 24 hours at room temperature. Refrigerate at 3–5°C (37–41°F) for approximately 2 hours prior to immediate use or else store at 3–5°C (37–41°F) and high humidity (90% if possible). Prolonged refrigeration will reduce fragrance. Display potted flowers in a cool, well-lit area. Keep growing medium moist. Hyacinths do not like warm conditions.

Hyacinthus orientalis L.   family: Asparagaceae (Hyacinthaceae)

hyacint (Dutch); *jacinthe* (French); *Hyazinthe* (German); *giacinto* (Italian); *jacinto* (Spanish)

Hydrangea macrophylla
hortensia

Hydrangea macrophylla pink

Hydrangea macrophylla blue

DESCRIPTION A hardy deciduous shrub with shiny leaves and large rounded flower heads. The heads comprise of groups of male and female florets, some fertile and some not (the infertile ones are more showy). Most cultivars and hybrids in the florist market are from *H. macrophylla*. The two main groups are mopheads (full rounded flower heads) and lacecaps (flat centre with an outer ring of full flowers). Certain cultivars are best grown for blue flowers, others for pink flowers.

ORIGIN & HISTORY Japan and Korea. In the language of flowers, hydrangeas represent a "boaster" or a "heartless" person.

PARTS USED Whole plants are used as potted flowers and flowering stems as cut flowers.

CULTIVATION Acid soils (pH 4.5–5.5) during cultivation produce intense blue flowers, while less acidic soils (pH 5.5–6.5) produce red to pink flowers.

PROPERTIES Vase life is average to good (7–10 days) for treated cut flowers. Flowers in pots last about 6 weeks.

QUALITY CRITERIA Check that plants are free of pests and diseases, especially aphids. Select compact, well-formed plants with full flower heads showing bright and clean colours. Leaves, especially in pink cultivars, should not be yellowing and flowers must be free of marks and botrytis. The bigger the pot, the more blooms per plant (up to 5 in a 200 mm or 8" pot). Cut flowers – select fully opened flowers on straight, sturdy stems.

CARE & HANDLING Display pots in maximum natural light, but avoid direct sunlight and draughts. Storing in the dark for more than 2–3 days can cause leaf drop. Water frequently and keep moist. Avoid condensation on flowers, which can cause botrytis. Use soft water, especially on blue flowers. Recut stems of cut flowers and immediately place in a hydrating solution, or warm water (43–49°C; 110–120°F) to revive. Use a floral preservative and avoid placing in floral foam.

Hydrangea macrophylla (Thunb.) Ser. (=*H. hortensis*)   family: Hydrangeaceae

hortensia (Dutch); *hortensia à grandes feuilles* (French); *Garten-Hortensie* (German); *ortensia* (Italian); *hortensia* (Spanish)

Hypericum androsaemum

hypericum • tutsan

Hypericum androsaemum 'Magical Beauty'

Hypericum androsaemum 'Magical Red'

Hypericum androsaemum 'Sugar Flair'

DESCRIPTION A deciduous shrub with erect branches of about 0.6 m (2′) high. The broad leaves are sometimes clasping the stem and may be tinted red. Star-shaped yellow flowers of 18 mm (⅓″) in diameter are followed by persistent brown or black fruits. Numerous cultivars are available, with many having red berries and green leaves. Cultivars can also differ in leaf colour and in the size and colour of berries (white, yellow, pink, green or orange, besides the standard red).

ORIGIN & HISTORY Europe, North Africa and western Asia. The name is thought to come from the Greek *hyper* (above) and *eikon* (picture) – flowers were once hung above pictures to ward off evil spirits.

PARTS USED Foliage with berries is used as cut foliage and whole plants as potted flowers.

CULTIVATION Hypericum is a long-day plant and flowering is initiated when day-length exceeds 14 hours. Growers use artificial lighting to extend day-length to 18–20 hours, which ensures better quality and higher yields of fruit (berries). *H. androsaemum* does poorly in hot, humid environments which results in rust and fungal diseases.

PROPERTIES Vase life is average to fairly good (7–10 days). Leaves are sensitive to fungal and bacterial diseases.

QUALITY CRITERIA Select cut stems with fully coloured, firm and shiny berries, turgid foliage and young (not too woody) stems. The leaves tend to go off quicker than the berries. Make sure leaves are free of disease, yellowing or damage. Select pots with compact plants, healthy leaves and plenty of blooms and/or berries.

CARE & HANDLING Recut stems and first hydrate in a hydrating solution, or in warm water and a commercial floral preservative for at least 2 hours before storage or usage. Remove all foliage below the water line. Cut stems can be stored for 2–4 days at 2–4°C (36–39°F).

Hypericum androsaemum L.   family: Hypericaceae (Clusiaceae)

hertshooi (Dutch); *androsème, toute-saine* (French); *Mannsblut* (German); *iperico* (Italian); *hipericón* (Spanish)

Iberis umbellata
candytuft • annual candytuft

Iberis umbellata purple

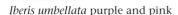

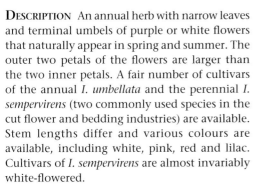

Iberis umbellata purple and pink

Iberis umbellata white and pink

DESCRIPTION An annual herb with narrow leaves and terminal umbels of purple or white flowers that naturally appear in spring and summer. The outer two petals of the flowers are larger than the two inner petals. A fair number of cultivars of the annual *I. umbellata* and the perennial *I. sempervirens* (two commonly used species in the cut flower and bedding industries) are available. Stem lengths differ and various colours are available, including white, pink, red and lilac. Cultivars of *I. sempervirens* are almost invariably white-flowered.

ORIGIN & HISTORY Southern Europe. Candytuft is an old favourite florist flower.

PARTS USED Flowers are used as cut flowers and whole plants as potted flowers.

CULTIVATION For cut flower production, annual candytuft is mostly grown. Propagation is from seeds. Candytuft requires excellent soil drainage and high light intensity during cultivation to produce good quality flowers in high yield. To ensure uniformity of flowering, the plants need to reach maturity before they flower. They also require a cold treatment – approximately 10 weeks at 2–7°C (36–45°F) – in order to induce flowering.

PROPERTIES Vase life is poor to average (5–7 days). Stems of cut flowers sometimes tend to be a bit short.

QUALITY CRITERIA Select stems with flower clusters in full bloom or potted plants that are well branched and fairly compact. Do not worry if some of the white flowers are pinkish. This is a normal reaction to cool day and night temperatures.

CARE & HANDLING Recut stems and place in a general preservative. Remove any foliage below the water line. Use within 2 to 3 days, as prolonged storage is not recommended. Flowers dry well. Display potted flowers in a well-lit, cool (18–20°C; 64–68°F) area and not in direct sunlight. Do not over-water but rather allow the medium to dry out slightly between watering.

Iberis umbellata L.   family: Brassicaceae

scheefbloem (Dutch); *thlaspi* (French); *Doldige Schleifenblume* (German); *iberis* (Italian, Spanish)

227

Ilex aquifolium

holly • common holly • Christmas holly

Ilex aquifolium leaves and berries

DESCRIPTION An evergreen shrub or tree of up to 25 m with glossy, often spiny leaves, small white flowers and bright red berries. Numerous cultivars of this species and hybrids of North American species such as *I. decidua* (possumhaw), *I. verticillata* (black alder) and the Japanese *I. serrata* (fine-tooth holly) have been used in the florist trade for many years.

ORIGIN & HISTORY Southern Europe, North Africa and western Asia. Medieval monks called this plant the *Holy Tree* and believed it gave protection from evil spirits and lightning. It has become a popular decoration during the Christmas season.

PARTS USED Leafy stems and stems with berries (with or without leaves) are used as florist greens and fillers.

CULTIVATION Propagation is chiefly from softwood cuttings. Plants are relatively slow growing and actually prefer heavy, swampy soils. Flower buds are formed a year prior to flowering and severe harvesting will retard future berry formation by a few years. Male and female plants need to be cultivated together and cross-pollination by insects is important. Berries are from the female plants and plants can be harvested for 30–50 years.

PROPERTIES Vase life is good to very good (10–20 days).

QUALITY CRITERIA Evergreen types – look for stems with fully mature, dark green, glossy leaves without spots or damage. Deciduous types – look for well-formed, well-branched stems full of brightly coloured berries and make sure not too many berries have dropped off. Do not worry if there are a few leaves still on the stems, simply remove them carefully.

CARE & HANDLING Handle with care to prevent berry loss. Evergreen types: Store in moisture-retentive boxes for 1–3 weeks at 0°C (32°F). Keep from drying out by misting occasionally or setting relative humidity to 95%. Leafless types: Store dry for 1–2 weeks in moisture-retaining boxes at 0°C (32°F).

Ilex aquifolium L.   family: Aquifoliaceae

gewone hulst (Dutch); *houx commun* (French); *Gewöhnliche Stechpalme, Hülse* (German); *agrifoglio* (Italian); *acebo* (Spanish)

Impatiens hawkeri
impatiens • busy lizzie

Impatiens hawkeri

Impatiens hawkeri variegated form

Impatiens walleriana double pink

DESCRIPTION A branched perennial herb of about 0.1 m (4″) high with reddish stems and toothed, dark green, bronze or purple leaves. The flowers are about 75 mm (3″) in diameter and may be red, pink, purple or white (and double or single). New Guinea hybrids are the best known, but "Spectra Mixed" are more compact plants with pink, lilac or orange flowers. A second species, *I. walleriana*, is often grown as an annual and numerous cultivars and hybrids are available in a wide range of colours.

ORIGIN & HISTORY New Guinea to Solomon Islands (*I. hawkeri*) and East Africa (*I. walleriana*). Impatiens have become fashionable as pot plants.

PARTS USED Whole plants are used as potted flowers, often in hanging baskets.

CULTIVATION Impatiens prefer a well-drained, slightly acidic (pH 6.0–6.8) soil. Over- or under-watering can cause problems. New Guinea impatiens are quite sensitive to salts and growers maintain low to moderate fertiliser programmes. Plants are day-neutral but as days lengthen, flowering increases. During the winter months, New Guinea impatiens benefit from supplementary lighting. Low temperatures (<15°C; 59°F) retard growth and high temperatures (>29°C; 84°F) shorten vase life and cause plants to stretch excessively.

PROPERTIES Flowers are very sensitive to ethylene.

QUALITY CRITERIA Select compact, well-branched plants that are full of buds (20–30% in colour), without curled leaves or lost buds. Bud loss is often a sign of ethylene damage but also rough handling. Make sure leaves have a uniform green colour – not blotchy or yellowish. Ensure that flowers and buds are free of spots caused by botrytis or bacteria.

CARE & HANDLING Display pots in a cool place (but above 13°C; 55°F) with bright light and partial shade. New Guinea impatiens can tolerate more sun. Water plants daily and regularly remove dead flowers and leaves.

Impatiens hawkeri W. Bull.   family: Balsaminaceae

vlijtig liesje (Dutch); *impatiens, balsamine* (French); *Fleißiges Lieschen* (German); *nouva guinea* (Italian); *alegria* (Spanish)

Iris hollandica

iris • Dutch iris

Iris ×hollandica 'Deep River'

Iris ×hollandica 'Golden Beauty'

DESCRIPTION A bulbous plant with sword-like leaves and a single stem bearing one or two flowers. Flower colour is mostly blue, yellow or white. There are hundreds of *Iris* species and cultivars but the Dutch iris is by far the most important florist flower. Bearded irises and the lesser known Siberian, Louisiana and Japanese irises are mostly grown as garden flowers. Cultivars of the Dutch iris have been placed into six groups. The cultivar 'Blue Magic' (from the Blue Magic Group) and some from the Miscellaneous Group account for almost 95% of all cut flower irises. Species such as *I. danfordiae* and *I. reticulata* and related cultivars are more suitable for potted flowers than the Dutch (or Spanish) iris.

ORIGIN & HISTORY Dutch irises are hybrids obtained by crossing *I. xiphium* (Spanish iris) with *I. tingitana*, *I. filifolia* and possibly *I. latifolia* – all of them western Mediterranean species.

PARTS USED Flowering stems are used as cut flowers and whole plants as potted flowers.

CULTIVATION Dutch irises need to be grown under cool conditions. Prolonged periods above 21°C (70°F) significantly reduce yields and quality and above 30°C (86°F) cause bulb dormancy.

PROPERTIES Vase life is poor (2–6 days). Flowers open quickly, especially under warm conditions. Irises are ethylene sensitive.

QUALITY CRITERIA Select flowers with sturdy, straight stems. Make sure stems are lively, uniform green and not pale or blotchy in colour. Select stems with closed buds, but which have emerged from the green sheath and are showing good colour.

CARE & HANDLING Unpack and loosen bunches as soon as possible. Place in a preservative with an anti-ethylene agent but no sugar. Use fluoride-free water as fluoride causes scorching of leaf tips. Flowers can be stored for a few days at 0–2°C (32–36°F). Once taken from the cooler they will start to open and last 2–5 days.

Iris ×hollandica Hort.

family: Iridaceae

Hollandse iris (Dutch); *iris* (French); *Holländische Iris* (German); *iris* (Italian); *lirio* (Spanish)

Ixia cultivars

African corn lily • wand flower

Ixia plants

Ixia flowers

DESCRIPTION A small round corm enveloped with a soft, fibrous brown tunic, with strap-shaped leaves and tubular flowers. The plant is deciduous in summer. Flowering occurs naturally in late winter and early spring. All the available flowers on the market are hybrids that have been bred over many years to give a wide range of colours and flower forms. There are many named cultivars.

ORIGIN & HISTORY *Ixia* species are indigenous to the winter rainfall area of South Africa. The cultivars used as florist flowers are complex hybrids with *I. maculata* as one of the parents.

PARTS USED Flowering stems are used as cut flowers.

CULTIVATION Plants do best in a well-drained, slightly sandy, moisture-retaining (but not waterlogged) soil. Flowers are grown in greenhouses or in open fields (then usually under a low percentage shade cloth to prevent sunburn and rain or hail damage). Mulching is often used to keep the corms cool and maintain a more constant soil temperature.

PROPERTIES Vase life is poor to average (5–7 days). Flowers are ethylene sensitive.

QUALITY CRITERIA Select stems with the bottom 1–2 flowers open and the rest of the buds showing colour (tightly closed buds often do not open). Stems should be straight and sturdy, with well-developed flowers. Ensure that the colour of foliage is good and uniform and that there are no marks, especially leaf-burn, on the edges of the leaves.

CARE & HANDLING Recut stems and place in a preservative containing a sugar as well as an anti-ethylene agent. The sugar ensures that most of the flowers along the spike will open. Flowers can be stored for a few days at 2–3°C (36–37°F). The top 2–3 buds can be broken off prior to use to further ensure that flowers along the full length of the spike will open fully.

Ixia cultivars   family: Iridaceae

ixia (Dutch); *fleur du soir, ixia* (French); *Klebschwertel* (German); *ixia* (Italian, Spanish)

Ixora coccinea

flame of the woods • jungle flame • red ixora

Ixora coccinea leaves and flowers

DESCRIPTION An evergreen shrub of up to 2.5 m high with elliptic to oblong leaves of 100 mm (4") long. The tubular flowers are 25–35 mm long and are borne in loose clusters. They are usually red but cross-breeding and hybridising has increased the colour range of the flowers from only red and orange to colours such as white, pink, yellow and salmon. Cultivars include 'Nora Grant' (pink-red), 'Fraseri' (salmon pink) and 'Orange King' (vivid orange). In addition to cultivars, several botanical varieties have also been described.

ORIGIN & HISTORY Tropical Asia (India and Sri Lanka). There are approximately 400 species spread across Africa and Asia. The name *Ixora* is said to have been derived from an Indian deity. *I. coccinea* is a favourite garden shrub because of the compact habit and abundance of colourful blooms.

PARTS USED The leafy stems with large flowering heads are used as florist flowers and fillers. Leaves are used as cut foliage.

CULTIVATION Plants prefer an organic-rich, acid soil that is well drained. Propagation is primarily by means of cuttings. While *Ixora coccinea* itself is best suited to full sun conditions, a number of the newer cultivars seem to prefer partial shade.

PROPERTIES Vase life is average to fairly good (6–10 days). Leaves are prone to premature yellowing and chlorosis. Some cultivars have a strong fragrance.

QUALITY CRITERIA Select stems with full, well-formed flowering heads. Leaves need to be healthy and bright green, free of yellowing. Flowering stems should be straight, sturdy and not too woody. Flowering heads should be 75% to almost fully open.

CARE & HANDLING Recut stems and place in a preservative with a sugar. Remove leaves below the water line and display in a cool, bright and well-ventilated area. Preferably use flowers promptly. If necessary, only store for 4–5 days at 2°C (36°F) and a high relative humidity (95%).

Ixora coccinea L.   family: Rubiaceae

ixora (Dutch); *ixora écarlate* (French); *Dschugelbrand* (German); *ixora* (Italian, Spanish)

Jasminum polyanthum

Chinese jasmine • jasmine

Jasminum polyanthum flowers

Jasminum officinale 'Affine'

DESCRIPTION A semi-evergreen climber with twining stems bearing glossy, compound leaves, each comprising five to seven leaflets. The exceptionally fragrant flowers are pink in the bud stage but white and star-shaped when open. This creates an attractive bicolour effect. Cultivated plants agree with the wild type – there are no well-known cultivars. The common jasmine or true jasmine (*J. officinale*) is a deciduous climber with minutely hairy leaflets. It is an Asian species that is commonly grown in gardens and is closely similar to *J. polyanthum*. Some cultivars of this species are known, such as 'Affine' (flowers very large, pink outside) and 'Aureum' (variegated leaves, blotched with gold).

ORIGIN & HISTORY South-western China. The jasmine has become a very popular garden plant in most parts of the world.

PARTS USED Whole plants are used as potted flowers and flowering stems with leaves are suitable as florist fillers.

CULTIVATION Plants are easily grown from cuttings in rich, well-drained soil. They grow well in full sun or partial shade.

PROPERTIES Jasmine is one of the most deliciously fragrant of all potted flowers. The plant should flower for 4–6 weeks in the pot, after which the flowering shoots can be pruned back and new shoots will appear the following year.

QUALITY CRITERIA Select plants with dark green leaves and many unopened flower buds.

CARE & HANDLING Potted flowers should be displayed in a well-lit, sunny position. A few hours of direct sunlight that is not too hot will do no harm. Water frequently and do not allow the potting medium to dry out. However, do not allow the pot to become waterlogged either. Maintain a humid atmosphere and spray the plant often. Be watchful as red spider mites can appear, especially in dry climates. Ideal temperatures range between a minimum of 5°C (41°F) and a maximum of 21°C (70°F).

Jasminum polyanthum Franch.　　　　　　　　family: Oleaceae

jasmijn (Dutch); *jasmin* (French); *Jasmin* (German); *gelsomino* (Italian); *jazmin* (Spanish)

Juniperus communis
juniper

Juniperus communis foliage

Juniperus communis leaves and berries

Thuja orientalis

DESCRIPTION The common juniper is an evergreen tall shrub or small tree of around 5 m (20′) high. The tiny leaves are needle-shaped, often silvery in colour and densely crowded on the branches. Male and female cones are borne on separate trees. Female trees bear small, berry-like fruits (juniper berries), which are actually modified fleshy cones – about 6 mm (¼″) in diameter and dark blue when ripe. Other conifers such as golden cypress (*Thuja orientalis*) are also used as florist greens.

ORIGIN & HISTORY Northern temperate regions of Europe, Asia and North America. Juniper berries are collected in Central Europe and used worldwide to flavour gin. The word gin is derived from 'genever', the Dutch word for juniper.

PARTS USED The leafy branches are used as florist greens.

CULTIVATION Propagation is from seeds or cuttings. Plants grow well even in warm temperate (but not tropical) regions. A cool climate, regular irrigation and full sun conditions

are preferred. Some forms are very slow growing and not really suited for foliage production.

CULTIVARS Numerous cultivars and species with different growth forms and foliage types are available mainly as ornamental and container plants.

PROPERTIES Vase life is very good (21–28 days). Stems and foliage tend to be sticky and leave the hands sticky and dirty. Juniper foliage is not usually allergenic.

QUALITY CRITERIA Select fully mature, but young stems with leaves in full colour. Dropping of needles (leaves) is an indication of dry stems or incorrect care and handling. Check that the tips of foliage are not brown or whitish.

CARE & HANDLING Recut and place in a bactericide to keep the water clean. If possible, display or store separately from cut flowers to avoid ethylene damage. Juniper can be stored dry in moisture-retentive boxes for 4–8 weeks at 0°C (32°F), or wet for 3–4 weeks at the same temperature and 95% relative humidity.

Juniperus communis L.   family: Cupressaceae

genever (Dutch); *geniévrier commun* (French); *Gewöhnlicher Wacholder* (German); *ginepro* (Italian); *enebro común* (Spanish)

Kalanchoe blossfeldiana

flaming katy • tom thumb

Kalanchoe blossfeldiana pink

Kalanchoe blossfeldiana double pink

Kalanchoe blossfeldiana salmon

DESCRIPTION A small perennial with succulent leaves borne in opposite pairs. Colourful flowers, each with four petals (or more in double flower forms), are borne in clusters at the stem tips. Many cultivars are grown commercially. Some of them may be hybrids derived from *K. flammea* and *K. pumila*. Cultivars react differently to season, day length and temperature, so that growers tend to produce a different mix of cultivars in winter than in summer.

ORIGIN & HISTORY Madagascar. It has become one of the top-selling pot plants worldwide.

PARTS USED Whole plants are used as potted flowers.

CULTIVATION Kalanchoes are short-day plants propagated from cuttings. Plants are forced to flower all year round, by inducing long days for vegetative growth, followed by induced short days to initiate flowering. Plants have a very fibrous root system and the potting medium needs to be well aerated, but at the same time able to retain moisture. Low temperatures (<16°C; 61°F) can lead to blind shoots and/or delayed flowering. Growers usually treat plants chemically (along with temperature control) to ensure that they remain compact.

PROPERTIES Shelf life is very good (6–8 weeks). Plants are sensitive to ethylene but are very easy to care for with a minimum of fuss.

QUALITY CRITERIA Select compact plants with a good volume of flowers, 30–50% of which should be open. Make sure leaves are a fairly dark, uniform green colour. Blotchy or reddish leaves are signs of stress. Avoid plants with "runaway" side shoots – with the terminal buds surpassed by the side shoots (plant reverting back to a vegetative state).

CARE & HANDLING Unsleeve pots and display in a bright, well-ventilated, moderately cool (15–24°C; 60–75°F) area, away from ethylene sources. Allow the pot to dry out slightly before watering. Continually remove dead flowers or leaves.

Kalanchoe blossfeldiana Poelln.　　　　　　　　　　family: Crassulaceae

kalanchoe (Dutch); *kalanchoe* (French); *Flammendes Käthchen* (German); *calancola* (Italian); *calanchoe, escarlata, kalancoe* (Spanish)

Kniphofia uvaria

red hot poker • torch lily

Kniphofia uvaria

Kniphofia yellow

DESCRIPTION Perennial herbs with tufts of long, soft, grass-like leaves arising from underground rhizomes. The yellow to orange or red flowers are borne in dense clusters at the tips of long, leafless stems. Summer flowering and winter flowering forms are available. Colours include pure white, yellow and cream, although the main cultivars are bright red or orange with a yellow base. Many cultivars are derived from *K. ×praecox* (a hybrid between *K. uvaria* or *K. linearifolia* and *K. bruceae*).

ORIGIN & HISTORY Africa. There are close to 70 species, mainly found in southern Africa, but also a few in Madagascar and the Arabian Peninsula. *K. uvaria* was one of the first Cape plants to be introduced into Europe. Red hot pokers are common garden plants with numerous hybrids and cultivars derived from South African species. The flowers are popular with florists.

PARTS USED Flowering stems are used as cut flowers.

CULTIVATION Most cultivation is done in open fields. Plants can be grown in full sun or partial shade and do best in well-drained, humus-rich soils. The rhizomes are best left in the ground for a few years after which they can be lifted, separated and replanted. The best flower quality is achieved if soils remain moist from flower initiation until harvest.

PROPERTIES Vase life is average to good (7–10 days). Flowers are sensitive to ethylene. The long thick stems and large flowers make red hot pokers ideal for large arrangements.

QUALITY CRITERIA Select stems with the bottom third to nearly all of the flowers on the spike showing colour, but not yet open. Look for long, straight and sturdy stems with well-developed flower spikes.

CARE & HANDLING Recut and place in a preservative containing an anti-ethylene agent. Store upright and away from ethylene-producing items such as ripening fruits. Flowers do not dry well.

Kniphofia uvaria (L.) Oken   family: Asphodelaceae

vuurpijl, fakkellelie (Dutch); *tritome* (French); *Schopf-Fackellilie* (German); *cnifofia, tritoma* (Italian); *tritoma, tritomo* (Spanish)

Lachenalia aloides
lachenalia • Cape cowslip

Lachenalia aloides 'Fransie'

Lachenalia aloides 'Rupert'

DESCRIPTION A bulbous geophyte easily recognised by its lance-shaped, usually heavily spotted leaves and spikes of cylindrical flowers in which the inner perianth segments protrude conspicuously. Several cultivars have already been developed and released in numerous colours (mostly shades of red, yellow and purple). Examples include 'Aurea', 'Luteola', 'Pearsonii', 'Quadricolor' and 'Tricolor'. Cultivars differ in their flowering times (winter or spring). Other cultivated species include *L. contaminata*, *L. liliiflora*, *L. rubida*, *L. unicolor*, *L. violacea* and *L. viridiflora*.

ORIGIN & HISTORY South Africa. Although breeding of *L. aloides* has been ongoing for a number of years, lachenalias are still very new as potted plants.

PARTS USED Whole plants are used as potted flowers.

CULTIVATION Flowering is initiated by high temperatures (20–25°C; 68–77°F) and inhibited at low temperatures (10–15°C; 50–59°F). Plants do best in a well-drained, fertile soil that is rich in organic matter. They prefer high daytime temperatures (20–30°C; 68–86°F) and are sensitive to frost. Plants are forced to flower year-round in greenhouses.

PROPERTIES Pots flower for 1–3 months. The attractive, multicoloured flowers are similar in appearance to hyacinths. Flowering stems become floppy under low light intensities. Flowers are sweetly scented and not sensitive to ethylene.

QUALITY CRITERIA Look for compact plants, with well-formed, full flower spikes which have the first (bottom) flowers just opening or open. Make sure flower spikes are sturdy and straight. Leaves must have good colour and be free of brown marks, damage and general blemishes.

CARE & HANDLING Unpack pots on arrival. Water them well (until water runs out the bottom of the pots) and then display in a brightly lit, warm area, out of any cold draughts. Keep the potting medium slightly moist, but never wet.

Lachenalia aloides (L.f.) Engl. (=*L. tricolor* Jacq. f)   family: Asparagaceae (Hyacinthaceae)

lachenalia (Dutch); *jacinthe du Cape* (French); *Kaphyazinthe, Lachenalie* (German); *lachenalia* (Italian, Spanish)

Lathyrus odoratus

sweet pea • sweetpea

Lathyrus odoratus mixed colours

DESCRIPTION Sweet pea is an annual climber (vine) of up to 2 m (6½') high. Typical are the winged stems, parallel veins in the leaves, leaflets that end in coiled climbing tendrils and clusters of multi-coloured, sweetly scented flowers. Countless cultivars have been bred over the years, differing in their tolerance of heat and light intensity, as well as their growth patterns, flower types (single or double, ruffled or not) and flower colours.

ORIGIN & HISTORY Southern Italy, including Sicily and Crete. Sweet peas have been sold since 1730 and were introduced to England in 1866 and to America in 1870. By the start of the 1900s, around 130 cultivars had already been bred from the original wild form, which had purple flowers. Although most peas are edible, sweet pea seeds are poisonous.

PARTS USED Flowers are used as cut flowers.

CULTIVATION Plants are sensitive to heat and are therefore typically grown during the cool winter months (both outdoors and in greenhouses). Day length (photoperiod) has little effect on flowering. However, high light intensities combined with cool growing conditions are necessary. Low light levels result in smaller and fewer flowers per stem, as well as bud abortion.

PROPERTIES Vase life is poor (3–5 days). Sweet peas are one of the most pleasantly scented florist flowers available (as reflected in the name *odoratus*). The flowers are very sensitive to ethylene.

QUALITY CRITERIA Select stems with 2–3 flowers open. Check to see that no flowers are damaged. Make sure the colour of stems, leaves and flowers is not mottled or pale – often a sign of disease and poor production practices.

CARE & HANDLING Flowers are easily damaged, so handle with care. Recut and place in a preservative with an anti-ethylene agent. Storage is not recommended, but if necessary store at 2–4°C (36–39°F) with at least 12 hours of lighting per day.

Lathyrus odoratus L.   family: Fabaceae

pronkerwt (Dutch); *pois de senteur* (French); *Duft-Wicke, Duftende Platterbse* (German); *pisello odoroso* (Italian); *jakou endou* (Japanese); *guisante de olor* (Spanish)

Lavandula angustifolia

lavender

Lavandula angustifolia

Lavandula dentata

DESCRIPTION An aromatic shrub of up to 1 m (40") high with brittle stems bearing narrowly oblong, silvery leaves in opposite pairs. The spikes of usually purple-blue flowers are very characteristic. The most common lavender is *L. angustifolia* (real lavender or English lavender), which is fragrant and showy. Several cultivars are available, including 'Alba' (white), 'Rosea' (pink), 'Hidcote Giant' (tall, deep purple) and 'Royal Purple' (lavender colour, long clusters). Several other species are also cultivated, including French lavender (*L. dentata*), lavandin (*L. ×intermedia*, a hybrid between *L. angustifolia* and *L. latifolia*) and Spanish lavender (*L. stoechas*).

ORIGIN & HISTORY Western Mediterranean region. Lavender is mainly used in the essential oils and herb industries but has always been popular as a filler in cut flower bunches or bouquets.

PARTS USED Flowering stems – filler. Whole plant – potted flower or herb.

CULTIVATION A well-drained soil that is slightly acidic (pH 5.5–6.2) is preferred and plants need to dry out between irrigations. Potted plants are trimmed at a young stage to encourage branching and obtain a more compact growth. Cold treatment (vernalisation) is necessary to induce flowering.

PROPERTIES Vase life of cut foliage is slightly poor to average (5–7 days). Leaves and flowers have a pleasant fragrance. Foliage is sensitive to rotting under humid conditions.

QUALITY CRITERIA Cut stems should be sturdy, with long flower spikes. Make sure the foliage is free of disease. Purchase pots with plants that are either green or with 1–3 flower spikes showing colour.

CARE & HANDLING Recut stems and remove foliage below the water line. Place in a preservative containing a bactericide. Display pots in high light, cool areas. Do not over-water, but allow medium to dry out slightly between waterings. The flowers air-dry well.

Lavandula angustifolia Mill. (=*L. officinalis* Chaix, *L. vera* DC.) family: Lamiaceae

echte lavendel (Dutch); *lavande vraie* (French); *Echter Lavendel* (German); *lavanda* (Italian); *lavanda* (Spanish)

Lavatera trimestris

mallow • rose mallow

Lavatera trimestris pink

DESCRIPTION A sparsely hairy annual herb of up to 1.2 m (4′) high bearing large, rounded to heart-shaped leaves, each with three, five or seven short lobes. There are three bracts (epicalyx lobes) below the flower, which is up to 50 mm (2″) in diameter. A number of cultivars are available, with a fair range of colours, including pink, rose, salmon, purple and white. The old-fashioned taller, bushy cultivars with pink flowers are the predominant ones found in florists. Examples are 'Loveliness' (trumpet-shaped, deep rose), 'Tanagra' (tall, pink) and 'Splendens' (large, white or red).

ORIGIN & HISTORY Mediterranean region. Annual mallow is a popular garden plant and is nowadays available in a range of dwarf cultivars.

PARTS USED Flowers are used as cut flowers.

CULTIVATION Mallow is susceptible to fungal and foliar diseases as well as numerous pests. Therefore production is best in areas with a cool, dry climate and well-drained soils. Plants are propagated from seed. They are not day length sensitive and do not require long days or short days to initiate flowering. High quality plants and flowers are realised under cool night temperatures of approximately 13–15°C (55–59°F). Mallow is primarily cultivated in open fields.

PROPERTIES Vase life is fairly poor to average (5–7 days). Flowers do not transport well. They are susceptible to a wide range of pests and diseases.

QUALITY CRITERIA Choose stems with flowers still closed, but beginning to uncurl or just opening. Avoid stems with more than 3–4 open flowers. Make sure the leaves are free of spots or damage.

CARE & HANDLING Recut stems, remove leaves below the water line and place in a preservative. Use a preservative containing a bactericide and a sugar. Display or hold flowers in a cool area to maintain vase life. Storage is not recommended. Flowers do not dry well.

Lavatera trimestris L.   family: Malvaceae

grootbloemige lavatera, bekermalve (Dutch); *lavatère d'un trimestre* (French); *Becher-Malve, Garten-Strauchpappel* (German); *malva regina* (Italian); *lavatera, malva real* (Spanish)

Leonotis leonurus

lion's ear

Leonotis leonurus white

Leonotis leonurus orange

Leonotis leonurus plant

DESCRIPTION An erect perennial herb (up to 2 m or 6½′) with woody branches arising at ground level. The oblong leaves are borne in opposite pairs on square stems. Dense, rounded clusters of stalkless flowers are borne at regular intervals along the flowering stems. They are usually bright orange (rarely reddish, yellow or white) and have a distinctive hairy tip that resembles a lion's ear. There are only a few cultivars. 'Harrismith White' has white flowers. Leonotis oxymifolia is smaller and has heart-shaped, hairy leaves. 'E.M. Rix' is a cultivar of this species with highly decorative white and reddish brown flowers.

ORIGIN & HISTORY South Africa. The plants are popular drought-hardy garden subjects and are also used in traditional medicine to treat fevers, headaches and coughs.

PARTS USED The flowering stems are used as cut flowers and the dried stems as ornaments. The long stems with spiky balls create interesting forms and lines in arrangements.

CULTIVATION Propagation is from seed, cuttings or division. Plants do best when grown in loamy soils and under full sun, summer conditions. They are cultivated as annuals or cut back completely after flowering and cultivated for a second year.

PROPERTIES Vase life of flower petals is poor (4–6 days). Dried stems can last for years. The foliage is aromatic.

QUALITY CRITERIA Select long, sturdy flowering stems. Flower clusters need to be well formed and numerous. Main flowering heads should be 75% to almost fully open. Fresh stems should not have lost any flower petals.

CARE & HANDLING Recut fresh stems and hydrate for 2–3 hours at room temperature before use. Place in a floral preservative and hold at room temperature or 2–4°C (36–39°F). Use fresh stems promptly – storage is not recommended. Stems are excellent for drying. Stand up straight in loose bunches in a well-ventilated area.

Leonotis leonurus (L.) R. Br.   family: Lamiaceae

wildedagga (Dutch); oreille-de-lion (French); Großblättriges Löwenohr (German); orecchio di leone (Italian); oreja de león (Spanish)

Leptospermum scoparium
tea bush • manuka

Leptospermum scoparium pink

Leptospermum scoparium white

DESCRIPTION A woody shrub of 2–3 m (up to 10′) in height, with small, elliptic, often silvery or purple leaves. The small flowers are up to 12 mm (½″) in diameter and are usually white but also red or pink in modern cultivars. Several cultivars are available, differing in growth form and flower colour. Examples include 'Album Flore Pleno' (white, double), 'Cherry Brandy' (leaves brown, flowers pink) and 'Roseum Multipetalum' (double pink flowers). Tall, erect cultivars are more useful for cutting than the dwarf types which are aimed at the garden and container industries.

ORIGIN & HISTORY Native to Australia, New Zealand and Tasmania. The name comes from the Greek words *leptos* (slender) and *sperma* (seeds). The name tea bush is derived from early Australian settlers who would soak the leaves to make a herbal tea that was thought to be rich in Vitamin C.

PARTS USED Flowering stems are used as florist fillers.

CULTIVATION Plants are grown from cuttings. They require well-drained slightly acid soils, full sun and good air movement. A lot of harvesting is still done in the wild.

PROPERTIES Vase life is average to good (7–10 days). Flowers tend to shatter easily and leaf drop can also be a problem. Flowers are ethylene sensitive.

QUALITY CRITERIA Look for cultivars with clean, vivid flower colours. Avoid cultivars that tend to drop petals. Check that chosen stems have not dropped any petals. Select well-branched, young stems with healthy, blemish-free leaves and large numbers of buds; 50–75% of the flowers should be open.

CARE & HANDLING Recut stems by 50–100 mm (2–4″) and place in a floral preservative. Handle with care to avoid damaging the flowers. Recut stems again when they are used. Storage is not recommended but if necessary, store for 4–5 days at 1–2°C and a relative humidity of 90–95%.

Leptospermum scoparium Forst. & Forst.
family: Myrtaceae

theeboom (Dutch); *leptospermum* (French); *Australischer Teebaum* (German); *manuka, leptospermum* (Italian); *leptospermo, arbol del te rosa* (Spanish)

Leucadendron salignum
conebush

Leucadendron 'Safari Sunset'

Leucadendron 'Jubilee Crown'

Leucadendron discolor

DESCRIPTION A shrub of about 1 m (40") high with narrowly oblong leaves that are often flushed yellow or red. Male and female flowers are borne on separate plants. The flowers form cone-like structures (about 16 mm or ¾" in diameter in female plants, much smaller in the male). Several natural species, hybrids and cultivars are cultivated commercially for their decorative foliage and cones. The natural variation in colour is astonishing. The most popular cultivar to date is 'Safari Sunset', a female selection from a hybrid between *L. salignum* and *L. laureolum*.

ORIGIN & HISTORY The 60 species are all endemic to South Africa. In the florist trade, conebushes are regarded as cut greens (foliage) and not as cut flowers.

PARTS USED Leafy stems with flower cones are used as cut foliage. Whole plants are used as potted flowers.

CULTIVATION Modern cultivars are grown from rooted cuttings. Plants grow best in well-drained, light soils with low concentrations of dissolved salts (a typical requirement of most Proteaceae) and fairly acidic (pH <5). Conebushes prefer a temperature range of 7–27°C (45–81°F) and good air movement through the plantation is important.

PROPERTIES Vase life is good to very good (14–25 days). Leaves have a tendency to blacken or brown before the flowers start to fade. Most of the preferred florist types are female (except *L. discolor* and certain of its hybrids).

QUALITY CRITERIA Select long straight stems with well-developed cones. Make sure the leaves are free of damage, blackening and marks, as well as insects.

CARE & HANDLING Recut stems and place in a preservative with a bactericide and sugar. Do not remove any foliage, except below the water line. Cut stems can be stored for 7–14 days at 0–2°C (32–36°F) and at a relative humidity of 90% (monitor, as botrytis can be a problem). Flowers are excellent for drying.

Leucadendron salignum Bergius

family: Proteaceae

leucadendron (Dutch, French, Italian, Spanish); *Leucadendron* (German)

Leucanthemum superbum

shasta daisy

Leucanthemum ×superbum single white

Leucanthemum ×superbum 'Snow Cap'

Leucanthemum ×superbum 'Esther Read'

DESCRIPTION A perennial plant (up to 1 m/40" or slightly taller) with erect stems bearing toothed and hairless leaves. The single flower heads are quite large (100 mm or 4" in diameter), with white ray florets surrounding the yellow disc florets. There are more than 50 cultivars, but most are aimed at the garden industry. Examples include 'Phyllis Smith' (single flowers), 'Esther Read' (semi-double) and 'Fiona Coghill' (fully double, with tall stems). Although attractive, the shasta daisy is not widely seen at florists or cut flower retailers. The closely related ox-eye daisy or moon daisy (*L. vulgare*) is used in much the same way as shasta daisies.

ORIGIN & HISTORY Garden origin. *Leucanthemum ×superbum* originated as a hybrid between *L. maximum* and *L. lacustre* (both are European species).

PARTS USED Fresh heads are used as cut flowers.

CULTIVATION Nearly all commercial production is in open fields. Plants need long days to initiate flowering. Shasta daisies benefit from a period of cold. Production from perennials lasts 3–5 years, with flowering taking place in the summer. Plants are usually lifted and divided after 2–3 years.

PROPERTIES Vase life is below average to average (5–8 days), with some cultivars lasting much longer. Botrytis and mildews can sometimes be a problem.

QUALITY CRITERIA Select sturdy, straight stems and check that flower heads are free of damage and disease. Although leaves are not that aesthetically important, still check to make sure those present are healthy and of good colour, as this is often a indication of overall flower quality and vase life.

CARE & HANDLING Petals can bruise fairly easily, so handle with care. Use a general preservative, but not with an anti-ethylene agent. Recut and remove any leaves below the water level. Storage is not recommended, but if necessary only store for 1–2 days at a temperature of 2–5°C (36–41°F).

Leucanthemum ×superbum (J. Ingram) Bergmans ex Kent   family: Asteraceae

magriet, shasta madeliefje (Dutch); *marguerite d'été* (French); *Garten-Margerite* (German); *margherita* (Italian)

Leucospermum cordifolium

pincushion

Leucospermum cordifolium 'High Gold'

Leucospermum cordifolium 'Succession'

Leucospermum 'Spider'

DESCRIPTION A shrub of up to 2 m (6½') high with broad, stalkless leaves and large flower heads of more than 100 mm (4") in diameter. The prominent parts of the flowers are the styles, which may be yellow, orange or red. Several cultivars and hybrids are available. Breeding is ongoing to develop cultivars that flower at different times and that are more resistant to root disease.

ORIGIN & HISTORY Cape fynbos of South Africa. Pincushions have long been popular in the florist trade because of their unusual shape and excellent vase life.

PARTS USED Flower heads are used as cut flowers. Whole plants are sometimes used as potted flowers.

CULTIVATION The plant occurs on nutrient-poor, coarse, slightly acidic sandy soils (the pH and low nutrient level are important). Commercial propagation is by means of cuttings or grafting (onto rootstocks that are more adaptable to variations in soil pH and less sensitive to root

diseases). Flower heads are harvested from late winter to late spring. Plants can remain commercially productive for many years.

PROPERTIES Vase life is very good (14–25 days) to excellent (35 days and longer in some cultivars). However, leaves tend to brown or blacken long before the flower head has started to deteriorate. Flowers do not really have a fragrance.

QUALITY CRITERIA Select long, straight stems with well-developed flower heads. Purchase heads where 75% of the "pins" (styles) have been released. Flowers that are harvested too closed will not open properly in the vase. Flower heads break off relatively easily, so check that all are firmly attached and handle with care. Make sure leaves are free of damage and marks or spots, as well as insects.

CARE & HANDLING Recut stems and place in a preservative containing a bactericide and a sugar. Flowers can be stored for 7–10 days at 2–4°C (36–39°F). Longer storage will reduce vase life. The flower heads dry well.

Leucospermum cordifolium (Knight) Fourc.   family: Proteaceae

leucospermum cordifolium (Dutch, French, Italian, Spanish); *Nadelkissen* (German)

Liatris spicata

gayfeather • blazing star • button snakewort

Liatris spicata purple

Liatris spicata white

DESCRIPTION A perennial herb (up to 1.5 m or 3' high) arising from a corm. It has slender leaves and small (usually purple) flower heads arranged in dense spikes that open from the top downwards. The plant is dormant in winter and flowers in mid- to late summer. The showiest and most common of the approximately 10 cultivars available is 'Callilepis'. Colour ranges from various shades of purple to white.

ORIGIN & HISTORY Eastern parts of North America. It has become a popular florist flower.

PARTS USED Flower spikes are used as cut flowers. Whole plants are grown as potted flowers.

CULTIVATION Commercial production is by means of corms, which takes about 8 weeks from planting to harvesting. Cold temperatures are essential for flowering, so corms are typically stored at temperatures of –2°C to 2°C (28–36°F) for 8–15 weeks prior to planting. Soaking them for one hour in a gibberellic acid solution will ensure 100% flowering. Corms planted upside down or on their sides take longer to flower and produce shorter stems.

PROPERTIES Vase life is average to good (7–10 days). There is no noticeable fragrance. Flower heads are not ethylene sensitive but susceptible to botrytis. Foliage declines more rapidly than the flowers.

QUALITY CRITERIA Select long, straight and sturdy stems with a good length flower spike. The top 30–50 mm (1–2") of flower heads should be open (in pre-treated stems) or otherwise the top 30–50%. Make sure the leaves are free of brown or black spots.

CARE & HANDLING Recut stems and place in a sugar-containing preservative to help open the flowers. Cool for 2–3 hours prior to use. Maintain good air movement between stems to prevent botrytis developing. Remove lower leaves as they quickly contaminate fresh water. Store flowers at 0–2°C (32–36°F), but only if really necessary. Flowers can be dried when fully open.

Liatris spicata (L.) Willd.   family: Asteraceae

kattestaart (Dutch); *plume du Kansas* (French); *Prachtscharte* (German); *liatris, liatride a spighe* (Italian); *serratula* (Spanish)

Lilium cultivars
asiatic lily

Lilium 'Royal Delight' (asiflorum)

Lilium 'Brunello' (asiatic)

Lilium 'Chiant' (asiatic)

DESCRIPTION Bulbous plants with glossy leaves and large flowers. The four main groups of lily cultivars are asiatics, orientals, hybrids between asiatics and longiflorums (LA's or asiflorums) and hybrids between orientals and asiatics (OA's). Asiatic lilies typically have a shorter flowering stem, but with many more buds than oriental lilies. Flowers also tend to be more star-shaped and open and are carried at the tip of the stem (in orientals typically trumpet-shaped and spread along the axis of the raceme). Cultivars typically remain fashionable for only a few years, so that new ones are continuously being developed.

ORIGIN & HISTORY Asia. Initially cultivars were derived from species native to Asia.

PARTS USED Flowering stems are used as cut flowers. Whole plants are used as potted flowers.

CULTIVATION Asiatics flower earlier than orientals, have smaller bulbs and are more accepting of soil variations. Most production takes place in greenhouses. Storage temperatures vary slightly between the different lily groups.

PROPERTIES Vase life is slightly below average to fairly good (5–9 days). Unlike oriental lilies, asiatic lilies have a wide range of colours, including white, yellow, orange, red and pink. Poor light during cultivation causes buds and flowers to fall off prematurely. Asiatic cultivars mostly lack fragrance, unlike oriental cultivars. Flowers are ethylene sensitive.

QUALITY CRITERIA Select sturdy, straight stems having leaves of uniform colour and with no brown tips, yellowing or twisting. Select stems with the first (bottom) flower bud fully coloured but still closed.

CARE & HANDLING Recut stems and place in a preservative as soon as possible. If leaves are wilted, first hydrate at room temperature for 1–2 hours. Stems can snap easily so handle with care. Flowers can be stored for 3–4 days at 0–2°C (32–36°F) and a relative humidity of 90–95%.

Lilium cultivars
family: Liliaceae

asiatische lelie (Dutch); *lis* (French); *Lilie* (German); *giglio* (Italian); *lirio, azucena* (Spanish)

Lilium cultivars

oriental lily

Lilium 'Siberia' (oriental)

Lilium 'Acapulco' (oriental)

Lilium 'Merostar' (oriental)

DESCRIPTION Bulbous plant with an inflorescence of large, outward-facing flowers and fleshy leaves. These lilies typically have larger but fewer and more trumpet-shaped flowers than asiatic lilies. New cultivars are released regularly (mostly white and pink). So much cross-breeding has occurred that the boundaries of the different lily groups (orientals, asiatics, longiflorums) are becoming vague.

ORIGIN & HISTORY Oriental cultivars are originally derived from crosses and breeding between *L. auratum* from Japan and *L. speciosum* from China and Japan.

PARTS USED Flowering stems are used as cut flowers and whole plants as potted flowers.

CULTIVATION Oriental lilies prefer a cool growing temperature (18–21°C; 64–70°F) and high light intensity. They are mostly grown in greenhouses. Growers force flowering through a process of cold treatment of the bulbs (vernalisation). After harvesting, bulbs are usually discarded.

PROPERTIES Vase life is from slightly below average to fairly good (5–9 days). Low light intensity during production results in buds falling off before they have opened. Direct sunlight and excessive heat result in bleaching of leaves and fungal infection. Flowers have a strong, pleasant fragrance. They are sensitive to ethylene.

QUALITY CRITERIA Select stems that are straight with leaves that have a "lively" green colour and no brown tips or yellowing. Select stems with flowers showing colour and the bottom 1 or 2 flowers starting to open.

CARE & HANDLING Cut off 10–20 mm (½–1") of stem and place in clean water with a preservative. Wilted flowers should first be hydrated for 1–2 hours before use or storage. The pollen stains, so be careful or remove the anthers by hand. Flowers can be stored for 3–4 days at 0–2°C (32–36°F) and a high relative humidity (90–95%). Display pots in a cool, bright area out of any direct draughts.

Lilium cultivars   family: Liliaceae

oriental lelie (Dutch); *lis* (French); *Lilie* (German); *giglio* (Italian); *kanokoyuri* (Japanese); *lirio* (Spanish)

Lilium longiflorum

Easter lily • St Joseph's lily

Lilium longiflorum 'Elegance'

Lilium longiflorum 'Snow Queen'

DESCRIPTION A bulb with stems up to 1 m (40") high and leaves up to 0.2 m (8") long. The white, funnel-shaped flowers are borne in groups of up to six at the tip of the flowering stalk. The few cultivars are all very similar and colour is limited to white.

ORIGIN & HISTORY Japan and Taiwan. *L. longiflorum* is in high demand during religious festivals such as Easter. The Madonna lily (*L. candidum*) is the actual lily of religious writings and paintings, but the Easter lily has largely replaced it because it is closely similar and far easier to cultivate. The Easter lily was one of the first florist flowers to be sold through mass-market outlets.

PARTS USED Flowering stems are used as cut flowers and whole plants as potted flowers.

CULTIVATION By reducing night temperatures to 13–14°C (55–58°F) during flower initiation for 1–2 weeks, growth is slowed but the number of buds per stem increases, giving better quality and higher prices. High temperatures often lead to bud abortion, leaf burn and thin stems.

PROPERTIES Flowers have a pleasant fragrance. They are sensitive to ethylene. Pollen stains clothing and skin.

QUALITY CRITERIA Select cut flowers and potted flowers with "puffy" buds that are white but still closed. Make sure leaves have a good colour, free of marks or "burnt" edges.

CARE & HANDLING Recut stems and place in a floral preservative. Display potted flowers and cut flowers in a bright but cool location (18–24°C; 64–75°F), away from ethylene-producing agents. Pollen of open flowers can be removed by carefully pulling off the pollen sacs. Be very careful as pollen will also stain the flower petals. Keep potted flowers moist, as drying may result in leaf and flower drop. Pots and flowers can be stored for 2–3 days at 2°C (36°F), high humidity (90–95%) and under lights.

Lilium longiflorum Thunb.   family: Liliaceae

kelklelie (Dutch); *lys, lilium* (French); *Oster-Lilie* (German); *giglio, giglio delle Bermude* (Italian); *teppouyuri* (Japanese); *azucena, lirio de Pascua* (Spanish)

Limonium sinuatum

statice • sea lavender

Limonium sinuatum 'QIS Yellow'

Limonium latifolium

Limonium perezii mixed colours

DESCRIPTION Perennial, hairy herbs (0.4 m or 16" high) with dissected leaves and winged flowering stems. The papery flowers occur in a wide range of colours and are borne in large clusters. The two main groups are the larger-flowered, thicker-stemmed *L. sinuatum* hybrids and the smaller, lacy-flowered, thinner-stemmed *L. latifolium* hybrids. *L. perezii* is similar to *L. sinuatum* but less important. Although many colours are available, the true blue colour is very popular.

ORIGIN & HISTORY Mediterranean region. Statice is one of the mainstays of the florist industry and is especially popular as dried flowers.

PARTS USED Flowering stems are used as cut flowers.

CULTIVATION Long days promote earlier flowering and larger yields and growers often use artificial lighting. High temperatures during the seedling stage inhibits flowering, while a cool period followed by a warmer period is necessary for good quality and high yields. Some

hybrids are grown as annuals, others as 2–3 year perennials.

PROPERTIES The vase life of *L. sinuatum* hybrids is good (10–12 days); in other species poor to average (4–7 days). All statice are ethylene sensitive. Many older hybrids have an unpleasant odour.

QUALITY CRITERIA Select stems with 80–90% of the flowers open and showing good colour. Stems should be long and not too flimsy (especially *L. latifolium* hybrids). Check to make sure the leaves and stems (especially *L. sinuatum* and *L. perezii*) are free of brown marks, the flowers free of botrytis and the stem ends not soggy.

CARE & HANDLING Recut stems and place in a floral preservative. Hold in a well-ventilated area. Flowers of *L. latifolium* and *L. perezii* hybrids can be stored for 2–3 days at 2–5°C (36–41°F). (*L. sinuatum* can be stored for twice as long.) Flowers are excellent for drying and retain their colour. Hang upside down in a well-ventilated, dark area.

Limonium sinuatum (L.) Mill.

family: Plumbaginaceae

statice (Dutch); *lavande de mer* (French); *Meerlavendel, Strandflieder, Widerstoß* (German); *statice* (Italian); *estatice* (Spanish)

Lobelia cardinalis

cardinal flower • scarlet lobelia

Lobelia cardinalis

Lobelia erinus purple

Lobelia erinus blue

DESCRIPTION A short-lived perennial herb (0.9 m or 3' high) with the stems and toothed leaves often flushed purple red. The flowers are about 50 mm (2") long and arranged in elongated spikes. They are usually bright scarlet but pink or white forms also occur. A related garden plant is *L. ×speciosa*, a hybrid between *L. cardinalis*, *L. siphilitica* and *L. splendens*. It has red to mauve or purple flowers. Numerous cultivars are available, including 'Alba' (white flowers), 'Compliment Scarlet' (red) and 'Rosea' (pink). Cultivars of *L. erinus* that have become popular as potted flowers include 'Sapphire' (deep purple blue with a white eye), 'Blue Cascade' (pale blue) and 'White Cascade' (white). Foliage colour varies (bronze, green, purple) depending on cultivar or species.

ORIGIN & HISTORY North America. The cardinal flower has become a popular garden plant. The South African *L. erinus* is an old favourite that has gained popularity as a potted flower.

PARTS USED Flowers are used as cut flowers or fillers and whole plants as potted flowers or hanging baskets.

CULTIVATION Lobelias used for cut flower production can be grown as annuals or perennials (but then must be over-wintered frost-free). They are typically grown from seed and prefer moderate to slightly warm temperatures 10–22°C (50–72°F).

PROPERTIES Vase life is average to good (7–10 days). Flowers are sensitive to ethylene.

QUALITY CRITERIA Select cut stems with 30% of the flowers open. Flowering stems need to be long, sturdy and straight. Check that leaves are of good colour and free of any blemishes. Potted flowers need to be compact, well branched and in full bud.

CARE & HANDLING Recut stems and place in a floral preservative. Flowers can be stored for 4–7 days at 1–2°C (34–36°F) and 95% relative humidity. Display potted flowers in a cool, bright area out of direct draughts. Do not over-water.

Lobelia cardinalis L.　　　　　　　　　　　　family: Campanulaceae

kardinaalsbloem (Dutch); *lobélie écarlate* (French); *Kardinals-Lobelia* (German); *lobelia rossa*, *lobelia cardinali* (Italian); *lobelia roja* (Spanish)

Lunaria annua

honesty • money plant • penny flower

Lunaria annua lilac

Lunaria annua fruits

Lunaria annua pink

DESCRIPTION A biennial plant of up to 1 m (40"), with heart-shaped leaves and purple to white flowers of up to 25 mm (1") long. The unusual fruit (a silique) is thin, flat and papery, about 50 × 25 mm (2 × 1") with a characteristic and persistent pearly white septum. The less popular perennial honesty (*Lunaria rediviva*) produces elliptical fruits in contrast to the more rounded fruits of *L. annua*. A few cultivars exist with white, purple or red flowers and green or variegated leaves. The colour and shape of the fruit is similar in all the cultivars.

ORIGIN & HISTORY Europe. The disc-shaped, transparent fruits are interesting and dry very well – they are traditionally used as decorations in winter. The flowers do not last well and although attractive, are not often seen in shops.

PARTS USED Stems with dried fruit are used as foliage or filler (and sometimes the flowers as cut flowers).

CULTIVATION Plants are grown from seed in open fields. A period of cold treatment (vernalisation) is required for effective flowering. Fruits form rapidly after flowering and can be green, translucent or purple as they dry on the plant. After the leaves are removed, stems are bunched and hung upside down in a warm, dark place to dry for about 4–5 weeks. The pods are ready when the papery outer covering is easily removed.

PROPERTIES Vase life of fresh flowers is poor (3–5 days). Shelf life of dried seed pods is at least a few years. Fresh flowers shatter easily.

QUALITY CRITERIA Select long, sturdy stems with fully developed, well-dried fruits. Make sure that none of the fruit discs are discoloured, damaged or broken off.

CARE & HANDLING Immediately recut fresh flowers and place in a preservative. Storage is not recommended. Handle dried pods with care to avoid damaging them.

Lunaria annua L.   family: Brassicaceae

tuinjudaspenning (Dutch); *monnaie du pape, lunaire* (French); *Einjähriges Silberblatt* (German); *medaglie del papa, monete del papa* (Italian); *lunaria, monedas del papa, planta de la plata* (Spanish)

Lupinus hartwegii
lupin • lupine

Lupinus 'My Castle'

Lupinus hartwegii

Russell lupins

DESCRIPTION Annuals or short-lived perennials with erect stems, characteristic palmately compound leaves (with 7–9 leaflets) and elongated spikes of clustered flowers. The flowers of the original form of *L. hartwegii* are lilac, blue and white. Many species and cultivars are used, including the famous Russell Lupins (Russell Hybrids). The taller types are preferred. Famous bicoloured cultivars include 'The Governor' (blue and white), 'The Chatelaine' (pink and white) and 'Monarch' (purple and yellow). 'Biancaneve' is a pure white cultivar.

ORIGIN & HISTORY Mexico (*L. hartwegii*); western United States (*L. arboreus* and *L. polyphyllus*). Lupins have become especially popular as garden plants in the 20th century. Russell Lupins were developed by George Russell of York over a period of 25 years and were introduced in 1937. They are derived from *L. ×regalis*, which is thought to be a hybrid between *L. arboreus* (tree lupin) and *L. polyphyllus* (garden lupin).

PARTS USED Flowering stems, as cut flowers.

CULTIVATION Lupins are easily propagated from seeds and adapt well to different soil types and to full sun or partial shade. Under commercial cultivation perennials are usually treated as annuals.

PROPERTIES Vase life is average (6–8 days). Flowers have a pleasant, strong fragrance. They are sensitive to ethylene but the sensitivity varies amongst cultivars.

QUALITY CRITERIA Select stems with 30–50% of the flowers open. Look for strong, straight stems with a full, evenly spaced spike of buds. Leaves must be bright green.

CARE & HANDLING Recut stems and remove leaves that will end up below the water line. Place all the stems in a preservative containing an ethylene inhibitor. Do not display lupins near ethylene-forming agents as this can cause flowers to shatter and buds to fall off. Preferably use promptly, although flowers can be stored wet at 4°C (39°F) for 3 days (relative humidity of 95%).

Lupinus hartwegii Lindl.   family: Fabaceae

lupine (Dutch); *lupin* (French); *Lupine, Wolfsbohne* (German); *lupino* (Italian); *altramuz* (Spanish)

Lycopodium cernuum
lycopodium • club moss

Lycopodium cernuum

Lycopodium clavatum

DESCRIPTION *Lycopodiums* are moss-like herbs with erect, branched stems bearing small stiff (cypress-like) leaves and small cone-like structures (strobili). *L. cernuum* has stiffly erect branches with pendulous smaller branchlets bearing small, awn-shaped, overlapping leaves and small strobili at the tips. Other species include the so-called ground pine (*L. clavatum* and *L. complanatum*), the ground pine or princess pine (*L. obscurum*), the shining club moss (*L. lucidum*) and the common lycopodium or club moss (*L. taxifolium*). Cultivated plants mostly agree with the original (wild) forms.

ORIGIN & HISTORY Cosmopolitan (temperate zones of both hemispheres): *L. cernuum* (tropics), *L. complanatum* (North America), *L. obscurum* and *L. clavatum* (northern hemisphere), *L. lucidum* (North America, China and Japan), *L. taxifolium* (tropical America) and *L. scariosum* (New Zealand). The spore-bearing leaf (sporophyll) is club-shaped, hence the name club moss.

PARTS USED Delicate stems with scale-like leaves

are used in posies, small arrangements and in wedding work. Some species are used as pot plants.

CULTIVATION Plants can be propagated by means of spores or rooted cuttings. Stems pegged down onto the growing medium root easily at every joint. Shady, warm and moist conditions are essential for good growth. Organic and compost rich growing mediums are also necessary. Foliage is predominantly wild-harvested.

PROPERTIES Stems are long lasting (10–21 days), depending on quality and care. They are not sensitive to ethylene and have no distinctive fragrance.

QUALITY CRITERIA Look for well-branched, full, straight and sturdy stems. The colour should be a fresh, even green, with no brown tips, yellowing or other blemishes.

CARE & HANDLING Handle with care as stems and leaves are relatively delicate. Hold in a cool place and keep moist. Store in moisture-retentive boxes or at a high relative humidity (95%). Keep free from draughts.

Lycopodium cernuum L.   family: Lycopodiaceae

wolfsklauw (Dutch); *lycopode* (French); *Bärlapp* (German); *enxofre vegetal, froco, licopodio brasileiro* (Italian); *licopodio* (Spanish)

Lysimachia clethroides
loosestrife • gooseneck loosestrife

Lysimachia clethroides white

Lysimachia 'Beaujolais'

DESCRIPTION A perennial plant with erect stem (up to 1 m or 40") and small white flowers borne in drooping (curling) racemes (hence the common name). The Eurasian species known as yellow loosestrife (*L. vulgaris*) is also used as a florist flower. Its yellow flowers are arranged in a broad panicle. No significant number of cultivars or hybrids is presently available. The flowers of the original species are beautiful, but the colours are limited to shades of white and yellow. The main cut flower colour is white.

ORIGIN & HISTORY Japan, China and Indonesia. *Lysimachia* species have become popular garden plants.

PARTS USED Flowering stems are used as cut flowers and the whole plant is sometimes grown as a potted flower or hanging basket.

CULTIVATION Production is predominantly by means of rhizomes. Flower yields and stem lengths tend to improve in the second year. Production takes place in open fields, under shade cloth and in greenhouses. Supplementary lighting is needed in areas with low light intensity during the winter months. Plants do not flower under continual short day conditions. At least 10 weeks of long day or night-break lighting is required.

PROPERTIES Vase life is below average to fairly good (5–10 days) and can vary significantly, depending on pre-treatment by growers.

QUALITY CRITERIA Select flowers with 30–50% of the florets open and make sure the closed buds are showing colour. Look for straight, sturdy stems with long racemes. Make sure that the leaves are in good condition, even though they are relatively insignificant to the overall aesthetic value of the flower.

CARE & HANDLING The use of a complete preservative is essential, as it makes a significant difference to vase life compared to flowers stored only in water. Recut stems and remove leaves below the water line. Store flowers at 3–5°C (37–41°F) and a relative humidity of 90–95%.

Lysimachia clethroides Duby   family: Primulaceae

wederik (Dutch); *lysimaque à feuilles de clétra* (French); *Entenschnabel-Felberich* (German); *lisimachia* (Italian); *lisimaquia* (Spanish)

Macrozamia communis

burrawang

Macrozamia communis plant

Macrozamia communis leaf

DESCRIPTION This palm-like plant is a cycad of up to 3 m (10′) high, with numerous compound leaves of 2 m (6½′) long, each having 100 to 130 leaflets. The leaflets (leaf segments) are widely spaced, linear in shape, 25 mm (1″) long, glossy green above, paler beneath, with a stiff texture and sharp tips. The female cones are broader than the male cones and comprise numerous spine-tipped cone scales bearing large, somewhat fleshy, egg-shaped seeds. It is one of 15 species indigenous to Australia. There appears to be as yet no distinct cultivars.

ORIGIN & HISTORY Australia. The seeds are rich in starch but very poisonous. Aborigines soak them in running water in a dillybag (a small bag or basket) for several days, before processing and eating.

PARTS USED The leaves are used as cut foliage.

CULTIVATION Cycads are relatively easy to cultivate, although they have the reputation of being difficult. Propagation is by means of seed or suckers (young plants that form at ground level from the parent plant). Both male and female plants are needed to produce seed. Plants need full sun, warm conditions and grow relatively slowly, although they remain productive for many years. A lot of foliage is still wild-harvested but nowadays an increasing percentage is produced through cultivation.

PROPERTIES Vase life is very good (21–28 days). Leaves have no definite fragrance and are not ethylene sensitive.

QUALITY CRITERIA Leaves need to be mature, relatively flat and well formed, with no leaflets missing or damaged. Leaves must have a uniform, deep, glossy green colour, free of any blemishes. Leaf stalks need to be sturdy.

CARE & HANDLING Keep the leaves cool and dry. There is no need to recut them or to place them in a floral preservative. Leaves can be held dry in the cooler or stored dry at low temperatures (0–2°C; 32–36°F). Loosen tied bunches to ensure good ventilation between fronds.

Macrozamia communis L. Johnson   family: Zamiaceae

burrawang (Dutch, French, Italian, Spanish); *Burrawang* (German)

Magnolia grandiflora
magnolia • large-flowered magnolia

Magnolia grandiflora leaves and flower

DESCRIPTION A large, evergreen tree of up to 30 m (100′). Twigs and young leaves are covered with rusty hairs. The glossy dark green leaves are stiff and leathery, and about 200 mm (8″) long. Large, erect, creamy white flowers of up to 0.4 m (16″) in diameter are borne on the branch tips. A large number of cultivars have been developed, differing in hardiness, growth form and leaf characteristics as well as in the size and shape of the flowers. 'Samuel Sommer' and 'Goliath' are cultivars with very large flowers, while 'Nantensis' has double flowers. Also important are the number of flowers produced and the time of flowering. 'Praecox' is an example of an early and long-flowering cultivar. 'Exmouth' is a cultivar derived from hybrids with *M. virginiana* (so-called Freeman hybrids).

ORIGIN & HISTORY South-eastern United States. This magnolia has become a popular ornamental tree in many parts of the world. It is particularly popular in gardens and parks in Italy.

PARTS USED Flowering stems are used as cut flowers and leafy stems as cut foliage.

CULTIVATION Plants are quite tolerant of drought and frost, but need regular watering in order to produce high quality flowers. For ease of harvesting, pruning is essential to develop low, well-branched plants.

PROPERTIES Vase life is poor to average (5–7 days). Flowers are very fragrant. Petals of open flowers tend to fall off easily.

QUALITY CRITERIA The flowers should be a uniform colour, with no blemishes or dry petal margins. Buds should be loosely closed and starting to open. Select cut foliage that has glossy leaves without any spots.

CARE & HANDLING Recut stems and hydrate for 2–3 hours before using. Place flowers and foliage in a floral preservative (without a sugar). Remove leaves below the water line. Use promptly or hold only for 3–4 days (2–4°C; 36–39°F; 95% relative humidity).

Magnolia grandiflora L.   family: Magnoliaceae

zuidelijke magnolia (Dutch); *magnolia à grandes fleurs* (French); *Immergrüne Magnolie* (German); *magnolia* (Italian); *magnolio* (Spanish)

Marsdenia floribunda

stephanotis • Madagascar jasmine • floradora

Marsdenia floribunda

DESCRIPTION An evergreen shrub with twining branches reaching 4 m (13′) in height bearing dark green, leathery leaves in opposite pairs. The waxy flowers are about 50 mm (2″) in diameter and occur in short-stalked clusters in the leaf axils. Colours are limited to pure white or ivory.

ORIGIN & HISTORY Madagascar. An old favourite cultivated ornamental and florist flower. The genus *Stephanotis* has been included in the genus *Marsdenia* but the plant is still listed under *Stephanotis* in most catalogues and textbooks.

PARTS USED The whole plant is used as a potted flower and the flowers for weddings and corsages.

CULTIVATION Propagation is primarily by means of cuttings and cultivation is usually in greenhouses. Plants require high light intensities, warm temperatures and fairly humid growing conditions. Good watering is required during the flowering season, but moderate watering during the dormant (winter) season favours the formation of new buds.

PROPERTIES Vase life of cut flowers is poor (3–4 days). Flowers are highly fragrant. The plant contains poisonous latex. Moving potted flowers around too much can result in bud drop.

QUALITY CRITERIA Select potted flowers that are full of well-coloured buds that are just beginning to open. Flowers must be pure white and have a waxy appearance, free of browning, bruising or any other blemishes. Select cut flowers at a more open stage than potted flowers (they are usually sold stemless and packed in air-tight bags).

CARE & HANDLING Handle cut flowers with care to avoid bruising. Store at 4°C (39°F) in original packaging, after first giving flowers a light spray (misting) of clean water, as flowers require constant moisture. Flowers can be stored for 7 days. Keep hands wet while working with flowers. Display pots in bright light (not direct sunlight or draughts). Keep moist and preferably water with soft, tepid water.

Marsdenia floribunda (Brongn.) Schltr. (=*Stephanotis floribunda*)   family: Apocynaceae (Asclepiadaceae)

bruidsbloem (Dutch); *jasmin de Madagascar* (French); *Kranzschlinge* (German); *gelsomino del madagascar* (Italian); *estefanotis* (Spanish)

Matthiola incana

stocks • Brompton stock • ten-week stock

Matthiola incana 'Lucida'

Matthiola incana lilac

Matthiola incana white

DESCRIPTION Biennial herbs (0.3–0.8 m or 12–32" high) with grey-green, hairy leaves borne on slightly woody branches. The fragrant flowers are about 25 mm (1") long and purple, pink or white. Cultivars (of which there are many) differ in their flowering time and the percentage double flowers. 'Ten-week Stock' is fast growing and is cultivated as an annual.

ORIGIN & HISTORY Mediterranean Europe. Stocks have long been a florist favourite due to their form, array of colours and fragrance.

PARTS USED Flowering stems are used as cut flowers.

CULTIVATION An important issue of stock breeding and production is selecting and cultivating higher value, double-flowered seedlings. After emergence, seedlings are exposed to cold temperatures (approximately 5°C; 41°F) for a few days, after which the double-flowered forms appear yellow and chlorotic, while the single forms remain green and vigorous. The sickly-looking double forms are kept (they

recover after a few days), while the healthy single forms are discarded.

PROPERTIES Vase life is poor (3–5 days). Flowers are scented. They are not sensitive to ethylene.

QUALITY CRITERIA Select flower spikes with the lower 50–75% of the flowers open. Look for straight, sturdy stems, compact spikes with no dry flowers and healthy leaves (dead tips are a sign of poor nutrition).

CARE & HANDLING Recut and place in a preservative. Keep out of the heat in a cool, dark place to prolong vase life and to avoid stem elongation and curving of the tips. Do not crush stems and recut frequently. Ensure good air movement between blooms, as stocks are susceptible to mildew. Prolonged cool storage may result in a loss of fragrance. Only store for 1–2 days at a temperature of 3–5°C (37–41°F). Flowers can be dried by hanging them upside down in small bunches (3–5 stems) in a warm area. If dried rapidly, flowers will retain their fragrance.

Matthiola incana (L.) R. Br.   family: Brassicaceae

violier (Dutch); giroflée, violier (French); Garten-Levkoje (German); violacciocca (Italian); alheli (Spanish)

Mimetes hirtus

pagoda flower

Mimetes hirtus

Mimetes cucullatus

DESCRIPTION A woody shrub of up to 2 m (6½′) high with spreading branches and oblong, hairy, overlapping leaves. The tubular, hairy flowers are crowded at the branch ends. Colours range from red to orange or yellow but these are naturally occurring forms and not cultivars. In this species, the upper leaves (bracts) are not much enlarged. Another species that is used as cut flower is *M. cucullatus*. It is commonly wild-harvested. The flower heads are decorated by the colourful upper leaves which are modified to serve as bracts.

ORIGIN & HISTORY South Africa. *Mimetes* is a genus of 12 shrubby species that are restricted to the Cape fynbos region in South Africa. Although the flowers have long been used locally as cut flowers, it is only relatively recently that the pagoda flower has become regularly available on international markets.

PARTS USED Stems with inflorescences are used as cut flowers (fresh or dried).

CULTIVATION *Mimetes* species are propagated from seeds or cuttings. However, growers generally purchase very young, rooted plants. Plants prefer open, well-ventilated, full sun conditions. Once established, they are fairly drought tolerant and can be productive for many years.

PROPERTIES Vase life is average to good (7–14 days). Flowers are not sensitive to ethylene. They are not scented.

QUALITY CRITERIA Look for long, straight and sturdy stems that are full of closely packed, healthy leaves. Leaves must be free of any black marks or other blemishes. Brightly coloured flowers must be present right around the stem tip (forming a complete "ring"). They must be closed or just opening.

CARE & HANDLING Recut stems and place in a preservative containing a bactericide and sugar. Do not display in a cold draught. Stems can be stored for 7–10 days at 2°C (36°F) and a relative humidity of 90%. Flowers dry well.

Mimetes hirtus (L.) Salisb. ex Knight   family: Proteaceae

mimetes (Dutch, French, Italian, Spanish); *Mimetes* (German)

Moluccella laevis

bells-of-Ireland • shellflower

Moluccella laevis

Moluccella laevis

DESCRIPTION Annual or short-lived perennial herbs (up to 1 m or 40") with hairless, toothed, rounded leaves and tall erect flowering stalks. The flowers are small, white or pale lilac and are surrounded by a characteristic bell-shaped green calyx. These "bells" are clustered fairly tightly together along single stems. There are four species but only one is commonly grown. Cultivated forms of *M. laevis* are similar to the original wild plant.

ORIGIN & HISTORY Western Asia (Cyprus, Syria, Iraq and the Caucasian region). Flowers are often used on St Patrick's Day celebrations, although the only real association with Ireland is in the name. The flowers are interesting rather than beautiful but have become very popular for flower arrangements. In the United States it is sometimes known as the shellflower.

PARTS USED Flowering stems are used as cut greens (fresh or dried).

CULTIVATION Plants are grown as annuals from seeds sown in early spring. Cultivation is uncomplicated – provide full sun and well-drained but moist soils that are moderately fertile.

PROPERTIES Vase life can vary from below average to above average (5–10 days). The small white or pale lilac flowers have a slight fragrance. The stems have small thorns that may cause skin irritation. Stems will bend towards any light source (phototropic).

QUALITY CRITERIA Look for straight stems with 80–90% of the bells open. Stems and flowers (calyces) are soft, so check for bruising and general damage due to handling. Make sure the green colour of the bells is uniform and not yellowish or blotchy.

CARE & HANDLING Recut stems and place in a floral preservative. Store upright and away from any strong side-lighting, as stems will bend towards the light. Flowers can be dried by hanging them upside down in small, loose bunches in a cool, dark place with good air movement.

Moluccella laevis L.   family: Lamiaceae

klokken van Ierland (Dutch); *clochette d'Irlande* (French); *Muschelblume* (German); *campanas de Irlanda*, *campanillas de Irlanda* (Italian); *campanas de Irlanda* (Spanish)

Monarda didyma

bergamot • bee balm • Oswego tea

Monarda didyma 'Cambridge Scarlet'

DESCRIPTION An aromatic perennial herb of about 1 m (40") high. The large leaves are minutely hairy and more or less broadly lance-shaped, with toothed margins. Flowers are borne in dense, rounded groups decorated with a circle of brightly coloured bracts. Each flower is tubular, two-lipped, gracefully arching and usually bright red. Several new colour forms have been developed, including the cultivars 'Alba' and 'Snow White' (white), 'Burgundy' (dark purple-red), 'Aquarius' (mauve to purple-lilac flowers and purplish green bracts), 'Cambridge Scarlet' (red), 'Prairie Night' (lilac), 'Croftway Pink' and 'Beauty of Cobham' (pale pink) and 'Salmonea' (salmon pink). *M. citriodora* is another popular cut flower species.

ORIGIN & HISTORY Eastern parts of the United States. The aromatic leaves were used by the Native Americans and early colonists to make herbal tea and are still used to some extent as a culinary herb (and in potpourris). Bee balm flowers are much loved by bees, hence this common name.

PARTS USED The flowering stems are used as cut flowers.

CULTIVATION Plants are propagated by means of seed or division of the rootstock. Bergamot thrives in moist soils under full sun or partial shade. They generally require a lot of feeding.

PROPERTIES Vase life is usually average (7 days). Flowers are not sensitive to ethylene. They are usually scented, depending on the cultivar.

QUALITY CRITERIA Select stems with flowers just starting to open. Look for long, straight and sturdy stems. Leaves should be of uniform colour, free of any brown tips or other blemishes.

CARE & HANDLING Recut stems and place in a floral preservative with a bactericide. Use fresh flowers promptly or hold them in a cooler at 2–4°C (36–39°F). Storage is not recommended. Remove leaves that will end up below the water line. Stems can be dried.

Monarda didyma L.   family: Lamiaceae

monarda, bergamotplant (Dutch); *monarde, thé d'Oswego* (French); *Scharlach-Indianernessel* (German); *bergamotto, tè d'Oswego* (Italian); *monarda escarlata* (Spanish)

Monstera deliciosa

ceriman • Swiss-cheese plant • windowleaf

Monstera deliciosa plant

Monstera deliciosa leaf

DESCRIPTION A robust climber (vine) with thick, sprawling stems that cling to rocks and tree trunks by means of aerial roots. The leaves are leathery and glossy green, up to 1 m by 0.5 m (40″ × 20″), with characteristic rows of oblong perforations between marginal perforations and the midrib. Costa Rican windowleaf (*M. epipremnoides*) has two to three ranks of perforations, with the outermost ones breaking the leaf margin. Variegated leaf forms are available, including 'Albovariegata' and 'Variegata'. Cultivated forms of *M. epipremnoides* are similar to the original form.

ORIGIN & HISTORY Mexico to Panama. *Monstera* species are old favourite houseplants, highly prized for their glossy, perforated leaves. The flower cluster (spadix) of the aptly named *M. deliciosa* becomes fleshy and delicious to eat, with a taste not unlike that of a mixed tropical fruit salad.

PARTS USED The leaves are used as cut greens.

CULTIVATION Propagation is typically by means of cuttings or division. Rich, well-drained soils are preferred. The best quality foliage is achieved under growing conditions of warm temperatures, high humidity and partial to heavy shade.

PROPERTIES Vase life is good (10–14 days, sometimes longer). Leaves have no fragrance and are not sensitive to ethylene.

QUALITY CRITERIA Select mature, glossy leaves that are fully opened and have a uniform deep green colour (not still opening or pale). Leaves must be free of blemishes (especially check the leaf margins). Leaf stalks must be sturdy.

CARE & HANDLING Recut leaf stalks and place in water in a bactericide. Make sure the leaf blade is not in the water. Do not physically pull open leaf holes that are still closed. Leaves can be held or stored wet or dry (in plastic or boxes), until needed or for 7–10 days at a high relative humidity (95%) and at 2–4°C (36–39°F). Wipe leaves clean before use.

Monstera deliciosa Liebm.

family: Araceae

gatenplant (Dutch); *cerima, philodendron* (French); *Fensterblatt* (German); *monsterio delicio* (Italian); *balazo, cerimán, costilla de Adán* (Spanish)

Muscari armeniacum

grape hyacinth

Muscari plants

Muscari armeniacum flowers

DESCRIPTION A clump-forming bulbous plant (up to 0.2 m or 8" high) with spikes of small, bell-shaped, usually blue flowers and slender, grass-like leaves. Flowers can also be mauve, purple or white, depending on the cultivar. Breeders focus on compact plants with dense flower spikes and deep, true blue colours. The popular 'Blue Spike' is compact, fully double, and deep blue, while 'Fantasy Creation' has unusual greenish-blue flowers. Several species are cultivated, including *M. neglectum* (=*M. atlanticum*, ="*M. racemosum*"), *M. botryoides*, *M. comosum* and *M. muscarimi* (=*M. moschatum*).

ORIGIN & HISTORY South-eastern Europe to the Caucasian region, and possibly also north-western Iran. There are 30 species, all from the Mediterranean and south-eastern Asia Minor. *M. muscarimi* is a Turkish species that has long been cultivated for the flowers that are used in scent-making.

PARTS USED Whole plants (as potted flowers).

CULTIVATION Plants flower naturally in winter and are dormant in summer. They like organic-rich, well-drained soils. The best quality is achieved under cultivation conditions of bright light and coolish temperatures. Irrigation is also a critical production factor and plants need to be kept moist but not wet, or else bulbs may rot.

PROPERTIES Deep blue flowers and short plants make this an ideal potted flower. Flowers are fragrant. Plants can last for at least three years in the same pot.

QUALITY CRITERIA Check to ensure that foliage has an even green colour and is not yellowish or blotchy. Select pots with well-formed foliage and long flowering spikes. Purchase plants with only 50% of the flowers open on the spike (flowers open from the bottom upwards).

CARE & HANDLING Keep the potting medium moist but do not over-water. Display in a coolish area with bright light (not in direct sunlight) and not in a cold draught.

Muscari armeniacum Leichtin ex Baker   family: Asparagaceae (Hyacinthaceae)

blauw druifje (Dutch); *muscari, jacinthe á grappes* (French); *Träubel, Traubenhyazinthe* (German); *cipollaccio* (Italian); *muscari(s), nazarenos* (Spanish)

Myosotis dissitiflora

forget-me-not

Myosotis dissitiflora plant

Myosotis dissitiflora flowers and fruit

DESCRIPTION Biennial or perennial herbs of up to 0.2 m (8″) high, with hairy leaves and deep sky blue flowers in multi-flowered clusters. Each flower is about 6 mm (¼″) in diameter and often has a small yellow or white "eye" in the middle. *Myosotis dissitiflora* hardly differs from the closely related garden forget-me-not (*M. sylvatica*) except in the smaller size of the plants (up to 0.5 m or 20″ in *M. sylvatica*). There are numerous cultivars of the latter and *M. alpestris*. Cultivars suitable for pot culture include 'Blue Ball' (rich indigo, without "eyes"), 'White Ball' (white) and 'Blue Basket' (blue, compact). 'Carmine King' is a carmine-pink cultivar of *M. alpestris*.

ORIGIN & HISTORY Switzerland (*M. dissitiflora*); North Africa, Europe and western Asia (*M. sylvatica*). The flowers are traditionally associated with love and remembrance.

PARTS USED The whole flowering plant is used as a potted flower, or the flowers as cut flowers or fillers, if sufficient stem length can be reached.

CULTIVATION Seeds are sown in moist soil and planted out into open fields in autumn. Growth and flowering is best in full sun but cool conditions (8–10°C; 46–50°F).

PROPERTIES Vase life of cut flowers is poor to average (4–8 days). Potted flowers should flower for 4–8 weeks. The flowers are not sensitive to ethylene and have no strong fragrance.

QUALITY CRITERIA Select potted plants with flowers beginning to open to 25% open. Select cut stems with half of the florets open. Make sure pot plants are compact and uniformly full of buds. Leaves need to have a uniform green colour with no yellowing or blemishes.

CARE & HANDLING Place flowers in a bactericide and use promptly. Storage is not recommended, although flowers can be held wet at 1–2°C (34–36°F) and 90–95% relative humidity. Display potted flowers in a cool, bright area (not direct sunlight). Keep soil moist.

Myosotis dissitiflora Bak. (=*M. sylvatica* Ehrh. ex Hoffm.?)   family: Boraginaceae

vergeet mij niet (Dutch); *myosotis, ne-m'oubliez-pas* (French); *Vergissmeinnicht* (German); *non-ti-scordar-di-me* (Italian); *miosotis* (Spanish)

Myrtus communis

myrtle

Myrtus communis foliage and flowers

Myrtus communis berries

DESCRIPTION An evergreen aromatic shrub of up to 3 m (10′) high. The leathery leaves are borne in opposite pairs – they are usually glossy dark green and 25–50 mm (1–2″) long but can also be much smaller and variegated, depending on the cultivar. White or pink-flushed flowers, each about 25 mm (1″) in diameter and solitary on a short, slender stalk, occur along the upper leaf axils. The small, edible fruits are usually dark reddish purple to black. Examples of garden cultivars include 'Albocarpa' and 'Leucocarpa' (both with white fruit), 'Buxifolia' (broad leaves), 'Flore Pleno' (double flowers) and 'Microphylla Variegata' (compact, with small, overlapping, variegated leaves).

ORIGIN & HISTORY Mainly found in the Mediterranean region and southern Asia but the exact origin is uncertain. Cultivated since ancient times and associated with Greek mythology and rituals. It is a symbol of purity and often used in bridal bouquets to signify marital love. Today, myrtle is grown as a hedge or topiary tree in all temperate regions of the world. It is a source of essential oil and has numerous culinary uses as flavour ingredient.

PARTS USED Leafy stems are used as cut foliage.

CULTIVATION Myrtle is usually propagated from cuttings. It thrives in a variety of soils and climates and is tolerant of mild frost. It responds well to regular pruning.

PROPERTIES Vase life is average to good (7–14 days). Stems have a slight lemon fragrance when cut.

QUALITY CRITERIA Select young stems that are not too woody and well branched. Look for healthy green foliage, free of damage or marks.

CARE & HANDLING Recut stems and remove any leaves below the water line. Place in a floral preservative or bactericide. Hold in a cool, ventilated area. Myrtle can be stored wet, or in moisture-retentive boxes, at 2–4°C (36–39°F) for 7 days (95% relative humidity).

Myrtus communis L.   family: Myrtaceae

myrthe (Dutch); *myrte* (French); *Echte Myrte, Brautmyrte* (German); *mirto* (Italian); *mirto común* (Spanish)

Narcissus cultivars

daffodil

Narcissus 'Tahiti'

Narcissus mixed

Narcissus white and yellow

DESCRIPTION A true bulb with strap-shaped leaves. The flowers (single or in clusters) have six petals and a characteristic outgrowth (corona) that forms a ring, cup or trumpet. Daffodils flower in winter and are dormant in summer. Many thousands of hybrids and cultivars have been bred over the centuries. Colours are mainly limited to white and yellow but there are countless sizes and shapes.

ORIGIN & HISTORY About 50 species in southern Europe, the Mediterranean region and Asia, including China and Japan. Daffodils have been the focus of songs, literature, art and legend for centuries. In Greek mythology, Persephone found daffodils more beautiful than any blooms she had ever seen.

PARTS USED Flowers are used as cut flowers and whole plants as potted flowers.

CULTIVATION Most daffodils require a sequence of warm–cool–warm periods. The cool period (15 to 20 weeks) is usually pulsed (9–5–1°C; 48–41–34°F).

PROPERTIES Vase life is poor to average (4–8 days). Most cultivars have a delicate scent. Cut stems exude a slimy sap that is toxic to many flowers, including roses, carnations, freesias and tulips. Flowers are ethylene sensitive.

QUALITY CRITERIA Purchase single, large flowers that are still closed but showing colour (gooseneck stage). Double-flowered cultivars should just begin to open. Ensure that stems are straight, sturdy and a uniform dark green colour and leaves are free of blemishes.

CARE & HANDLING Recut and hydrate as soon as possible and place in a preservative. Do not hydrate or store in the same water as other flowers. First place in own water for 24 hours before using together in an arrangement with other flowers and then do not recut, or else more sap will exude. Flowers can be stored for 2–3 days at 0–3°C (32–37°F). Display potted flowers in a cool, bright area away from ethylene-forming agents. Keep moist but not wet.

Narcissus cultivars   family: Amaryllidaceae

affodil (Dutch); *narcisse* (French); *Narzisse, Osterglocke* (German); *narciso* (Italian, Spanish)

Nelumbo nucifera

lotus • sacred lotus

Nelumbo nucifera white

Nelumbo nucifera pink

Nelumbo nucifera dry fruits

DESCRIPTION A water plant with thick, fleshy rhizomes that grow in the mud and very large, umbrella-shaped leaves on long stalks. The large, tulip-like flowers are solitary and pink or white and are borne high above the water surface. They are followed by characteristic and highly decorative cup-shaped, flat-topped fruits. Several cultivars have been developed, differing mainly in the colour of the flowers. They range from single to fully double forms and include pure white to pink or even deep red, with various bicolour patterns. 'Kamal Krishna' is an extremely beautiful cut flower cultivar. The American lotus (*N. lutea*) is very similar but has yellow flowers.

ORIGIN & HISTORY Asia (Iran to India, China, Japan and Australia). Lotus was once grown in Egypt but it is no longer there except on ancient walls and pillars. It is sacred in the Hindu and Buddhist religions and is a symbol of vitality, purity and eternal life. Lotus has become a popular ornamental plant for cultivation in dams and ponds in warm regions of the world.

PARTS USED The flowers are used as cut flowers and dried fruit capsules as ornaments in dry decorations.

CULTIVATION Propagation is by means of seed or rhizomes. The rhizomes are planted in shallow water. They grow rapidly and can reach a length of 20 m in one season.

PROPERTIES Vase life is poor (4–5 days). The flowers are very fragrant. Fruit capsules dry well and last for many years. The flowers, seeds and leaves are edible.

QUALITY CRITERIA Select flowers with long stems that are sturdy and straight. Petals must be free of bruises, marks and other blemishes. Select flowers that are still closed, but starting to open.

CARE & HANDLING Handle flowers with care. Place in deep water with a bactericide and hold in the cooler at 4°C (39°F). Use promptly – storage is not recommended. Store or display seed capsules dry.

Nelumbo nucifera Gaertn.   family: Nelumbonaceae

lotus (Dutch); *nelumbo* (French); *Lotosblume* (German); *nelumbo* (Italian); *loto* (Spanish)

Nepenthes cultivars

pitcher plant

Nepenthes 'Superba'

Nepenthes alata

DESCRIPTION Perennial, carnivorous climbers or herbs with inconspicuous purple or brownish flowers but remarkable "pitchers" that are borne on slender stalks on the leaf tips. Above the opening is a flat, rounded "lid" that has nectar-secreting glands. Insects attracted to the lids fall into the liquid inside the pitcher and serve as a source of nitrogen for the plant. Numerous species, hybrids and cultivars are grown. Trumpet- to flask-shaped pitchers include *N. ×chelsonii, N. ×coccinea, N. ×dormanniana* and *N. ×intermedia.* 'Henry Shaw' has large, pale green pitchers spotted with maroon red, while 'Superba' has green and yellow pitchers with red blotches and a red-striped lid fringed with red hairs.

ORIGIN & HISTORY About 70 species, from Madagascar to tropical Asia and Australia. Most of the cultivated species originated from Borneo, Sumatra and other parts of Indonesia. In the previous century, pitcher plants became a popular novelty.

PARTS USED The whole plant is grown as a potted "flower" or novelty item.

CULTIVATION Propagation is from seeds, air-layering or cuttings. Species from lowland regions require a minimum temperature of 18°C (64°F), while those from tropical highlands can withstand 10°C (50°F). Other requirements are a moist, fertile growing medium, high air humidity and partial shade.

PROPERTIES Potted plants are highly variable in the colour, size and shape of the pitchers. They are sensitive to salt build-up in soils. Plants can be "fed" with insects.

QUALITY CRITERIA Plants should be compact and healthy with bright green leaves and unblemished or physically damaged pitchers.

CARE & HANDLING Display in a warm area out of direct sunlight. Keep humid by regular misting and watering. Do not allow soil/medium to dry out. Handle with care, as excessive touching or handling will damage the pitchers.

Nepenthes cultivars   family: Nepenthaceae

bekerplant (Dutch); *nepenthes, tasse-de-singe* (French); *Kannenstrauch* (German); *nepenthes* (Italian); *nepentes, plantas jarro* (Spanish)

Nephrolepis exaltata
sword fern • Boston fern

Nephrolepis exaltata plants

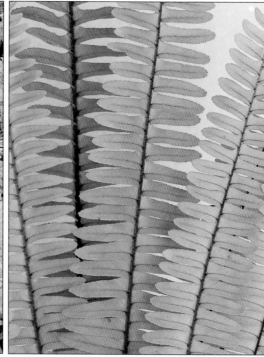

Nephrolepis exaltata leaves

DESCRIPTION A medium-sized fern with tapered fronds arranged in false rosettes. Several named cultivars are available, differing mainly in the structure of the leaf divisions. Cultivar selection is focused on container plants and hanging baskets.

ORIGIN & HISTORY All tropical regions of the world. It is an "old-fashioned" plant, once commonly found in parlours. In 1894 a Philadelphia grower shipped 50 000 sword ferns to a Boston distributor. The plants looked slightly different from the traditional sword ferns and thus became know as *N. exaltata* 'Bostoniensis', the Boston fern.

PARTS USED Leaf fronds are used as cut greens. Whole plants are popular for pots and hanging baskets.

CULTIVATION Cultivation is easy but tends to be time-consuming. Use a very loose, organic growing medium and avoid high pH or salty soil. The best growth and quality is achieved at a minimum day/night temperature of 22°C (72°F). During summer growers normally provide 50% shade, while in winter production the short days are often artificially modified by the use of interruption lighting to encourage fronds to lengthen.

PROPERTIES Vase life is average to good (7–14 days). Fronds are sensitive to ethylene.

QUALITY CRITERIA Fronds must have a uniform green colour – grey indicates water stress, while a pale colour indicates too much light. Select leaves with no broken tips or missing leaflets. For cut foliage, make sure there are no spores on the undersides of the leaves.

CARE & HANDLING Cut foliage can be kept in shipping cartons and stored at 2–4°C (36–39°F) and 95% humidity. Foliage that is going to be used in the next day or two can be recut and placed in a bucket containing preservative. Remove lower leaflets that are below the water line. Display pots in a well-lit area but avoid direct sunlight and cold draughts. Spray the leaves with mist and water the plants regularly.

Nephrolepis exaltata (L.) Schott

family: Lomariopsidaceae (Nephrolepidaceae)

krulvaren (Dutch); *néphrolépis* (French); *Schwertfarn, Aufrechter Schwertfarn* (German); *felce* (Italian); *helecho de boston* (Spanish)

Nerine bowdenii

Guernsey lily

Nerine bowdenii pink

Nerine sarniensis 'Alba'

DESCRIPTION A bulbous perennial with leaves produced with or soon after the flowers in late summer. The slender, tubular, two-lipped and often frilly flowers are borne in dense umbels. *Nerine bowdenii* is one of the most commonly available species and practically all of the numerous cultivars have the flowers in various shades of pink (rarely white). Examples are 'Alba' (white), 'Mark Fenwick' (pink) and 'Pink Triumph' (dark pink). *Nerine sarniensis* has bright red or rarely white flowers.

ORIGIN & HISTORY South Africa. Nerines are called Guernsey lilies because *N. sarniensis* has become naturalised on Guernsey Island in the Channel Islands, where it has grown since the 17th century. It is speculated that bulbs washed ashore after a shipwreck.

PARTS USED Flowering stems are used as cut flowers.

CULTIVATION Plants will tolerate poor soils but they do best in well-drained, loose, organic-rich soils. They tolerate full sun but are usually cultivated under low percentage shade cloth to prevent sun scorch on very hot days and for general protection from the elements. Most of the species do not flower readily after transplanting and thus are often left in the ground for a few years before lifting and processing. During active growing and flowering the soil needs to be kept moist. Growers often use mulch, which helps to retain moisture and maintain a constant soil temperature.

PROPERTIES Vase life is good (10–14 days). Flowers have no significant fragrance and they are not sensitive to ethylene.

QUALITY CRITERIA Select stems with 1–2 open buds and the rest showing good colour. Look for strong, straight stems free of marks and with a healthy green colour.

CARE & HANDLING Recut and place flowers in a preservative containing a sugar, to assist in bud opening. Do not store below 5°C (41°F) as this will cause the flowers to turn blue and ruin their coloration. Flowers do not dry well.

Nerine bowdenii W. Watson

family: Amaryllidaceae

nerine (Dutch); *nérine* (French); *Nerine* (German); *nerine, nerina* (Italian); *nerina, nerine, azucena de Guernesey* (Spanish)

Nertera granadensis

bead plant • coral moss • English babytears

Nertera granadensis

Soleirolia soleirolii

DESCRIPTION A creeping perennial herb with thread-like stems bearing opposite pairs of small, rounded leaves of less than 6 mm (¼") long. The plant forms moss-like patches of 0.3 m (1') or more in diameter. Flowers are solitary and greenish-white but minute and inconspicuous. They are followed by colourful, fleshy, bead-like fruits of about 5 mm (nearly ¼") in diameter. The usual colour of the fruit is bright orange but dark red forms are also known. Cultivated forms differ in the colour of the fruits but there are only a few well-known or named cultivars, such as 'Astrid' (small orange-red berries). When not in fruit, the plant may be mistaken for another moss-like creeper (*Soleirolia soleirolii*), which is variously known as peace-in-the-home, mind-your-own-business, baby's tears, angel's tears or Irish moss. *Nertera granadensis* is nowadays usually included in the genus *Coprosma* (as *Coprosma granadensis*).

ORIGIN & HISTORY South America, Taiwan, Southeast Asia, Australia, Tasmania and New Zealand. It has become popular as a pot plant and is often seen in florist shops in most parts of the world.

PARTS USED The whole plant is used as a potted "flower" or novelty ornamental.

CULTIVATION Plants are propagated by division of the clumps or seed. A rich, well-drained soil is essential for good results. Under natural conditions flowering occurs in summer, followed by berries in autumn. Plants are sensitive to frost.

PROPERTIES Plants are fairly unattractive until berries appear. The berries have no distinctive fragrance and are not sensitive to ethylene.

QUALITY CRITERIA Select plants with densely leafy stems and an abundance of berries. Plants should be compact and berries evenly dispersed. Select plants with mature, well-coloured berries, but make sure none have blackened or deteriorated. Foliage should be bright green, with no yellowing.

CARE & HANDLING Display pots in good light and out of direct draughts. Mist leaves occasionally. There is no need to water with tepid water, but avoid ice-cold water.

Nertera granadensis (Mutis) Druce (=*N. depressa*)   family: Rubiaceae

koraalmos (Dutch); *plante-perle* (French); *Korallenmoos* (German); *nertera* (Italian); *planta de las canicas, baya de coral, coralito* (Spanish)

Nigella damascena

love-in-a-mist

Nigella damascena flower

Nigella damascena 'Jekyll Blue'

Nigella damascena fruits

DESCRIPTION An annual herb with erect stems of about 0.5 m high and characteristic slender, thread-like leaf segments. The bracts surrounding the single flowers are finely divided and hair-like, creating a "halo" or "mist" around the colourful petals. Flowers are traditionally blue and about 40 mm in diameter (nearly 2"). The fruits are inflated, 10-locular capsules. A number of cultivars are grown, but visually they differ mainly in stem length and flower colour and only some in fruit shape, size or colour. Flowers may be single or double and the colours are mainly blue but also white and various shades of purple, mauve or rose pink.

ORIGIN & HISTORY Southern Europe and the Mediterranean region, including North Africa. Love-in-a-mist is an old favourite garden plant.

PARTS USED Flowering stems are used as cut flowers. The fruit capsules are popular as fillers (fresh or dried) or for potpourri.

CULTIVATION Seeds are sown direct, because seedlings do not transplant well. Plants are mainly grown to produce and sell the dried ornamental fruits. These "pods" are harvested when they are green or purple and air-dried in the dark. Drying in the light causes unwanted bronzing.

PROPERTIES Vase life is poor to average (5–8 days). Dried fruits ("pods") have a shelf life of many years.

QUALITY CRITERIA Dried stems – select stems that have fruit with a vibrant green or purple colour but avoid those with a bronze colouration. Fresh flowers – select stems with flowers fully coloured, that are still closed and only starting to open. Make sure flowers and/or fruits are free of any pests, diseases or damage.

CARE & HANDLING Recut the flower stems and place them in a preservative. Storage is not recommended, but if absolutely necessary, then hold the flowers for 2–3 days at 3–5°C (37–41°F). Flowers may be dried if harvested and sold fully open. Handle dried fruits with care to avoid damage.

Nigella damascena L.

family: Ranunculaceae

juffertje in't groen (Dutch); *nigelle de damas* (French); *Braut in Haaren, Gretel im Busch, Jungfer im Grünen* (German); *damigella, fanciullaccia* (Italian); *arañuela, flor d'aranya* (Spanish)

Nymphaea cultivars
water lily

Nymphaea red

Nymphaea nouchali var. *caerulea*

Nymphaea white

DESCRIPTION Perennial herbs with rhizomes that grow in the mud in shallow fresh water. The large, umbrella-shaped leaves are borne on slender stalks. Both the leaves and the large, rose-like flowers usually float on the water surface but are typically emergent in some species. Flower colour varies greatly, from white to yellow, pink, orange, red, purple and blue. Numerous cultivars have been developed from several species and hybrids. The three basic groups are the tropical night-flowering cultivars, the tropical day-flowering cultivars and hardy cultivars, which are mostly day-flowering.

ORIGIN & HISTORY Garden origin. Cultivated species occur on all continents. Many of the cultivars originated from hybrids between Old World and New World species. The African blue water lily (*N. nouchali* var. *caerulea*) was used as a narcotic in ancient Egypt and wreaths made from it were found on the mummy of Rameses II. The genus is named after the Greek goddess Nymphe.

PARTS USED The flowers are used as cut flowers and novelty flowers.

CULTIVATION Temperature and water quality are important considerations in cultivation. Plants need full sun conditions and still water. Ideal water depths vary, depending on cultivar and species.

PROPERTIES The vase life is poor to average (5–8 days). Most of the cultivars have fragrant flowers. Flowers are sensitive to ethylene.

QUALITY CRITERIA Flower petals must be free of black marks or any other blemishes. Flower stalks must be straight, sturdy and of good length. Flowers must be well formed, compact and have a good petal count. Select flowers that are just starting to open.

CARE & HANDLING Keep most of the flower stalk submerged in clean water. Do not use any additives. Replace water daily. Display the flowers in a cool, bright area, or hold at 4–6°C (39–43°F). Use promptly – do not store.

Nymphaea cultivars

family: Nymphaeaceae

waterlelie (Dutch); *nénuphar* (French); *Seerose* (German); *ninfea* (Italian); *nenúfar* (Spanish)

Odontoglossum cultivars
lace orchid

Odontoglossum 'Violetta Von Holms'

Odontoglossum 'Yellow Dream'

DESCRIPTION A clump-forming plant, with flattened pseudobulbs bearing two strap-like leaves each. Up to 12 flowers, each about 75 mm (3″) in diameter, are borne on short to long spikes. They typically have broad segments, are white to pale pink and are variously spotted and blotched with red or purple. There are many intergeneric hybrids (with *Miltonia*, *Cochlioda* and *Oncidium*) and numerous cultivars. *Odontocidiums* (intergeneric hybrids between *Odontoglossum* and *Oncidium*) have become popular potted flowers, with long-lasting blooms and a range of colours.

ORIGIN & HISTORY Central America (Colombia). The species and related hybrids are old favourite florist flowers.

PARTS USED The whole plant is used as a potted flower, or the flowers as cut flowers.

CULTIVATION *Odontoglossum* can adapt to a range of temperatures provided the humidity is kept high. Avoid direct sunlight. Grow the plants in a mixture of sphagnum moss, fine-grade bark and perlite, and keep them well watered at all times.

PROPERTIES Vase life of fresh *Odontoglossum* flowers is average to good (7–14 days) and potted flowers can last even longer (2–5 weeks). Flowers are ethylene sensitive.

QUALITY CRITERIA Select plants with numerous blooms that are free of blemishes. In winter 3–4 buds should be open, while in summer only 1–2 need to be open. Make sure none of the pollinia of the flower have been damaged, as pollinated flowers deteriorate very quickly. In the case of cut stems, look for fully opened flowers.

CARE & HANDLING Check that cut flower vials have adequate water. Cut off stem ends that have turned black. Handle carefully as touching can cause bruising of petals, or pollination of flowers. Display pots in a warm area, out of direct sunlight and draughts. Do not over-water pots. Flowers can be stored wet at 1–2°C (34–36°F) and 95% relative humidity for 7 days. Water on the petals can leave marks.

Odontoglossum cultivars   family: Orchidaceae

odontoglossum (Dutch, French, Italian); *Odontoglossum, Zahnzunge, Tigerorchidee* (German); *odontoglossa, orquídea tigre* (Spanish)

Oenothera fruticosa

sundrops

Oenothera fruticosa

Oenothera missouriensis

Oenothera biennis

DESCRIPTION A biennial or perennial herb that varies from 0.6 to 1 m in height (about 2–3'). It typically has erect, reddish stems and narrow leaves that may also be red-tinted. The flower buds are orange or reddish, opening to golden yellow. Sundrops are closely related to the well-known evening primrose (*Oenothera biennis*). The flower buds of the evening primrose open at dusk and shrivel before noon, while those of sundrops tend to open by day. Several cultivars of *O. fruticosa* are available, including well-known ones such as 'Fireworks' (purple-tinged leaves and yellow flowers), 'Golden Moonlight' (tall, with large, bright yellow flowers) and 'Yellow River' (red stems with canary yellow flowers). Missouri primrose (*O. missouriensis*) is used as a potted flower.

ORIGIN & HISTORY Eastern parts of North America. Sundrops are popular garden plants and are also used to some extent in the cut flower trade. One of the common names for *Oenothera*, "King's cure-all", reflects the wide range of healing powers that have been ascribed to this plant.

PARTS USED The flowering stems are used as cut flowers or fillers.

CULTIVATION Propagation is from seeds, softwood cuttings or by division. A sandy, well-drained soil and full sun to partial shade are essential. Plants are usually cut back after flowering.

PROPERTIES Vase life is poor to average (5–7 days). Flowers are not heavily scented and are sensitive to ethylene.

QUALITY CRITERIA Cut stems need to be sturdy and straight. Leaves should be healthy, of a uniform green colour and free of any blemishes. Select stems with 30–50% of flowers open or opening and most of the buds having good colour.

CARE & HANDLING Recut stems and place in a floral preservative. Remove any leaves that are below the water line. Storage is not recommended, although if necessary keep flowers at 2–4°C (36–39°F) and 90–95% relative humidity for only a few days.

Oenothera fruticosa L.   family: Onagraceae

teunisbloem (Dutch); *onagre, onagre tétragone* (French); *Nachtkerze, Rotstängelige Nachtkerze* (German); *enothera* (Italian); *enotera* (Spanish)

Oncidium flexuosum

dancing doll orchid

Oncidium flexuosum cultivar

Oncidium flexuosum 'Dancing Lady'

DESCRIPTION A clump-forming perennial with pseudobulbs that are oval to oblong in shape and up to 90 mm (nearly 4") long. Leaves are strap-shaped, somewhat leathery and about 25 mm (1") wide. Flowers are borne in a multi-flowered, large cluster of up to 1 m (40"). They are relatively small and usually bright yellow with reddish brown bars and blotches. There are numerous cultivars of *O. flexuosum* and related species. Orchid hybrids such as *Wilsonara* arose from cross-breeding between *Odontoglossum* (large, shapely flowers), *Cochlioda* (vivid red flowers) and *Oncidium* (many-flowered scape).

ORIGIN & HISTORY Argentina, Brazil, Paraguay and Uruguay. The dancing doll orchid has become very popular as a potted flower.

PARTS USED The whole plant is used as a potted flower and the flowering stems as cut flowers.

CULTIVATION *Oncidium* cultivation is lengthy and more difficult than for most florist flowers. Propagation from seed is rare and virtually all plants are grown from meristems and tissue culture. It is essential to start off with high quality plant material and good quality irrigation water.

PROPERTIES Vase life of fresh flowers is average to good (7–14 days). Vase life of potted flowers is very good (2–5 weeks). Flowers are sensitive to ethylene.

QUALITY CRITERIA Select stems with fully opened blooms that are not showing any signs of ageing or blemishes. Make sure none of the pollinia of the flower have been damaged, as pollinated flowers deteriorate quickly. Choose potted flowers with 3–4 open buds (winter) or 1–2 open buds (summer).

CARE & HANDLING Check that flower vials are filled with water. Cut off stem ends that have turned black. Avoid touching petals, which can cause bruising. Cut flowers can be stored wet at 1–2°C (34–36°F) and 95% relative humidity for 7 days. Water drops cause marks on the petals. Display pots in a bright cool, humid area, away from ethylene-forming agents.

Oncidium flexuosum Sims   family: Orchidaceae

oncidium (Dutch, French, Italian, Spanish); *Oncidium* (German)

Onopordum acanthium

giant thistle • Swiss mountain thistle • silver thistle

Onoopordum acanthium

DESCRIPTION A robust and spiny biennial herb (up to 3 m or 10′) with strongly ribbed and winged stems bearing spines of up to 10 mm (nearly ½″) long. The large leaves are variously lobed and dissected, with the teeth ending in sharp spines. The surface is sparsely woolly and silvery grey. Thistle-like, spiny capsules are borne in leafy clusters at the stem tips. The purple or white florets are relatively large – 25 mm (1″) long. Flowering occurs in summer. There are no well-known named cultivars.

ORIGIN & HISTORY Europe, Central Asia and North Africa (naturalised in North America). The common name Scotch thistle is sometimes used for this species and it is claimed that this is the one depicted on the Scottish royal emblem. However, the true (original) Scotch thistle is more likely to be the indigenous *Cirsium vulgare* or *Carduus nutans*, as the giant thistle does not occur naturally on the British Isles.

PARTS USED Flowering stems with flower heads are used as cut flowers.

CULTIVATION The plants form a compact clump of foliage in the first year and rapidly develop the typical branched and winged flowering stems in the second year. Propagation is by seed and plants prefer well-drained soils and full sun conditions. However, they require a cold period to produce quality blooms with good colour.

PROPERTIES Vase life is poor to average (5–7 days). Flowers have no strong fragrance and are not ethylene sensitive.

QUALITY CRITERIA Look for stems with at least 75% to all flower heads showing good colour. Select strong, well-branched stems with well-formed "cones". Check that leaves are healthy and free of any blemishes.

CARE & HANDLING Recut stems and place in a floral preservative. Display or hold in a cool, draught-free area. Cut stems can be stored for 1 week at 0–2°C (32–36°F) and a high relative humidity. Stems are suitable for drying.

Onoopordum acanthium L.

family: Asteraceae

wegdistel (Dutch); *chardon aux ânes* (French); *Gewöhnliche Eselsdistel* (German); *onopordo, acanzio* (Italian); *alcachofa borriquera* (Spanish)

Origanum vulgare

wild marjoram • oregano

Origanum vulgare purple

Origanum vulgare pink

DESCRIPTION A perennial herb of up to 0.9 m (3') high. The leaves are in opposite pairs, about 25 mm (1") long and aromatic. Loose clusters of small flowers (purple to pink in the wild forms) are borne on the branch ends, surrounded by brightly coloured flower bracts. Cultivars differ in the colour of the leaves as well as the flowers (white to pink, purple or lilac). Examples of taller cultivars suitable for cut flowers include 'Album' (white flowers, pale green leaves), 'Bucklands' (upright, flowers and bracts pink) and 'Heiderose' (upright, pink flowers). Oregano should not be confused with marjoram (*O. majorana*) or pot marjoram (*O. onites*).

ORIGIN & HISTORY Europe. Oregano has been used since prehistoric times as a culinary herb and medicinal plant and nowadays it provides the distinctive flavour to the popular pizza. Oregano or wild marjoram is also a minor florist flower.

PARTS USED The leafy, fragrant stems are often used by florists and flower retailers as foliage or fillers, when available.

CULTIVATION Oregano is easily cultivated from seed or cuttings. The plant prefers a slightly alkaline soil and a mild to warm, Mediterranean climate, with full sun conditions.

PROPERTIES The vase life of the cut flowers is average (6–8 days), while the foliage is slightly better (10 days). Leaves are aromatic and edible.

QUALITY CRITERIA Select flowering stems with 50% of flowers open. Stems need to be well-branched and of good length. Make sure that the leaves have a uniform green colour (leaves should not be pale or yellowish) and that they are free of blemishes.

CARE & HANDLING Treat oregano as a cut foliage or filler. Recut stems, remove leaves below the water line and place in a bactericide. Display in a bright, cool area. Stems can be stored wet for 4–5 days at 1–2°C (34–36°F) and a high relative humidity 90%.

Origanum vulgare L.   family: Lamiaceae

marjolein (Dutch); *origan, marjolaine* (French); *Gewöhlicher Dost, Wilder Majoran* (German); *origano* (Italian); *mejorana* (Spanish)

Ornithogalum thyrsoides

chincherinchee • star-of-Bethlehem

Ornithogalum thyrsoides 'Mt Fuji'

Ornithogalum saundersiae

Ornithogalum dubium

DESCRIPTION A bulbous plant with strap-shaped leaves of up to 0.3 m (1') long that are minutely hairy along their margins. The flowers are white to ivory or golden yellow and often tinted with bronze or green. Almost all cultivars suited to florists are derived from only a few of the species, namely O. *arabicum* (Arabian star flower), O. *saundersiae* (giant chincherinchee), O. *thyrsoides* (chincherinchee) and O. *umbellatum* (star-of-Bethlehem). Cultivars of O. *thyrsoides* include 'Album' (flowers white with a darker eye) and 'Flavescens' (flowers golden).

ORIGIN & HISTORY South Africa. The real chincherinchee is the best known of the four species that have become popular as cut flowers.

PARTS USED Flowering stems are used as cut flowers.

CULTIVATION Best quality flowers are produced under high light intensity and cool temperatures (13–17°C; 55–63°F) in greenhouses. Bulbs are "programmed" and then forced to flower at specific times by putting them through a number of temperature changes at varying time intervals.

PROPERTIES Vase life is very good (14–21 days). Flower tips will bend and twist towards light (phototropic). All parts of the plant are poisonous. Flowers are ethylene sensitive.

QUALITY CRITERIA Ideally select flower spikes with only 2–3 of the basal flowers open. Look for strong, straight stems with a good flower spike length. Make sure foliage is free of spots and not pale or mottled in colour (due to viruses).

CARE & HANDLING Flowers continue to open in plain water and vase life is good, so a preservative is not necessary, but can do no harm. Store at 5–10°C (41–50°F). To prevent bending towards light, the spikes must be stored upright and the tips can be cut off. Flowers can be dried by desiccation – cover them gently with a 1:1 borax and sand mixture in a closed container for 10–14 days.

Ornithogalum thyrsoides Jacq.   family: Asparagaceae (Hyacinthaceae)

vogelmelk (Dutch); *dame d'onze heures* (French); *Milchstern* (German); ornitogallo (Italian); *leche de gallina* (Spanish)

Ozothamnus diosmifolius

rice flower

Ozothamnus diosmifolius

DESCRIPTION The plant is an erect shrub of up to 3 m (9′) high. The small, narrow leaves are densely hairy or woolly. Small flower heads are borne in large, multi-flowered clusters. The persistent bracts are papery and usually white but the outer ones are often tinged with pink. There are as yet no well-known cultivars and the colour range is limited to white and pink. Significant volumes of stems are still wild-harvested. *Ozothamnus obcordatus* has a wider colour range, from pale lemon to bright yellow and mustard, and occasionally red-brown bracts.

ORIGIN & HISTORY Australia (New South Wales and south-eastern Queensland). *Ozothamnus* species are similar to the well-known everlasting flowers of the genus *Helichrysum* but the latter are typically herbs and not woody plants. These flowers are old favourites in the florist industry and the rice flower is one of several relatively recent novel introductions.

PARTS USED The flowering stems are used as fillers and dried flowers.

CULTIVATION Propagation is by means of seed or cuttings. Plants prefer well-drained soils and full sun conditions and are fairly drought tolerant.

PROPERTIES Vase life of fresh stems is average to good (7–10 days). Flowers have no distinct fragrance. The flowers and leaves are ethylene sensitive.

QUALITY CRITERIA Select young stems with 30–50% of flower heads open. Look for straight, well-branched stems. Check that no flowers have started to brown, fade or have any blemishes. The leaves should be fresh and of good colour, with no blackening of the tips or other blemishes.

CARE & HANDLING Recut stems and place in a floral preservative with a bactericide. Remove leaves below the water line. Loosen bunches to improve ventilation. Stems can be stored for 7–8 days at 1–2°C (34–36°F) and a high relative humidity (90%). Cut stems are excellent for drying.

Ozothamnus diosmifolius (Vent.) DC. (=*Helichrysum diosmifolium*)   family: Asteraceae

ozothamnus (Dutch, French, Italian, Spanish); *Ozothamnus* (German)

Paeonia lactiflora

peony • common garden peony

Paeonia cultivar

Paeonia lactiflora white

Paeonia cultivar

DESCRIPTION A perennial herb of 0.6 m (2′) high with red stems bearing compound (triternate), dark green leaves. The large flowers were originally white but modern cultivars are multi-coloured. Commercial cultivars are mostly crosses between *P. lactiflora* and *P. officinalis*. Peonies are categorised by their flower type (single, Japanese, anemone, semi-double and double). Cultivars are further categorised by their flowering times.

ORIGIN & HISTORY China, Siberia and Tibet. Peonies have a longer history as garden plants than as florist flowers.

PARTS USED Flowers are used as cut flowers and whole plants as potted flowers.

CULTIVATION Plants are propagated from root division and can be harvested for up to seven years, but yields peak after three years. A cold period is required to initiate flowering and well-drained soils with good ventilation result in high quality flowers. Large, single flowers can be produced by removing all the lateral flower buds,

or a spray of smaller flowers can be obtained by removing the central flower bud.

PROPERTIES Vase life is poor to average (5–7 days) and very short once the flower is fully open. Flowers are lightly scented. Plants and flowers are fairly susceptible to botrytis.

QUALITY CRITERIA Select cut flower stems with tight buds, but that are showing good colour. Doubles and reds need to be slightly more open. Do not purchase flowers that are 50% or more open, as they will not last. Select potted flowers with flowers still closed. Make sure that leaves are in a good condition.

CARE & HANDLING Recut flowers and hydrate in a citric acid solution at 21°C (70°F) for 2–3 hours, and then place in a preservative with a bactericide but without sugar. Keep flowers in a cool (preferably 2–5°C; 36–41°F), dark place to retard bud opening. Display potted flowers in a cool, light (not direct sunlight) area. Keep potting medium moist, but not wet.

Paeonia lactiflora Pall. (=*P. albiflora*)   family: Paeoniaceae

pioen (Dutch); *pivoine* (French); *Chinesische Pfingsrose, Päonie* (German); *peonia* (Italian); *peonia* (Spanish)

Papaver nudicaule
Iceland poppy

Papaver somniferum flowers

Papaver nudicaule orange

Papaver somniferum fruits

DESCRIPTION A perennial herb, 0.3 m (1') high, with a basal tuft of dissected, grey-green and hairy leaves. Solitary colourful flowers occur on slender stalks of up to 0.8 m (nearly 3'). The Asian opium poppy (*P. somniferum*) is a more robust plant and the flowers usually have a purple basal blotch. There are many cultivars with stunning colours. Some have long stems, ideal for florist flowers, while others are more compact and suitable as potted flowers.

ORIGIN & HISTORY Subarctic regions. Poppies are old favourite cut flowers and the fruits of opium poppies are popular in dried arrangements. Laws pertaining to opium production sometimes make it problematic for flower growers to grow opium poppies. Red poppies (*P. rhoeas*) are worn in the weeks preceding Remembrance Day (11 November) or Memorial Day.

PARTS USED Flower stems are used as cut flowers and whole plants as potted flowers.

CULTIVATION Seed germination is often erratic so that growers usually prefer to buy seedlings in plugs. Plants are cultivated in open fields or in greenhouses during winter months. Iceland poppies grow best in low temperatures of 10–15°C (50–59°F) – above 21°C (70°F), the quality and size of the flowers are seriously reduced. Watering is critical – foliage must be dry by nightfall to prevent diseases.

PROPERTIES Vase life of cut flowers is poor (3–5 days). Cut stems exude a milky sap.

QUALITY CRITERIA Select flowers that are only about half open (with the fuzzy sheath split and the coloured petals busy unfolding). Flowers cut and sold in the bud stage may fail to open. Choose pots with buds showing some colour.

CARE & HANDLING Recut stems and scald them in hot water to stop any latex flow. Place in a preservative and keep in a cool place (10–15°C; 50–59°F). Storage is not recommended, due to poor vase life and thin stems. Display potted flowers in a well-lit, cool area (under 21°C; 70°F). Avoid direct sunlight and draughts. Allow the pots to dry out slightly before watering again.

Papaver nudicaule L.   family: Papaveraceae

klaproos (Dutch); *pivot d'Islande* (French); *Island-Mohn* (German); *papaveri d'Islanda* (Italian); (Japanese); *amapola de Islandia* (Spanish)

Paphiopedilum cultivars
slipper orchid • Venus's slipper

Paphiopedilum red

Paphiopedilum pink

Paphiopedilum yellow

DESCRIPTION Slipper orchids are perennial herbs with fleshy, strap-shaped leaves arranged in two ranks. Unlike many orchids, they have no swollen stem bases (pseudobulbs). Some have variegated (mottled) foliage. The spectacular and distinctive flowers are often solitary but some have clusters of a dozen or more flowers. The flower typically has the lip modified to form a hollow "pouch" or "slipper". A multitude of colour forms are available, with the petals beautifully decorated with stripes and spots. New hybrids and cultivars are continuously being developed. There are three basic styles. "Maudiae"-type hybrids have bicolour leaves and large, single flowers that are conspicuously striped on the dorsal sepal. Multifloral hybrids typically have several large and spectacular flowers. "Complex hybrids" or "exhibition"-style hybrids are single-flowered with very large, rounded flowers.

ORIGIN & HISTORY Garden origin. Approximately 80 species occur naturally in India, China and Southeast Asia, as far as the Solomon Islands. The name is derived from Paphos (the place where the temple of Aphrodite, better known as Venus, is situated) and *pedilon*, the Greek word for slipper.

PARTS USED The whole flowering plant is used as a potted flower.

CULTIVATION Propagation is by division. Pots should contain well-drained, loose medium. The plants are planted deeply to prevent them from being pushed out as the roots develop. Species and cultivars differ in their temperature requirements.

PROPERTIES Potted flowers can last for 1–3 months. Flowers are very sensitive to ethylene.

QUALITY CRITERIA Select a healthy plant with no blemishes on the leaves or flower(s). Look for fully opened flowers, which are well formed and free of bruising or brown edges.

CARE & HANDLING Handle with care to avoid damage to the flowers. Keep plants shaded and moist. Mist the foliage regularly.

Paphiopedilum cultivars

family: Orchidaceae

venusschoentje (Dutch); *sabot de Vénus* (French); *Venusschuh* (German); *zapatilla de venus* (Spanish)

Pelargonium domesticum

regal pelargonium • regals

Pelargonium ×domesticum

DESCRIPTION Shrubby plants with erect, woody stems and deeply divided, toothed leaves. The flowers are very large and showy. The two upper petals have characteristic dark veins and blotches. Amongst the very numerous cultivars are 'Carisbrooke' (large pink, with maroon marks), 'Pompeii' (dark purple-black with narrow white margins) and 'White Chiffon' (white). Rose geranium (*P. graveolens*) is similar but has more deeply lobed, glandular, aromatic leaves and much smaller flowers – 'Rosé' is the most famous cultivar.

ORIGIN & HISTORY Garden origin (original species all from South Africa). The name *Pelargonium ×domesticum* was given to the hybrid group known as regals, Lady Washington pelargoniums or show pelargoniums. They originated as hybrids between *P. grandiflorum, P. cucullatum* and other species and are sometimes also referred to as *Pelargonium ×hybridum*. Rose geranium is grown as a source of essential oils used in the perfume industry.

PARTS USED Whole plants, as potted flowers.

CULTIVATION Plants require cool production temperatures of 13–18°C (55–65°F) for best results. At high humidity levels (more than 70%), plants tend to remain vegetative, even with ideal temperatures and light intensities. Plants are sensitive to drying out and their growing medium must remain moist.

PROPERTIES Regals have a short flowering season of only about one month. The leaves and flowers are not fragrant. Flowers are very sensitive to ethylene, which causes petal drop.

QUALITY CRITERIA Select plants with compact flowering heads and healthy leaves. Purchase plants pretreated against ethylene and avoid plants with discoloured leaves.

CARE & HANDLING Place pots in bright light but avoid direct sunlight. Cool temperatures (16–21°C; 61–70°F) are ideal. Keep away from draughts and sources of ethylene. Maintain potting medium uniformly moist and do not allow to dry out. Regularly remove dead flowers.

Pelargonium ×domesticum L. H. Bail.   family: Geraniaceae

geranium (Dutch); *géranium* (French); *Geranie* (German); *geranio* (Italian); *geranio* (Spanish)

Pelargonium peltatum

ivy geranium • ivy-leaved geranium • hanging geranium

Pelargonium peltatum

DESCRIPTION A trailing and climbing perennial herb with fleshy (succulent), five-lobed and hairless leaves. The white to pink, red or purple flowers typically have the upper two petals marked with darker veins (in single-flowered forms – the petals of modern double forms are mostly uniform in colour). There are numerous cultivars, including 'Crocodile' (single, pink), 'Galiliee' (double, pink), 'La France' (semi-double, mauve with white and purple veins) and 'L'Elégante' (single, white with purple veins and pink-tinted leaves). The common name geranium is misleading – these plants should not be confused with the genus *Geranium* (the related stork's bill).

ORIGIN & HISTORY South Africa. Plants have been grown for generations, mainly for their beautiful flowers. In the language of flowers, dark geraniums represent melancholy, while scarlet ones represent comfort. The ivy geranium has become a popular container plant, as the creeping stems cascade over the edges of balconies, windowsills and hanging baskets.

PARTS USED Whole plants are used as potted flowers and are especially popular for use in hanging baskets.

CULTIVATION Ivy geranium is a hardy and drought-tolerant plant that can be grown successfully under a range of temperatures and in any good soil medium. Flowers should be kept dry to prevent botrytis infection.

PROPERTIES Plants flower for several months (especially when the dead flower heads are regularly removed). The flowers are sensitive to ethylene and susceptible to botrytis.

QUALITY CRITERIA Select well-branched plants with many flower heads and numerous healthy new buds emerging. Leaves and petals should be firm, fleshy and healthy, free from spots or signs of disease. Avoid plants with discoloured leaves.

CARE & HANDLING Pots or containers should be placed in a warm position – plants can tolerate direct sunlight as long as the soil is kept moist. Dead flower heads should be removed to prevent fungal diseases and to encourage more flowering.

Pelargonium peltatum (L.) L'Hérit.   family: Geraniaceae

hanggeranium (Dutch); *géranium lierre* (French); *Efeublättrige Pelargonie* (German); *geranio edera* (Italian); *geranio de hiedra* (Spanish)

Pelargonium zonale

geranium • zonal geranium • zonal pelargonium

Pelargonium zonale

DESCRIPTION An aromatic perennial subshrub (up to 1 m or 3′) with succulent stems and rounded leaves that are often marked with a darker zone (hence *zonale*). The flowers vary from white to pink, red or purple. These are the common container and bedding "geraniums". The main cultivar groups are (1) cactus-flowered pelargoniums (quilled petals); (2) American Irene types (large flower heads, used as cut flowers); (3) stellar and startel pelargoniums (small plants, with star-shaped, zoned leaves and forked petals); (4) miniature and dwarf pelargoniums (less than 200 mm or 8" high and popular as potted flowers); (5) rosebud pelargoniums (small double flowers resembling rose buds).

ORIGIN & HISTORY Garden origin. The zonal pelargonium (sometimes called *P. ×hortorum*) is a complex hybrid derived mainly from *P. zonale* and *P. inquinans*, both from South Africa. Zonal pelargoniums have decorated windowsills and balconies (especially in Europe and North America) for more than a century.

PARTS USED Whole plants are used as potted flowers. Flower heads of large types can be used as cut flowers.

CULTIVATION Propagated from seed or cuttings, but cuttings are easy and preferred when selected cultivars are grown. Cool temperatures and moist soils are essential. Flowers are very susceptible to botrytis and plants are usually grown under cover where the foliage and flowers can be kept dry.

PROPERTIES Plants continue to flower for months on end. They are ethylene sensitive. The leaves are usually slightly fragrant.

QUALITY CRITERIA Select healthy plants with leaves and flowers free from blemishes and disease, especially botrytis. Avoid plants with discoloured leaves.

CARE & HANDLING Place in a bright, but cool area (4–13°C; 39–55°F) to maintain vase life. Avoid draughts and sources of ethylene. Keep potted plants moist but do not over-water and regularly remove dead flowers and leaves.

Pelargonium zonale (L.) L'Herit. ex Aiton   family: Geraniaceae

geranium (Dutch); *pélargonium zonale, géranium des balcons* (French); *Zonal-Pelargonie, Geranie der Gärtner* (German); *geranio* (Italian); *geranio* (Spanish)

Pennisetum alopecuroides

Chinese fountain grass • swamp foxtail grass

Pennisetum alopecuroides

Pennisetum alopecuroides flower spikes

DESCRIPTION A perennial grass of up to 1.5 m (3'), with erect, slender culms. Leaves are up to 12 mm (½″) wide and vary in colour from bright green to yellow or variegated, to reddish or bronze. The inflorescences are cylindrical and yellow-green to dark purple or black. Numerous cultivars have been developed, differing in the size of the plant and in the colour of both the leaves and the inflorescences. Examples are 'Burgundy Giant' (bronze and reddish leaves), 'Woodside' (dark purple inflorescences) and 'Moudry' (glossy green leaves and dark purple to black inflorescences).

ORIGIN & HISTORY Korea, Japan and the Philippines to western Australia. The colourful Chinese fountain grass has become a popular garden plant all over the world.

PARTS USED The leafy culms are used as fillers and ornamentals.

CULTIVATION *Pennisetum* is propagated mainly by means of seed. A well-drained soil and full sun conditions are necessary. Proper feeding and watering are essential to produce high-quality stems and plumes. The plant is a beautiful ornamental grass that is mainly cultivated for the garden industry, but it is also popular in the florist industry.

PROPERTIES Vase life of fresh stems is good (7–10 days) and the grass stays attractive as it dries in the vase. It is not scented or sensitive to ethylene. The plumes seldom cause allergic or hay fever reactions.

QUALITY CRITERIA Look for long, straight and sturdy feathery spikes. Plumes should be well formed and full and have a bright colour. Make sure that plumes, leaves and stems are clean and free of any damage or blemishes.

CARE & HANDLING There is no need to recut the stems or to place them in a preservative. Hold or display them dry, in a cool area. Preferably use fresh stems promptly. Loosen tight bunches to improve ventilation and do not get the plumes wet. The stems and plumes dry well and remain attractive.

Pennisetum alopecuroides (L.) Spreng. (=*P. japonicum*)   family: Poaceae

lampenpoetsersgras (Dutch); *pennisétum* (French); *Japanisches Federborstengras* (German); *chikara-shiba* (Japanese)

Penstemon hartwegii
penstemon • beard-tongue

Penstemon 'Garnet Dark Red'

Penstemon purple

DESCRIPTION Perennial herbs or shrubs producing tubular flowers arranged in clusters. The colourful flowers are two-lipped, with the lower lip often decorated with yellow hairs, hence the common name beard-tongue. Two other species important in horticulture are the true beard-tongue (*P. barbatus*) and the large beard-tongue (*P. grandiflorus*). Several species are cultivated and many hybrids and cultivars have been developed. 'Scarlet Queen' (bright scarlet) is a cultivar derived from *P. hartwegii*. Examples of tall *P. barbatus* cultivars include 'Albus' (white), 'Carneus' (pale pink) and 'Coccineus' (bright red or orange-scarlet).

ORIGIN & HISTORY *Penstemon hartwegii* is a Mexican species. Most species (including *P. barbatus* and *P. grandiflorus*) are indigenous to the western parts of the United States.

PARTS USED The flowering stems are used as cut flowers or as fillers in mixed bouquets.

CULTIVATION A summer flower that is grown mainly from seed sown directly (often outdoors in open fields). Plants are sensitive to water-logging and require well-drained soils. Temperatures need to be moderate to warm (12–15°C; 54–59°F) and not too hot.

PROPERTIES Vase life is fairly average (6–8 days). Flowers are sensitive to ethylene.

QUALITY CRITERIA Flowering stems should be long, straight and sturdy, with good length flowering spikes. Select stems with only 2–3 flowers opening (and closed buds showing colour) or with 30% of the flower spike open. Leaves must be a uniform green colour, free of any brown marks, brown tips or other blemishes.

CARE & HANDLING Recut stems and place in a floral preservative. Remove leaves below the water line. Allow flowers to hydrate at room temperature for 2–3 hours before using or storing (a hydrating solution can be used). Flowers can be stored for 4–5 days at 2°C (36°F) and 95% relative humidity.

Penstemon hartwegii Benth. family: Plantaginaceae (Scrophulariaceae)

penstemon (Dutch, Italian, Spanish); *galane, penstemon* (French); *Bartfaden* (German)

Pericallis hybrida
cineraria • florist cineraria

Pericallis ×hybrida mixed colours

DESCRIPTION A perennial herb (grown as an annual) up to 1 m (40") high with large, rounded, soft, often pale green leaves. Large and brightly coloured flower heads of about 50 mm (2") in diameter are borne in flat-topped clusters. The ray florets are almost any colour and are often bicoloured, giving an attractive halo effect. Several seed races of dwarf types have become popular for use as potted flowers. Names include Amigo Hybrids, Dwarf British Beauty Mixed, Elite Hybrids, Erfurt Dwarf Mixture, Jubilee Dwarf Mixture, Moll Improved Hybrids, Multiflora Nana Goldcentre, Saucer Series, Starlet Mixture, Superb Series and Tosca Hybrids.

ORIGIN & HISTORY *Pericallis ×hybrida* originated in Britain as a hybrid between *P. cruenta*, *P. lanata* and possibly other species (all indigenous to the Canary Isles). It has become one of the most important potted flowers in the world.

PARTS USED The whole flowering plant is used as a potted flower.

CULTIVATION Plants grow best in partial shade and require bright but cool conditions. Fairly rich, well-drained and slightly acidic soil is an important requirement. Proper irrigation is critical – soils must remain slightly moist at all times but not be over-watered.

PROPERTIES Plants remain in flower for 1–2 months, depending on handling and cultivar. They are sensitive to ethylene.

QUALITY CRITERIA Select well-branched, compact plants with a good volume of buds and 5–10 open flower heads. Avoid plants with deformed or mottled leaves or burnt leaf tips. Wilting can be due to damaged root systems and not necessary lack of water.

CARE & HANDLING Water well on arrival, but keep leaves dry. Display pots in a bright, but cool area (13–16°C; 55–61°F) with good ventilation (away from draughts or direct sunlight). Keep the soil moist and continually remove dead leaves and flowers.

Pericallis ×hybrida R. Nordenstam (=*Senecio ×hybridus*)   family: Asteraceae

kruiskruid (Dutch); *cinéraire* (French); *Aschenblume, Cinerarie* (German); *cineraria* (Italian); *cineraria híbrida* (Spanish)

Phalaenopsis cultivars

moth orchid • dove orchid

Phalaenopsis 'Lennestadt'

Phalaenopsis 'Gold'

DESCRIPTION Epiphytic orchids with a few dark green leaves and clusters of spectacular flowers with broad segments and a relatively small lip. Many cultivars are available to florists with a wide range of colours, bicolours and buds per stem.

ORIGIN & HISTORY Asia to northern Australia. It is the most widely cultivated and commercially important orchid. Orchids are protected under the convention for international trade of endangered species (CITES) and special permits are required when importing plant material.

PARTS USED Whole plants are used as potted flowers. Flowering stems or individual flowers are used as cut flowers.

CULTIVATION Propagation is by means of tissue culture, seeds or division. The long production time, high heat and humidity requirements result in most production being done in countries with low labour costs and suitable climates. Plants require a day-night temperature differential of 8–11°C (15–20°F) in order to flower.

PROPERTIES Potted flowers can last 10–14 weeks. They are extremely sensitive to ethylene. Cut flowers last significantly shorter (5–7 days). Over-watering can cause damage to the soft, fleshy storage roots.

QUALITY CRITERIA Look for well-formed flowers with no bruising or brown edges. Select potted flowers with dark green leaves and sturdy spikes with plenty of blooms. Do not worry if the plant is pot bound.

CARE & HANDLING Cut flowers: Temperature sensitive, so store at 10–13°C (50–55°F). Store the individual flowers in a water tube with sufficient preservative solution. Water on the petals may leave marks. Ensure that blooms do not rub against each other. Potted flowers: Display in medium light, away from fruit and draughts, especially cold air. Weekly feeding is recommended. Keep moist and mist regularly. Botrytis can occur on flowers in high humidity and poor ventilation.

Phalaenopsis cultivars

family: Orchidaceae

vlinderorchidee (Dutch); *orchidée-papillon* (French); *Malayenblume, Schmetterlingsorchidee* (German); *phalaenopsis* (Italian); *orquídea alevilla* (Spanish)

Philodendron pinnatifidum

philodendron • spit-leaf philodendron

Philodendron pinnatifidum 'Xanadu'

Philodendron pinnatifidum plant

Philodendron pinnatifidum 'Xantal'

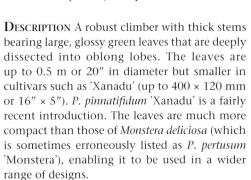

DESCRIPTION A robust climber with thick stems bearing large, glossy green leaves that are deeply dissected into oblong lobes. The leaves are up to 0.5 m or 20" in diameter but smaller in cultivars such as 'Xanadu' (up to 400 × 120 mm or 16" × 5"). *P. pinnatifidum* 'Xanadu' is a fairly recent introduction. The leaves are much more compact than those of *Monstera deliciosa* (which is sometimes erroneously listed as *P. pertusum* 'Monstera'), enabling it to be used in a wider range of designs.

ORIGIN & HISTORY Central and South America (Brazil to Venezuela and Trinidad). The "Split-leaf" philodendron has been a popular houseplant since the early 1960s, but has only fairly recently made its way into the floral trade as a large cut green. *P. pinnatifidum* 'Xanadu' is available year round and sold in 10-stem bunches. It is often listed by the old name (*P. selloum*) or misspelled as "Zanadu".

PARTS USED Leaves are used as cut greens.

CULTIVATION Plants require a well-drained, acidic soil (pH 6.0). They are sensitive to frost and require a minimum growing temperature of around 16°C (61°F). Much higher temperatures between (18–29°C; 64–84°F) are preferred. Growers routinely spray with a calcium/magnesium foliar feed to ensure good quality plants and leaves (to prevent yellowing). Commercial production is usually outdoors under shade cloth.

PROPERTIES Vase life of 'Xanadu' is average to good (7–14 days). They are fairly sensitive to ethylene, which will cause the leaf to yellow.

QUALITY CRITERIA Select leaves with a deep green, uniform colour. Make sure leaves are free of marks, disease and general handling damage. With larger leaves make sure that the stems are sturdy enough to support the leaf.

CARE & HANDLING Recut stems and place in a bactericide. Display in a cool, shaded area. Leaves do not dry well.

Philodendron pinnatifidum (Jacq.) Schott (=*P. selloum*)   family: Araceae

philodendron (Dutch, French, Italian, Spanish); *Philodendron* (German)

Phlox paniculata

phlox • perennial phlox • summer phlox

Phlox paniculata 'White Missy'

Phlox paniculata 'Bright Missy'

Phlox paniculata '21st Century Blue Star'

DESCRIPTION An erect perennial of up to 1 m (40") high with crowded, slightly hairy lance-shaped leaves and topped with a large cluster of variously coloured flowers. Each flower is about 25 mm (1") in diameter. The natural flowering time is summer. Many of the popular cultivars have flowers that are bicoloured, having darker centres ("eyes"). For example, pastel pink petals with deep rose-pink centres, or lilac petals with white "eyes". However, single-toned, large-flowered cultivars are also in demand.

ORIGIN & HISTORY North America. Phlox has long been popular as a cut flower due to its vigorous growth, large inflorescences and wide variety of colours. The flowers are useful as fillers in arrangements.

PARTS USED Leafy flowering stems are used as cut flowers and whole plants as potted flowers.

CULTIVATION Growers first cool young plants and then provide a period of long days (by using artificial lighting) to ensure longer stems

and higher yields. In outdoor production, the plants are usually harvested over a period of two years. Good air movement is important, as phlox is susceptible to fungal diseases – especially powdery mildew.

PROPERTIES Vase life of cut flowers is poor (3–5 days). Flowers are fragrant and sensitive to ethylene. *P. paniculata* hybrids are very susceptible to powdery mildew. *P.* ×*arendsii* (Arend's phlox), a hybrid between *P. paniculata* and *P. divaricata*, is less sensitive to powdery mildew.

QUALITY CRITERIA Select stems with 50% open flowers. Do not purchase if too few flowers are open. Stems should be sturdy, straight and have a good volume of flowers. Check that flowers and leaves are free of marks and damage.

CARE & HANDLING Recut stems and place in a preservative with a bactericide and an anti-ethylene agent. Store (only if absolutely necessary) for 1–2 days in a preservative solution at 3°C (37°F). Flowers do not dry well.

Phlox paniculata L.

family: Polemoniaceae

vlambloem (Dutch); *fléole* (French); *Stauden-Phlox, Flammenblume* (German); *flox* (Italian, Spanish)

Phoenix roebelinii

miniature date palm • pygmy date palm

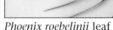

Phoenix roebelinii leaf

Phoenix roebelinii fruits

Phoenix roebelinii plant

DESCRIPTION A small palm of up to 2 m (6½') high, with the stem slender at the base but becoming thicker towards the crown of pinnate leaves. Each leaf is about 1.2 m (4') long and has about 50 regularly spaced and somewhat drooping grey-green leaflets (250 × 10 mm; 10" × ½") on each side of the midrib. The ellipsoid fruits are about 10 mm (½") long and black in colour. The cultivated form closely agrees with the original wild form and there appear to be no well-known cultivars.

ORIGIN & HISTORY Native to Laos. The miniature date palm has long been used as an elegant pot plant and has also become popular in recent years as a source of foliage for the florist industry. It is related to the well-known date palm (*Phoenix dactylifera*).

PARTS USED The leaves are used as cut foliage or the fruits as decorative fillers.

CULTIVATION Propagation is usually by means of seed, although growers would normally purchase young, rooted plants. Pygmy date palms prefer full sun to partial shade conditions and well-drained soils. To obtain top-quality fronds, humidity levels must not be too low or temperatures too extreme. Most commercial cultivation is, however, for the garden and container industries.

PROPERTIES Vase life is good to very good (14–21 days). Leaves are not sensitive to ethylene and have no strong fragrance.

QUALITY CRITERIA Select fully mature leaves that are well formed and fairly flat. Make sure that the colour is a uniform dark green. Leaves must have no brown or dry margins or tips or any other blemishes.

CARE & HANDLING Recut stems and place in clean water with a bactericide. There is no need to use a floral preservative. Check that the leaflets are not touching the water. Loosen bunches to improve ventilation. Cut leaves can be stored for 1–2 weeks at 1–2°C (34–36°F) and a high relative humidity 95%. Leaves do not dry well.

Phoenix roebelinii O'Brien   family: Arecaceae (Palmae)

dwergdadelpalm (Dutch); *palmier dattier miniature, phoenix roebelen* (French); *Zwerg-Dattelpalme* (German); *palmera enana* (Italian); *palmera de Roebelen* (Spanish)

Phormium tenax

New Zealand flax • New Zealand hemp

Phormium tenax plant

Phormium tenax variegated leaves

DESCRIPTION A large, robust tuft with long and broad, grass-like leaves up to 4 m (more than 12') high. The leaves are two-ranked to form large "fans". The original wild form has dull yellowish green leaves but modern forms are variously coloured. The tall flowering stalks bear tubular, dull red flowers. A large number of dwarf forms have been developed as named cultivars for garden use. For the florist industry, the original large-leaved green flax, the old-fashioned variegated forms and the purple-leaved forms are the most useful and popular.

ORIGIN & HISTORY New Zealand. The plant is a traditional source of bush flax, a fibre used by the Maoris for textiles and to make ropes and nets. It has become a popular garden plant and the leaves also have a long history of use in flower arrangements.

PARTS USED The leaves are used as cut greens.

CULTIVATION Plants can be grown in most soil types as long as they are fairly well drained.

Cultivation usually takes place in open fields or under low percentage shade cloth. Plants require a moist soil and are hardy and able to be grown in most regions, except very cold areas.

PROPERTIES Vase life is very good (21–28 days). Leaves have no distinctive scent and are also not sensitive to ethylene. Their relatively large size makes them ideally suited for large arrangements.

QUALITY CRITERIA Leaves are often available in various lengths and sizes, so select as desired. Leaf colour, whether solid or variegated, needs to be bright and even. Make sure leaves are healthy, with no dry or discoloured tips or other blemishes.

CARE & HANDLING Loosen bunches to improve ventilation. Leaves can be displayed dry and do not need to be recut or placed in a preservative. They can be stored dry in a cold-room at 1–6°C (34–43°F), depending on the needs of other stored flowers or foliage.

Phormium tenax J.R. Forst. & G. Forst.   family: Hemerocallidaceae (Phormiaceae)

nieuw-zeelands vlas (Dutch); *lin de Nouvelle-Zélande* (French); *Neuseelandflachs* (German); *canapa della nuova zelanda* (Italian); *nyuusairan forumiumu* (Japanese); *formio, lino de nueva zelanda* (Spanish)

Phylica ericoides

white phylica • Cape myrtle

Phylica ericoides plant

Phylica lasiocarpa

Phylica plumosa

DESCRIPTION A shrub of up to 1 m (40″) high with hairy stems and small leaves of 6–12 mm (¼–½″) long. Each leaf is typically heart-shaped, dark glossy green above and densely white-woolly beneath, with rolled in margins. The small white flowers are borne in heads, surrounded by a halo of dense wool. Another popular florist flower is the featherhead (*P. plumosa*, previously known as *P. pubescens*). This is an erect shrub with slender, tapering leaves of about 25 mm (1″) long. The small flower spikes are surrounded by a large number of golden yellow to pale brown, hairy and feathery bracts. *Phylica lasiocarpa* is sometimes used as a filler.

ORIGIN & HISTORY South Africa. *Phylica* species have long been wild-harvested in the Cape mountains but they have become popular as florist flowers and are now also cultivated.

PARTS USED Flowering branches are used as fillers.

CULTIVATION *Phylica* requires a well-drained, sandy soil that is acidic. Plants are sensitive to pH imbalances as well as incorrect feeding. Sunny, well-ventilated growing conditions are also necessary. A fair amount of foliage is wild-harvested.

PROPERTIES Vase life is average to fairly good (7–10 days). Flowers are not sensitive to ethylene. Many of the types do not have a scent.

QUALITY CRITERIA Select cut stems or bunches with 50% of the florets open. Look for young stems that are well branched and full. Flowers must show no signs of browning or ageing. Leaves must have good colour and not be pale or have brown or dry tips.

CARE & HANDLING Recut stems and hydrate in a floral preservative or hydrating solution at room temperature for 2–3 hours before using or storing. Cut stems can be stored for 5–7 days at 1–2°C (34–36°F) and 90–95% relative humidity. Flowers are excellent for drying. Hang upside down in a dark, well-ventilated area.

Phylica ericoides L.   family: Rhamnaceae

phylica (Dutch, Italian, Spanish); *myrte du Cap* (French); *Kapmyrte* (German)

Physalis alkekengi

Chinese lantern

Physalis alkekengi plant

Physalis alkekengi fruits

DESCRIPTION A perennial herb of up to 0.6 m (2′) high with heart-shaped, glandular leaves. The flowers are inconspicuous and pendulous but they develop into brightly coloured "lanterns" (formed by the persistent and much enlarged calyx that completely hides the round, fleshy fruit). There are two varieties: var. *alkekengi* (the wild form) and var. *franchetii* (the ornamental, cultivated form). Cultivars and variation within them are limited, but some have variegated leaves and others (such as 'Gigantea' or 'Monstruosa') produce much larger fruits than the original species.

ORIGIN & HISTORY Central and southern Europe, as well as Korea, Japan and northern China. There are many species but only *P. alkekengi* is used to any extent in the floral industry.

PARTS USED Stems with fruits are used as fresh or dried fillers.

CULTIVATION Plants require good watering but at the same time well-drained soils. Flowering is not initiated by day length, but simply by the plant maturing. Warm, sunny conditions result in faster growth and flowering. However, continued high temperatures of above 27°C (80°F) will reduce yields and quality, resulting in small fruit that lack good colour.

PROPERTIES Vase life of fresh lanterns is good to very good (10–18 days). Dried lanterns last for years.

QUALITY CRITERIA Select sturdy stems with well spaced and numerous lanterns. Make sure lanterns are large and have a bright colour. Check that the fruits are free of marks, disease or general damage.

CARE & HANDLING Recut the stems and remove leaves below the water line. Place in clean water. There is no need to use a preservative. Stems can be stored for a number of days at 3–5°C (37–41°F). Fruits are excellent for drying. Simply remove leaves and hang the stems to air-dry, or alternatively, place them in a container that is then properly closed and kept in a horizontal position. Be aware that rodents are particularly fond of eating *Physalis*.

Physalis alkekengi L. (=*P. franchetii*)   family: Solanaceae

blaaskersen, lampionplant (Dutch); *armour en cage* (French); *Lampionpflanze, Lanternen-Judenkirsche* (German); *alcachengi* (Italian); *alquequenje, capulí* (Spanish)

Physostegia virginiana

obedient flower • obedient plant • false dragon head

Physostegia virginiana plant

Physostegia virginiana flowers

DESCRIPTION An erect perennial herb (up to 1.8 m or 6′) with leafy stems. The flowers are tightly or loosely spaced and are reddish-violet, pink or white, often conspicuously spotted or streaked. Numerous cultivars with different stems lengths are available as bedding plants or cut flowers.

ORIGIN & HISTORY North America. The common name comes from the notion that the flower will retain the shape that it is bent into – which would be great for florists – but this seldom appears to be the case!

PARTS USED Flowering stems are used as cut flowers.

CULTIVATION A photoperiod of 12–16 hours is required to initiate flowering (long-day plant). Cold periods are not necessary to break dormancy but result in uniform flowering. Furthermore, cold treatment of a number of weeks at around 4°C (39°F) can initiate flowering regardless of day length. Plants are cultivated in open fields as well as in greenhouses and remain productive for 3–5 years. However, after 3 years yields tend to decline and plants need to be lifted, separated and replanted.

PROPERTIES Vase life is slightly poor to average (5–7 days). Pink flowers have a better vase life than white flowers. As flowers age, the petals turn brown (more visible and unsightly in white flowers).

QUALITY CRITERIA Purchase stems with 0–5 flowers open. Make sure none of the basal flowers have started to deteriorate, especially if purchasing stems with more than 5 open flowers. Select straight, sturdy stems with well-formed flower spikes. Make sure cut stems are free of disease and damage as production is often in open fields.

CARE & HANDLING Recut stems and place in a preservative, the use of which significantly improves vase life. Flowers can be stored for up to a week in a cold-room at a temperature of 4°C (39°F). However, make sure they are treated before and after storage. Flowers do not dry well.

Physostegia virginiana (L.) Benth.

family: Lamiaceae

scharnierbloem (Dutch); *cataleptique* (French); *Gelenkblume* (German); *fisostegia* (Italian); *planta de bisagra* (Spanish)

Pinus strobus

white pine • Weymouth pine • eastern white pine

Pinus strobus

Pinus sylvestris

DESCRIPTION A large tree of up to 40 m (150′) with a broad crown and brown, fissured bark. The needles are borne in fascicles of five. They are blue-green and about 75–125 mm (3–5″) long. The pinkish brown cones are narrowly cylindrical, pendulous and borne in groups. There are numerous dwarf cultivars for garden use. Some cultivars ('Pendula' and 'Inversa') have weeping branches. Others have colourful blue or golden foliage ideal for florists, such as 'Hillside Winter Gold' (golden needles) and 'Alba' (white new growth). The Scotch pine (*P. sylvestris*) is used in Europe.

ORIGIN & HISTORY North America (Canada and the eastern parts of the United States). This pine with its highly decorative foliage and cones has become a popular garden plant. The branches are used as Christmas greens.

PARTS USED Leafy branches are used as cut foliage and the cones as ornaments.

CULTIVATION Many species are fast growing. Most require light, well-drained soils and prefer to be cultivated in open sites and not in shady positions. Propagation is by means of seed or cuttings, although most growers simply find it easier to purchase young, well-rooted saplings. Foliage and cones are also wild-harvested.

PROPERTIES Vase life is very good (21–28 days). The foliage is sensitive to ethylene. Resin from handling can leave hands sticky and dirty, but seldom causes allergic reactions.

QUALITY CRITERIA Select stems with leaves in full colour. Dropping of needles (leaves) is an indication of dry stems or incorrect care and handling. Preferably select young, well-branched stems and make sure leaf-tips have not browned or dried out.

CARE & HANDLING Recut the stems and place them in a floral preservative. Remove all the needles below the water line. Loosen bunches to improve ventilation. Foliage can be stored at 0–2°C (32–36°F) and 95% relative humidity for 1–2 weeks. Stems should be stored separately from other foliage or cut flowers to avoid ethylene damage.

Pinus strobus L.   family: Pinaceae

weymouthden (Dutch); *pin weymouth* (French); *Strobe, Weymouths-Kiefer* (German); *pino strobo* (Italian); *pino blanco, pino de weymouth* (Spanish)

Pittosporum tobira

Japanese mock orange • Japanese pittosporum • tobira

Pittosporum tobira (variegated)

DESCRIPTION A shrub or small tree of up to 5 m (more than 15') high, with leathery, glossy dark green leaves. The creamy white or lemon yellow flowers have an orange-blossom scent. Most cultivars are dwarf forms developed for garden use. Cultivars with dark green leaves or variegated leaves (narrow white or cream leaf margin) are available as florist greens. Variegated leaves can be small as in 'Silver Queen' or large, broad and rosette-forming, as in 'Tobira'. *Pittosporum tenuifolium* is also used commercially.

ORIGIN & HISTORY China, southern Korea and Japan. The name *Pittosporum* is derived from the Greek word "pitt" and means "pitch seed". Several species are used as garden ornamentals in most parts of the world.

PARTS USED Stems with leaves are used as cut foliage. Occasionally stems with seed heads are used as fillers.

CULTIVATION Plants are usually propagated by means of cuttings, although seed or division is also possible. A well-drained, loose and fairly rich soil with regular feeding results in good quality foliage. Plants need to be well watered and require warm temperatures for strong, active growth. Most species and cultivars are not suitable for outdoor production in cold climates.

PROPERTIES Vase life is average to good (7–14 days). Leaves are not sensitive to ethylene and do not have any distinctive fragrance.

QUALITY CRITERIA Select full, leafy stems that are well branched and not too woody or large. Make sure leaves have a bright green colour, are open and flat and free of brown or white marks, and any other damage.

CARE & HANDLING Recut the stems and place them in a floral preservative. Remove any leaves below the water line. Allow stems to hydrate for 2–3 hours at room temperature before using or storing. Stems can be stored at 1–2°C (34–36°F) and a high relative humidity (95%) for 7–10 days.

Pittosporum tobira (Thunb. ex Murray) W.T. Aiton   family: Pittosporaceae

pittosporum (Dutch, French); *Chinesischer Klebsame, Pechsame* (German); *pittosporo* (Italian); *pitosporo del japón* (Spanish)

Platycodon grandiflorus
balloon flower • Chinese bellflower

Platycodon grandiflorus plant

Platycodon grandiflorus flowers

DESCRIPTION An attractive perennial with rigid, upright stems bearing alternate, ovate to ovate-lanceolate leaves of about 25–75 mm (1–3″) long. The leaves have a blue-green colour and neatly toothed margins. The flower buds swell up like balloons. Once open, the 5-petalled, saucer-shaped flowers look similar to those of *Campanula* (bellflower) species. Flowering occurs naturally in late spring. Cultivars have single or double flowers and vary in stem length, flower colour and profusion of flowering. The clean, vivid colours range from white, pink, lavender and purple to blue. The flowers of some cultivars do not open.

ORIGIN & HISTORY China, eastern parts of Siberia, Japan and northern Korea. It is a popular garden plant that is used in Chinese traditional medicine.

PARTS USED The flowering stems are used as cut flowers, while the whole plants of dwarf cultivars (these have been developed since the 1990s) have become very popular as potted flowers.

CULTIVATION Plants need moist, well-drained soils and will not survive in waterlogged soils. They can be grown in full sun or under low percentage shade, but prefer moderate production temperatures and slightly acidic soils. Growers often use supplementary lighting to increase the number of shoots and flowers but if the process is not well managed, the extra light can cause plants in pots to stretch too much.

PROPERTIES Vase life is poor to average (4–6 days). The leaves have a tendency to turn yellow.

QUALITY CRITERIA Select straight, sturdy cut stems with 2–4 open flowers. Make sure the leaves show no yellowing. Look for pots with well-branched, compact plants with a good volume of buds.

CARE & HANDLING Recut the stems and place them in a preservative. Storage is not recommended. Display potted flowers in a coolish, well-lit area, but not in direct sunlight. Do not over-water, but allow the potting medium to dry out slightly between waterings.

Platycodon grandiflorus (Jacq.) A. DC.   family: Campanulaceae

ballonbloem (Dutch); *platycodon à grandes fleurs* (French); *großblütige Ballonblume* (German); *campanula grandiflora* (Italian); *campanula, campaneta* (Spanish)

Podocarpus macrophyllus

yew pine • big leaf yew pine • kusamaki

Podocarpus macrophyllus foliage

DESCRIPTION An evergreen woody plant, ranging from shrubs of 2 m (about 6′) high to tall trees of up to 15 m (more than 45′). The leaves have a distinct midrib and are about 150 × 12 mm (6 × ½″), dark glossy green above and tinted yellowish below. The female cones are represented by bright red, fleshy receptacles. There are several named cultivars, differing in the size, shape and colour (variegation) of the leaves. Examples are 'Angustifolia' (narrow leaves) and 'Argenteus' (green with a narrow white border). *Podocarpus gracilior* (now known as *Afrocarpus gracilior*) and *P. nagi* (now known as Nageia nagi) are another two species that are often used as cut foliage in the floral industry.

ORIGIN & HISTORY Southern China and Japan. Some forms are very popular as hedge plants in Japan.

PARTS USED Leafy branches are used as cut foliage.

CULTIVATION Propagation is by means of seed or cuttings. Plants prefer to be grown in open, sunny positions with fairly rich, well-drained soils. Young trees are susceptible to heavy frost and cold winters and outdoor production is thus not suited to cold regions. Commercial cultivation is seldom solely for the cut foliage industry.

PROPERTIES Vase life is sometimes average but mostly very good (7–21 days). Foliage is not sensitive to ethylene and does not have a distinctive aroma.

QUALITY CRITERIA Look for young, well-branched, bushy stems that are not too large or woody. Check to ensure that leaves are not damaged, yellowing or browning. They must have a uniform, dark green colour.

CARE & HANDLING Recut stems and place in clean water with a bactericide. There is no need to use a full floral preservative. Remove leaves below the water line. Place in a cool, well-ventilated area. Stems can be stored for 7–10 days at 2–4°C (36–39°F) and a high relative humidity 90–95%.

Podocarpus macrophyllus (Thunb.) D. Don   family: Podocarpaceae

grootbladige podocarpus (Dutch); *podocarpus* (French); *Buddhisten-Steineibe, Großblättrige Steineibe* (German); *podocarpo* (Italian); *kusamaki* (Japanese); *podocarpo, tejo chino* (Spanish)

Polianthes tuberosa

tuberose

Polianthes tuberosa plant

Polianthes tuberosa flowers

DESCRIPTION A perennial herb with thinly succulent, tough leaves that form a basal rosette. The waxy white flowers are borne in a spike of up to 1 m (40") high. Various cultivars and double forms are grown, including 'Pearl'. The bright orange twinflower (*P. geminiflora*) appears to have potential as a florist flower.

ORIGIN & HISTORY Mexico. Tuberose is a cultigen (not found in the wild) of pre-Columbian Mexico (called "omixochitl", added as flavouring to chocolate). It has been grown in Europe for more than 200 years – the flower oil is used in the perfume industry.

PARTS USED Flowering stems are used as cut flowers.

CULTIVATION Tubers are planted in greenhouses or open fields (after the danger of frost has passed). They can be left in the soil for at least 3 years (but stem length declines every year) so they need to be lifted, divided and treated. Warm temperatures of around 20–24°C (68–75°F) are ideal. Thrips can be a major problem but there are few other pests and diseases. Too wet conditions during flowering may result in speckled flowers with brown spots.

PROPERTIES Vase life is average to good (7–10 days). Single-flowered cultivars last better than double-flowered ones. Some people find the strong gardenia scent too overpowering. Only high levels of ethylene are detrimental.

QUALITY CRITERIA Select straight, healthy stems with only 2–3 basal flowers open and the rest of the buds showing colour. If absolutely necessary, stems with as many as 50–75% of flowers open can be purchased, but make sure the basal flowers have not started to fade and are free of marks and damage.

CARE & HANDLING Recut and place in a sugar-containing preservative, but do not use an anti-ethylene agent. Prolonged refrigeration may reduce fragrance. Optimum storage temperature is 0–5°C (32–41°F), although storage is not recommended. Flowers do not dry well.

Polianthes tuberosa L.   family: Asparagaceae (Agavaceae)

tuberoos (Dutch); *tubéreuse* (French); *Nachthyazinthe, Tuberose* (German); *tuberosa* (Italian, Spanish)

Portulaca grandiflora

moss rose • common portulaca

Portulaca grandiflora mixed

Portulaca grandiflora white

DESCRIPTION An annual succulent herb of up to 0.3 m (1') high and wide. The fleshy, cylindrical leaves are about 25 mm (1") long and the large, single or double flowers are available in red, pink, violet, orange, yellow or white (often striped). Flowers open in sunlight and close under rainy or dark conditions, but breeders are trying to develop new cultivars that stay open longer. The numerous hybrids and seed races include Calypso, Cloudbeater, Extra Double, Magic Carpet, Sundance, Sunny Boy and Wildfire Hybrids.

ORIGIN & HISTORY Brazil, Uruguay and Argentina. Portulaca has been used in the landscaping business and as a hanging basket plant for many years, but has gradually lost some of its popularity. Renewed breeding efforts in the 1990s and especially the 'Yubi' range (with their large flowers and bright colours) have rejuvenated this species.

PARTS USED Whole plants are used as potted flowers and for hanging baskets.

CULTIVATION Portulaca prefers warm, dry conditions and a high light intensity. Plants are propagated from cuttings or seed and need to be grown in a well-drained medium that is slightly acidic (pH 5.5–6.2). Short days delay flowering in some cultivars, causing them to form rosettes. Once plants have formed rosettes then flowering is significantly delayed.

PROPERTIES Flowers close at night and under poor light and/or rainy conditions. They are not ethylene sensitive. Potted flowers are quite drought tolerant.

QUALITY CRITERIA Select well-branched, compact plants with a good volume of buds. Be careful not to buy plants that have excessive vegetative growth and very few flowers. Check that foliage colour is healthy and uniform and not yellowish or blotchy.

CARE & HANDLING Do not over-water the growth medium or allow it to remain wet for long periods. Display plants in a bright, warm area. Flower buds may not open if light levels are too low.

Portulaca grandiflora Hook.

family: Portulacaceae

portulakroosje (Dutch); *pourpier à grandes fleurs* (French); *Portulakröschen* (German); *porcellana grandiflora* (Italian); *portulaca, verdolaga de flor, flor de seda* (Spanish)

Primula vulgaris

primrose • polyanthus

Primula vulgaris blue

Primula vulgaris red

Primula malacoides

Primula obconica

DESCRIPTION Annuals or short-lived perennials with large basal leaves and attractive flowers borne in groups on slender stalks. *P. vulgaris* (the common primrose with yellow flowers) is unsuitable as a houseplant but modern hybrids are grown for indoor use and produce large, colourful blooms in many shades of yellow, pink, red and blue. The most popular type is the so-called polyanthus (sometimes referred to as *Pruhonicensis* Hybrids) – there are countless hybrids and named cultivars. Other commonly cultivated species include *P. malacoides*, with dainty flowers arranged in 2–6 tiers along the flower stalk and *P. obconica*, with large rounded flowering heads and hairy leaves.

ORIGIN & HISTORY Europe. The name primrose literally means "first rose". In the language of flowers, primroses signify "early youth".

PARTS USED Whole plants are very popular as potted flowers.

CULTIVATION Plants are propagated from seed, which takes a long time and requires cool temperatures. For these reasons, most growers purchase seedlings in plug form from suppliers. Good drainage is critical and pots need to dry out between irrigations. Erratic irrigation leads to plants developing dry, brown leaf edges.

PROPERTIES Potted plants flower for about 2 weeks. Flowers are fragrant and sensitive to ethylene. *P. obconica* may cause an allergic reaction and skin rashes in some people due to the presence of primine in the leaves.

QUALITY CRITERIA Select plants without yellowish (chlorotic) leaves or discoloured leaf margins. Avoid large, leafy plants with long, weak flower stems (due to over-feeding with nitrogen). Make sure the plants have a good volume of flowers with a uniform stage of opening.

CARE & HANDLING Display in a cool area (below 21°C; 70°F), with good light, but out of direct sunlight. Water daily. Do not display with fruit, as they are ethylene sensitive.

Primula vulgaris Huds. (=*P. acaulis*)　　　　　　　　　　　　family: Primulaceae

sleutelbloem (Dutch); *primevére acaule* (French); *Kissen-Primel, Stängellose Schlüsselblume* (German); *primavera* (Spanish)

Protea cynaroides

king protea • giant protea

Protea cynaroides

Protea cynaroides

DESCRIPTION A resprouting shrub of up to 2 m (about 6½') high with hairless, spoon-shaped leaves and large flower heads resembling globe artichokes (but with red or pink bracts). A number of cultivars and hybrids (with *P. repens* and *P. compacta*) are available in the florist trade.

ORIGIN & HISTORY South Africa (fynbos area of the Cape). The king protea is the national flower emblem of South Africa.

PARTS USED Flower heads are used as cut flowers (less often the whole plant as a potted flower).

CULTIVATION Plants are propagated from cuttings and take 1–2 years to establish, after which they are productive for many years. The most critical factor is the soil – it needs to be well drained, sandy and acidic. Even moderate levels of calcium and phosphorus can destroy the complex root systems. In their natural habitat, plants occur in soils with a pH as low as 3.5. They require full sun and good air-circulation. Protea bushes are generally not cut or pruned back to below the previous season's growth but king proteas are an exception and benefit from being cut back hard.

PROPERTIES Vase life is sometimes average but most often very good (7–16 days). Proteas are not tropical flowers and are therefore not chill sensitive. Leaves tend to turn brown or black often long before the flowers have declined. This is as a result of water stress and loss of carbohydrates. Stem length tends to be a bit short.

QUALITY CRITERIA Select straight, young stems with large, well-developed flower heads.

CARE & HANDLING Recut stems and hydrate in an acidified water (pH 3.5). Remove leaves below the water line and place in a preservative containing a bactericide and sugar (carbohydrate). Flowers can be stored for 7–10 days at 2–4°C (36–39°F) and at a relative humidity of 90%. Longer storage will reduce vase life. Flowers are excellent for drying.

Protea cynaroides (L.) L.   family: Proteaceae

koningsprotea (Dutch); *protée* (French); *Königs-Protee* (German); *protea cynaroides* (Italian, Spanish)

Protea neriifolia

bearded protea • oleander leaf protea

Protea neriifolia

Protea magnifica hybrid 'Susara'

DESCRIPTION An erect shrub of up to 3 m (10′) high, with narrowly oblong, leathery leaves and goblet-shaped flower heads. The bracts are yellow to pale pink or red and each has a conspicuous tuft of black hairs at the tip. Modern cultivars tend to be less prone to leaf blackening. A number of hybrids with other species (such as *P. magnifica*) are available as florist flowers.

ORIGIN & HISTORY South Africa (fynbos region of the Cape). It is one of the most common and popular species and is widely cultivated.

PARTS USED Flowering heads are used as cut flowers.

CULTIVATION Proteas have an intricate root system, so that the soil around the bushes should not be worked – disturbing the roots can kill the plants. Proteas require poor, leached soils and are highly sensitive to phosphates. Plants stay productive for many years. Correct pruning during and after harvesting is vital to future production. Growers do not usually cut or prune

below the previous season's growth because the plants rarely form new growth from old wood.

PROPERTIES Vase life is usually very good (7–16 days). Proteas are not chill sensitive. Leaves tend to blacken before the flower heads deteriorate as a result of water stress and loss of carbohydrates. *Protea neriifolia*, *P. repens* and *P. eximia* are especially prone to leaf blackening.

QUALITY CRITERIA Select long, straight stems with well-formed flower heads. Purchase heads with florets starting to open. Tightly closed buds will open satisfactory, but will have poorer colouring than flowers harvested at a more mature stage. Check that leaves are free of blackening, damage and disease.

CARE & HANDLING Recut the stems and place in an acidic solution (pH 3.5) to hydrate. Remove any leaves below the water line. Use a preservative with a bactericide and a sugar. If necessary, store for 7–10 days at 2–4°C (36–39°F) and a relative humidity of 90%. The flower heads are ideal for drying.

Protea neriifolia R. Br.   family: Proteaceae

blauwe suikerbos (Dutch); *protée* (French); *Oleander-Protee* (German); *protea neriifolia* (Italian, Spanish)

Protea repens
sugarbush

Protea repens red

Protea repens white

DESCRIPTION An erect shrub of up to 3 m (10′) high bearing narrowly linear, hairless and somewhat leathery leaves. The cone-shaped flower heads persist on the shrubs after flowering. A number of named hybrids and cultivars are available in shades of red, pink, cream and white.

ORIGIN & HISTORY South Africa (Cape fynbos region). The plant is exceptionally common and is still being wild-harvested to some extent, but these days improved cultivars are mostly grown for the florist industry.

PARTS USED Flowering stems, usually with only a few leaves attached, are used as cut flowers (fresh or dried).

CULTIVATION Commercial propagation is mainly by means of cuttings grown in full sun and well-drained, phosphate-poor soils. Like most *Protea* species, *P. repens* is sensitive to soil disturbance and to variations in soil pH. Once established, shrubs are hardy and require little attention. However, correct harvesting and pruning is important to maintain long stems and good yields.

PROPERTIES Vase life is usually very good (10–16 days). Some cultivars are prone to leaf-blackening. Flower heads are nectar-rich (not allergenic) and neither chill-sensitive nor ethylene-sensitive.

QUALITY CRITERIA Look for long, straight stems with well-formed flower heads. Buds must be closed, with outer bracts just starting to loosen and open. Leaves must be free of blackening or blemishes. Flower stalks should not be too woody.

CARE & HANDLING Recut stems and remove leaves that will be below the water line. Hydrate in an acidified solution (pH 3.5) at room temperature for 2–3 hours prior to use or storage. Place in a preservative containing a bactericide and a low sugar concentrate (it helps prevent leaf-blackening and assists in bud opening). Flower heads can be stored for 7–10 days at 2–4°C (36–39°F) and a relative humidity of 90%. They are excellent for drying.

Protea repens L.

family: Proteaceae

gewone suikerbos (Dutch); *protea repens* (French, Italian, Spanish); *Echte Zuckerbusch* (German)

Prunus glandulosa

Chinese bush cherry • dwarf flowering almond

Prunus glandulosa dark pink

Prunus glandulosa light pink

DESCRIPTION The plant is a deciduous shrub of up to 2 m (6½′) high with erect stems bearing finely toothed leaves which are hairy below. The flowers are solitary or borne in few-flowered clusters. They are at first reddish but fade to pink or white. The fruits are round, dark red and 10 mm (nearly ½″) in diameter. There are several cultivars, differing in leaf and flower colour. Examples include 'Alba' (single, white), 'Alba Plena' (double, large, white) and 'Sinensis' (also called 'Rosea Plena') – with large, double, bright pink flowers. There are many species of *Prunus* (especially flowering cherries, apricots, almonds, plums and peaches) that are occasionally used as florist flowers.

ORIGIN & HISTORY Central and northern China and Japan. It is a popular garden shrub.

PARTS USED Budding, leafless stems (or flowering stems) are used as fillers.

CULTIVATION Shrubs can be propagated from seed or cuttings. Growers normally obtain 1–2 year-old saplings from nurseries. Well-drained, loamy soils and full sun conditions are preferred. Proper watering and feeding are also essential. The plants can be productive for many years but require proper harvesting and pruning techniques.

PROPERTIES Vase life of open flowers (blossoms) is poor (3–5 days). Flowers are sensitive to ethylene. Budding stems harvested at the end of winter will flower in 3–4 weeks, while those harvested in early spring will flower in 1–2 weeks.

QUALITY CRITERIA Select young, long and straight stems. Budding stems should have many well-formed buds. Most of the blossoms on flowering stems should be 50% open with closed buds showing good colour.

CARE & HANDLING Recut stems and place in a floral preservative. Do not store stems in flower but use promptly. Budding stems can be stored for 3–5 days in a preservative at 5°C (41°F) and a high relative humidity (90–95%).

Prunus glandulosa Thunb. ex Murray   family: Rosaceae

chinese kers, witte amandel (Dutch); *amandier à fleurs du Japon* (French); *Drüsenkirsche* (German); *mandorlo ornamentale, pruno da fiore* (Italian)

Pteris tremula

trembling fern • shaking brake • Australian bracken

Pteris tremula

Pteris cretica

DESCRIPTION The plant is an erect fern with 3–4-pinnate fronds of up to 0.9 × 0.6 m (about 3 × 2'). The pinnules and ultimate segments of the fronds are oblong to linear and distinctly toothed. There are several cultivars of this species and its relatives, especially *P. cretica* (Cretan brake), *P. ensiformis* (sword brake) and *P. umbrosa* (jungle brake).

ORIGIN & HISTORY New Zealand, Australia and Fiji. *Pteris* species have been used in traditional medicine (as vermifuge) and some are old favourite cultivated ornamentals.

PARTS USED The fern fronds (leaves) are used as cut greens.

CULTIVATION Plants are usually cultivated under a high percentage shade cloth and are harvested for many years. Growers normally lift, separate and replant every few years. Compost-rich, well-draining loam soils are best for production. Ferns require good watering and benefit from their leaves being watered from time to time. Warm, fairly humid conditions result in good growth and plants slow down considerably during colder seasons.

PROPERTIES Vase life is average to good (7–14 days). Fronds have no fragrance and are not sensitive to ethylene. Stem length and frond size can vary considerably.

QUALITY CRITERIA Select mature leaves with sturdy stalks, but make sure that they have not yet formed spores under the leaves. Look for stiff fronds that have no browning or curling tips. Colour must be good and uniform.

CARE & HANDLING Foliage is most often sold in cartons. Store fronds in these moisture-retaining cartons. Cover loosely with the plastic bags containing the foliage to keep the fronds moist. Storing flat in the cartons will help to prevent leaf-curl. Alternatively, recut stems and place in water with a preservative or bactericide and hold at 4–5°C (39–41°F) and a high relative humidity (95%). Mist fronds regularly to prevent them from drying out.

Pteris tremula R. Br.   family: Pteridaceae

wortelloofvaren (Dutch); *Australischer Saumfarn* (German)

Ranunculus asiaticus

buttercups • garden ranunculus

Ranunculus asiaticus pink

Ranunculus asiaticus orange

Ranunculus asiaticus white

DESCRIPTION A deciduous perennial herb (0.3 m or 1′ high) with claw-like tubers, lobed basal leaves and flowers of 25–50 mm (1–2″) in diameter. True petals are absent but the sepals are brightly coloured and resemble petals. The anthers are typically black. Thousands of cultivars have been developed from *R. asiaticus*. Popular cut flower types include large-flowered Tecolote and Victoria hybrids. 'Color Carnival' has large double flowers in a wide range of colours. Bloomingdale hybrids are a seed race of dwarf plants suitable for potted flowers.

ORIGIN & HISTORY South-eastern Europe to south-western Asia. The species was once a prime florist flower. It was first developed in Turkey – by 1777 there were already 1 100 named cultivars.

PARTS USED Flowering stems are used as cut flowers and whole plants as potted flowers.

CULTIVATION Plants grow best in bright light. Soil temperatures should not exceed 15°C (60°F). Commercial growers purchase tubers from specialist suppliers and first soak them for 2–4 hours in water containing a fungicide. Flower yields are directly proportional to the size of the tuber. Most buttercups are grown in greenhouses or plastic-covered tunnels.

PROPERTIES Vase life of cut flowers is poor to average (5–7 days). Potted flowers last 1–2 weeks. The flowers have no scent and are fairly sensitive to ethylene. Stems are hollow, fairly brittle and easily damaged.

QUALITY CRITERIA Purchase cut stems with at least one flower half to fully open. Make sure flowers are free of marks and damage. Select pots with one or two flowers open (and no sign of mildew).

CARE & HANDLING Recut stems and place in water with a preservative that will assist flower opening (no need for an anti-ethylene agent). Store in a preservative at 1–2°C (34–36°F), but only if absolutely necessary. Display potted flowers in a cool (maximum 21°C / 70°F) and bright area.

Ranunculus asiaticus L.   family: Ranunculaceae

ranonkel (Dutch); *renoncule* (French); *Ranunkel* (German); *ranuncolo* (Italian); *ranúnculo* (Spanish)

Rhodanthe manglesii
paper daisy • Swan River everlasting

Rhodanthe manglesii 'Timeless Rose'

Rhodanthe manglesii 'Alba Pura'

DESCRIPTION The plant is an erect annual herb of up to 0.8 m (nearly 3') high. The broad, greyish green leaves are alternately arranged and have wide, heart-shaped bases that clasp the stems. The flower heads are solitary, up to 40 mm (about 1½") in diameter, with pale pink, papery bracts. Individual florets are pink, but the main attraction is the persistent, radiating bracts. The best-known cultivar is 'Maculatum', which has distinctive and decorative red spots on the bracts. Others include 'Alba Pura' (white flowers) and 'Roseum Maculatum' (pink with a dark eye). *Acroclinium roseum* (previously *Helipterum roseum*) is a similar plant known as pink and white everlasting or pink paper daisy.

ORIGIN & HISTORY Western Australia. There are several species but only *R. manglesii* has become well known as a garden plant and florist flower.

PARTS USED The flower heads are used as cut flowers or dried flowers, while the whole plant is sometimes used as a potted flower.

CULTIVATION Flowers are usually cultivated outdoors in summer and in greenhouses in the colder seasons. Propagation is mainly by means of seed that is sown direct. Plants are sensitive to frost and do best in a fairly rich, well-drained soil.

PROPERTIES Vase life is average to good (7–14 days). Flowers are not sensitive to ethylene.

QUALITY CRITERIA Select fresh cut stems with 50% of flower heads open. Make sure that the fresh (or dried) flower heads and leaves are brightly coloured and well shaped, with no noticeable blemishes or damage.

CARE & HANDLING Recut fresh stems, place in a floral preservative and allow to hydrate for 2–3 hours. Stems tangle easily so do not simply pull apart, but first hold upside down and shake gently to loosen. Fresh cut flowers can be stored for 7–10 days at 1–2°C (34–36°F) and 95% relative humidity. Flower heads are excellent for drying.

Rhodanthe manglesii Lindl. (=*Helipterum manglesii*)   family: Asteraceae

rhodante (Dutch); *immortelle, rhodanthe* (French); *Rosen-Immortelle* (German)

Rhododendron simsii
azalea • Indian azalea

Rhododendron simsii red

Rhododendron 'Desert Sun'

DESCRIPTION An evergreen shrub (up to 3 m or 9') with oblong leathery leaves and usually red, spotted, broadly funnel-shaped flowers of about 25–50 mm (1–2") in diameter. Rhododendrons are amongst the most hybridised of all flowering plants – at least 500 of the 850 species are cultivated. The numerous cultivars used in the florist trade are better known as azaleas and are grouped by their flowering times.

ORIGIN & HISTORY Myanmar, China and Taiwan. One of the premier potted flowers. Also popular is *R. ×obtusum* – semi-evergreen, with smaller leaves and funnel-shaped flowers.

PARTS USED Whole plants are used as potted flowers.

CULTIVATION Cuttings are taken from "mother stock". Flowering is initiated by short days and warm temperatures. Growers use growth-retarding chemicals to keep the plant shorter – it delays flowering slightly, but increases the number and uniformity of flower buds. Plants grow best at temperatures between 15–18°C (59–64°F).

PROPERTIES Flowers last 2–4 weeks. Lack of humidity or light, water stress and ethylene build-up can all cause leaf drop. Azaleas are sensitive to ethylene and botrytis.

QUALITY CRITERIA At least 25–30% of the flowers should be open and/or in the "candle" stage. Flowers that are too tightly closed may never open indoors or have a pale, washed out colour. Leaves and flowers should have no blemishes (botrytis may develop if plants with wet leaves or flowers are shipped). Look for well-formed plants, full of brightly coloured flowers that are fairly uniform in distribution, opening and bud stage.

CARE & HANDLING Unpack immediately and display in a cool, bright location, but avoid direct sunlight. Avoid draughts but ensure good ventilation (to prevent ethylene build-up). Water daily and do not allow potting medium to dry out. Temperature: minimum (10°C; 50°F); maximum (16°C; 61°F).

Rhododendron simsii Planch. (=*Azalea simsii*)   family: Ericaceae

azalea (Dutch); *azalée* (French); *Indica-Azalee* (German); *azalea* (Italian); *azalea* (Spanish)

Rhodohypoxis baurii
red star • spring starflower • rosy posy

Rhodohypoxis baurii

DESCRIPTION. The red star is a small geophyte of up to 100 mm (4") high with strap-shaped leaves which are folded, keeled and somewhat hairy. The flowers are solitary or in pairs and are usually combinations of white, pink or red (rarely yellow in some hybrids). In addition to several natural varieties and natural hybrids, many new hybrids and cultivars are being developed. Well-known examples include 'Stella' (pink with rose-pink eye and margins), 'Pixie' (white with pink rim) and 'Red Star' (red).

ORIGIN & HISTORY South Africa (Drakensberg mountains). *Rhodohypoxis* became popular amongst growers of alpine plants and is now a commercial florist flower, also known as spring starflower or rosy posy.

PARTS USED The whole plant is used as a potted flower.

CULTIVATION Propagation is by means of bulbs (corms). *Rhodohypoxis* are often cultivated for the garden industry. They prefer full sun and do best in organic-rich, well-drained soils that are slightly acidic. Growing conditions of moderate to warm temperatures and high light intensities are needed to produce high quality potted flowers. During the active growing season, plants require regular watering. The plants are dormant in winter.

PROPERTIES Potted plants can flower for many weeks. Flowers are sensitive to ethylene. Potted flowers are best treated as annuals.

QUALITY CRITERIA Select pots with well-formed, evenly balanced plants. Leaves should have a uniform green to silver-green colouration and be free of any yellowing. Make sure that leaf tips and edges are not brown or discoloured.

CARE & HANDLING Display pots in high light areas such as filtered or partial sun, but avoid full sun indoors. Water regularly and keep potting soil moist while in flower. However, do not allow plants to stand in water or become waterlogged. Avoid cold draughts and ethylene producing agents.

Rhodohypoxis baurii (Bak.) Nel   family: Hypoxidaceae

rhodohypoxis (Dutch, French, Italian, Spanish); *Rhodohypoxis* (German)

Rosa cultivars
hybrid tea rose

Rosa 'Royal Renate'

Rosa mixed

Rosa 'Grand Gala'

DESCRIPTION Perennial shrubs with thorny stems, compound leaves, single or double flowers and fleshy, edible fruits. Thousands of cultivars have been bred. Categories are: hybrid teas (more than 90 mm or 3½" in diameter); sweethearts (less than 90 mm or 3½") and spray roses. Hybrid teas are classified as large, intermediate and small, although categories are becoming vague.

ORIGIN & HISTORY Garden origin. Roses have a long and complicated history as source of rose petal oil and as garden ornamentals and cut flowers. There is little argument that the number one florist flower is the red rose.

PARTS USED Flowering stems are used as cut flowers.

CULTIVATION Most growers use grafted plants, resulting in higher yields, less soil-borne diseases and better quality flowers. Planting densities are important, along with good ventilation, good light and moderate temperatures.

PROPERTIES Vase life varies from 5–14 days,

depending on quality and cultivar. Bentneck (buds that fall over without opening) is caused by poor growing conditions, harvesting too early or water stress. Roses are sensitive to ethylene and bacteria.

QUALITY CRITERIA The picking stage is critical but varies among cultivars: too closed and buds do not open; too open and vase life is reduced. Select stems with the following general opening stages: red and pink cultivars – first 2 petals beginning to unfold; calyx reflexed below a horizontal position; yellow cultivars – slightly tighter; white cultivars – slightly more open. Buds should be more open in winter than in summer.

CARE & HANDLING Recut, remove lower leaves (but leave the thorns), hydrate in acidified solution and transfer to a preservative with bactericide. Use cold water (0°C; 32°F). Check daily that water is clean. Store for 7 days at 0–2°C (32–36°F) and a relative humidity of 80–90%. Most roses dry well.

Rosa cultivars   family: Rosaceae

roos (Dutch); *rosier* (French); *Rose* (German); *rosa* (Italian); *ruusu* (Japanese); *rosa* (Spanish)

Rosa cultivars

spray rose • cluster rose

Spray rose 'Viviane'

Spray rose 'Pink Flash'

DESCRIPTION Spray roses are similar to hybrid tea roses but have multiple flowers per stem. Many cultivars are being developed (but still not as many as with tea hybrids). Cultivars include 'Macarena' (yellow), 'Diadeem' (pink), 'Viviane!' (white) and 'Tamango' (red), to name just a few. As with other rose types, new cultivars tend to come into fashion, while others go out.

ORIGIN & HISTORY Garden origin. The influence of supermarkets (chain stores) and their increasing share in the bouquet market has in recent times created awareness, possibilities and a large demand for spray roses.

PARTS USED Flowering stems as cut flowers or fillers, especially for use in bouquets.

CULTIVATION Roses require growing conditions of high, uniform light and moderate temperatures. Good ventilation between plants is important to prevent disease. Too low night temperatures or low light levels can cause plants to drop their leaves. Plants are also sensitive to high salt concentrations and low nitrogen levels in the growing medium/soil.

PROPERTIES Vase life varies from 10 to 21 days, depending on quality and cultivar. Some cultivars are scented, but not all. Spray roses are sensitive to ethylene.

QUALITY CRITERIA Select compact, well-branched stems with a full and even spray of blooms. Leaves should have a healthy sheen and colour and be free of spots, chemical residue and damage. Select stems with blooms all at the same stage of opening and all having the same length, so that when used in bouquets blooms all show uniformly in the top.

CARE & HANDLING Recut, remove lower leaves, hydrate in an acidified solution (pH 3.5) and then place in a floral preservative with a bactericide. Preferably do not remove thorns (if present) as wounds can become infected. If necessary, store for 7–10 days at 0–2°C (32–36°F) and 80–90% relative humidity.

Rosa cultivars · family: Rosaceae

roos (Dutch); *rosier* (French); *Rose* (German); *rosa* (Italian); *ruusu* (Japanese); *rosa* (Spanish)

Rosa cultivars

pot rose • mini rose

Potted rose 'Portofino'

Potted rose 'Venise'

DESCRIPTION Potted roses are similar to hybrid tea and spray roses but they are bred to be small and compact. Numerous cultivars and hybrids are available, with new ones continually being released. Potted roses are not as sensitive to changes in fashion as are hybrid tea cultivars. Cultivars include 'Mistral Parade' (yellow); 'Chica Kordana' (pink); and 'Isabel Hit' (red).

ORIGIN & HISTORY Garden origin. Potted roses are part of a general increase in the popularity of potted flowers.

PARTS USED Whole plants are used as potted flowers.

CULTIVATION Propagation is mainly by means of cuttings, which take 7–10 days to root. Plants require a well-drained, acidic potting medium (pH 5.5–6.2) and bright, full sun conditions (but moderate temperatures). Plants need to be kept uniformly moist, as they tend to drop their leaves if they dry out and wilt. Gradually lowering growing temperatures towards the end of cultivation increases production time, but improves vase life. Plants are pinched numerous times during cultivation to produce a well-branched, compact plant.

PROPERTIES The flowers last for 2–6 weeks, depending on quality and cultivar. Some cultivars are scented. They are sensitive to ethylene and fungal infection and buds often fail to open.

QUALITY CRITERIA Select plants with at least 2 flowers open and 2–3 buds showing good colour. Look for well-branched, compact plants with a good bud count and even flowering (and no dropped leaves or buds). Leaves should be bright green and healthy.

CARE & HANDLING Unpack immediately if in boxes. Display in a well-ventilated, bright and coolish area (20°C; 68°F), away from ripening fruit or vegetables. Water carefully to avoid getting foliage wet. Do not over-water. Continually remove any dead flowers or leaves. Plants can be held for a few days at 2–4°C (36–39°F) if necessary, but not in the boxes.

Rosa cultivars   family: Rosaceae

roos (Dutch); *rosier* (French); *Rose* (German); *rosa* (Italian); *ruusu* (Japanese); *rosa* (Spanish)

Rudbeckia hirta

coneflower • black-eyed Susan

Rudbeckia hirta 'Goldsturm'

Rudbeckia fulgida

DESCRIPTION A biennial plant of up to 2 m high that is often grown as an annual. It has three-ribbed leaves and large solitary flower heads on long stalks. Each head has a distinctive central "cone" of dark purple-brown florets surrounded by a circle of bright yellow ray florets. Fully double forms are also available. The numerous cultivars vary from tall to dwarf, with single or double flower heads, yellow to reddish ray florets and purple to brown disc florets (that form the cone). Famous examples include 'Gloriosa' and 'Double Gloriosa'. Certain cultivars are grown for their cones.

ORIGIN & HISTORY Central United States. The old-fashioned coneflower has long been a favourite cut flower but perennial species such as *R. fulgida* and *R. laciniata* (widely known as black-eyed Susan) have also become popular.

PARTS USED Fresh flower heads: cut flowers. Flower heads without ray florets (flower cones): cut flowers or dried flowers. Whole plant:

infrequently as a potted flower (but not as common as fresh flowers).

CULTIVATION Nearly all commercial production is in open fields. Plants need long days to initiate flowering. The perennial rudbeckias benefit from a period of cold, while this is not necessary for the annuals. Production from perennials may last up to five years.

PROPERTIES Vase life is below average to average (5–8 days), with some cultivars lasting much longer. Botrytis and mildew can sometimes be a problem.

QUALITY CRITERIA Select sturdy, straight stems. Check to ensure that flower heads are free of damage and disease.

CARE & HANDLING Handle fresh cut flowers carefully as ray florets bruise easily. Use a general preservative, but not with an anti-ethylene agent. Storage is not recommended, but if necessary only store for 1–2 days at a temperature of 2–5°C (36–41°F). For drying, remove the ray florets and hang the stems upside down in a well-ventilated place.

Rudbeckia hirta L. (=*R. bicolor*) family: Asteraceae

zonnenhoed (Dutch); *rudbeckia* (French); *Rauer Sonnenhut* (German); *rudbekia, margherita gialla* (Italian); *rudbeckia* (Spanish)

Rumohra adiantiformis
leather leaf fern

Rumohra adiantiformis plant

Rumohra adiantiformis leaf

DESCRIPTION A fern of 0.9–1.5 m (3–5') with stiff, triangular fronds and a wiry midrib. Pale coloured spore sacs on the undersides of mature fronds become black as the spores mature. No significant cultivar selection has occurred as the naturally occurring plant fulfils the requirements of florists and consumers. The so-called "Cape-form" from South Africa has slightly longer fronds of up to 1.5 m (5').

ORIGIN & HISTORY Central and South America, South Africa, Madagascar, Australia, New Zealand and New Guinea. Leather leaf is one of the most important foliages (cut greens, florist greens) in the florist trade.

PARTS USED Leaves are used as cut foliage.

CULTIVATION Plants are usually cultivated under a high percentage shade cloth. Leather leaf ferns require well-drained soils, rich in organic matter and humus. They need regular watering and benefit from misting. New plants take 2–3 years to come into full production and are lifted and divided after a few years. Growth slows down considerably during autumn and winter.

PROPERTIES Vase life is normally above average to good (7–14 days). Stem length and frond size can vary considerably. There is no fragrance or leaking sap and fronds are very easy to work with.

QUALITY CRITERIA Select foliage that does not have any signs of mature, black spores under the leaves. Look for stiff fronds of an even green colour with no browning or curling tips (the first sign of old or poor quality leaves).

CARE & HANDLING Store fronds in the moisture-retaining cartons that they are sold in. Cover with damp newspaper or leave in the plastic bags to keep the fronds moist. Keep the humidity very high (90%+). Storing flat in the cartons will help to prevent leaf-curl. Alternatively, recut stems and place in water with a preservative at 4–5°C (39–41°F). Mist fronds regularly to prevent them from drying out.

Rumohra adiantiformis (G. Forst.) Ching (=*Arachniodes adiantiformis*) family: Dryopteridaceae

rumohra (Dutch, French); *Lederfarn* (German); *felce cuoio* (Italian); *hoja de helecho de cuero* (Spanish)

Ruscus hypoglossum
spineless butcher's broom

Ruscus hypoglossum foliage

Ruscus hypoglossum plant

Ruscus aculeatus fruit

DESCRIPTION An evergreen perennial herb of about 1 m (40") high with leafy stems arising from creeping rhizomes. The "leaves" are actually flattened stems that fulfil the same function as a true leaf. These structures are called cladophylls. The true leaves are very small and reduced to scales (a small group of them is often visible in the middle upper surface of the cladophyll). The plant bears small greenish white flowers on the midrib of the cladophyll that after pollination develops into a red berry. Species cultivated for florist foliage differ mainly in the size and shape of the cladophylls and flowering time. They include the common broom (*R. aculeatus*) as well as *R. hypoglossum*, *R. hypophyllum* and a hybrid between the two, known as *R. ×microglossa*. Some cultivars have small or variegated "leaves".

ORIGIN & HISTORY Europe and Asia. Butcher's broom has a long history as traditional medicine and as decoration for meat (hence the common name). It is said to be the "laurel" worn by Caesar.

PARTS USED Stems with "leaves" (cladophylls) are used as cut greens (sometimes with berries).

CULTIVATION *Ruscus* prefers rich, loose, well-drained soils. Soils need to be kept relatively moist and temperatures at the root zone moderate and constant. Plants need heavy shading to ensure good stem length and good ventilation to prevent disease problems.

PROPERTIES Vase life is good (10–14 days). Stems sometimes tend to be a bit short. Leaves are not ethylene sensitive.

QUALITY CRITERIA Select stems with mature, dark green leaves (cladophylls). "Leaves" must be clean, have a uniform colour and not be pale, or have whitish or brown marks, or any other blemishes. Select straight, sturdy stems with evenly spaced "leaves".

CARE & HANDLING Recut stems and place in clean water with a bactericide. Remove "leaves" below the water line. Stems can be stored for 1 week at 1–2°C (34–36°F) and 95% relative humidity.

Ruscus hypoglossum L.   family: Asparagaceae (Ruscaceae)

muizedoorn (Dutch); *epine de rat, fragon, petit houx* (French); *Hadernblatt* (German); *rusco* (Italian); *brusco de hojas anchas, laurelillo* (Spanish)

Sabal palmetto

palmetto • cabbage palmetto • palmetto palm

Sabal palmetto leaves

DESCRIPTION A large palm of up to 30 m high, with a rough stem of about 0.6 m at maturity. The rounded, hand-shaped green leaves are 2 m in diameter and are divided into about 60 narrow segments. The palmetto should not be confused with the well-known saw palmetto (*Serenoa repens*), the berries of which are a traditional medicine for prostate hypertrophy. It is a much smaller palm bearing greyish green, fan-shaped leaves that are thorny along the leaf stalk. There are no well-known cultivars but several related species are occasionally harvested for foliage.

ORIGIN & HISTORY South-eastern United States to the Bahamas. This palm has numerous traditional uses as palm cabbage (edible young stem hearts), thatch, mats, furniture and wharf-piles. Many of the famous palm avenues in Los Angeles and Miami (United States) are of *Sabal* species.

PARTS USED Leaves are used as cut greens.

CULTIVATION Propagation is primarily by means of seed. The trees are sun-loving and do best in subtropical and tropical areas. They also prefer a sandy soil.

PROPERTIES Vase life of fresh leaves is average (6–8 days). Leaves are not sensitive to ethylene, nor do they have any distinct fragrance. They work well in large designs but the heavy stems need extra securing.

QUALITY CRITERIA Select young but fully mature leaves that are relatively flat. Look for clean, unmarked and undamaged leaves that are well formed. Unopened leaves (palm buds) are usually yellowish-green in colour. Make sure they are free of disease and damage.

CARE & HANDLING Recut leaf stalks and place in a preservative. Leave at room temperature for a few hours before using or storing. Fronds can be stored or held for a few days at 4°C (39°F) and a high relative humidity. Palm buds should be kept dry and can be stripped into individual "leaflets" if desired.

Sabal palmetto (Walter) Lodd. ex Schult. & Schult. f.　　　　　　　　　　　family: Arecaceae (Palmae)

palmetto (Dutch); *palmette, sabal* (French); *Gewöhnliche Palmettopalme* (German); *palmetto* (Italian); *parumetto yashi* (Japanese); *sabal, sabal de carolina* (Spanish)

Saintpaulia ionantha

African violet

Saintpaulia ionantha pink

Saintpaulia ionantha mixed

Saintpaulia ionantha blue

DESCRIPTION A subtropical perennial with a short rosette of fleshy, hairy leaves. The soft, delicate flowers are borne on short stems in loose clusters. There are more than 2 000 hybrids and cultivars (single, semi-double or double, frilled or not). The large range of flower forms and colours (white, pink, violet or blue) resulted from breeding with *S. confusa* and other species.

ORIGIN & HISTORY Tanzania (East Africa). African violets are old favourite potted flowers that resemble common violets (*Viola odorata*).

PARTS USED Whole plants are used as potted flowers.

CULTIVATION Commercial propagation is from cuttings. Irrigation is critical. Overhead irrigation helps to maintain high humidity, but the temperature of the water must be within 3°C of the leaf temperature to avoid damage. Once the plants start to flower, irrigation must be from below. Plants do not tolerate high salt levels. Too much fertiliser results in leafy plants with few flowers.

PROPERTIES Plants are sensitive to temperatures below 10°C (50°F) and are fairly difficult to grow well, but once mature, are quite easy to maintain in the home environment. Flowers are sensitive to ethylene.

QUALITY CRITERIA Look for a well-formed crown of flowers with five or more open. Only purchase plants with protective sleeves. Make sure the flowers and especially the leaves are free of marks and damage.

CARE & HANDLING Plants respond well to fluorescent lighting, which encourages flowering. Draughts may result in leaf drop. Water on the leaves causes blemishes or rotting and direct sunlight often results in large brown patches on the leaves. Temperature: minimum (10°C; 50°F); maximum (21°C; 70°F). Keep the soil moist and maintain humidity by placing the pot on pebbles over a saucer of water (but not in direct contact with the water). Regularly pinch off old flowers and flower stalks. Plants do not store well.

Saintpaulia ionantha H. Wendl.

family: Gesneriaceae

Kaaps viooltje (Dutch); *violette d'Usambara* (French); *Usambaraveilchen* (German); *violetta africana* (Italian); *violeta africana* (Spanish)

Salix discolor

willow • pussy willow

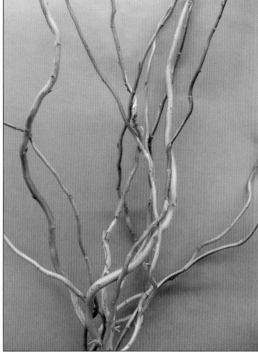

Salix discolor

Salix alba (contorted willow)

DESCRIPTION A deciduous shrub or small tree with purple-brown stems, bright green tapering leaves and dense oblong catkins of 25 to 70 mm (about 1–3") long. Many cultivars and a few hybrids are available. Stem colours range from yellow or red to dark brown or black. Species and related cultivars typically grown for their buds (pussy willows) include *S. caprea* (goat willow), *S. discolor* (the true pussy willow) and *S. chaenomeloides* (Japanese pussy willow). Willows grown for their contorted stems include *S. alba* (white willow), *S. ×erthroflexuosa* (*S. alba × S. matsudana*) and *S. matsudana* (Hankow willow).

ORIGIN & HISTORY Canada and the United States. Willows are among the most common cut stems used by florists around the world and form an important part of the "cut branch" market.

PARTS USED Stems are used as fillers or ornamentals.

CULTIVATION Propagation is from soft- or hardwood cuttings. Stems are most colourful and contorted when still young. Cool temperatures and high light intensities result in better stem colour. Severe pruning in late winter results in good stems (form and colour) in the following season.

PROPERTIES Vase life is very good (14–21 days – buds) and indefinite with regard to contorted stems. The interesting colour and form add variety to florist fillers.

QUALITY CRITERIA Select leafless stems with good colour. Pussy willow stems should be young, fresh looking and straight with several large and evenly spaced buds. Check stems for damage and disease.

CARE & HANDLING Recut, remove any foliage and place in water with a bactericide. Alternatively, hold budded stems dry to prevent catkins from opening and leaves developing. To keep contorted willow and weaving willow stems flexible, do not allow to dry out but keep wrapped in plastic or at a very high humidity. Stems can be stored for at least a week at 2–4°C (36–39°F).

Salix discolor Muhl.

family: Salicaceae

wilg (Dutch); *saule* (French); *Weide, Verschiedenfarbige Weide* (German); *salice* (Italian); *suace* (Spanish)

Salvia leucantha

sage • Mexican bush sage

Salvia officinalis

Salvia leucantha

Salvia splendens

DESCRIPTION A perennial herb or subshrub (up to 1 m) bearing opposite pairs of prominently veined leaves which are densely white-hairy below. Flowers are grouped in rounded clusters along the flowering stalk. They are densely hairy and have a purplish calyx and white petals fused into a tube. There are many garden cultivars but not much focus on the breeding of cultivars specifically as florist flowers.

ORIGIN & HISTORY Mexico and tropical America. Hundreds of species are grown as garden plants. The true sage (*S. officinalis*) is an important culinary herb. *Salvia leucantha* and *S. ×superba* (meadow sage) are two of the more common species grown as florist flowers. The popular red bedding salvia (*Salvia splendens*) is often sold as a potted flower.

PARTS USED Flowering stems are used as cut flowers and whole plants as potted flowers.

CULTIVATION Sage is grown from seeds or terminal cuttings. Long days result in vegetative growth and flowering is initiated when days

become shorter than 12 hours. Plants are forced to grow and flower year round in greenhouses by controlling temperature and day length by means of black screens and artificial lighting.

PROPERTIES Vase life is poor to average (5–7 days). Foliage declines more rapidly than the flowers. Stems are often short, flowers shatter easily and are very sensitive to ethylene.

QUALITY CRITERIA Look for stems with the bottom 3–5 flowers opening (with petals emerging from the sepals). Make sure foliage is fresh and of uniform colour, free of damage or disease. Potted plants should be compact with well-formed but closed flowers.

CARE & HANDLING Recut and hydrate immediately. Place flowers in a preservative containing an ethylene inhibitor. Avoid ethylene-forming products. If absolutely necessary, store for only 2–3 days at 2–4°C (36–39°F). Display pots in bright light and out of draughts. Flowers dry well – hang loose bunches upside down in a well-ventilated area.

Salvia leucantha Cav.   family: Lamiaceae

salie (Dutch); *sauge à fleurs blanches* (French); *Strauchiger Salbei* (German); *salvia a fiori bianchi* (Italian); *espiga lavanda* (Spanish)

Sandersonia aurantiaca

Christmas bells • Chinese lantern lily

Sandersonia aurantiaca yellow

Sandersonia aurantiaca orange

DESCRIPTION A perennial herb with erect branches (up to 0.6 m or 2' long) growing from a tuberous root. The glossy green leaves are spirally arranged along the stems and have characteristic curled tips that are modified to form climbing tendrils. The attractive, lantern-shaped flowers are solitary and hang down from a slender stalk in each of the leaf axils along the stem. Each flower is about 25 mm (1") long and orange or orange-yellow in colour. There appears to be as yet no named cultivars.

ORIGIN & HISTORY South Africa. This attractive plant has become a popular florist flower but cultivation on a commercial scale started only recently.

PARTS USED The leafy, flowering stems are used as cut flowers.

CULTIVATION Propagation is by means of corms. Plants require partial shade and well-drained soils. Watering is increased as plants grow taller and if corms are to be re-used, then watering needs to continue until foliage dies down and dormancy sets in. Plants are fairly sensitive to frost.

PROPERTIES Vase life is average to good (7–10 days). Flowers are not sensitive to ethylene. There is no strong or distinctive fragrance.

QUALITY CRITERIA Select stems with 1–4 flowers starting to open or open, and the rest showing good colour and shape. Flower colour fades as they age, so check that the colour is good. Leaves must be a bright, uniform green and not pale, yellowish or blotchy. The "bells" must be evenly spaced along the length of the flowering stalk. Make sure that the slender stalks are sufficiently sturdy.

CARE & HANDLING Recut stems and place in a bactericide or hydrating solution. Remove leaves below the water line. Allow to hydrate for 2–3 hours at room temperature before using or storing. Stems can be stored for 1–2 weeks at 0–1°C (32–34°F) and a high relative humidity (95%).

Sandersonia aurantiaca Hook.   family: Colchicaceae

chinese lantaarnbloem (Dutch); *cloche de Noël, lanterne chinoise* (French); *Lanternenlilie* (German); *sandersonia, lampioncino cinese* (Italian); *sandersonia* (Spanish)

Sansevieria trifasciata

mother-in-law's tongue • bowstring hemp

Sansevieria trifasciata 'Variegata'

Sansevieria cultivar

DESCRIPTION Evergreen, rhizomatous perennials with fleshy, stiff, sword-like leaves of up to 0.8 m (32") high. Leaves are often banded pale and dark green or yellow in variegated forms. The fragrant, tubular flowers are borne in large numbers on sturdy stems but cultivated plants seldom flower. About five or six of the approximately 50 species and their cultivars are used in the pot plant and garden industries. However, these are seldom used in the florist trade as foliages. The most common cultivar used as florist filler is 'Variegata', also known as 'Laurentii'.

ORIGIN & HISTORY West Africa (Nigeria). The genus is named after the 18th century Italian prince, Raimondo di Sangro of San Severo. Plants are widely used as traditional sources of strong fibres. They tolerate extreme conditions and have therefore become popular office and indoor plants.

PARTS USED Leaves are used as a filler (and whole plants as pot plants).

CULTIVATION Plants tolerate dry conditions and prefer a low humidity. They are quite sensitive to over-watering, especially during the winter (dormant) months. Every few years they are lifted and divided. Leaf cuttings are also successful, but the yellow-edge cultivars will revert back to the green form.

PROPERTIES Flowers have a pleasant fragrance, but are seldom seen in florist shops. The leaves are exceptionally long-lasting.

QUALITY CRITERIA Make sure leaves are free of brown or yellow marks or other signs of damage. Select leaves with a bright green and yellow colour – a pale colour results from poor light intensity. Plants like to be a bit pot-bound.

CARE & HANDLING Display pots in bright light or full winter sun. Do not over-water and allow the soil surface to dry out slightly before watering again. Keep pot plants at temperatures above 10°C (50°F). Cut greens should be recut and kept in clean water with a bactericide.

Sansevieria trifasciata Prain   family: Asparagaceae (Dracaenaceae)

vrouwetong (Dutch); *langue de belle-mére* (French); *Schwiegermutterzunge, Bogenhanf* (German); *espada de san jorge* (Spanish)

Sarracenia flava

yellow pitcher plant • yellow trumpet

Sarracenia flava yellow

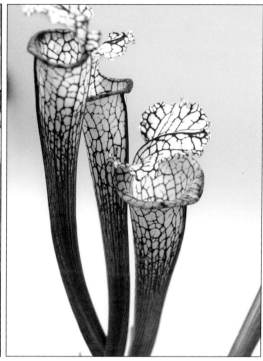

Sarracenia flava red

DESCRIPTION A carnivorous plant that typically grows in marshy areas. It is a perennial herb with hollow, trumpet-shaped leaves (pitchers) of up to 1.2 m (4') long, each bearing a wing or ridge that ends in an erect lid above the wide mouth. The pitchers are yellow-green and often decorated with red veins (or they can be completely maroon or red). The flowers are yellow and about 100 mm (4") in diameter. There are few cultivars. 'Maxima' has yellow-green pitchers of up to 75 mm (3") long that have red veins in the upper parts. 'Red Burgundy' has long pitchers with a deep wine-red colour.

ORIGIN & HISTORY United States (Virginia to Florida and Louisiana). Carnivorous plants have become very popular in recent years. The trumpets take on a yellow hue when grown in full sun, hence the common names of the species.

PARTS USED The whole plant is used as a potted "flower" or novelty.

CULTIVATION Propagation is primarily by division of the rhizomes. Plants require a nutrient-free soil with good drainage. Rich soils or fertiliser will kill them. Pitchers tend to be smaller at first after plants have been divided, but get progressively larger. A dormancy period is required, which is triggered by the onset of cold temperatures (below 10°C; 50°F).

PROPERTIES Vase life of cut flowers is poor to average (3–7 days). The actual flowers on the plant last about 2 weeks. Flowers have a faint, unpleasant smell. Pitchers on the plant last about 6 months.

QUALITY CRITERIA Look for healthy plants with well-formed pitchers. Pitchers must have good, definite colour and markings or variegation. Avoid pitchers with marks and bruising, especially on the edges.

CARE & HANDLING Place the pot in standing water to keep the soil moist at all times. Do not allow the soil to dry out completely. Do not fertilise and preferably use mineral-free water.

Sarracenia flava L.   family: Sarraceniaceae

Amerikaanse bekerplant (Dutch); *sarracénnie* (French); *Gelbe Schlauchpflanze* (German); *pianta insettivora* (Italian)

Scabiosa caucasica

sweet scabious • pincushion flower

Scabiosa caucasica

Scabiosa atropurpurea scarlet

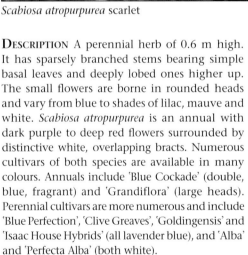
Scabiosa atropurpurea 'Deep Red'

DESCRIPTION A perennial herb of 0.6 m high. It has sparsely branched stems bearing simple basal leaves and deeply lobed ones higher up. The small flowers are borne in rounded heads and vary from blue to shades of lilac, mauve and white. *Scabiosa atropurpurea* is an annual with dark purple to deep red flowers surrounded by distinctive white, overlapping bracts. Numerous cultivars of both species are available in many colours. Annuals include 'Blue Cockade' (double, blue, fragrant) and 'Grandiflora' (large heads). Perennial cultivars are more numerous and include 'Blue Perfection', 'Clive Greaves', 'Goldingensis' and 'Isaac House Hybrids' (all lavender blue), and 'Alba' and 'Perfecta Alba' (both white).

ORIGIN & HISTORY Caucasian region (*S. caucasica*) or Europe and Africa (*S. atropurpurea*). The dark flowers of *S. atropurpurea* symbolised death (hence the common name "mournful widow").

PARTS USED Flowering stems: cut flowers. Whole plant: potted flowers.

CULTIVATION Both annual and perennial species are mainly grown in open fields. High yields and superior quality flowers are obtained under conditions of cool summers and cold winters.

PROPERTIES Vase life is poor to average (4–7 days). White forms tend to have thinner stems than blue or darker forms. Flower heads bruise easily, so handle with care.

QUALITY CRITERIA Select sturdy stems with flowers in full colour. Most flowers are field-grown so check for damage, diseases and soft stems. Stems are sometimes crooked, but this gives them character.

CARE & HANDLING Recut and place in a preservative. Storage is not recommended, but keep for 1–2 days at 3–5°C (37–41°F) if necessary. Potted flowers can be displayed in bright light (even full sun), provided temperatures are cool (<21°C; <70°F). Keep potting medium moist. Cut back after flowering – the plant will flower again in 4–6 weeks.

Scabiosa caucasica M. Bieb.   family: Caprifoliaceae (Dipsacaceae)

duifkruid (Dutch); *scabieuse de Caucase* (French); *Skabiose* (German); *scabiosa* (Italian); *escabiosa* (Spanish)

Schlumbergera buckleyi

Christmas cactus

Hatiora gaertneri

Schlumbergera ×buckleyi

Disocactus ×hybridus

DESCRIPTION An epiphytic cactus, producing flat, succulent stems and small thorns instead of leaves. The large, delicate flowers are usually red, pink or white and pink. There are more than 200 named cultivars of the Christmas cactus alone. Similar-looking cacti sold by florists include the Easter cactus (*Hatiora gaertneri*, previously *Rhipsalidopsis gaertneri*) and the well-known epiphyllum (*Disocactus ×hybridus*)

ORIGIN & HISTORY Garden origin (a hybrid between *S. russeliana* and *S. truncata*, both Brazilian species). Stem segments are scalloped along their margins, not saw-toothed as in *S. truncata* (the crab cactus or Thanksgiving cactus). Millions of plants are sold each year.

PARTS USED Whole plants are used as potted flowers.

CULTIVATION Flowering is controlled by day length and temperature. Growers control plant height in the pot by twisting off leaf segments at a certain growth stage. When done correctly, this leads to a uniform plant height and numerous buds.

PROPERTIES Flowering continues for about eight weeks, with individual flowers lasting 3–4 days. Flowers are very sensitive to ethylene and have no fragrance. They damage easily during packing and shipping.

QUALITY CRITERIA Avoid plants with light green or yellowish leaves. Ensure that flowers are free of botrytis or any other marks and that the stem base is free of lesions or a wet sliminess (all indicating diseases). Purchase well-branched compact plants full of brightly coloured flowers still in bud stage.

CARE & HANDLING Display in maximum natural light, but avoid direct sunlight and draughts. Water when potting medium feels dry and do not allow plant to stand in excess water in the potholder. Do not feed the plant while in bloom. Display at cool temperatures of 16–20°C (61–68°F). When flowering is over, allow the plant to become quite dry, as a dry period is necessary to induce flowering. Resume regular watering once new growth starts.

Schlumbergera ×buckleyi (T. Moore) Tjaden   family: Cactaceae

kerstcactus (Dutch); *cactus de Noël* (French); *Gliedercactus, Weihnachtskaktus* (German); *cactus di natale* (Italian); *cactus de navidad* (Spanish)

Scilla peruviana
Cuban lily • Peruvian scilla

Scilla peruviana

DESCRIPTION A bulb of about 75 mm (3") in diameter with strap-shaped, hairy leaves. About 50 to 100 small flowers are borne on long stalks in a rounded or conical cluster of up to 100 mm (4") in diameter. The flowers are usually purple or violet blue, rarely white or pink. A few cultivars have been developed, including 'Alba' (with white flowers). Also well known is 'Spring Beauty', a cultivar derived from the Siberian squill (*S. siberica*). It has sterile flowers so they tend to last longer. Another cultivated species is *S. hyacinthoides*, originally from Europe and the Middle East.

ORIGIN & HISTORY Europe and Northwest Africa. Many of the species occur naturally in woodland areas, growing under trees.

PARTS USED The flowering stems are used as cut flowers or the whole plant as a potted flower.

CULTIVATION Plants require rich, loose and well-drained soils. Shading is often provided during cultivation and cool growing conditions

are needed, with the soils kept moist. Plants are quite hardy to frost.

PROPERTIES Vase life of cut flowers is average (6–7 days). Potted flowers should last 2–3 weeks if kept in a fairly cool area. Flowers are not sensitive to ethylene. Unfortunately, stem length often tends to be a bit short so that Peruvian lily is not suitable as a cut flower for large arrangements.

QUALITY CRITERIA Select cut stems with half open flowers. Stems should be straight, as long as possible and free of discolouration or blemishes. Select potted flowers with flowers just starting to open. Plants should be compact and stems and leaves should have a bright green colour.

CARE & HANDLING Recut stems and place in a floral preservative. Display in a bright, cool area and avoid direct sunlight or draughts. Flowers can be stored dry, in moisture-retentive boxes or at 95% relative humidity at 0–1°C (32–34°F) for 7–10 days. Display pots in a cool, bright area and keep the soil/medium moist.

Scilla peruviana L.   family: Asparagaceae (Hyacinthaceae)

peruviaanse sterhiacint (Dutch); *scille* (French); *Peruanischer Blaustern* (German); *flor de la corona, flor de la piña* (Italian); *jacinto estrellado* (Spanish)

Sedum spectabile
ice plant

Sedum spectabile

Sedum aizoon

Sedum 'Autumn Joy'

DESCRIPTION An erect perennial herb (0.7 m high) with large, blue-green succulent leaves in opposite pairs (or in groups of three) and clusters of bright pink to dull red (rarely white) flowers. Cultivars include 'Snowqueen' (white), 'Brilliant' (pink), 'Indian Chief' (dark pinkish red) and 'Variegatum' (dark pink, variegated leaves). *S. aizoon* is a compact plant with toothed leaves and yellow flowers. *S. telephium* (orpine) has alternate leaves and reddish purple flowers – a famous cultivar is 'Autumn Joy' or 'Herbstfreude'(*S. telephium × S. spectabile*).

ORIGIN & HISTORY Northern Asia, mainly China and Korea (naturalised in northern and central Europe). The ice plant and many related species and cultivars have become popular pot plants.

PARTS USED The flowering stems are used as cut flowers or dried flowers and the whole plant as a potted flower.

CULTIVATION Propagation is mainly by means of cuttings, but plants can also be divided and some species grow well from seed. Plants require full sun and very well-drained soils that are slightly acidic (pH 5.8–6.5). They need to dry out well between irrigations. Some cultivars and species require long days to flower.

PROPERTIES Vase life of fresh flowers is average (6–8 days). They are sensitive to ethylene. The mature seed heads are excellent for drying.

QUALITY CRITERIA Select pots with plants that are well established and just beginning to flower. Select cut flowers with all the florets beginning to open to fully opened. Make sure leaves and stems are free of blemishes and damage.

CARE & HANDLING Display pots in bright, well-ventilated areas, out of direct draughts. Allow them to dry out slightly before watering again. Recut flowers and place in a floral preservative. Remove leaves below the water line. Handle with care to avoid damage to fleshy leaves and stems. Storage is not recommended.

Sedum spectabile Boreau (=*Hylotelephium spectabile*) family: Crassulaceae

hemelsleutel (Dutch); *orpin remarquable* (French); *Schöne Fetthenne* (German); *sedum spectabile* (Italian, Spanish)

Serruria florida

blushing bride

Serruria florida

Serruria florida × *S. rosea*

DESCRIPTION A lanky shrub of up to 2 m (about 6′) bearing deeply dissected leaves with needle-shaped lobes. The flower heads have inconspicuous florets surrounded by leafy white bracts that are flushed with reddish pink (hence "blushing bride"). Some species with smaller bracts are known as spider heads. The main commercial species are *S. florida* and the similar-looking *S. rosea*, as well as hybrids between these two species. Only a handful of cultivars have been bred and are as yet not commercially well known.

ORIGIN & HISTORY South Africa (Cape Floral Kingdom). The blushing bride and other species have very localised natural distributions. It has long been a popular cut flower and is often used in bridal bouquets.

PARTS USED Flower heads are used as cut flowers or whole plants as potted flowers.

CULTIVATION Propagation is by means of cuttings. The main limiting factor in cultivation is the soil, which needs to be well drained,

relative sandy and acidic, with a low salt and phosphorus content. Shrubs prefer full sun conditions.

PROPERTIES The vase life of cut flowers is average to good (7–10 days). They are not ethylene sensitive. Potted flowers bloom for 1–2 months. There is no noticeable fragrance.

QUALITY CRITERIA Select cut stems with 50% of the flower heads half to fully open. Potted flowers can be more closed. Make sure flower heads and leaves are free of any marks or blemishes. Look for compact plants that are well branched and full of blooms.

CARE & HANDLING Recut and use a floral preservative. Use the flower heads promptly, but if necessary store them in light for 3–5 days at 2–3°C (36–37°F) and 90% relative humidity. Flower heads are excellent for drying. Water potted flowers well on arrival and display in a bright, well-ventilated area (not in direct sunlight or draughts). Allow medium to dry out slightly before watering again.

Serruria florida Knight   family: Proteaceae

serruria (Dutch, French, Italian, Spanish); *Serruria* (German)

Silene chalcedonica

Maltese cross • cross of Jerusalem • lychnis

Silene chalcedonica red

Silene chalcedonica flowers

DESCRIPTION A herbaceous perennial herb up to 1 m (40"), with unbranched stems and opposite pairs of simple leaves, each about 25–125 mm (1–5") long. The flowers are borne in clusters of 10 to 50. Each flower is 10–30 mm (about ½–1") in diameter and has a deeply five-lobed corolla. The lobes are further split into two smaller lobes, which create a shape similar to the Maltese cross. Flowers are a brilliant scarlet colour, although white and pink forms occur. The best-known cultivars are 'Grandiflora' (large, red), 'Red Tiger' (bright red), 'Flore Plena' (double red), 'Rosea' (pink), 'Salmonea' (salmon pink) and 'Alba' (white).

ORIGIN & HISTORY Europe, Russia and north-western China. The plant has become naturalised in various regions of North America. Thomas Jefferson is known to have sown it at Monticello (United States) in 1807. This popular garden ornamental is better known as *Lychnis chalcedonica* (the old name) and is readily used by florists when available.

PARTS USED The flowering stems are used as cut flowers or fillers.

CULTIVATION Cultivation is from seed, cuttings and division. Plants grow well in most soils, as long as they are well drained. Full sun to partial shade conditions and regular watering are required. Double-flowered cultivars are propagated by division.

PROPERTIES Vase life is slightly poor to above average (5–8 days). Flowers have a faint scent. They are sensitive to ethylene and water stress.

QUALITY CRITERIA Select stems with full, compact heads and several flowers open. Avoid faded flowers and pale green leaves.

CARE & HANDLING Recut stems and hydrate for 2–3 hours prior to use. Place in a floral preservative with a bactericide and display in a cool, bright area or hold in a cooler at 4–6°C (39–43°F) and a high relative humidity (90%). Stems will potentially pollute water so do not hold with pollutant-sensitive flowers.

Silene chalcedonica (L.) E. Krause (=*Lychnis chalcedonica*)　　　　　　family: Caryophyllaceae

brandende liefde (Dutch); *croix de malte, croix de jérusalem* (French); *Brennende Liebe* (German); *croce di malta* (Italian); *cruz de malta* (Spanish)

Sinningia speciosa
florist's gloxinia • gloxinia

Sinningia speciosa purple

Sinningia speciosa white

Sinningia speciosa pink

DESCRIPTION A perennial herb (up to 0.3 m or 1′) with a rounded tuber. It has large, soft, finely hairy leaves flushed with red below. The attractive flowers are typically solitary, bell-shaped and available in a multitude of colours. Most cultivars belong to the Fyfiana Group and have large, erect flowers. Examples include 'Blanche de Meru' (white and pink), 'Chic' (red) and 'Mont Blanc' (white). The Maxima Group has large nodding flowers, often with blotches and spots.

ORIGIN & HISTORY Brazil. The most popular species is *S. speciosa* and its numerous hybrids and cultivars. Potted gloxinias used to be a year-round favourite in florist shops but are nowadays mostly available as a summer crop.

PARTS USED Whole plants are used as potted flowers.

CULTIVATION Seedlings take very long (16–17 weeks) before they can be potted so growers purchase plugs and use only one per pot. Overhead irrigation with cold water (below 10°C; 50°F) causes spots on the leaves. Too much nitrogen leads to inferior plants with cupped, curled or twisted and off-colour blue-green leaves.

PROPERTIES Flowering continues for many weeks. Viruses and botrytis can sometimes be problematic.

QUALITY CRITERIA Select plants with well-formed, dark and uniform green leaves that are not twisted, curled or blemished (and free from botrytis). Select plants with 3–5 flowers open. Some older cultivars have brittle leaves so handle with care.

CARE & HANDLING Do not store in the dark as this can cause unopened buds to fall off. Display in bright light in a warm spot (18–24°C; 65–75°F) but out of direct sunlight. Keep the potting medium moist, but not soaked. Water from the bottom, preferably with tepid water and do not get the flowers or leaves wet. Continually remove dead flowers and leaves to encourage continued flowering. Gloxinias are related to African violets and like the same treatment.

Sinningia speciosa (Lodd.) Hiern

family: Gesneriaceae

gloxinia (Dutch); *gloxinia* (French); *Gartengloxinie* (German); *gloxinia* (Italian); *gloxinia* (Spanish)

Solanum pseudocapsicum
winter cherry • Jerusalem cherry • Madeira winter cherry

Solanum pseudocapsicum

DESCRIPTION A shrub of 1–2 m (40–80") with bright green leaves and single, small, white, star-shaped flowers. The fruits are up to 25 mm (1') in diameter and usually bright orange when ripe or sometimes marked with shades of white, yellow or red. Several cultivars are available, including 'Patersonii' (dwarf, with many orange fruits), 'Giant Red Cherry' (large orange-red fruits) and 'Cherry Jubilee' (white, yellow and orange fruit). This species (and all other members of the genus) have anthers which open by terminal pores (and not longitudinal slits as in most other plants).

ORIGIN & HISTORY Madeira (but widely naturalised and a common garden weed in many countries). It is a very popular potted "flower", grown for the highly decorative (but poisonous), cherry-like fruits.

PARTS USED The whole flowering and fruiting plant is used as potted "flower".

CULTIVATION Propagation is mainly by means of seed. Plants require high light intensities and warm growing temperatures (they are sensitive to frost). The growing medium or soil needs to be loose and well drained and plants require regular watering, especially during flowering and fruiting.

PROPERTIES Vase life of fruit is very good and they change colour as they ripen. Plants are sensitive to ethylene (causing leaf and fruit drop) and have no fragrance. The fruits contain toxic alkaloids so keep them away from small children and pets.

QUALITY CRITERIA Look for compact and well-branched plants. They must be full of well-formed and colourful berries (fruit). Make sure no fruit drop has occurred. Foliage must be dark green (not pale or yellowish) and fruits must be free of any marks or blemishes. Purchase plants treated against ethylene.

CARE & HANDLING Unpack immediately and water well. Display in bright light (not direct sunlight) and avoid draughts. Keep potting soil moist, but do not over-water. Mist occasionally, especially in hot weather, even though plants are tolerant of dry air. Do not hold or store plants at temperatures below 10°C (50°F).

Solanum pseudocapsicum L.   family: Solanaceae

appeltje der liefde (Dutch); *pommier d'amour* (French); *Jerusalemkirsche, Korallenstrauch* (German); *solanum pseudocapsicum* (Italian); *cerezo de Jerusalén* (Spanish)

Solidago canadensis

golden rod • goldenrod

Solidago canadensis

Solidago 'Tara'

DESCRIPTION An erect perennial herb (up to 1.5 m or 5') with tapering leaves and small yellow flower heads of 6 mm (¼") in diameter. At present cultivars differ mainly in the size and shape of the flowering stem and the number of flowers – flower colour is limited to shades of yellow and gold.

ORIGIN & HISTORY North America and Canada (naturalised in Europe). *Solidago canadensis* is still the most common garden species in Europe and America. Nowadays there are numerous hybrids derived from this species, the European goldenrod (*S. virgaurea*) and *S. cutleri* (north-eastern United States), resulting in excellent florist cultivars.

PARTS USED Flowering stems are used as cut flowers.

CULTIVATION More than 90% of the world production is based on hybrids produced from cuttings or tissue culture. Although plants are perennials, growers replace them every 2–3 years, with most production being all year round in greenhouses. Hybrids are particularly sensitive to photoperiod and require "short" days of 14 hours light to initiate flowering (less than 12 hours of daylight result in poor quality flowers and inferior yields). No cold treatment is required to initiate flowering, but temperatures above 27°C (80°F) will delay flowering and reduce quality.

PROPERTIES Vase life is poor to average (5–7 days).

QUALITY CRITERIA Select colourful stems with 33–50% of the flower heads open. Check carefully for brown or dry flower heads. Select stems with an even leaf colour and no signs of yellowing.

CARE & HANDLING Recut and hydrate immediately in a solution containing a bactericide. Use a preservative with a sugar to assist in further flower opening and to help prevent premature leaf yellowing. Stems drink a lot of water so check water levels daily. Flowers may be stored for 5 days at 2–4°C (36–39°F). They are suitable for drying – wait for flower heads to open fully then dry by standing them straight up.

Solidago canadensis L.   family: Asteraceae

guldenroede (Dutch); *verge-d'or* (French); *Goldrute* (German); *pioggia d'oro* (Italian); *vara de oro* (Spanish)

Solidaster luteus

golden aster

×*Solidaster luteus*

×*Solidaster luteus*

DESCRIPTION An erect perennial herb of about 1 m (40") high – similar to *Solidago* but with larger, canary yellow flower heads of up to 10 mm (nearly ½") in diameter. The ray florets typically fade to creamy white. The best-known cultivar of ×*Solidaster luteus* (especially popular in the Netherlands) is 'Lemore' (a spontaneous hybrid found in a nursery in Lyon in 1910).

ORIGIN & HISTORY Garden origin. It is an intergeneric hybrid, usually said to be *Solidago × Aster*, but actually between *Euthamia graminifolia* (previously *Solidago*) and *Oligoneuron album* ("Aster") that looks very similar to goldenrod (*Solidago*) and has similar properties. Excellent florist cultivars of solidago have been developed over the last few years so that the production and use of solidaster has all but disappeared.

PARTS USED Flowering stems are used as cut flowers.

CULTIVATION Commercial propagation is from cuttings or tissue culture and plants are replaced every two to three years (even though they are perennials). Flowering is forced by initially elongating stems through exposure of the plants to long days of around 16 hours light per day, followed by "short" days of 14 hours light. However, golden aster has been shown to flower even after photoperiods of 16 hours or more. Cultivation in an environment hotter than 27°C (80°F) will delay flowering and reduce quality.

PROPERTIES Vase life is poor to average (5–7 days).

QUALITY CRITERIA Select stems with bright green (not yellowing) leaves and colourful flower heads, about a third of which should be open. There should be no browned or dried out flower heads.

CARE & HANDLING Recut the stems and rehydrate immediately. The preservative should have a bactericide and a sugar (which helps flower opening and prevents leaf yellowing). Add water daily or preferably replace with fresh water. Store flowers for 5 days at 2–4°C (36–39°F). Fully open flower heads dry well – simply air dry them in an upright position.

×*Solidaster luteus* M.L. Green ex Dress   family: Asteraceae

solidaster (Dutch, French, Italian, Spanish); *Goldrutenaster* (German)

Sparaxis tricolor

harlequin flower

Sparaxis tricolor

Sparaxis tricolor mixed

Sparaxis tricolor

DESCRIPTION A small, deciduous bulbous plant bearing a corm. The bright green, sword-shaped leaves are arranged in a fan. The flowering stalks are up to 0.4 m (16") high and bear up to five flowers, each about 25–33 mm (1–1½") long. The segments are typically bicoloured and also marked with black, giving a "tricolour" effect. Flowering occurs in late winter to early spring. Most cultivars are derived from *S. tricolor*, but *S. elegans*, *S. fragrans* and *S. grandiflora* are also used to some extent in breeding work. A seed race known as Magic Border Hybrids has become very popular, especially as garden plants. Cultivars include 'Alba' (white and yellow with dark stripes) and 'Honneur de Haarlem' (red, yellow and black).

ORIGIN & HISTORY South Africa (all six species). The most commonly cultivated *Sparaxis* is *S. tricolor* and its cultivars – the multicoloured flowers are reminiscent of the traditional clothing worn by harlequins.

PARTS USED Flowering stems are used as cut flowers and whole plants as potted flowers.

CULTIVATION *Sparaxis* grows fairly well in most soils, although some organic matter is preferable. Drainage needs to be good, but the soil must remain moist. Most commercial production that is done outdoors is under a low percentage shade, although some direct sunlight is beneficial.

PROPERTIES Vase life of individual flowers is short (3–5 days), but flowers continue to open, giving a lasting display. Flowers are fragrant and sensitive to ethylene.

QUALITY CRITERIA Select stems with buds showing good colour but still closed. Leaves and stems should have a bright green colour and not be pale or blotchy. Potted flowers must be compact, well formed and full of buds.

CARE & HANDLING Place recut stems in a floral preservative and hold in a cool area until used. Cut flowers can be stored for 4–7 days at 0–2°C (32–36°F). Display pots in a bright, cool area. Keep the soil moist but do not over-water.

Sparaxis tricolor (Schneev.) Ker-Gawl.   family: Iridaceae

harlekijnbloem (Dutch); *fleur arlequin, sparaxis* (French); *Dreifärbiges Fransenschwertel* (German); *sparaxis tricolor* (Italian); *arlequina, esparaxis* (Spanish)

Spathiphyllum wallisii
peace lily

Spathiphyllum wallisii

Spathiphyllum 'Chopin'

DESCRIPTION An evergreen perennial plant that grows from a rhizome below the ground. It has glossy green leaves on long stalks and a distinctive arum-type inflorescence – a finger-shaped spadix that bears numerous tiny white florets, surrounded by a large white spathe that becomes partly green. Cultivars mostly have white flowers and differ only in growth form, leaf shape and the colour, length and shape of the flower spathe. The best-known cultivar is 'Clevelandii' but there are quite a few of hybrid origin, including 'Mauna Loa', 'Marion Wagner' and 'McCoy'.

ORIGIN & HISTORY Panama, Costa Rica and Colombia. Peace lilies are old favourite florist flowers.

PARTS USED Flowering stems are used as cut flowers and whole plants as potted flowers.

CULTIVATION Peace lilies require time, heat and humidity. Commercial production is by means of tissue-cultured plants, cuttings or seed. Until fairly recently seed production, although more economical, did not give commercial growers the uniformity they required.

PROPERTIES Flowers are fragrant. Even without flowers it makes an attractive foliage plant.

QUALITY CRITERIA Check to ensure that leaves have an even, glossy green colour. Yellowish leaves or leaves with golden-yellow margins indicate nutrient deficiencies. Select compact plants with well-formed leaves, straight sturdy stems and an adequate number of flowers (which can vary depending on the cultivar). Poor production conditions can result in narrow leaves (strap leaf), loss of colour and reduced flower quantities and quality.

CARE & HANDLING Unpack and water plants immediately. Display in bright light but not direct sunlight (semi-shade in summer). A humid environment is ideal, so place the pot on pebbles in a water-filled tray and/or mist the foliage often. Water freely and regularly, but avoid fluorinated water as it can damage the leaves. Keep out of cold draughts.

Spathiphyllum wallisii Regel   family: Araceae

lepelplant (Dutch); *spathyphyllum* (French); *Zwerg-Blattfahne* (German); *espatifilo* (Spanish)

Spathoglottis plicata
Philippine ground orchid • spathoglottis

Spathoglottis plicata flowers

DESCRIPTION A ground orchid of up to 1 m (40") high with sparse tufts of long, slender and characteristically pleated leaves. The flowers are 35 mm (1½") in diameter and are borne on tall inflorescences. They are usually pink or purple, sometimes yellow or white. Cultivated forms flower throughout the year. There are as yet no well-known named cultivars.

ORIGIN & HISTORY India, Southeast Asia, the Philippines and Australia. It is naturalised in Hawaii and has become a popular orchid in the florist industry.

PARTS USED The flowering stems are used as cut flowers and the whole plant as a potted flower.

CULTIVATION Propagation is primarily by means of tissue culture. Plants prefer full sun to light shade, with warm, moist conditions. *Spathoglottis* is relatively fast growing and requires more feeding than other orchids. Plants have a vigorous root system and need a deep growing medium. Frost will kill plants and temperatures persistently below 4–8°C (39–46°F) will cause leaf loss and dormancy.

PROPERTIES Potted flowers can last for 2–3 months, with new buds opening periodically. Cut flowers last for 4–6 weeks. They are sensitive to ethylene.

QUALITY CRITERIA Select potted flowers with a few buds open or opening. Make sure flowers and buds are free of marks, blemishes and other damage. Check that leaves are healthy and free of disease and damage.

CARE & HANDLING Avoid touching flowers as this may cause bruising or pollination, which will reduce vase life. Store flowers at 10–13°C (50–55°F) and 95% relative humidity. Store the individual flowers in a water tube with sufficient preservative solution. Water may leave marks on the petals. Keep potted flowers evenly moist, but do not over-water. Display pots in a bright, warm area (16–24°C; 61–75°F), with good ventilation, but avoid direct sunlight and draughts. Maintain a high humidity around the plant.

Spathoglottis plicata Blume (=*S. vieillardii*)   family: Orchidaceae

spathoglottis (Dutch, French, Italian, Spanish); *Spathoglottis* (German)

Stoebe plumosa
stoebe

Stoebe plumosa plant with flowers

Stoebe plumosa foliage

DESCRIPTION The plant is a silvery-white, dense, much-branched and often matted shrub of about 0.9 m (3') high. The minute, densely hairy leaves are clustered along the slender stems. Inconspicuous flowers are borne in tiny heads along the branch tips. Little or no breeding and hybridising has been done to date and there are as yet no well-known cultivars.

ORIGIN & HISTORY South Africa (fynbos region of the Cape). *Stoebe plumosa* is an exceptionally common shrub and has been wild-harvested for many years. Fresh and dried foliage hardly differ in appearance, so that stoebe has become popular as a filler.

PARTS USED The silvery, almost leafless stems are used as fillers or cut foliage in arrangements and mixed bouquets.

CULTIVATION The plants grow best in full sun conditions. They occur naturally in clay soils, but are tolerant of most soil types. Cultivated plants are sensitive to excessive salts and fertilisers but remain productive for many years if well managed. A large part of the annual production is still wild-harvested.

PROPERTIES Vase life of fresh foliage is good (10–14 days). Foliage remains attractive and usually retains its colour as it ages and dries in an arrangement or bouquet. It is not sensitive to ethylene. Stems have no strong or distinctive fragrance.

QUALITY CRITERIA Select straight stems with good length and that are well branched and full of dense silvery foliage. Preferably choose young stems that are not too woody, but with fully matured foliage. Foliage must have a bright silvery-grey colour with no blemishes or insect galls.

CARE & HANDLING Recut stems and place in a bactericide – there is no need to use a full floral preservative. Remove foliage below the water line. Stems can be stored at 0–2°C (32–36°F) and 90% relative humidity for 5–10 days. The stems are excellent for drying.

Stoebe plumosa (L.) Thunb.   family: Asteraceae

slangbos (Afrikaans); *stoebe* (Dutch, French, Italian, Spanish); *Stoebe* (German)

Strelitzia reginae

bird-of-paradise • crane flower

Strelitzia reginae 'Mandela's Gold'

Strelitzia reginae

DESCRIPTION A perennial, robust, evergreen herb with flowering stems and leaves rising directly from the ground. Large, shield-shaped leaves are borne on long, strong and straight stalks. The "flower" is actually a closed sheath containing numerous blue and orange bicoloured flowers that emerge one at a time over a period of 1–2 weeks. There are as yet only a few cultivars. Well-known examples are 'Kirstenbosch Gold' and 'Mandela's Gold' (a golden-yellow flower named for the former South African president, Nelson Mandela).

ORIGIN & HISTORY South Africa. A popular and attractive garden plant with a long history of use as a cut flower for large arrangements.

PARTS USED Flowering stems are used as cut flowers and the leaves as cut foliage.

CULTIVATION Plants are cultivated in large, open fields. The plants take 2–3 years to come into full production but persist for many years.

PROPERTIES Vase life is good (7–14 days), with new flowers continually emerging one after the other. Colours are limited to blue and orange or blue and yellow. The flowers have no noticeable fragrance and are not ethylene sensitive.

QUALITY CRITERIA Look for straight, sturdy stems and large, undamaged sheaths. Purchase stems with tight closed sheaths, but showing some colour or with the first flower emerging. Closed flowers transport with less damage and open easily in a floral preservative.

CARE & HANDLING Recut the stems by 50–100 mm (2–4"). Use tall buckets or support rings, as flowers are top-heavy. Use a preservative with a carbohydrate to assist in flower opening. *Strelitzia* is not a tropical flower. Store flowers at 2–4°C (36–39°F), not above 10°C (50°F). Tight sheaths can be "forced to flower in a hurry" by soaking them for 15–20 minutes in warm water. Afterwards, physically open the sheath with a sharp knife or thumbnail and gently lift out some of the individual flowers.

Strelitzia reginae Banks ex Dryand.   family: Strelitziaceae

paradijsvogelbloem (Dutch); *oiseau de paradis* (French); *Paradiesvogelblume* (German); *uccello del paradiso* (Italian); *ave del paraiso* (Spanish)

Streptocarpus hybridus

florist streptocarpus • Cape primrose

Streptocarpus ×hybridus

DESCRIPTION A small perennial herb with broad, strap-shaped leaves close to the ground. The leaves are shortly hairy and puckered, with toothed and wavy margins and prominent veins visible on both surfaces. One or two trumpet-shaped flowers (rarely up to 6) are borne on a slender stalk emerging at or near the leaf base. Flower colour is typically lilac or mauve-purple, but various shades of blue, mauve, red, pink or white are nowadays available in modern cultivars. These are mainly from *S. ×hybridus*, a group of hybrids derived from *S. rexii* crossed with *S. dunnii*, *S. cyanus*, *S. polyanthus*, *S. saundersii*, *S. wendlandii* and *S. woodii*. The Tanzanian *S. saxorum* is also well known.

ORIGIN & HISTORY Garden origin. (*S. rexii* and the other listed species are from South Africa.) *Streptocarpus* is an old favourite florist flower.

PARTS USED Whole plants are used as potted flowers.

CULTIVATION Plants require bright, indirect sunlight and warm temperatures during flowering. During the active growing season, regular watering is essential. They are sensitive to frost.

PROPERTIES The plant is attractive even after flowering has finished and before it becomes semi-dormant. The leaf sap may cause skin irritation. Flowers are sensitive to ethylene.

QUALITY CRITERIA Select plants with a well-formed growth of leaves and full of buds and opening flowers. Make sure leaves are undamaged and have a healthy green colour and that flower stems are at least 200 mm (8") long and carried well above the rest of the plant. Purchase plants that have been pretreated against ethylene.

CARE & HANDLING Display pots in bright light but not in direct sunlight. Mist leaves occasionally, but do not soak them. Water freely, especially during flowering and feed once a week. Display at a minimum temperature of 13°C (55°F), but preferably at room temperature (20–21°C; 68–70°F). Regularly remove the dead flowers as well as their stalks.

Streptocarpus ×hybridus Voss.   family: Gesneriaceae

kaapse primula (Dutch); *primevère du Cap* (French); *Drehfrucht* (German); *primula del capo* (Italian); *primavera de cabo* (Spanish)

343

Symphoricarpos albus

snowberry

Symphoricarpos albus flowers and fruit

DESCRIPTION A deciduous shrub of up to 1.2 m (4′) high with slender shoots bearing oval leaves and small pink flowers in spikes or clusters. The distinctive berries are about 12 mm (½″) in diameter and snow-white. There are several cultivars that have been developed for their ornamental value, including 'Constance Spry', which bears a copious crop of large, round berries. The common snowberry is well known as a garden plant but at least 10 other species and hybrids are regularly cultivated.

ORIGIN & HISTORY Western parts of North America. Naturalised in Britain. The plant is rich in saponins and has been used as fish poison and as traditional medicine by several North American Indian tribes.

PARTS USED The flowers as cut flowers or fillers and the fruit (berries) as fillers and ornamentals.

CULTIVATION Propagation is by means of seed, cuttings and suckers. Snowberry can be cultivated in heavy clay and nutritionally poor soils. It can grow in full shade, semi-shade or full sun conditions, although full sun is preferable. The plants can also tolerate the salty air encountered at the coast.

PROPERTIES Vase life of flowers is poor to average (4–7 days). Berries are poisonous but poorly absorbed by the body. Flowers are sensitive to ethylene.

QUALITY CRITERIA Select stems with flowers half to almost fully open. Make sure flowers have not started to fade or deteriorate. Look for stems with well-formed and brightly coloured berries. Leaves must be dark green and free of blemishes.

CARE & HANDLING Recut stems of flowers and berries and allow to hydrate for 2–3 hours at room temperature before use. Remove leaves that are below the water line. Hold or store in a floral preservative. Storage of fresh flowers is not recommended – use promptly. Berries can be stored for 4–7 days at 1–2°C (34–36°F) and 90–95% relative humidity.

Symphoricarpos albus (L.) S.F. Blake

family: Caprifoliaceae

sneeuwbes (Dutch); *symphorine* (French); *Gewöhnliche Schneebeere* (German); *sinforicarpo bianco* (Italian); *bola de nieve* (Spanish)

Syringa vulgaris
common lilac

Syringa vulgaris 'Schöne von Moskau'

Syringa vulgaris 'Nadezhda'

Syringa vulgaris 'Andenken an Ludwig Späth'

DESCRIPTION A small deciduous tree of up to 7 m high with large, oval leaves in opposite pairs and branched clusters of small, lilac, highly fragrant flowers, each about 10 mm (nearly ½") long. There are a multitude of hybrids and cultivars, including early and late flowerers, single or double flowers, green or variegated leaves, and flower colours ranging from the original lilac to pink, magenta, mauve, blue and white.

ORIGIN & HISTORY South-eastern Europe. Lilacs (from the Persian *nilac* = bluish) are old-fashioned garden plants, highly prized for the attractive fragrant flowers. Since 1850, more than 1500 cultivars have been developed in Europe (mainly France) and the USA.

PARTS USED Flowering stems are used as cut flowers or fillers.

CULTIVATION Lilacs prefer well-drained, organic rich soils and benefit from being well mulched. Plants are hardy and require cold, dormant winter conditions to flower well the following season. As a result, they are not suitable for cultivation in warm regions of the world. Propagation is mainly by means of layering or cuttings.

PROPERTIES Vase life is poor to good, depending on the cultivar (normally 3–7 days, but sometimes up to 14 days). Flowers are extremely fragrant. However, the stronger the fragrance, the shorter the vase life. Flowers are sensitive to ethylene.

QUALITY CRITERIA Select stems with tight blossoms that are just starting to loosen or break towards the panicle base. Stems need to be long, straight and sturdy and flowering heads full. Make sure buds are free of blemishes or damage.

CARE & HANDLING Recut stems and place in a floral preservative. Allow to hydrate for 2–3 hours before using or storing. Leaves can be removed for design purposes, but leave the leaf cluster nearest the blooms to assist in water uptake. Preferably avoid using in floral foam, which tends to inhibit water uptake. Stems can be stored at 2–4°C (36–39°F) and 90–95% relative humidity for 4–6 days.

Syringa vulgaris L.

family: Oleaceae

sering (Dutch); *lilas commun* (French); *Gewöhlicher Flieder* (German); *lillà comune* (Italian); *lila, lilo* (Spanish)

Tagetes erecta

African marigold • American marigold

Tagetes erecta 'Promise Orange'

Tagetes erecta 'Promise Yellow'

DESCRIPTION Robust annuals of up to 1.5 m (5′) high with sparsely gland-dotted, compound leaves and large, solitary (often double and rounded), orange to yellow flower heads of 50–125 mm (2–5″) in diameter. French marigold and striped Mexican marigold are smaller plants with smaller flower heads. The large pompom types are particularly popular as cut flowers. Numerous cultivars are available, including taller ones such as Inca Hybrids (orange, gold or yellow) and Jubilee Hybrids (white, cream, yellow, lemon or orange). There is also a wide range of dwarf types that are used as potted flowers.

ORIGIN & HISTORY Mexico and Central America. African marigolds have larger flowers and longer stems than other species, making them more suited to use as cut flowers.

PARTS USED Flower heads: cut flowers. Whole plants: potted flowers.

CULTIVATION Marigolds tend to flower quicker under short days. Plants prefer a well-drained, slightly acidic growing medium (pH 6.2–6.5).

They are susceptible to micronutrient toxicity, especially at low pH levels. Crops are typically grown under moderate to warm temperatures of between 16–26°C / 13–16°C (61–79°F / 55–61°F) day / night.

PROPERTIES Vase life is average to fairly good (6–8 days). Flowers are edible (used in salads) and the foliage is usually scented. Marigolds are sensitive to ethylene.

QUALITY CRITERIA Select cut flowers that are 75% to fully open. Make sure leaves of cut stems and pots are free of yellow spots (iron toxicity) as well as diseases and damage in general. Reddish foliage is often the result of production temperatures that were too low. Select compact plants.

CARE & HANDLING Recut stems and place in a preservative with a bactericide. Store flowers at 4°C (39°F). Display pots in bright light or even full sunlight (if temperatures are moderate). High temperatures cause undesired stretching of plants.

Tagetes erecta L.   family: Asteraceae

grote Afrikaantje (Dutch); *oeillet d'Inde, tagète* (French); *Hohe Studentenblume* (German); *rosa d'India* (Italian); *cempasúchil, flor de muerto* (Spanish)

Tagetes patula
French marigold

Tagetes patula bicolor

Tagetes patula yellow

Tagetes patula orange

DESCRIPTION A bushy annual of about 0.2–0.5 m (8–20″) high with solitary yellow to brown flower heads of up to 50 mm (2″) in diameter. The leaves are pinnately compound and strongly aromatic. Cultivars are mostly bred for the bedding plant industry. Examples include Disco Hybrids (compact, single) and Pretty Joy Hybrids (compact, double, red to pale yellow). Dwarf African marigolds include Lady Hybrids (orange and yellow), Super Star Orange Hybrids (0.4 m, bright orange) and the Nugget Hybrids – a cross between African and French marigolds (0.3 m, fully double, orange or yellow). The striped Mexican marigold (*T. tenuifolia*) has clusters of small heads (25 mm or 1″ in diameter) in a range of colours.

ORIGIN & HISTORY Mexico and Guatemala. Marigolds are old favourite bedding plants and the smaller, more compact types are popular as potted flowers.

PARTS USED Whole plants are used as potted flowers.

CULTIVATION Plants are easily propagated from seeds and for optimal growth requires a well-drained, slightly acidic (pH 6.2–6.5) growth medium. Temperatures of 16–26°C / 13–16°C 61–79°F / 55–61°F day / night are ideal, but growers of potted flowers typically lower the night temperatures to 10°C (50°F) to increase shelf life.

PROPERTIES Flowering can continue for several weeks. Leaves are scented.

QUALITY CRITERIA Select pots of French marigolds with the first or second flower heads open. In the case of African marigolds, the buds can be either still green or just beginning to open. The first flower head of most cultivars is usually smaller than the rest. Select well-formed, compact plants with dark green, undamaged leaves, free from yellow spots or diseases.

CARE & HANDLING Display pots in a cool (10–21°C; 50–70°F) area, as high temperatures cause stretching. Choose a bright area, even full sun, provided temperatures are moderate. Do not over-water pots and allow them to dry out slightly.

Tagetes patula L.   family: Asteraceae

klein afrikaantje (Dutch); *tagète* (French); *Studentenblume* (German); *garofano d'India* (Italian); *clavel de indias, flor de muerto* (Spanish)

Telopea speciosissima
waratah

Telopea speciosissima plant

Telopea speciosissima flower head

DESCRIPTION A woody shrub of up to 3 m (10′) high bearing large rounded flower heads with numerous (usually red) florets of 25 mm (1″) long, surrounded by showy bracts. A few cultivars and hybrids are available as florist flowers, mainly from *T. speciosissima*, *T. oreades* and *T. truncata*. The flower colour is predominantly red, but pink, yellow or white forms are occasionally encountered.

ORIGIN & HISTORY Australia and Tasmania. It is the flower emblem of New South Wales. The "kiwi rose" of New Zealand flower exporters has become a popular cut flower.

PARTS USED Flowering stems are used as cut flowers.

CULTIVATION Waratahs can be successfully grown on a variety of soil types as long as it is well aerated and well drained. Full sun, some fertilisation and correct pruning methods are essential for maximum yields and high quality. Protection against strong wind is important (especially during flowering).

PROPERTIES Vase life is average to good (7–13 days), depending on the cultivar. Flowers are not chill-sensitive but avoid high humidity (botrytis) and heat (flowers may not open). Cool promptly after harvest to 4°C (39°F) and keep at this temperature during transportation to prolong vase life. Cut stems are generally very long (unlike many other Proteaceae). Browning of the flower bracts can be a problem.

QUALITY CRITERIA Look for fully mature flower heads with only 5–10% of individual florets open. Select long, straight stems with large, well-formed heads. Make sure the tips of the bracts are not brown or discoloured. Check that the leaves are free of marks, disease or general damage.

CARE & HANDLING Recut stems, remove leaves below the water line and hydrate in acidified water (pH 3.5). Place in a preservative containing a bactericide and sugar (carbohydrate). Store for 4–5 days at 1–2°C (34–36°F). Flowers are excellent for drying.

Telopea speciosissima (Sm.) R. Br.

family: Proteaceae

waratah (Dutch); *télopéa* (French); *Waratahprotee* (German); *waratah* (Italian, Spanish)

Thalictrum aquilegiifolium

meadow-rue • columbine meadow-rue

Thalictrum aquilegiifolium flowers

DESCRIPTION A clump-forming perennial of up to 1 m (40") high with compound leaves resembling those of *Aquilegia* species. The clustered, fluffy flowers have no petals but brightly coloured stamens (usually pink or purple). More than 20 species have potential as florist flowers and some useful cultivars have been bred. Colours in this species are usually pink or purple but may also be lilac, yellow, orange or white.

ORIGIN & HISTORY Europe and Asia. Several species have become popular garden plants.

PARTS USED Flowering stems are used by florists as filler in bouquets and arrangements.

CULTIVATION Plants are grown from seed or by division of the rootstocks. Germination is significantly improved when the seeds are given a chill treatment for a few weeks. Growers also increase their cultivation areas by lifting and dividing the plants every 2–3 years. Spacing and supporting of stems are important as flowers tend to become badly entangled and are then damaged during harvesting. Production is best from the second year on. Flower quality and yields improve after a period of cold treatment.

PROPERTIES Vase life is poor (3–5 days). Flowers cut too early (in the bud stage) do not open. Flowers tend to shatter very easily and are sensitive to ethylene.

QUALITY CRITERIA Purchase stems with 80–90% of flowers open (avoid when fully open or less than 50% open). Select sturdy, fresh stems with numerous, evenly spaced flowers that are not damaged (or with some broken off).

CARE & HANDLING Recut stems immediately and place in a preservative with an ethylene inhibitor. The poor vase life of meadow-rue can be significantly improved by the use of a floral preservative. Storage is not recommended, but if necessary, first pre-treat and then store for 2–3 days at 3–5°C (37–41°F). Flowers can be air-dried (upright to retain shape) but will lose their colour after a few months.

Thalictrum aquilegiifolium L.   family: Ranunculaceae

akeleibladige ruit (Dutch); *pigamon à feuilles d'ancolie* (French); *Akeleiblättrige Wiesenraute* (German); *pigamo colombino* (Italian)

Thunbergia alata

black-eyed Susan • black-eyed Susan vine

Thunbergia alata 'Suzie' yellow

Thunbergia alata 'Suzie' mixed

DESCRIPTION A perennial twining herb that is grown as an annual. It has heart-shaped leaves and attractive yellow to orange flowers that usually have a purplish brown throat (hence the common name). Cultivars include 'Alba' (white with dark centre), 'Aurantiaca' (orange with dark centre), 'Bakeri' (pure white) and the popular 'Suzie' hybrids.

ORIGIN & HISTORY Tropical Africa. The exact origin is unclear as the plant has been cultivated in Africa since ancient times.

PARTS USED The whole plant is used in window boxes, hanging baskets and trellises. Trailing, leafy branches with or without flowers are sometimes used in floral arrangements.

CULTIVATION When grown as container plants seeds are most often sown directly into the final containers. Growers do not normally pinch plants out, as branching occurs along the main stem. Black-eyed Susan prefers an acidic growing medium (pH 5.5–6.2) and a relatively low soil-salt concentration. Plants are sensitive to frost, but also do not like hot, dry conditions.

PROPERTIES Although a tall climber, it remains small when grown in a container or hanging basket. Indoors, the plant is treated as an annual but flowering continues for many months.

QUALITY CRITERIA Check that all foliage is of a good, uniform, deep green colour and that there are no blemishes, damage or yellowing of leaves. Look for well-branched plants with healthy foliage and many, well-dispersed buds in various stages of opening.

CARE & HANDLING Display plants in bright light but avoid direct sunlight, especially if kept indoors. Ideal temperatures are 16–24°C (61–75°F). Water well but allow the top layer of soil to dry out between waterings. Avoid cold draughts, but allow for good ventilation. Make sure creeping plants are securely supported and trellised. Routinely remove any dead or dying flowers.

Thunbergia alata Bojer

family: Acanthaceae

suzanne met de mooie ogen (Dutch); *suzanne aux-yeux-noirs* (French); *Schwarzäugige Susanne* (German); *susanna dagli occhi neri* (Italian); *susana de los ojos negros, ojo de poeta* (Spanish)

Tillandsia cyanea

pink quill • tillandsia

Tillandsia cyanea plant

Tillandsia cyanea potted flower

DESCRIPTION An epiphytic perennial herb with curved, grass-like leaves and long, paddle-shaped flower clusters. Each cluster comprises numerous overlapping bracts that produce a succession of small pink, violet or blue flowers. Many new hybrids, cultivars and colours (shades of red, pink and purple) are released every year as a result of improved tissue culture techniques.

ORIGIN & HISTORY Ecuador and Peru. The pink quill has become a popular pot plant due to the unusual shape and bright colours of the flower clusters.

PARTS USED Whole plants are used as potted flowers.

CULTIVATION Although most bromeliads are naturally epiphytic, they adapt well to potting mediums. However, some grey-leaved *Tillandsia* species (so-called air plants) do not, and they are mounted onto pieces of wood or fern slabs. *Tillandsia* thrives on good ventilation, high humidity and warm growing conditions. Mature plants are forced to flower using water that contains dissolved ethylene gas.

PROPERTIES The flowering spike and bracts can last for many months. They are fairly sensitive to botrytis. The plant is hardy and tends to thrive under a certain amount of neglect.

QUALITY CRITERIA Select plants with well-formed, long flowering spikes that have only 0–2 of the true flowers open. (Spike length and thickness can vary depending on cultivar.) Choose plants with healthy, light green coloured leaves and brightly coloured flowering spikes, free of damage and marks.

CARE & HANDLING Place the container in maximum natural light away from direct sunlight and draughts. Do not over-water, as it will shorten the life of the plant. The plant performs best if the potting medium is kept on the dry side. Use soft, tepid water and keep the central "vase" of the plant filled. Mist plants occasionally as they do best in a high humidity environment. The temperature requirements are: minimum (16°C; 61°F); maximum (27°C; 81°F).

Tillandsia cyanea Lind. ex K. Koch

family: Bromeliaceae

bromelia (Dutch); *fille de l'air* (French); *tillandsie* (German); *figlie dell'aria* (Italian); *tillandsia* (Spanish)

Trachelium caeruleum
blue throatwort

Trachelium caeruleum 'Dafne'

Trachelium caeruleum 'Helios'

DESCRIPTION A perennial herb with erect stems of up to 1 m (40") high, growing from a somewhat woody base. The lance-shaped leaves have toothed margins. Small, tubular flowers (blue, purple, pink or white) are borne in umbellate clusters. There are a number of cultivars available, but from the florist's point of view there is very little to choose between them. Flowers of white cultivars tend to decline more rapidly than the blue or purple forms, and tend to show petal blackening.

ORIGIN & HISTORY Western and Central Mediterranean region (Europe and North Africa). The name is derived from *"trachelos"* meaning neck, because the plant was once thought to be a cure for diseases of the throat (hence also the common name "throatwort").

PARTS USED Flowering stems are used as cut flowers and whole plants as potted flowers.

CULTIVATION *Trachelium* is grown in greenhouses as well as in open fields. They require rich, well-drained soil. Short days tend to inhibit flowering and the plants flower faster under long days of at least 14 hours light. They perform best at cool growing temperatures of 15–21°C (59–70°F) and do not do well if temperatures fluctuate or increase too much.

PROPERTIES Vase life is average to good (7–10 days). The stage of harvesting affects vase life. Flowers are fairly sensitive to ethylene.

QUALITY CRITERIA Select cut stems with 30–50% of flowers open. Flower clusters that are harvested and sold too early will result in many of the flowers not opening properly. Look for straight, sturdy and well-branched stems with full flowering heads. Ensure that the leaves are damage and disease free and that the colour is a uniform green.

CARE & HANDLING Recut the stems and place them in a sugar-containing preservative. There is no need to use an ethylene inhibitor. The flowers can be stored for a few days at around 2–4°C (36–39°F). Flowers can be air-dried but they tend to lose much of their colour.

Trachelium caeruleum L.

family: Campanulaceae

halskruid (Dutch); *trachélium* (French); *Blaues Halskraut* (German); *traquelio* (Italian); *flor de la viuda* (Spanish)

Trachymene coerulea
blue lace flower • didiscus

Trachymene coerulea white

Trachymene coerulea blue

Trachymene coerulea rose

DESCRIPTION The plant is an annual or biennial herb of about 0.6 m (2') high. The leaves are characteristically divided in three equal parts, each of which is again equally divided in narrow segments. The delicate, white and blue florets are borne in rounded clusters, surrounded by decorative bracts. It is similar in appearance to Queen Anne's Lace. Cultivated forms resemble the original (wild) form of the species and only a few commercial cultivars presently exist. Flower colour includes pure white, blue, pale pink and bright pink.

ORIGIN & HISTORY Western Australia. The name is derived from the Greek *trachys* (rough) and *meninx* (membrane), in reference to the rough fruit surface. The plant has become a popular cultivated ornamental.

PARTS USED The flower heads are used as cut flowers or fillers in bouquets and arrangements.

CULTIVATION Production is primarily by means of seed, which can be sown directly in the required spot or the seedlings can be transplanted. Plants do best in well-cultivated, well-drained soils and a full sun to partial shade environment. Plants self-seed easily and naturally flower from midsummer to autumn.

PROPERTIES Vase life is average to usually good (7–10 days). Flowers are sensitive to ethylene. Leaves and stems are sticky to the touch.

QUALITY CRITERIA Select fairly closed flower umbels (heads) that are only 25–30% open. Look for well-branched, sturdy stems with many full flowering heads. Check that the flowers, stems and small leaves are free of any blemishes or damage.

CARE & HANDLING Remove all foliage that will be below the water line. Hydrate in a solution of warm, acidified (pH 3–3.5) water and then treat with a commercial floral preservative (preferably one that contains an ethylene inhibitor). Hydrate for at least two hours before storage or usage. Store the flowers at 2–3°C (36–37°F) and a high relative humidity (90–95%).

Trachymene coerulea Graham (=*Didiscus caeruleus*) family: Apiaceae (Umbelliferae)

blauwe kantbloem (Dutch); *trachymène bleu* (French); *Blaudolde, Blaue Raudolde* (German); *trachymene, didiscus* (Italian, Spanish)

353

Tricyrtis hirta
Japanese toad lily

Tricyrtis hirta

Tricyrtis hirta flowers

Tricyrtis hirta leaves

DESCRIPTION A perennial herb with clusters of longitudinally folded (plicate) leaves arising from creeping rhizomes. The flowering stems are up to 0.6 m (2′) high and characteristically densely hairy. Each axil bears up to three star-shaped flowers of about 25 mm (1″) in diameter that are white with large purple spots. There are several cultivars that differ mainly in flower colour: 'Miyazaki' (white spotted with lilac), 'Miyazaki Gold' (similar but leaves are gold-edged), 'Alba' (white with a green tinge), 'White Towers' (white) and 'Lilac Towers' (lilac). Cultivars of the Taiwanese *T. formosana* and the Chinese *T. macropoda* (sometimes grown as *T. hirta*) are also available.

ORIGIN & HISTORY Japan. Toad lilies are very popular in Asian countries and are slowly gaining in popularity in other parts of the world.

PARTS USED The flowering stems are used as cut flowers or fillers.

CULTIVATION Plants prefer a sandy loam soil that is well drained and slightly acidic. Correct watering is important and soils need to remain moist during cultivation but not waterlogged. Best quality flowers are achieved in semi-shade to full shade. Full sun and high temperatures can result in damage to leaves and flower buds and poor quality in general.

PROPERTIES Vase life is average to good (6–9 days). Flowers are sensitive to ethylene and are said to be poisonous when ingested.

QUALITY CRITERIA Look for straight, sturdy stems with large buds showing colour but still closed. Make sure leaves have a uniform colour and are free of burnt (brown) tips or edges. Buds must be free of any marks, spots or blemishes.

CARE & HANDLING Recut and hydrate stems in an acidic (pH 3–3.5) solution for 2–3 hours prior to use or storage. Hold or store flowers in a floral preservative. Flowers can be stored for 5–7 days at 0–2°C (32–36°F) and 90–95% relative humidity.

Tricyrtis hirta (Thunb.) Hook.   family: Liliaceae (Tricyrtidaceae)

paddenlelie (Dutch); *lis des crapauds* (French); *Borstige Krötenlilie* (German); *hototogisu* (Japanese)

Triteleia laxa

grassnut • triplet lily • brodiaea

Triteleia laxa plant

Triteleia laxa flowers

DESCRIPTION A perennial herb with one or two narrow, strap-shaped leaves growing from an underground corm. The long-stalked flowers are usually violet-blue and are borne on a stem of 0.75 m (30″) high. There are only a few species and cultivars used as cut flowers. 'Queen Fabiola' (derived from *T. laxa*) has several large, pale violet blue flowers. A hybrid between *T. laxa* and *T. peduncularis* (known as *T. ×tubergenii*) produces beautiful dark blue flowers.

ORIGIN & HISTORY North America. The species most used as florist flowers, were previously classified in the genus *Brodiaea*, and are still commonly known as brodiaea. Brodiaeas are not so often seen in florist's shops. One of the reasons is that agapanthus offers basically the same colour and flower shape, but with much more impressive flowering heads.

PARTS USED Leafless flowering stems are used as cut flowers.

CULTIVATION Production is normally by means of mature corms. Growing from seed requires two years to maturity, plus a third year to produce a saleable florist flower. Flowers are grown in greenhouses as well as in open fields. Growth is affected by soil temperature and although plants prefer sunny production areas, photoperiod (day length) has little effect on flower initiation. Good drainage is essential.

PROPERTIES Vase life is average to good (7–10 days). Colours are more intense when grown under cool conditions. Flowers are not scented.

QUALITY CRITERIA Select stems with 25–50% of florets showing full colour and a few open or opening. Do not purchase stems with all the flowers still in tight, green bud. Look for sturdy, straight stems of a uniform green colour and no soft spots.

CARE & HANDLING Recut stems and place in a sugar and anti-ethylene containing preservative. Cut stems can be stored for a number of days at 3–5°C (37–41°F). Flowers do not dry well.

Triteleia laxa Benth. (=*Brodiaea laxa*)   family: Asparagaceae (Alliaceae)

brodiaea (Dutch); *triteleia* (French); *Blaue Triteleie, Brodiaea* (German); *fabiola* (Italian)

Triticum spelta

spelt • spelt wheat

Triticum spelta

Triticum aestivum

DESCRIPTION The plant is a clump-forming annual grass with robust but narrow leaves and graceful flowering ears borne at a height of about 1.5 m (5'). There are several cultivars but these are really of more interest to farmers than florists.

ORIGIN & HISTORY The exact origin is unknown. It was already widely grown in the Near East, Europe and the Balkans during the Bronze Age (4000–1000 BC). Spelt wheats are ancient cultivars and, along with other wheat types such as einkorn and emmer, are the ancestors of modern bread wheat (*T. aestivum*). Spelt is making a comeback as human food in the health food industry. The ears of both bread wheat and spelt have always been popular as cut "flowers", as they symbolise prosperity and abundance.

PARTS USED The flowering spikes or "ears" are used as cut foliage or filler. Both fresh (green) and dried (brown) spikes are used.

CULTIVATION Propagation is by means of seed that is sown direct. Plants prefer full sun with cool temperatures. Soils need to be well drained and plants require good, frequent watering. Once seed has set, watering is halted to allow stems to dry out.

PROPERTIES Vase life of fresh stems is usually good (10–14 days) depending on quality and handling. Stems are not ethylene sensitive and do not have a strong fragrance.

QUALITY CRITERIA There are no real quality criteria. However, look for long, straight, sturdy stems with well-formed, full spikes (ears). Check that the ears are free of disease, blemishes and general damage. Rather purchase stems that have dried on the land than to try drying them afterwards.

CARE & HANDLING There is no need to recut stems and no need for preservatives. Simply store the stems upright in a cool area. Handle dried stems with care, as flower spikes (ears) tend to be slightly brittle. Store or hold in a dry place to avoid disease and rotting.

Triticum spelta L. (=*T. aestivum* subsp. *spelta*)   family: Poaceae

dinkeltarwe, spelt (Dutch); *épeautre* (French); *Dinkel, Spelz* (German); *spelta* (Italian); *superuto komugi* (Japanese); *espelta, spelta* (Spanish)

Tritonia crocata

tritonia • flame freesia • garden montbretia

Tritonia crocata mixed

DESCRIPTION The plant bears a fan of sword-shaped leaves arising from a corm below the ground. Flowering stems of 0.2–0.5 m (8–20") high emerge in spring to early summer. The flowers are cup-shaped, bright orange to reddish or pinkish orange, with the lower three lobes marked with a yellow stripe in the middle. There are several colour forms in cultivation and a number of hybrids and cultivars, although not many are well known named cultivars. The modern, hybrid garden tritonias resemble freesias. Colours range from orange to salmon and from cream to white. At least 16 species are regularly grown in gardens.

ORIGIN & HISTORY Southern Africa. *Tritonia* is closely related to *Crocosmia* (falling stars) and is sometimes confused with it. Both have become popular garden plants.

PARTS USED Whole plants are used as potted flowers or the flowering stems as cut flowers or fillers.

CULTIVATION Propagation is by means of corms and plants prefer well-drained, light soils. Cultivation is best under full sun conditions and moderate to cool temperatures, although the plants need some protection in areas of severe frost (especially for the new, young foliage).

PROPERTIES Vase life of flowers is average (6–8 days). Flowers are sensitive to ethylene and are not strongly scented.

QUALITY CRITERIA Select stems with only 1–3 flowers open or opening and the rest of the buds showing colour. Stems tend to be slender so check that selected ones are sturdy enough and none are broken. Flower spikes need to be of good length and leaves free of burnt or dry tips and buds free of any damage or blemishes.

CARE & HANDLING Recut the stems and place them in a floral preservative. Display in a bright, cool area. Preferably use as soon as possible. Store only if necessary for a few days (3–5) at 1–2°C (34–36°F) and a 90% relative humidity.

Tritonia crocata (L.) Ker-Gawl.   family: Iridaceae

tritonia (Dutch, French); *Safranfarbige Tritonie* (German); *tritonia* (Italian); *tritonia, tritomes* (Spanish)

Trollius europaeus

globeflower • European globe flower

Trollius europaeus flower

Trollius europaeus plants

DESCRIPTION A perennial herb with thick, fibrous roots and flowering stalks of 0.8 m (32″) high. The lobes are markedly lobed and occur mainly in a basal rosette. The ball-shaped flowers are up to 50 mm (2″) in diameter and lemon yellow. Large-flowered cultivars of *T. europaeus* include 'Giganteus', 'Grandiflorus' and 'Loddigesii'. There are many cultivars of *T. ×cultorum*, including 'Fire Globe' (dark orange), 'Lemon Queen' (pale yellow) and 'Pritchard's Giant' (golden orange).

ORIGIN & HISTORY Europe, Asia and North America. The common globeflower is one of several species that are cultivated as garden flowers and cut flowers. These include *T. asiaticus* (widespread in Asia) and *T. chinensis* (from Russia and China). A hybrid between these two species and *T. europaeus* is known as *T. ×cultorum*. This garden hybrid has long flowering stems of up to 1 m (40″) long.

PARTS USED Flowering stems are used as cut flowers or whole plants as potted flowers.

CULTIVATION Globeflowers prefer partial shade to full sun, provided temperatures are cool to moderate. Well-drained, rich and loamy soils are required and need to be kept moist during cultivation. Plants take longer to flower under cool temperatures but stem strength and flower size are better.

PROPERTIES Vase life is poor to sometimes average (5–8 days). Flowers are sensitive to ethylene. Parts of the plant are poisonous if ingested.

QUALITY CRITERIA Select straight, sturdy stems, with large, well-formed flowers. Flowers should be closed, but fully mature with petals just starting to loosen. Check that stems have no soft spots and that buds are free of any blemishes or damage.

CARE & HANDLING Recut the stems and hydrate them for a few hours at room temperature before using or storing. Place in a floral preservative with an ethylene-inhibitor and a bactericide. Flowers can be stored for a few days at 1–2°C (34–36°F) and 90–95% relative humidity.

Trollius europaeus L.   family: Ranunculaceae

kogelbloem (Dutch); *trolle d'Europe, boule d'or* (French); *Europäische Trollblume* (German); *botton d'oro* (Italian); *calderones, flor de san pallari* (Spanish)

Tropaeolum majus
garden nasturtium • Indian cress

Tropaeolum majus

DESCRIPTION An annual creeper with soft fleshy stems and hairless, umbrella-shaped leaves. The large, bell-shaped flowers each have a characteristic long, nectar-bearing spur. They vary from pale yellow to orange or dark red and may be single, semi-double or double, depending on the hybrid or cultivar. Pot culture cultivars include 'Empress of India' (dwarf, bright red flowers) 'Dwarf Cherry Rose' (semi-double, pink), 'Hermine Grashoff' (double, orange-red) and 'Nanum' (dwarf and compact with variously coloured, small flowers).

ORIGIN & HISTORY A cultigen from Colombia, Ecuador and Peru. Garden nasturtium is thought to be a hybrid between *T. minus* and *T. ferreyae*. It was introduced into Europe from Peru in 1684. The nasturtium symbolises patriotism in the language of flowers. The flowers, leaves and seeds are edible and have a sharp taste due to the presence of mustard oils.

PARTS USED The whole plant is used as potted flower.

CULTIVATION Cultivation is easy from seed grown in full sun in moist, fertile soil. Regular feeding improves quality but over-fertilisation results in masses of leaves with very few flowers. Growers often spray plants with chemicals to control height.

PROPERTIES Flowering continues for many weeks. The flowers do not have a distinctive fragrance and are not ethylene sensitive.

QUALITY CRITERIA Check that the leaves are free of black spots (often due to iron toxicity), yellowing and other blemishes. Select compact plants full of buds and about 25% of flowers opening or open. Avoid large, leafy plants with few flowers or tall spindly plants.

CARE & HANDLING Unpack and check plants on arrival. Remove any dead or dying leaves and flowers. Water well if potting medium is dry. Display in a bright and cool to warm area. Allow soil to dry out slightly on the surface between waterings.

Tropaeolum majus L.　　　　　　　　　　family: Tropaeolaceae

oostindische kers (Dutch); *capucine* (French); *Kapuzinerkresse* (German); *nasturzio, cappuccina, tropeolo* (Italian); *capuchina* (Spanish)

Tulbaghia violacea
wild garlic

Tulbaghia violacea flowers

Tulbaghia violacea plants

Tulbaghia simmleri

DESCRIPTION A clump-forming perennial herb with numerous narrow bulbs bearing slender, strap-shaped leaves. All parts of the plant smell strongly of garlic. The flowering stalks are up to 0.6 m (24″) high and end in an umbel of bright lilac to purple (rarely white) flowers. A few cultivars have been developed, including 'Silver Lace' (with large flowers) and 'Variegata' (leaves with cream-coloured stripes). Other species commonly cultivated include sweet garlic or so-called pink agapanthus (*T. fragrans*) and Simmler's wild garlic (*T. simmleri*).

ORIGIN & HISTORY South Africa. Wild garlic is an old favourite garden plant that is very hardy and drought tolerant, requiring minimal care.

PARTS USED Flowering stems are used as cut flowers or fillers.

CULTIVATION Propagation is mainly from bulbs or seed. Clumps of bulbs are lifted, divided and replanted every few years. Although plants will do best in well aerated, rich soils they grow with ease in most soils, provided they are well drained. Plants prefer full sun and moderate temperatures but they are extremely frost hardy.

PROPERTIES Vase life is average (6–8 days). Flowers are sweetly scented and do not have an overpowering garlic smell as might be expected. They are not sensitive to ethylene.

QUALITY CRITERIA Select stems with mainly closed florets, but all the buds showing good colour. Make sure that the stems are straight, long and sturdy and have a well-shaped, compact flowering head full of buds. Stems and buds must be free of any marks, soft spots or blemishes.

CARE & HANDLING Recut stems and place in a bactericide or floral preservative containing a low percentage sugar, to assist in bud-opening. Display flowers in a bright, cool location. Flowers can be stored for 7 days at 4°C (39°F) and 95% relative humidity. Storing at lower temperatures will improve vase life but may result in red-tinted florets.

Tulbaghia violacea Harv.   family: Alliaceae

wilde knoflook (Dutch); *tulbaghia* (French); *Knoblauchs-Kaplilie, Tulbaghie* (German); *tulbaghia* (Italian, Spanish)

Tulipa cultivars
tulip

Tulipa orange (goblet type)

Tulipa pink (parrot type)

DESCRIPTION A true bulb that is deciduous, winter growing and summer dormant. Most tulips produce a single, 6-petalled flower. There are thousands of cultivars and hybrids. Parrot tulips have broken, serrated incurved blooms, while lily-flowered types have pointed petals that curve outwards. Some have double flowers but the most common tulip is the waxy, goblet-shaped, single flower.

ORIGIN & HISTORY Middle East. A long period of cultivation and breeding occurred in Iran and Turkey before introduction into Europe in the 16th century. Nowadays, nearly all hybrid flower bulbs come from Holland.

PARTS USED Flowers: cut flowers; whole plants: potted flowers.

CULTIVATION Most tulips require a cold climate and a warm-cool-warm sequence. Commercial growers purchase treated bulbs and grow them as annuals. Optimum greenhouse temperatures are 17–20°C (63–68°F) – temperatures above 20°C (68°F) may result in flower abortion and/or flower topple. Retardants are used to reduce the height (stem length) of potted tulips.

PROPERTIES Vase life is average (1–3 days in opening stages and a further 5–7 days once open). Flowers are not sensitive to ethylene. Stems continue to elongate after harvesting.

QUALITY CRITERIA Choose flowers with closed buds showing half to full colour. Purchase potted flowers with the first flower still in the "green-bud" stage.

CARE & HANDLING Recut stems and place in a germicide-containing hydration solution. Avoid sugar or else flowers will open too fast (blow). Do not store or display tulips in the same container as daffodils (their sap is toxic to cut tulips). Keep stems upright and in good lighting as flowers bend towards the light. Bent flowers can be straightened by wrapping in wet paper and standing them in water directly under lights. Display pots in the coolest possible area and keep moist, not wet. Flowers and pots can be stored at 0–2°C (32–36°F) to maintain flower life.

Tulipa cultivars

family: Liliaceae

tulp (Dutch); *tulipe* (French); *Tulpe* (German); *tulipano* (Italian); *tulipán* (Spanish)

Tweedia caerulea

tweedia

Tweedia caerulea flowers

DESCRIPTION A sparse, twining perennial with heart-shaped leaves borne on slender stems that exude milky latex. The star-shaped flowers of 25 mm (1") in diameter are heavenly blue when they open but become lilac when faded. Only a few cultivars are available and some have darker blue flowers than the original species. An example is 'Heavenborn' which has deep blue flowers.

ORIGIN & HISTORY Brazil and Uruguay. The genus *Tweedia* is named after James Tweedie (1775–1862) who was head gardener at the Royal Botanic Garden in Edinburgh, Scotland. He later lived in Buenos Aires, Argentina and routinely collected plants right across South America and sent them back to Scotland.

PARTS USED Leafy flowering stems are used as cut flowers or fillers.

CULTIVATION Best quality and yields are achieved within a temperature range of 18–24°C (65–75°F). Growth slows below 15°C (60°F), while flower abortion, spindly stems and poor colour results from high temperatures (>30°C; >86°F). Flower stems naturally tend to be a bit short. Cultivation under low percentage shade cloth helps to increase stem length, although too much shade causes stems to be thin and lanky.

PROPERTIES Vase life is below average to slightly above (5–9 days). Stems exude a milky sap when cut. The fragrance of the foliage can be unpleasant.

QUALITY CRITERIA Select stems with at least 6 individual groups (cymes) of flowers per cut stem. Ensure that only 1–3 of the cymes have open flowers and the rest closed but all showing colour. Check to see that no flowers have been damaged or broken off during handling and that leaves have a uniform colour.

CARE & HANDLING Recut the stems and hydrate them for 2–3 hours at room temperature in a hydrating solution or preservative before using. It is best to keep tweedia separate from other flowers as the cut stems exude a milky sap. Store the stems at 2–4°C (36–39°F) and 95% relative humidity.

Tweedia caerulea D. Don (=*Oxypetalum caeruleum*) family: Apocynaceae (Asclepiadaceae)

tweedia (Dutch); *tweedia, étoile du sud* (French); *Tweedia* (German); *tweedia* (Italian, Spanish)

Typha angustifolia
bulrush • lesser bulrush • narrow-leaved reed mace • narrow leaf cattail

Typha plants

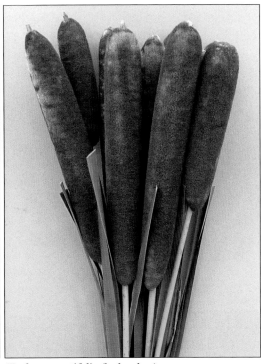

Typha angustifolia (bulrushes)

DESCRIPTION A robust, grass-like, perennial herb (up to 2 m or 6½' high) with narrow, strap-shaped leaves that are firm in texture. The characteristic flowering stems are shorter than the leaves and bear numerous florets in a velvety, club-shaped spike. Male and female florets are separated (male above, female below). There are no well-known cultivars – the original species are used in various parts of the world.

ORIGIN & HISTORY Northern hemisphere (America, Europe, North Africa, North and Central Asia). The starch-rich rhizomes are used all over the world as an emergency food. Pollen is produced in large quantities and is eaten as a food or, in ancient China, added to honey to make a sweetmeat. Some species have medicinal uses. The plush of the female flowers is used as stuffing for pillows, while the leaves are traditionally used for weaving mats and chair seats (natural "rush"). Fresh or dried flowering stalks with their distinctive shape have long been a component of flower arrangements.

PARTS USED The fresh or dried flowering stems are used as fillers, especially in large arrangements. The long leaves are used as cut greens and fillers.

CULTIVATION Stems are usually wild-harvested and found almost anywhere soil remains saturated or flooded. Plants grow on a variety of soil types – pure sand, peat, clay and loamy soils.

PROPERTIES Stems last very well. Mature flower spikes shatter (fall apart) easily. They are not ethylene sensitive.

QUALITY CRITERIA Select long, straight and sturdy stems with well-formed, mature flower spikes. Check carefully to ensure that flowering heads are not damaged or falling apart and that stems are free of soft spots. Check that leaves and stems are free of disease and pests.

CARE & HANDLING Handle with care as the flowering spikes can fall apart easily. Preferably spray the spikes with a fixative to prevent breaking apart and spreading fluff. Display or store dry at low humidity with good ventilation. Stems dry well.

Typha angustifolia L.   family: Typhaceae

kleine lisdodde (Dutch); *massette à feuilles étroites* (French); *Schmalblättriger Rohrkolben* (German); *tifa, tifa a foglie strette* (Italian); *espadaña* (Spanish)

Ulex europaeus
gorse • furze • whin

Ulex europaeus

DESCRIPTION A dense, spiny shrub (up to 2 m or 6½') with leaves modified to form thorns of about 12 mm (½") long. Normal (trifoliate) leaves occur on seedlings only. Flowers are solitary or borne in small clusters throughout the year. They are bright yellow and pea-like, with red marks at the base. A few cultivars are available, including 'Strictus' (dense, erect), 'Flore Pleno' or 'Plenus' (with double flowers) and 'Aureus' (with the stem golden yellow).

ORIGIN & HISTORY Western Europe. Gorse is a common plant of Atlantic Europe where it is adapted to regular fires. It has become naturalised in other parts of the world, notably Scandinavia, East Europe, the United States and New Zealand. The plant has become an invasive weed in some of these regions.

PARTS USED The straight, green foliage is used as cut foliage or filler in bouquets and arrangements.

CULTIVATION *Ulex* is usually wild-harvested. It thrives in poor, dry acid soils and sunny conditions. Plants are often grown as a hedge and can thus be pruned back hard to continually produce slender, young stems. They do not like dense shade, waterlogged or chalky soils.

PROPERTIES Vase life is poor to average (5–7 days). The flowers are fragrant, with a distinct coconut smell. Stems are prone to premature wilting and poor water uptake.

QUALITY CRITERIA Stems should have a bright green colour and not be pale or yellowish (except when it is obviously a golden colour form). Make sure foliage tips are not limp, dry or dead (often due to being out of water for too long).

CARE & HANDLING On arrival immediately recut stems and hydrate for at least 2–3 hours in a hydrating solution or floral preservative at room temperature. Use promptly as storage is not recommended. Stems can be held at low temperatures and high humidity (1–2°C; 34–36°F and 95% relative humidity).

Ulex europaeus L.   family: Fabaceae

gaspeldoorn (Dutch); *ajonc* (French); *Stechginster* (German); *ginestrone* (Italian); *tojo* (Spanish)

Vaccinium ovatum

huckleberry • Californian huckleberry • shot huckleberry

Vaccinium ovatum leaves and berries

DESCRIPTION A deciduous shrub of 1–4 m high and wide. It has small oval leaves of 12–25 mm (½–1") long that are toothed along the margins, sparingly hairy on the upper surfaces and more densely so on the lower surface, especially along the midrib. The small, bell-shaped flowers are 6 mm (¼") long, with white petals that are flushed red. The fruits are small black berries that are edible but have a sour taste. There are no well-known, named cultivars of *V. ovatum* but numerous cultivars of mixed or uncertain origin that are commonly seen in gardens. Florists commonly use two types – green huckleberry or red huckleberry (red-tinged leaves on red stems).

ORIGIN & HISTORY North America (British Columbia to California). The plant is one of a large number of *Vaccinium* species that are grown as garden plants and as sources of edible berries (variously known as huckleberries, cranberries,

blueberries, cowberries, foxberries, deerberries or bilberries, depending on the species).

PARTS USED Leafy stems are used as cut foliage or the fruited stems as decorative filler.

CULTIVATION Huckleberry foliage is most often wild-harvested. The plants grow well in full sun and partial shade and usually prefer well-drained, sandy soils that are acidic.

PROPERTIES Vase life is usually good to very good (10–20 days). It is not sensitive to ethylene.

QUALITY CRITERIA Select stems with a dense and even distribution of leaves along the stem. Ensure the leaves are dark green, clean and free of damage or marks. Preferably purchase young, fresh stems that are not too woody.

CARE & HANDLING Unpack the foliage as soon as possible. Recut stems by at least 30–50 mm (1–2") and place in water with a bactericide. Foliage can be stored for 1–2 weeks at 0–2°C (32–36°F). Cover with wet paper or put in plastic film to maintain a high humidity.

Vaccinium ovatum Pursh.   family: Ericaceae

blauwe bes (Dutch); *airelle à feuilles ovées* (French); *Kalifornische Heidelbeere* (German); *arándano* (Spanish)

Vanda coerulea

vanda orchid • blue vanda

Vanda coerulea plants

Vanda coerulea flowers

DESCRIPTION This orchid is a so-called monopodial species that grows upwards from a single, usually unbranched stem. Pseudobulbs are absent. Flowering stalks with 10–30 flowers and strap-shaped, leathery leaves are produced along the same stem. The flowers are usually bluish-lavender or nearly white. There are 50 species but breeding and hybridisation focus on *V. coerulea* (the origin of all so-called "blue" hybrids) and *V. sanderiana* (the origin of the large, rounded flower shape and pink or brownish flower colours). Famous cultivar names include 'Rothchildiana' (a primary hybrid between the two species) and 'Bangkok Pink' (with pinkish purple spotted flowers).

ORIGIN & HISTORY India to China (*V. coerulea*). The vanda orchid is the national flower emblem of Singapore and the basis of a large cut flower industry in Thailand and Singapore.

PARTS USED Flowering stems: cut flowers; whole plant: potted flower.

CULTIVATION Plants are propagated from cuttings (with at least three roots attached). They are grown in wooden baskets or pots and require bright, humid (70–80%) and warm conditions. Plants grow and flower throughout the year and don't have a rest period. Temperature fluctuation is necessary to initiate flowering.

PROPERTIES Plants can bloom for 1–3 months, with individual flowers lasting 2–3 weeks. The fragrant flowers do not last as long as cut flowers and are sensitive to ethylene.

QUALITY CRITERIA Plants should have bright, medium green, firm leaves – not dark green, yellowish, reddish or with any marks or damage. Check that no buds have dropped off.

CARE & HANDLING Cut flowers can be stored for up to 5 days at 13°C (55°F) and 90–95% relative humidity. Display flowers in a bright place but not in direct sunlight. Make sure there is good ventilation, but avoid draughts. Water plants daily with tepid water, especially during the warm summer months and keep the potting medium moist.

Vanda coerulea Griff. ex Lindl.

family: Orchidaceae

blauwe vanda (Dutch); *vanda* (French); *Vanda* (German); *vanda-orchidee* (Italian); *vanda orquidea* (Spanish)

Verbascum chaixii
mullein • nettle-leaved mullein

Verbascum chaixii 'Southern Charm'

Verbascum hybrid cultivar

DESCRIPTION A perennial with large, hairy leaves in a basal rosette and erect flowering stems of 1 m (40") high. The flowers are up to 25 mm (1") in diameter and are borne small groups along the stalk. They are yellow with decorative violet-purple hairs on the stamens. A few cultivars have been developed, including 'Album' (white with mauve eyes), 'Neele's Beauty' (creamy-white with purplish-blue centre) and 'Vernale' (tall, yellow). Flowers of hybrids such as *V.* ×*hybrida* and their cultivars may be salmon, lavender and rose.

ORIGIN & HISTORY Europe. At least 30 species are regularly cultivated in gardens and the plants are notoriously difficult to identify. Dried flower spikes were once used as lamp wicks.

PARTS USED The flowering spikes are used as cut flowers or fillers in arrangements and the seed pods in decorative work and arrangements.

CULTIVATION Propagation is mainly from seed (or root cuttings in the case of the sterile hybrids). Plants tolerate a wide range of soil types and growing conditions, but not wet or waterlogged soils. Full sun to partial shade is also necessary and plants require long days to flower. Harvesting of stems encourages further blooming of plants.

PROPERTIES Vase life of flowers is average (6–8 days). They are fairly sensitive to ethylene. Flowers open randomly along the flowering spike.

QUALITY CRITERIA Look for long, straight, sturdy stems with well-formed, compact and full flowering spikes. Flowering stems must be free of any marks, blemishes and disease. Select stems with a few flowers open or opening and numerous buds showing good colour.

CARE & HANDLING Recut stems and hydrate for 2–3 hours at room temperature before using. Remove leaves below the water line. Place in a floral preservative and display in a cool, bright area. Flowers can be stored for 4–5 days at 2°C (36°F) and 90% relative humidity.

Verbascum chaixii Vill.   family: Scrophulariaceae

toorts (Dutch); *molène de Chaix* (French); *Chaix-Königskerze* (German); *verbasco di chaix* (Italian); *verbasco* (Spanish)

Verbena bonariensis

tall verbena • purple top • South American vervain

Verbena bonariensis flowers

Verbena bonariensis flowers

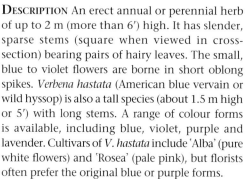

Verbena bonariensis plants

DESCRIPTION An erect annual or perennial herb of up to 2 m (more than 6′) high. It has slender, sparse stems (square when viewed in cross-section) bearing pairs of hairy leaves. The small, blue to violet flowers are borne in short oblong spikes. *Verbena hastata* (American blue vervain or wild hyssop) is also a tall species (about 1.5 m high or 5′) with long stems. A range of colour forms is available, including blue, violet, purple and lavender. Cultivars of *V. hastata* include 'Alba' (pure white flowers) and 'Rosea' (pale pink), but florists often prefer the original blue or purple forms.

ORIGIN & HISTORY Brazil and Argentina (naturalised in the United States, West Indies, Australia and South Africa). The two tall species are used as fillers but florist verbena (*V. ×hybrida*) is a lax, trailing plant grown as border plant and potted flower. The name *bonariensis* refers to Buenos Aires (Argentina).

PARTS USED Flowering stems are used as a filler.

CULTIVATION *Verbena bonariensis* and *V. hastata* are exceptionally easy to cultivate and thrive under almost any conditions, as long as the soil is well drained. The plants can be grown as perennials but the crowns should then be protected from frost.

PROPERTIES Vase life is average (6–8 days). The flowers are not ethylene sensitive but they are susceptible to powdery mildew. Some cultivars are fragrant. Flowers have a tendency to shatter.

QUALITY CRITERIA Cut stems should have healthy green foliage with no signs of yellowing or powdery mildew. Select sturdy stems full of flowers. A third to half the flowers should be open.

CARE & HANDLING Cut stems, hydrate for several hours and place in a floral preservative. Stems tangle and flowers fall off easily, so handle with care. Shake gently upside down to loosen and remove dropped flowers just prior to use. Store at 2–4°C (36–39°F).

Verbena bonariensis L.   family: Verbenaceae

ijzerhard (Dutch); *verveine* (French); *Eisenkraut, Verbene* (German); *verbena* (Italian); *hierba santa* (Spanish)

Verbena hybrida

florist verbena • common garden verbena

Verbena ×hybrida pink

Verbena ×hybrida blue

Verbena ×hybrida red

DESCRIPTION A hairy perennial usually grown as an annual. It is variable in growth form but usually has spreading and trailing stems of up to 1 m (40") high and wide. The leaves are coarsely hairy and toothed. The tubular florets are borne in oblong or more usually flat-topped clusters, in almost any colour and typically have a white or yellow "eye". Tall cultivars are suitable as florist fillers and the more popular creeping and cascading cultivars as potted flowers and hanging baskets. Modern cultivars have high germination percentages, greater uniformity and a wide range of clear colours, including red, pink, white and blue.

ORIGIN & HISTORY Garden origin. The florist verbena is a complex hybrid thought to be derived from *V. incisa*, *V. peruviana*, *V. phlogiflora* and *V. teucroides*. It is widely grown as border plant and has become very popular as a potted flower.

PARTS USED Whole plant: potted flower or hanging basket. Tall types are used as cut flowers and fillers.

CULTIVATION Verbenas prefer cool temperatures and bright light. Plants are sensitive to over- and under-watering, and both result in damage to roots and leaves. When cultivated for hanging baskets, plants are routinely pinched to improve branching and shape. The amount of accumulated light energy, not day length, initiates flowering.

PROPERTIES Plants are fairly sensitive to powdery mildew (new cultivars less so). The flowers are fragrant.

QUALITY CRITERIA Avoid potted flowers or baskets with excessive vegetative growth and lack of buds. Especially check that the leaves are a healthy green colour with no yellowing or burnt edges and especially no signs of powdery mildew.

CARE & HANDLING Display pots or baskets in bright light, cool temperatures and limit exposure to direct sunlight. Keep containers moist but not too wet. Maintain good ventilation and avoid high humidity.

Verbena ×hybrida Groenl. & Ruempl.

family: Verbenaceae

ijzerhard (Dutch); *verveine* (French); *Eisenkraut, Verbene* (German); *verbena* (Italian, Spanish)

Veronica longifolia

speedwell • garden speedwell

Veronica longifolia blue

Veronica longifolia pink

DESCRIPTION A perennial herb (0.4–1.2 m or 16" to 4' high) with branched clusters of small flowers that are usually pale blue to lilac but sometimes purple or white. Garden speedwell and its cultivars are most suitable for the florist trade. Spiked speedwell (*V. spicata*) has a broader range of colours but the short stems are problematic. The big draw card of speedwell as a florist item is of course its blue flowers. Various other hybrids and cultivars are available in the garden and landscaping industries.

ORIGIN & HISTORY Europe (naturalised in the United States). Speedwell is an old favourite garden plant and cut flower.

PARTS USED Flowers: cut flowers. Whole plant: potted flowers.

CULTIVATION Veronicas prefer cool temperatures of 15/21°C (59/70°F) night/day, and well-drained, loose soil. Heavy soils are acceptable if the drainage is good. Irrigation is important – long periods of drying between irrigation lead to poor

yields and flower quality. Plants produce larger yields in the second year of production.

PROPERTIES Vase life is poor to average (5–7 days). Veronicas are quite susceptible to powdery mildew and botrytis. Flowers are sensitive to ethylene. A problem with cut stems is that the bottom flowers open and deteriorate before the top ones have even opened.

QUALITY CRITERIA Purchase cut stems with no more than 30–50% of the florets open. Make sure the leaves are turgid and not soft or limp. Select stems that are free of any sign of disease or damage. Especially check the leaves for powdery mildew and the flowers for botrytis.

CARE & HANDLING Recut stems and immediately place in a preservative containing a bactericide and an anti-ethylene agent. Bacteria build-up in the vase can prevent water uptake. Storage of cut stems is not recommended. If absolutely necessary, store for only 1–2 days at 3–5°C (37–41°F). Flowers do not dry well.

Veronica longifolia L. (=*Pseudolysimachion longifolium*)   family: Plantaginaceae (Scrophulariaceae)

langbladige ereprijs (Dutch); *véronique à longues feuilles* (French); *Blauweiderich, Langblättriger Ehrenpreis* (German); *veronica* (Italian, Spanish)

Veronicastrum virginicum
culver's root

Veronicastrum virginicum plant

Veronicastrum virginicum flowers

DESCRIPTION A perennial herb reaching approximately 1.2–1.8 m (4–6') in height, with slender stems and lance-shaped, serrated leaves arranged in groups of five at each node. Flowers are tubular, purple-blue or white in colour, borne in dense spikes and naturally bloom in summer. The purplish-blue original colour form of the species is commonly cultivated and is still popular. Well-known cultivars grown as florist flowers include 'Album' (pure white) and 'Roseum' (pale pink).

ORIGIN & HISTORY Eastern parts of the United States. *Veronicastrum* means "resembling veronica" and it is indeed closely related. There is only one species. Culver's root is a traditional medicine but is now grown commercially as an ornamental plant.

PARTS USED Flowering stems: cut flowers. Whole plant: potted flower.

CULTIVATION Plants are propagated from seed or by division. They can be productive for many years and are normally lifted and divided after 2–3 years. The best flower quality and yield are achieved under moderate to cool night/day temperatures of around 15/21°C (60/70°F). Plants thrive in full sun to partial shade and do best in poor but moist soil. It can tolerate boggy conditions but over-fertilisation results in weak stems.

PROPERTIES Vase life is slightly poor to average (4–7 days). If harvested too early, the foliage will decline before all the flowers have opened. Leaf browning is often a problem.

QUALITY CRITERIA Purchase stems with inflorescences 30–50% open. Check that the leaves are free of spots, diseases and damage.

CARE & HANDLING Recut stems and remove leaves below the water line. Place in a preservative containing a bactericide and sugar. The sugar not only helps buds open more fully, but also inhibits premature browning of the leaves. Storage is not recommended but if necessary, flowers can be held for 2–3 days at 3–5°C (37–41°F). Flowers do not dry well.

Veronicastrum virginicum (L.) Farw.   family: Plantaginaceae (Scrophulariaceae)

Virginische ereprijs (Dutch); *véronique de Virginie* (French); *Arzneiehrenpreis* (German); *veronicastrum* (Italian, Spanish)

Viburnum opulus

Guelder rose • snowball • crampbark

Viburnum opulus flower cluster

Viburnum opulus leaves and fruit

DESCRIPTION A woody shrub of up to 4 m (about 13′) high. The deeply lobed, toothed leaves are woolly below and turn bright red in autumn. The creamy white flowers are either small and fertile or sterile and showy, borne in flat-topped clusters that are typically rounded (globose) in some cultivars. The fleshy fruits are bright red and about 8 mm (⅓″) in diameter. Many cultivars have been developed for garden use. They differ in growth form and in the colour of the leaves, flowers and fruits. The most popular cultivar for use as a cut flower is the original 'Roseum' (sometimes listed as 'Sterile' or 'Snowball'). The flowers are white with a greenish tint and sometimes turn pinkish.

ORIGIN & HISTORY Europe, Asia and the Mediterranean region. The original Guelder rose grown near Guelders is a sterile cultivar, 'Roseum' (sometimes called Whitsuntide boss or snowball tree). It is also known as the European cranberry bush because the edible berries were once used as a substitute for cranberries.

PARTS USED The flowering stems are used as flowers or fillers, especially in large arrangements.

CULTIVATION A hardy shrub that thrives in shade and partial shade conditions. It prefers well-drained, relatively light soils that remain moist (not waterlogged) during active growth.

PROPERTIES Vase life is very poor (2–4 days). Flowers are scented. They are sensitive to ethylene.

QUALITY CRITERIA Select stems with open flowers that show no signs of bruising or browning. It is important to know that immature flowers often have a greenish tinge, but they whiten beautifully when fully open.

CARE & HANDLING Recut and hydrate stems promptly for a few hours at room temperature before using. Place in a floral preservative. Storage is not recommended, but hold in a cooler at 2–4°C (36–39°F) and 90% relative humidity until used. Handle with care to avoid damage to flower clusters.

Viburnum opulus L.   family: Caprifoliaceae

gelderse roos (Dutch); *viorne obier* (French); *Gewöhnlicher Schneeball* (German); *palla di neve* (Italian); *bola de nieve* (Spanish)

Viola odorata
sweet violet • florist violet

Viola odorata

DESCRIPTION A stoloniferous perennial herb (to 150 mm or 6″ high) with heart-shaped leaves borne on slender stalks. The flowers are single or double and have a nectar spur of about 6 mm (¼″) long. The colour varies from violet to lilac, white or yellow. It is thought that most of the many cultivars are derived from hybrids between *V. odorata*, *V. suavis* (Russian violet) and a French cultivar known as 'La Violette de Quatre'. The basic cultivar groups are Single Scented, Scented Semi-double, Scented Parma, Hybrids Violas and Hybrid Violettas.

ORIGIN & HISTORY Europe, Asia and North Africa. The flowers have been used as a source of perfume, flavouring and as an ingredient of skin creams and expectorant medicine. The flowers are crystallised for use as food and cake decorations. Sweet violets symbolise modesty in the language of flowers.

PARTS USED Whole plants are used for potted flowers and hanging baskets.

CULTIVATION Sweet violet is very sensitive to high salt levels in the soil, especially during germination. Plants require cool temperatures during production. Many growers use light shade to help reduce temperatures, but excessive shade and warm temperatures cause plants to stretch. If over-watered, plants are more susceptible to disease.

PROPERTIES Plants continue to flower for several weeks (6–8 weeks). One of the main attractions of sweet violets is their strong and characteristic sweet fragrance. They are sensitive to ethylene.

QUALITY CRITERIA Select healthy, compact plants with some open flowers (to check colour) and many flower buds. The leaves should not be distorted and free from blotches, damage or signs of disease.

CARE & HANDLING Display potted plants in a bright but cool area (16–24°C; 61–75°F), with good ventilation. Keep moist but do not over-water. Continually remove dead flowers as this also stimulates further flowering.

Viola odorata L.   family: Violaceae

maarts viooltje (Dutch); *violette* (French); *März-Veilchen, Wohlriechendes Veilchen* (German); *viola* (Italian); *violeta* (Spanish)

Viola wittrockiana

pansy • Johnny jump-up

Viola ×wittrockiana 'Princess'

Viola ×wittrockiana cultivar

Viola ×wittrockiana black

DESCRIPTION An annual or short-lived perennial (to 0.3 m or 1') with rounded to heart-shaped leaves. The flowers are more than 50 mm (2") in diameter, with brightly coloured overlapping petals. Commercial cultivars are nowadays almost exclusively F_1 hybrids and not open-pollinated. Cultivars are grouped into blotchy or solid types and autumn (fall) or spring flowering.

ORIGIN & HISTORY Garden origin. It is a hybrid between several species that was created around 1830. The vibrant colours of pansies have become a common sight during autumn or early spring.

PARTS USED Whole plants are used as potted flowers and for hanging baskets.

CULTIVATION The seedling stage is very demanding and therefore most growers prefer to purchase plugs from specialists. Plants are not day length sensitive, but flowering is more profuse under long days. Growers control plant height by manipulating temperature, nutrition and irrigation, as well as using growth-stunting chemicals. However, pansies require bright light conditions, along with moderate to cool temperatures.

PROPERTIES Flowers are somewhat sensitive to ethylene. They are also prone to a number of leaf spot diseases, typically aggravated by warm, humid conditions. During production pansies are sensitive to both a deficiency and toxicity of certain micronutrients, which can result in twisted or discoloured and blotchy leaves.

QUALITY CRITERIA Look for compact plants with short, sturdy flowering stems. Make sure that leaves are not distorted, yellowish, blotchy or spotted. Check that flowers are free of botrytis.

CARE & HANDLING Display in full sun to partial shade, provided that cool temperatures can be maintained (16–24°C; 61–75°F). Do not over-water. Pansies transpire slowly and dry out more slowly than most potted flowers. Continually remove dead or dying flowers.

Viola ×wittrockiana Gams ex Kappert   family: Violaceae

viooltje (Dutch); *pensée* (French); *Garten-Stiefmütterchen* (German); *viola del pensiero* (Italian); *viola* (Spanish)

Vriesea splendens

flaming sword

Vriesea splendens yellow

Vriesea splendens orange

Aechmea fasciata

DESCRIPTION An epiphytic bromeliad with overlapping leaves forming a rosette. The leaves have dark purple bands and form a natural container in which rainwater is collected. Small yellow flowers are borne in between numerous bright red to orange, overlapping bracts. Many cultivars exist, with differing flower spike shapes. Some have variegated leaves ('Splenriet' and 'Fire'), others dark green leaves ('Christine' and 'Annie'). *Vriesea* is sometimes confused with *Aechmea fasciata*, which is also an important florist bromeliad.

ORIGIN & HISTORY Central and South America. It is named after the 19th-century Dutch botanist, W.H. de Vriese. Several species and hybrids have become popular as potted flowers.

PARTS USED Whole plant: potted flower.

CULTIVATION Cultivars with stiff leaves need to be grown under high light to ensure colourful "flowers" and leaves. However, direct sunlight will burn the leaves of most types. Soft-leaved types require up to 85% shade, if not more, to grow properly. Plants need frequent feedings of potassium, as they do not store it, yet it is essential for their growth.

PROPERTIES Plants only flower once and then die, but every year new growth is produced at soil level. The coloured spikes can last for many months. Plants tend to thrive on neglect. Flowers are not scented.

QUALITY CRITERIA Select plants with well-formed, long flowering spikes, which are still closed. (Keep in mind that spike length also depends on cultivar.) Choose plants where the spike originates in the funnel of the plant. Make sure leaves and flowers are free of damage and marks.

CARE & HANDLING Place in maximum natural light away from direct sunlight and draughts. Do not over-water. The potting medium should be kept slightly dry. Use soft, tepid water and keep the central "vase" of the plant filled. Mist plants occasionally, as they prefer a high humidity environment. Keep temperature above 16°C (61°F) and below 27°C (81°F).

Vriesea splendens (Brongn.) Lem.   family: Bromeliaceae

bromelia (Dutch); *vriesea* (French); *Flammendes Schwert* (German); *vriesea* (Italian); *vriesia*, *pluma de indio* (Spanish)

Vuylstekeara cultivars
vuylstekeara orchid • cambria orchid

×*Vuylstekeara* cultivar

Colmanara 'Massai Splash'

DESCRIPTION A sympodial hybrid with strap-shaped leaves arising from a creeping rhizome. Several flowers are borne on an arching inflorescence. The flower is white and heavily spotted with maroon, with a yellow blotch on the base of the lip. There are a large number of named cultivars in a range of colours and flower shapes. 'Cambria' is by far the best-known and most popular cultivar and is grown on a large commercial scale.

ORIGIN & HISTORY Garden origin. *Vuylstekeara* is a cross between three genera (*Cochlioda*, *Miltonia* and *Odontoglossum*). The last two of these genera, crossed with Oncidium, resulted in another popular hybrid genus, *Colmanara*.

PARTS USED The whole flowering plant is used as a potted flower. The flowers are used as cut flowers.

CULTIVATION Plants are mass propagated by means of modern tissue culture techniques but they can also be increased by division. Light is a key factor in the cultivation of healthy plants and flowers, along with humidity and temperature.

PROPERTIES The flowers last for several weeks and the plant remains in flower for 2–3 months. Flowers are sensitive to ethylene.

QUALITY CRITERIA Select a healthy plant with bright green leaves and a robust inflorescence bearing several well-coloured buds. Only a few flowers should be open. Check that buds are healthy and none has dried out or dropped off.

CARE & HANDLING Handle cut flowers with care. Touching of petals can cause bruising or damage pollinia – both reduce vase life. Gloves or wet hands are recommended when working with flowers. Store flowers at 10–12°C (50–54°F) and 95% relative humidity. Display plants in a warm, bright environment (avoid direct sunlight). Ensure good ventilation, but avoid cold draughts. Do not store with or near ethylene-producing products. Allow potting medium to dry out quite a bit before watering again.

×*Vuylstekeara* 'Cambria'   family: Orchidaceae

cambria orchidee (Dutch); *cambria* (French); *Cambria-orchidee* (German); *cambria* (Italian); *cambria orquidea* (Spanish)

Watsonia cultivars

watsonia • bugle lily

Watsonia plants

Watsonia flowers

DESCRIPTION Perennial herbs with a fan of sword-shaped leaves arising from a large underground corm. The sturdy flowering stems are up to 2 m (6½′) long and end in a two-ranked spike of tubular, curved flowers. A number of cultivars and hybrids exist, with a variety of colours and shades, ranging from orange and red, to pink, purple and white.

ORIGIN & HISTORY Southern Africa. Breeding of *Watsonia* started in the early 20th century – mainly in Australia and California. Species are usually interfertile, so that the lineages of cultivars are not always clear. Many of the first cultivars had flowers in various shades of pink, salmon and red. Hybrid watsonias tend to be tall, lanky plants, flowering more sparsely over a longer period than gladioli and are therefore less popular.

PARTS USED Flower spikes are used as cut flowers.

CULTIVATION Watsonias prefer well-aerated soils with plenty of organic matter and full sun conditions, although partial shade is tolerated. The evergreen types require moisture throughout the year, while the winter-growing deciduous plants flower in spring and require regular, deep watering during winter but a dry summer rest period. In contrast, the summer-growing deciduous types need water during summer and flower in late summer.

PROPERTIES Vase life is average to good (6–10 days). Flowers are sensitive to ethylene.

QUALITY CRITERIA Flowers must be free of damage and disease, especially rust on the leaves and botrytis on the blooms. Leaves must have a uniform colour and not be yellowish or have "burnt" tips. Select sturdy stems with most closed buds showing good colour and only 1–2 flowers open.

CARE & HANDLING Recut stems and place in a floral preservative with an ethylene inhibitor and a low sugar concentrate, to assist in bud-opening. Flowers can be stored at 1–2°C (34–36°F) and 90% relative humidity for 5–7 days.

Watsonia cultivars   family: Iridaceae

watsonia (Dutch, French, Italian, Spanish); *Watsonie* (German)

Xanthorrhoea australis

grass tree • steel grass • black boy

Xanthorrhoea australis plant

Xanthorrhoea australis leaves

DESCRIPTION A slow-growing, evergreen, fire-tolerant plant with a thick stem and a dense crown of slender, fibrous leaves. Small white flowers are borne in cylindrical spikes. There are no well-known cultivars specifically bred for use in the florist industry.

ORIGIN & HISTORY South-eastern Australia. The plants are also known as black boy because they are often blackened by fire. The stems exude a resin that is used as varnish and the soft wood is traditionally used to carve bowls and utensils. The flowers contain considerable amounts of nectar, which was used by aborigines to produce a sweet drink by soaking the flowers in water. Grass trees are commonly cultivated as accent plants. Steel grass is still a fairly unknown florist green but is gaining in popularity.

PARTS USED The long leaves are used as cut greens or as foliage for use in small or large arrangements.

CULTIVATION Propagation is primarily by means of seed. Growth is slow and seedlings take many years to develop into large, mature plants. The leaves are very strong and can grow up to 2 m (6½') high. Plants prefer full sun conditions and well-drained, moist soils. Most of the product is still wild-harvested.

PROPERTIES Leaves are long lasting (2–4 weeks). Leaves have no distinctive fragrance and are not sensitive to ethylene.

QUALITY CRITERIA Select long, mature leaves with uniform, dark green colour. Check that tips are not dry or brown. Inspect for general damage, blemishes, pests and disease. Make sure foliage is clean and properly graded.

CARE & HANDLING Recut leaves by 50–100 mm (2–4") and place in clean water with a bactericide. Keep cool and prevent from drying out. Leaves can be stored for 2 weeks at 1–2°C (34–36°F) and 95% relative humidity. Check daily and replace treated water every few days. Recut leaves again before use.

Xanthorrhoea australis R. Br.   family: Xanthorrhoeaceae

grasboom (Dutch); *black boy* (French); *Grasbaum, Südlicher Grasbaum* (German); *xanthorrhoea* (Italian, Spanish)

Xeranthemum annuum

immortelle • common immortelle

Xeranthemum annuum mixed

DESCRIPTION A non-spiny annual herb (up to 0.7 m or 28" high) with erect stems bearing oblong leaves that are densely white hairy below. The flower heads are 25–50 mm (1–2") in diameter and are usually pink or white. Modern cultivars and seed races are available in a range of colours (white, purple, pink and red). 'Purple Violet' has semi-double, dark purple flower heads. 'Snowlady' has single, pure white flower heads.

ORIGIN & HISTORY South-eastern Europe to Iran. The plants are popular as cultivated "everlasting" flowers in gardens and for florists.

PARTS USED Fresh flowers are used as cut flowers or fillers but it is mainly the dried flowers that are popular for mixed arrangements and dried flower bouquets.

CULTIVATION Propagation is mostly by means of seed, that can either be sown direct or transplanted out as seedlings. Plants prefer full sun conditions and well-drained, moderately fertile soils. Seedlings are sensitive to frost. If flowers are left to dry on the plant they tend to turn a light brown or tan colour.

PROPERTIES Vase life of fresh flowers is very good and they remain attractive as they dry. When drying out, the blossoms and buds more or less keep the shape in which they were picked.

QUALITY CRITERIA Look for cut flowers that are fully open, or stems with most of the flower heads open. Stems should be straight, well branched and sturdy, even though they are fairly thin. Dried flowers – make sure that they have completely dried and that no flower heads or stems are broken or damaged. Flower colour must be vivid (not brown). Flower heads must be free of any blemishes or fungus.

CARE & HANDLING Place fresh flower heads in a floral preservative. Flowers are excellent for drying and hold their shape and colour well. Handle dried flower heads carefully as the delicate bracts damage easily. Store dried flowers in a cool, ventilated area with low humidity.

Xeranthemum annuum L.   family: Asteraceae

papierbloem (Dutch); *immortelle annuelle* (French); *Einjährige Papierblume* (German); *immortelle* (Italian, Spanish)

Xerophyllum tenax

bear grass • elk grass • Indian basket grass

Xerophyllum tenax (bunches)

Xerophyllum tenax leaves

DESCRIPTION A perennial, grass-like tuft of up to 1.8 m (6′) high. It has a dense rosette of basal leaves – long, linear, 0.9 m (3′) long and 6 mm (¼″) wide, with rough edges. The plant flowers in late summer, producing a large single cluster of long-stalked, cream-coloured flowers of 15 mm (just over ½″) in diameter. There are no well-known cultivars – the cultivated form of the species agrees closely with the wild type.

ORIGIN & HISTORY Western parts of North America. The leaves were once used by Native Americans to weave watertight baskets. Grizzly bears sometimes use the leaves as nesting material for winter dens, hence the common name. In the garden industry, bear grass is popular as an ornamental, grass-like plant. In the florist trade the leaves are used as durable and attractive fillers.

PARTS USED Leaves are used as foliage and filler.

CULTIVATION Propagation is by means of division or seed. Bear grass is not a true grass but is closely related to lilies and has similar cultivation requirements. Plants do best in bright light and cool, well-drained soils that are well aerated.

PROPERTIES Vase life is good to very good (10–21 days). The leaves are not ethylene sensitive and have no distinctive fragrance.

QUALITY CRITERIA Select leaves with a healthy, even green colour. Ensure that there is no browning, especially on the tips. Look for fully mature, long blades and make sure bunches are free of disease, blemishes and general dirt.

CARE & HANDLING Recut stems and place in a preservative containing a bactericide, which is aimed not so much at increasing the vase life of the leaves but rather at keeping the water clean and free of bacteria (so as not to infect more sensitive flowers). Hold or display in a cool, ventilated area (not in any direct draughts). The leaves dry well.

Xerophyllum tenax (Pursh) Nutt.　　　　　　　　　　　　　　　　　　　family: Melanthiaceae

beregras (Dutch); *xérophylle* (French); *Bärengras, Truthahnbart* (German); *xerophyllum* (Italian, Spanish)

Yucca aloifolia

Spanish bayonet • dagger plant

Yucca aloifolia 'Variegata'

Yucca aloifolia leaves

DESCRIPTION An aloe-like plant with a slender stem (up to 8 m or nearly 27') that may be sparsely branched and a large rosette of stiff, sword-shaped leaves. Each leaf is about 0.6 m (2') long, 60 mm (2½") wide, flat, sharp-tipped and minutely toothed along the margins. The large, white or purple-flushed flowers are borne in enormous clusters of up to 6 m (about 20') long. Several cultivars with different leaf colours are available, including 'Marginata' (margins yellow), 'Tricolor' (striped yellow with a white line along the midrib) and 'Quadricolor' (striped yellow and white on green background).

ORIGIN & HISTORY South-eastern United States and the West Indies. This and several other species have become popular garden plants. The erect stems, attractive flowers and decorative foliage have made them ideal accent plants. The tough, fibrous leaves are also a source of rope fibre. Leaves are popular with florists.

PARTS USED Leaves: cut foliage (flowers are seldom used).

CULTIVATION Flowers are only pollinated by specialised moths found in the plant's natural habitat. Propagation is therefore by means of stem cuttings. High temperatures and high light intensities are required for active, healthy growth. Plants are tolerant of most soil types and weather conditions.

PROPERTIES Vase life of leaves is very good (10–21 days). Leaves have no distinctive fragrance and are not sensitive to ethylene.

QUALITY CRITERIA Leaves must have a good, uniform green colour or vivid variegated colours. Select mature leaves that are free of any yellowing, blackening, pests, diseases or damage.

CARE & HANDLING Handle with care – leaf tips are very sharp. Display in a cool, ventilated area – either dry or in clean water with a bactericide. Replace water every few days. Store for 1–2 weeks at 1–2°C (34–36°F) and 90–95% relative humidity.

Yucca aloifolia L.   family: Asparagaceae (Agavaceae)

palmlelie (Dutch); *yucca* (French); *Graue Palmlilie* (German); *tronco dell'amicizia* (Italian); *yuca* (Spanish)

Zantedeschia aethiopica

calla lily • arum lily

Zantedeschia aethiopica (winter calla)

Zantedeschia cultivars (summer calla)

DESCRIPTION A perennial herb with large, soft leaves and tiny flowers borne on a finger-like structure (the spadix), enclosed by a large, fleshy bract (the spathe). Summer callas are deciduous and brightly coloured hybrids have been bred from these species. Winter callas are evergreen and mainly white. The colourful summer callas are much more popular in the florist trade.

ORIGIN & HISTORY South Africa. Calla lilies are old favourites and are commonly used at weddings and funerals.

PARTS USED Flowering spathe: cut flower. Whole plant: potted flower.

CULTIVATION Calla lilies like rich, well-composted soil and full sun, but are usually grown in shade to increase stalk length. *Zantedeschia aethiopica*, unlike some of the other species, can be grown in full shade (even submerged in a pond). Warm temperatures result in faster flowering but also increase the incidence of disease.

PROPERTIES Vase life of cut flowers is poor to good, depending on cultivar and environment

(3–14 days). There is no fragrance. The pollen does not stain clothing. Flowers pack and ship poorly.

QUALITY CRITERIA Select long, straight and sturdy stems, with flowers unrolled and almost fully open. Handle carefully, as open flowers damage very easily. Look out for marks and damaged or soft stems. Select pots with about half the flowers showing colour.

CARE & HANDLING Recut the stems and place them in a preservative with a disinfectant to reduce stem splitting. Be careful when using a sugar, as microbes can quickly multiply and harm the soft stems. Only if absolutely necessary, store white cultivars at 3°C (37°F) and coloured ones at 6–8°C (43–46°F) (lower temperatures will cause chill damage). Flowers do not dry well (except perhaps when microwaved or processed in some other way). Keep potted flowers moist but not wet. Display potted plants in a cool area in bright light but avoid direct sunlight.

Zantedeschia aethiopica (L.) Sprengel

family: Araceae

aronskelk (Dutch); *calla, arum* (French); *Kalla, Zimmerkalla* (German); *calla* (Italian); *cala* (Spanish)

Zea mays

maize • corn

Zea mays leaves

Zea mays – ornamental maize (cobs)

DESCRIPTION A robust annual grass with large sheathing leaves and distinctive female and male ears. The female flowers with silky styles are borne in a thick ear lower down on the plant, while the male flowers occur in tassels at the tip of the plant. Unusual ear and leaf colour forms have been developed as ornamental plants. 'Fiesta' has long grains in a patchwork of colours – purple, blue, yellow, red, and white; 'Harlequin' has red grains and leaves striped green and red; and 'Cutie Blues' has small, dark blue grains.

ORIGIN & HISTORY Central America (Mexico). Maize or corn is an ancient cultigen and has been cultivated for more than 5 000 years. Forms with coloured grains have become popular for decorative work.

PARTS USED The fresh leafy stems are used as cut foliage and the dried fruits as ornaments.

CULTIVATION Propagation is by means of seed, which germinates very easily and is sown direct. Plants are frost sensitive and germination temperatures need to be warm (18°C; 64°F). Maize prefers full sun conditions and thrives in rich or poor soils.

PROPERTIES Vase life of fresh foliage is fairly good (10–14 days). Dried fruits can last for years. Foliage or fruits are not scented and are not sensitive to ethylene.

QUALITY CRITERIA Look for stems with a full, compact volume of leaves. Make sure desired colours or variegations of leaves are vivid and clean. Check that leaf tips are not dried out. Foliage and dried fruits must be free of disease, pests or damage.

CARE & HANDLING Recut the stems and remove all leaves below the water line. Place in clean water with a bactericide. Display in a cool, bright area. Leaves become brittle when dried and do not usually make good dried material. Keep dried fruits in a dry, low humidity area. Check occasionally as they may attract or be damaged by vermin.

Zea mays L.
family: Poaceae

siermais (Dutch); *maïs* (French); *Mais* (German); *granoturco* (Italian); *toumorokoshi* (Japanese); *maíz* (Spanish)

Zingiber spectabile

beehive ginger • nodding gingerwort

Zingiber spectabile plant

Zingiber spectabile inflorescences

DESCRIPTION A herbaceous perennial producing large, dark green leaves from underground rhizomes and very attractive, yellowish flower heads that turn red when they age. The peculiar heads with large bracts that surround the flowers are distinctive and reminiscent of an old-fashioned beehive (hence beehive ginger). The flowers are yellow and white with a dark purple lip decorated with yellow spots. There are numerous cultivars and hybrids of *Zingiber* species available as florist flowers. Vase life and colours are fairly limited so that attempts are ongoing to breed cultivars with more long-lasting flowers in a wider range of colours.

ORIGIN & HISTORY Malaysia. The beehive ginger is commonly cultivated as a garden plant in tropical regions. It is closely related to common ginger (*Z. officinale*).

PARTS USED Flowering spikes are used as cut flowers or decorative fillers.

CULTIVATION Propagation is by division, cuttings or seed. Bracts become reddish as they mature,

especially if exposed to full sun. Plants prefer well-aerated soils rich in organic material. Poor drainage and water-logging will result in rhizome rot and a reduction in flower yields and quality.

PROPERTIES The vase life of beehive ginger is usually average to good (7–12 days), but may be poor in some cultivars. Flowers and foliage have a strong ginger fragrance.

QUALITY CRITERIA Make sure the flower clusters have no discolouration or blackening on the tips. Bracts must be mature with good colour, but with no true flowers having emerged. Stems must be straight, sturdy and long enough for practical use.

CARE & HANDLING Recut stems on arrival and place in a floral preservative. Display in a bright, warm area and avoid cold draughts. Do not display or store flowers below 10°C (50°F), as this will cause cold damage. Flowers can be stored for 4–7 days at 13°C (55°F) and 90–95% relative humidity.

Zingiber spectabile Griff.   family: Zingiberaceae

maracas (Dutch); *gingembre, maracas* (French); *Nickender Ingwer* (German); *maracas* (Italian); *maracas, micrófono de oro* (Spanish)

Zinnia elegans

youth-and-old-age • zinnia

Zinnia elegans plants

Zinnia elegans flower heads

DESCRIPTION Erect annual (up to 1 m or 40") with hairy leaves and large, colourful, single or double flower heads. More than 80 cultivars are available, especially for the garden industry. Dahlia- and cactus-flowered forms are popular as cut flowers and are available to growers mostly as mixed hybrids and not individual colours.

ORIGIN & HISTORY Mexico. Zinnias are old favourite garden plants.

PARTS USED Flower heads are used as cut flowers.

CULTIVATION Zinnia is regarded as a cheap summer crop and is propagated by seed. Plants require high light intensities and flower poorly on spindly stems if grown under low light (winter) conditions. Persistent cold – under 15°C (60°F) – results in yellowish, unhealthy foliage and delayed flowering. The denser the plant spacing, the taller and less branched the flowering stems will be. Zinnias are seldom grown in greenhouses, but most often in open fields.

PROPERTIES Vase life is poor (4–7 days). There is no fragrance. "Zinnia meltdown" is a term used by many growers to describe the rapid (within 24 hours) deterioration of perfectly good-looking flowers – the stems turn brown and mushy. Bacterial infection is the most likely cause. Plants are also very susceptible to powdery mildew. There are many different and vivid flower colours – practically any colour except blue.

QUALITY CRITERIA Select stems with fully opened heads and pollen starting to form. Make sure stems are sturdy and straight, with healthy green leaves that are free of marks and damage.

CARE & HANDLING Flower heads and stems collapse easily, so recut and rehydrate in a preservative as soon as possible. Stems are hollow just below the head, so for design work, push a short piece of wire through the centre of the flower down into the stem to help keep it sturdy. Keep in the dark at 5°C (41°F) for 3–5 hours prior to use. Storage is not recommended.

Zinnia elegans Jacq. family: Asteraceae

zinnia (Dutch); zinnia (French); *Zinnie* (German); *zinnie* (Italian); *zinia* (Spanish)

GLOSSARY

Actinomorphic – an actinomorphic flower is radially symmetrical in all directions when viewed from above

Anthocyanins – the most common red or purple pigments found in leaves and flowers

Antibiotic – a substance that kills or inhibits the growth of micro-organisms

Antioxidant – a substance that protects cells or counteracts the damage caused by oxidation and oxygen free radicals

Apetalous – without petals

Aromatherapy – the medicinal use of aroma substances, mainly by inhalation, bath and massage

Arrangement – artistic and intentional placement of flowers

Bactericide – a chemical compound used to kill bacteria

Bent-neck – a problem occurring in certain cut flowers, especially common in roses, where the flower bud droops over causing the flower stem to be bent

Berry – a fleshy fruit with numerous small seeds

Bicolour – flowers that have a two-toned colouration

Biotechnology – the manipulation of living organisms (usually micro-organisms) for beneficial effects (such as production of nutrients, hormones, enzymes, etc.)

Botrytis – a genus of bacteria that causes quality and vase-life problems in cut flowers

Bouquet – an arrangement of flowers

Bract – a leaf-like structure found at the base of a flower

Bud drop – a physiological problem, especially with lilies, where the flower bud drops off before it has opened

Bud opening stage – refers to the various stages as a flower bud opens; often used as an indicator as to when a flower should be harvested

Bulb – a rounded or elongated structure formed from fleshy overlapping leaf bases borne on a very small underground stem

Bunch – numerous cut stems of a single type of flower or foliage tied together

Calyx – the outer (usually green) leaf-like structures in a flower that surrounds the petals

Capsule – a dry, dehiscent fruit formed from several carpels, which splits open along more than one suture

Carpels – the leaf-like structures from which a fruit is formed (often fused into a single unit)

Catkin – a pendulous (hanging), elongated flower cluster comprising numerous, inconspicuous, sessile flowers

Chlorophyll – the green pigment in leaves that is able to convert sun energy into sugars through the process of photosynthesis

Clock – refers to the clock pricing or bidding system used at flower auctions

Clock system – *see* Clock

Cold chain – refers to the entire process and movement of cut flowers from harvesting to the consumer, during which the flowers must be kept cold

Corolla – a collective term describing the structure formed by the petals of a flower (*see also* Petals)

Creeper – a plant that grows upwards by twining or using tendrils (= climber, vine)

Cultigen – a form of a plant (usually a mutation) originating from human selection, which is not found in nature

Cultivar – a **culti**vated **vari**ety (a form of a plant that originated from human selection or plant breeding, which is maintained in cultivation and not found in nature)

Cultivation – the growing and nurturing of plants or flowers

Cut flower – a term that can be used to describe any flower that is cut or harvested

Cut greens – leaves cut or harvested, often green in colour and used in the florist industry

Deciduous – a term used to describe the annual shedding of leaves (*see also* Evergreen)

Domestication – the process of converting a wild plant into a crop

Double – refers to flowers that have two or multiple whorls of petals and are much fuller than single varieties

Drupe – a fleshy fruit containing a single seed

Essential oil – a mixture of volatile terpenoids with the flavour and odour of the plant from which it was extracted

Ethylene – a plant hormone and naturally occurring gaseous by-product that causes the undesirable effects of premature aging, bud drop and leaf yellowing in cut flowers

Evapotranspiration – the process of losing water from the plant or cut flower caused by evaporation of water from the surfaces of the leaves

Evergreen – a term used to describe plants that retain their leaves during the dormant season (*see also* Deciduous)

Fillers – refers to various types of plant material such as leaves, twigs or small-flowered multi-stems that are typically used along with the more traditional flowers to fill out an arrangement

Floral design – the art of creating flower arrangements or designing and working with cut flowers

Floral foam – a stiff foam, typically in brick form, used in arrangements into which the stems are pushed and thereby held in place

Floral preservative – a chemical compound in powder, tablet or liquid form which is typically added to the water in which the flowers are standing to prolong vase life

Floriculture – breeding and cultivation of ornamental plants and cut flowers

Flower – the reproductive shoot or organ of a flowering plant (usually angiosperms) that typically contains colourful petals

Flower quality – *see* Quality

Foam – *see* Floral foam

Foliage – typically refers to leafy cut greens used in the cut flower industry; also refers to the leaves on the flower stem

Garland – a decorative wreath or cord of flowers typically used for festive occasions, which is either hung somewhere or placed around a person's neck

Germicide – a product or compound, typically chemical in nature, which is used to kill germs (fungi or bacteria) in flower water or to disinfect work areas

Grading – flowers are graded or sorted into different categories depending on the quality

Grafting – the process of propagation in horticulture by which a small piece of plant tissue of the desired plant (scion) is made to unite with an established plant (the stock or rootstock)

Gum – a sticky plant excretion that forms a viscous mass when dissolved in water

Harvest – the process of picking (harvesting) cut flowers

Herb – a non-woody, annual or perennial plant

Humidity – *see* Relative humidity

Hydrate – harvested flowers lose their source of water and are therefore placed in water to keep them turgid and hydrated (*see also* Rehydrate)

Ikebana – traditional Japanese method of arranging flowers

Inflorescence – the system of stalks of a plant on which the flowers are borne

Language of flowers – flowers have a strong association with human sentiments and over the ages certain flowers have become synonymous with certain sentiments or ceremonies – this has become known as the "language of flowers"

Leaf yellowing – the yellowing or fading of green colouration in the leaves of flowers or cut greens; typically refers to poor quality or premature aging, not to the natural aging process

Mixed bunch – a bunch of flowers containing a mix of flower types

Organic – relating to a substance or food produced without the use of chemical fertilisers or chemical pesticides

Peduncle – the stalk of a whole inflorescence

Percentage relative humidity – the amount of water held within the air as a percentage of total saturation, total saturation being 100%

Perianth – the outer whorls of the flower not directly involved in reproduction, that is the calyx and corolla

Petals – the inner, usually brightly coloured, leaf-like structures in a flower

Phloem – the conducting tissue in higher plants that distributes nutrients from the leaves to other parts

Phytochemicals – chemical compounds found in plants

Plant breeding – the processes of selection, hybridisation or genetic manipulation through which new plant cultivars are developed

Polysepalous – flowers with sepals that are not united

Postharvest care and handling – refers to all the processes and steps in the handling and caring for flowers after they have been harvested, from the grower to the consumer

Posy – small flower bouquet or tussie-mussie

Preservative – *see* Floral preservative

Quality – the quality of a cut flower is determined by factors such as number of buds, bud size, stem length, colour, damage; the main indicator of quality being vase life

Raceme – a flower cluster with stalked flowers arranged along a single axis and opening from the bottom up

Rehydrate – flowers stored or transported dry, will wilt and internal water needs to be reintroduced by placing them in cold water or water containing preservatives to rehydrate them

Relative humidity – the amount of water in the air, which is directly related to temperature; relative humidity therefore changes as temperature changes

Rhizome – a stem (often fleshy) that grows horizontally below or partly above the ground

Rootstock – (1) an alternative name for a rhizome; (2) a rooted plant used as stock in grafting

Selection – refers to the plant and flower cultivars that plant breeders have chosen (selected) for cultivation through a process of breeding and growing trials

Senescence – the technical term referring to the process of maturing and aging in plants and flowers, culminating in their death

Sepals – the outer leaf-like structures (usually green) that surround the petals

Series – refers to a group (series) of related cultivars that might only differ in flower colour and are marketed under one commercial (not necessary botanical) name

Sessile – without a stalk (used to describe leaves or flowers)

Single – refers to flowers that have a single whorl of petals, or a few close whorls of petals in a single or flat plane

Single stems – refers to certain flower types, such as chrysanthemums or carnations, that have only a single flower per stem

Sleepiness – refers to flowers that are damaged by ethylene and then close and shrivel as if going to sleep; typically found in carnations

Sleeve – a plastic covering in which a bunch of cut flowers are placed (sleeved) mainly to offer protection

Spike – a type of flower cluster with sessile (stalk-less) flowers along an elongated axis

Spray – refers to certain flower types, such as chrysanthemums and carnations, which have multiple blooms on a single flower stem; for example "spray carnations"

Stamen – the male reproductive organ in a flower consisting of a stalk (filament) with a head (anther) in which the pollen is formed

Stem block – refers to micro-organisms or air-bubbles that block the xylem vessels in the stem and prohibit the uptake of water

Stigma – the terminal part of the style on the ovary of a flower where the pollen is deposited during pollination

Style – the structure in a flower that connects the stigma(s) to the ovary

Syncarp – a fleshy compound fruit formed from the fused carpels of one or several flowers

Taproot – the main root of the plant that grows vertically downwards (often bearing smaller lateral roots)

Tepal – the leaf-like structure in flowers where there is no difference between the calyx and the corolla

Transpiration – the movement of water through the plant and out of the leaves due to evaporation

Tuber – swollen underground part of a stem or root

Turgidity – caused by the pressure of the water inside the cells of the plant tissue, the variation of which causes the leaves, flowers and stems to be stiff (turgid) or droopy (wilted)

Umbel – a flower cluster which has all the flowers arising at the same point (typical for the family Umbelliferae or Apiaceae)

Variegated – refers typically to cut foliage or leaves with patches, strips or regions of different colours

Vase life – an important indicator of flower quality, it refers to the length of time in days that a flower lasts from being placed in a vase until it is aesthetically unacceptable

Vernalisation – promotion of flowering by means of naturally or artificially applied periods of extended low temperature

Wilt – as more water is lost due to transpiration than is taken up, flowers and leaves lose turgidity and start to droop or wilt

Wreath – flowers and foliage arranged in a flat ring or other shape, which is often hung during festive occasions or laid at ceremonies such as military processions or funerals

Xylem – the vascular system consisting of vessels that translocate water and nutrients from the roots to the rest of the plant, or from the flower stem to the leaves and flowers

Yellowing – *see* Leaf yellowing

Zygomorphic – a flower that is only symmetrical in one direction, in other words, bilaterally symmetrical

FURTHER READING

Armitage, AM, Laushman, JM (2003) *Specialty Cut Flowers – The Production of Annuals, Perennials, Bulbs, and Woody Plants for Fresh and Dried Cut Flowers*. 2nd ed. Timber Press, Portland.

Austin, D (1992) *Old Roses and English Roses*. Antique Collector's Club, Suffolk.

Bailey, LH (1925) *Manual of Cultivated Plants*. MacMillan, New York.

Bangs, DH (2002) *The Business Planning Guide – Creating a Winning Plan for Success*. 9th ed. Dearborn Trade Publishing, Chicago, Illinois.

Barnhoorn, F (2005) *Growing Bulbs in Southern Africa*. 2nd ed. Struik Publishers, Cape Town.

Beales, P (1992) *Roses*. Harvill, London.

Blanchette, R, van der Velde (eds) (2000) *Green Profit on Retailing*. Ball Publishing, Batavia, Illinois.

Blessington, TM, Collins, PC (1993) *Foliage Plants – Prolonging Quality*. Ball Publishing, Batavia, Illinois.

Bloom, A (1956) *Hardy Perennials*. Faber and Faber, London.

Bretschneider, E (1962) *History of European Botanical Discoveries* (2 Volumes). Leipzig.

Bullivant, E (1989) *Dried Fresh Flowers from Your Garden*. Pelham Books, London.

Coats, AM (1971) *Flowers and Their Histories*. 2nd ed. McGraw-Hill, New York.

De Hertogh, AA (1996) *The Commercial Bulb Forcer's Guide*. 5th ed. International Flower Bulb Centre, Hillegom.

Deutch, Y (1981) *Popular Houseplants – All about Your Plants and How to Look After Them*. Galley Press, Leicester.

Dickerson, BC (1992) *The Old Rose Advisor*. Rimer Press, Oregon.

Dirr, MA (1998) *Manual of Woody Landscape Plants – Their Identification, Ornamental Characteristics, Culture, Propagation, and Uses*. 5th ed. Stripes Publishing, Champaign, Illinois.

Duthie, P (2000) *Continuous Bloom & Continuous Color*. Ball Publishing, Batavia, Illinois.

Emberton, SC (n.d.) *Garden Foliage for Flower Arrangement*. Faber and Faber.

Floralife, Inc. *Care and Handling of Fresh Cut Flowers* (www.floralife.com). Walterbora, South Carolina.

Gast, KLB (1997) *Postharvest Handling of Fresh Cut Flowers and Plant Material*. Kansas State University, Agricultural Experiment Station and Cooperative Extension Service.

Genders, R (1948) *Cut Flowers and Bulbs – for Pleasure and Profit*. Littlebury and Company, Worcester.

Griffith, LP (1998) *Tropical Foliage Plants*. Ball Publishing, Batavia, Illinois.

Halevy, AH (ed) (1985–1989) *The Handbook of Flowering*. 6 Volumes. CRC Press, Boca Raton, Florida.

Hamrick, D (ed) (2003) *Ball Redbook – Crop Production*. 17th ed. Volume 2. Ball Publishing, Batavia, Illinois.

Hay R, Synge, PM (1969) *The Dictionary of Garden Plants – In Colour with House and Greenhouse Plants*. Royal Horticultural Society, London.

Holstead, CL (1985) *Care and Handling of Flowers and Plants*. 2 Volumes. The Society of American Florists (SAF), Alexandria, Virginia.

Horton, A, McNair, J (1986) *All About Bulbs*. Robert L Iacopi, San Francisco.

Huxley, A (ed) (1992) *Dictionary of Gardening*. 4 volumes. Royal Horticultural Society, Macmillan, London.

John Henry Company, The (1989) *Fresh Flowers – Book 2*. Floraprint, USA.

Krüssmann, G (1982) *Roses*. Batsford, London.

Massingham, B (1976) *Homes and Gardens Book of Flower Arrangement*. Hamlyn Publishing Group, Middlesex.

McHoy, P (1996) *The New Houseplant A-Z – Everything You Need to Know to Identify, Choose, and Care for the 350 Most Popular Houseplants*. Anness Publishing, London.

Nell, TA (1993) *Flowering Potted Plants – Prolonging Shelf Performance*. Ball Publishing, Batavia, Illinois.

Nowak, J, Rudnicki, RM (1990) *Postharvest Handling and Storage of Cut Flowers, Florist Greens, and Potted Plants*. Timber Press, Portland.

Oakes, AJ (1990) *Ornamental Grasses and Grasslike Plants*. Van Nostrand Reinhold.

Phillips, R, Rix, M (1993) *The Quest for the Rose*. BBC Books, London.

Pokon Chrysal International (2004) Cut Flower Care & Handling – *75 Frequently Asked Questions*. 2nd ed. Pokon & Chrysal BV, Naarden.

Riley, Hall, R (1990) *Refrigeration and Controlled Atmosphere Storage for Horticultural Crops*. Cornell University, Ithaca, New York.

Sacalis, JN (1993) *Handling and Storage of Cut Flowers, Florist Greens and Potted Plants*. Timber Press, Portland, Oregon.

Salunkhe, DK, Bhat, NR, Desai, BB (1990) *Postharvest Biotechnology of Flowers and Ornamental Plants*. Springer-Verlag, Berlin.

Staby, G (1994) *SAF Flower and Plant Care Manual – A Contemporary Approach*. The Society of American Florists (SAF), Virginia.

Stanley, J (2002) *Complete Guide to Garden Center Management*. Ball Publishing, Batavia, Illinois.

Stevenson, V (1955) *Dried Flowers for Decoration*. Collingridge, London.

Stevenson, V (1973) *The Encyclopaedia of Floristry*. Drake, New York.

Strong, V (1996) *Foliage for Florists*. Strong's Greenery, Worchestshire.

Tampion, J, Reynolds, J (1971) *Botany for Flower Arrangers*. Pelham Books, London.

Terril NA, Reid, MS (2000) *Flower and Plant Care – The 21st Century Approach*. Society of American Florists, Alexandria, Virginia.

Van Wyk B-E, Wink, M (2004) *Medicinal Plants of the World*. Briza Publications, Pretoria.

Vaughan, MJ (1988) *The Complete Book of Cut Flower Care*. Timber Press, Portland, Oregon.

Vogts, M (1982) *South Africa's Proteaceae – Know Them and Grow Them*. Struik, Cape Town.

ACKNOWLEDGEMENTS

Our special thanks goes to the flower breeders, nurseries, seed merchants, flower traders, wholesalers, private photographers, plant collectors, botanical gardens, flower auctions and various associations for graciously supporting us in this project. Also to the following people and institutes for providing us with photos we were not able to use in this edition: **Plant Delights Nursery**, Tony Kosky (**Floratrade International**), Monique van Luijk (**Chiltern Seeds**), Rob Broekhuis (**Robsplants.com**) and **The Begavalley.com**. Finally, to Briza Publications, the University of Johannesburg and the supporting staff, and our families and spouses (Christine Maree and Mariana van Wyk) for always being there for us.

Photographic contributions

Johannes Maree: 13a,b,c,d,e,f,g,h, 15a,b,c,d,e,f,g,h,I,j,k,l,m,n,o,p,q,r,s,t, 17b, 19b,c,d,e, 21b–h, 23, 25, 27, 29b, 31, 33, 35a,b, 37a,b,c,d, 39a,b,c, 41b, 43, 45, 55a, 59a, 62a,b, 70a,b,c, 71b, 75a,b, 76a, 77b, 78a,b, 79b, 81a, 83a,b, 88, 89a,b,c, 90a,b,c, 91a, 92, 93a,b, 97b, 100a, 102a,b,c, 103a,b, 104a,b, 110a, 111, 113b, 115b, 116a, 118c,124b,c, 125a,b, 131a,b, 132a,b, 133a,b,c, 134a,b, 137b, 139a,b, 140a,b, 141b, 146a,b, 150a,b, 152a, 154b, 155a, 156a,b, 158a, 159c, 160a,b, 165a,b, 167a,b,c, 168a,b, 169a, 170b, 171a,b, 174a,b, 175a, 178a, 180a, 182a, 185, 186a,b,c, 187a,b,c, 188c, 190b,c, 199a,b,c, 200b, 201a, 202b, 203a,b, 205a,b, 207a,c, 209a, 213a,b, 215a, 216b, 218a, 221a, 222a,b, 223b, 224a, 226a,b,c, 229a,c, 230a,b, 232, 233a, 235a,b,c, 236b, 238, 239b, 242a, 243a, 244a, 245a,b,c, 246b, 247a,b,c, 248a,c,c, 249a,b, 250b,c, 255a, 256a,b, 259b,c, 261a,b, 263b, 267c, 270a,b, 277a,b, 280a, 283a, 284a,b, 289a,b, 290, 292a,b,c, 294a,b,c, 295a,b, 301b, 303b, 304a,b, 306b, 307b, 310a,b, 311a,b,c, 315a,b,c, 316b, 318a, 319b, 321, 322a,b,c, 323a,b, 325a,b, 326a,b, 334b,c, 338a,b, 339a,b, 341b, 342b, 347a, 348b, 351b, 363b, 370a,b, 372a, 375a,b,c, 380b, 381b, 382a,b, 383a. **Prof. Ben-Erik van Wyk** (University of Johannesburg): 13a,d,h, 19a,f, 21a, 29a, 39d, 41a, 55b,c, 65a, 66a, 67b, 68a,b, 69a,b, 72, 79a, 80a,b, 85a,b,c, 86a,b, 87a,c, 91b, 93c, 94a,b, 95a,b,c, 97a, 99b, 107a, 108a,b, 109b, 110b, 113c, 114c, 117, 118a,b, 120a,b, 121b,c, 128c, 129a,b,c, 137a, 138a,b, 142, 143a,b, 144c, 148b,c, 149, 151a,c,d, 152b,c, 153a, 154a, 155b, 157, 158b, 159a,b, 161a,b, 163a,b, 169b,c, 170a, 173a, 175b, 176a,b, 177c, 180b, 181a,b,c, 182b, 183a,b, 188a,b, 189, 192a,b,c, 193a,b,c, 196, 201b, 206, 209b, 210a,b,c, 214a, 215b,c, 216a, 218b,c, 220, 221c, 223a,c, 225a,b, 227a,b,c, 228, 229b, 233b, 234a,b,c, 236a, 239a, 240, 241a,b,c, 242b, 243c, 244b,c, 246a, 251a,b,c, 253a, 257, 258, 260a,b, 262, 263a, 264a, 265a,b, 266a,b, 268a,b,c, 269a,b,c, 272b, 273b, 274a,b, 279a,b, 280b,c, 282a,b,c, 283b,c, 284c, 285, 286, 287, 288a, b, 288a,b, 296c, 297a,b, 298a,b, 299a,b, 301a, 305a,b,c, 306a, 308a, 309c,d, 313a,b, 314, 318b, 319a, 320a,b,c, 324a,b, 327a, 328b, 329a,b,c, 331a,c, 332a,b, 335, 336a, 341a, 342a, 343, 344, 345a,b,c, 347b,c, 348a, 354a,b, 355b, 356a,b, 359, 360a,b,c, 361a,b, 362, 363a, 366a,b, 367b, 368b,c, 369a,b,c, 371a,b, 372b, 373, 374a,c, 377a,b, 378a, 380a, 381a, 383b, 384a,b, 385a,b.

Agricultural Research Council (Vegetable and Ornamental Plant, Roodeplaat, South Africa): 237a,b. **Anthura B.V.** (www.anthura.nl, Plant breeders, Bleiswijk, The Netherlands): 291a,b, 376b. **Ball Horticultural Company** (www.ballhort.com, Plant breeders, Illinois, USA): 57a,b, 63a,b, 64a,b,c, 84a,b, 87b, 105, 119a,b, 128a,b, 144a,b,c, 166, 211, 221b, 293c, 350a,b, 367a, 374b. **Bartelsstek** (www.bartelsstek.nl, Plant breeders, Aalsmeer, The Netherlands): 141a, 293a,b. **Benary** (www.benary.de, Hann Muenden, Germany): 74a, 116b, 334a. **Bestelink, Jaqi** (Galago Graphics, Johannesburg, South Africa): 17a. **Boshoff, Stephanus** (Nelspruit, South Africa): 179. **Breen, Pat:** 309a. **Brendler, Thomas:** 151b. **Collins, Phil** (Collins.Phil@saugov.sa.gov.au, State Flora Nursery, Australia): 61, 98. **Combifleur Seeds and Plants** (www.combifleur.com, Suppliers of seed and plants, Maasdijk, The Netherlands): 273c. **Crownsville Nursery:** 172b. **Danziger Flower Farm** (www.danziger.co.il, Breeders of young plants, Beit Dagan, Israel): 207b. **Fayyaz, Mo:** 358c. **Fial, Liz** (California Flora Nursery): 337a, 354c,d. **Flogaus-Faust, Robert:** 358a. **Dr Ori Fragman-Sapir** (Jerusalem Botanical Garden): 191b, 194, 376a, 252a, 275a,b, 364, 376a. **Gardino Nursery** (www.gardinonursery.com): 184. **George, Jean-Claude:** 340. **Hackney, Paul** (Botanic Gardens Belfast): 197. **Hadeco** (www.hadeco.co.za, Breeders and suppliers of flowerbulbs, Roodepoort, South Africa): 13c, 76b, 162, 200a, 224b, 231a,b, 264b, 267a,b, 271a,b, 303a, 338c, 353a, 355a, 357. **Hammond, Roger** (roger@themagnolias.co.uk): 58. **Harman, Simon** (Lilieswatergarden.co.uk): 358b. **Harten, Chris:** 333b. **Höggemeier, Annette** (Botanical Gardens Ruhr University of Bochum): 191b. **Hugh, Nicole M:** 195a,b. **Intellectual Property Office (TIPO)** (Ministry of Economic Affairs, Taipei, Taiwan. biotech.tipo.gov. tw): 254a,b, 300, 302. **Kieft Seeds** (www.kieftseeds.com, Plant and flower breeders, Venhuizen, The Netherlands): 59b,c, 66b, 71a, 73a,b, 77a, 82a,b, 96, 113a, 119a,c, 122a,b,c, 127a,b, 148a, 164a,b, 178b,c, 202a,c, 212a,b,c, 250a, 255b, 259a, 273a, 276c, 312a,b, 328a,c, 346a,b, 352a,b, 353b,c, 379. **Lerner, Rosie** (Purdue University, Department of Horticulture and Landscape Architecture): 145, 252b,c. **Logee's Greenhouses** (logee-info@logess.com, Source of the plant material listed): 198. **Maloney, Peter** (Department of Agriculture and Food, Perth, Australia): 208b, 378b. **Maree, Christine** (Johannesburg, South Africa): 274c. **McLachlan-Evans, Rhys** (Rosendal Farms, South Africa): 115a. **Misiurewicz, Michal:** 74b. **Missouri Botanical Gardens** (Plantfinder): 74c, 114a, 147a,b,c, 276a,b, 309b, 337b. **Nirp International** (www.nirpinternational.com, Rose breeders, Menton, France): 317a,b. **Nutile, Pete** (Johnny's Selected Seeds): 253c. **O'Connell, Jo** (Ventura, California, USA): 204b,c, 208a. **Peace, Janet** (Hot Tomato Graphics, Johannesburg, South Africa): 272a, 327b, 251a. **Pustovrh, Davor** (Vrtnarstvo.pustovrh@siol. net): 56a,b. **Sahin Seeds** (www.sahin.nl, Breeders and wholesalers of flower seeds, Alphen aan den Rijn, The Netherlands): 67a, 99a, 107b, 130, 136, 217, 253b, 331b, 333a, 368a. **Sakata Ornamentals** (www.sakata.com, Plant and seed breeder, Marslev, Denmark): 305d. **Schreurs Gerberas & Roses** (www.schreurs.nl, Breeders of gerberas and roses, De Kwakel, The Netherlands): 316a. **Selamoglu, Handan** (Terrapin-gardens.com): 123a,b. **Sessions, Andrea** (Sunlight Gardens): 172a. **Smith, David G** (Delaware Wildflowers): 219. **South African Protea Producers and Exporters Association (SAPPEX)** (www.sappex.org.za, Botrivier, South Africa): 101a,b, 106a,b, 177a,b, 243b, 307a, 308b. **Steffen, Richie** (Great Plant Picks): 365. **Stewart, Bianca** (Sydney, Australia): 204a. **USDANRCS Plants Database** (http://plants.usda.gov): 114b,d, 278, 349.

Name and page entries in **bold print** indicate main entries and illustrations.